Women in American History

Series Editors
Mari Jo Buhle
Nancy A. Hewitt
Anne Firor Scott
Stephanie Shaw

The Working Class in American History

Editorial Advisors
David Brody
Alice Kessler-Harris
David Montgomery
Sean Wilentz

Lists of books in the series appear at the end of this book.

Marching Together

Marching Together

WOMEN OF THE BROTHERHOOD
OF SLEEPING CAR PORTERS

Melinda Chateauvert

University of Illinois Press
Urbana and Chicago

This book is printed on acid-free paper.

Frontispiece: From the cover of "Marching Together," the official anthem of the Ladies'
Auxiliary to the Brotherhood of Sleeping Car Porters. Artist unknown; words and
music by Rosina Corrothers-Tucker. (Rosina Corrothers Tucker Papers, Leadership
Conference on Civil Rights, Washington, D.C.)

Library of Congress Cataloging-in-Publication Data
Chateauvert, Melinda.
Marching together: women of the Brotherhood of Sleeping Car Porters / Melinda
Chateauvert.
p.   cm.— (Women in American history) (The working class in American history)
Includes bibliographical references and index.
ISBN 0-252-02340-4 (acid-free paper). — ISBN 0-252-06636-7 (pbk. : acid-free paper)
1. Brotherhood of Sleeping Car Porters. Ladies Auxiliary—History.
2. Trade-unions—United States—Afro-American membership—History.
3. Women in trade-unions—United States—History.
4. Discrimination in employment—United States—History.
5. Race discrimination—United States—History.
6. Pullman porters—History.
I. Title.
II. Series.
III. Series: The working class in American history.
HD6515.R362B763   1998
331.4'781138522'0973—dc21   97-4579   CIP

Marching Together*

When the brotherhood in nineteen twenty-five was organized,
Some wives were prompt to lend a hand because they realized
That they must in this fight take part and with their husbands try
To bring truth and justice nigh.

CHORUS:
> We're the Ladies' Auxiliary,
> The Ladies' Auxiliary of the BSCP.
> Together we are marching proudly;
> Proudly marching as one pow'rful band;
> Singing our Union songs so loudly
> That they vibrate throughout the land.
> We are determined and won't turn away,
> But will steadfastly face the new day;
> And courage and unity shall lead us to victory.

Injustice of all kinds and vile reaction we have fought;
All efforts for the Union was with manly hardships fraught;
But it was our aim a bona fide Union to achieve
Our bondage to relieve.

CHORUS

All tyranny, reaction and abuses we decry;
The Union gives us power, makes us brave you'll not deny;
We take our stand for freedom, justice and stability;
So we march with agility.

CHORUS

We have the only Union, Sisters, by our group controlled;
So we urge all porters and their wives to be enrolled.
Arise ye women nothing fear, a great campaign begin;
This battle we will win.

CHORUS

*Words and music © 1939 by Rosina Corrothers-Tucker

Contents

Preface

In 1939, Rosina Corrothers Tucker, the recently elected International Secretary-Treasurer of the Ladies' Auxiliary to the Brotherhood of Sleeping Car Porters, wrote and set to music "Marching Together," the anthem of the women's organization. Mrs. Tucker believed the union won because "Some wives were prompt to lend a hand because they realized / That they must in this fight take part and with their husbands try / To bring truth and justice nigh." In the fight against the Pullman Company, women's "efforts for the Union w[ere] with manly hardships fraught." For "the Union gives us power, makes us brave you'll not deny . . . We have the only Union, Sisters, by our group controlled . . . Arise ye women nothing fear, a great campaign begin; This battle we will win."[1]

Mrs. Tucker and her union sisters considered themselves members of the Brotherhood. But neither she nor other Auxiliary members worked for the Pullman Company; rather, they were wives and female relatives of sleeping car porters. These labor conscious, organized women, many of whom worked for pay and some who did not, joined the Ladies' Auxiliary of the Brotherhood to demand their rights as citizens, as consumers, and as workers. By taking action through their husbands' labor union, Mrs. Tucker and her sisters negotiated the traditional boundaries of their race, gender, and class. These African American women implemented their own political agenda by exploiting concepts of black manhood, female respectability, and class consciousness.

The Ladies' Auxiliary was the distaff side of the Brotherhood of Sleeping Car Porters, the most influential black labor union in the United States and Canada in the mid-twentieth century. Organized in 1925 by A. Philip Randolph, Milton P. Webster, and a small core of men and women, the union cast itself as the new manhood movement. Randolph's propaganda stressed black manhood rights, calling for better working conditions, a family wage, respect from fellow workers, and equal citizenship. But for men to achieve manhood, women must be feminine; Brotherhood rhetoric depicted women as admiring wives, rarely noting their pivotal role in the twelve-year struggle for unionization.

The Ladies' Auxiliary constituted the largest and most visible group of women in the union, but the BSCP also had female members who worked as Pullman maids, car cleaners, and porterettes. The position of working women in the BSCP was ambiguous. Not only were their numbers few, given the union's masculine emphasis, many believed a working woman's demand for "manhood" was deviant. BSCP leaders generally regarded these railwaywomen as temporary workers, and agreed to Pullman's request to deny them seniority rights. Nor did Auxiliary members support female unionists; rather than providing a forum for Pullman maids, Brotherhood wives stressed domesticity and male support, obsuring their own participation in the labor force.

Auxiliary women saw their husband's union as their own, sometimes demanding that BSCP officials handle their job grievances with other employers. They complained of racial discrimination, but the circumstances they described might also be interpreted as sex discrimination. African American women earned less than white women and African American men. They believed such wage differences were the result of racism not sexism, because in their eyes, employers refused to give them the same respect given to white women. During World War II, African American women sought to racially integrate the "pink collar ghetto" only to be offered the opportunity to break down sex segregation by doing jobs commonly given to African American men. They wanted to be recognized as women and to receive the same benefits and privileges white women enjoyed in the workplace. Denial of that respect constituted race discrimination.

The Auxiliary's attention to female respectability reflected members' consciousness about their class and political status. To be respected by whites, these African American women believed they should heed society's strictures for proper female behavior, particularly in the conservative post–World War II period. Almost every member identified herself as a housewife, whether or not she held paid employment. Even the way a woman dressed for Auxiliary affairs served as an index of respectability. Through their ladylike behavior, Auxiliary women sought to contradict the stereotypes of Mammy and Sapphire and thus gain their rights as first-class citizens. Respectability established the political authority of African American women.

These sometimes conflicting but often compatible concerns regarding black manhood, female respectability, class consciousness, and citizenship are the principal themes of this book. In particular periods, and in specific political campaigns, one concern might appear to overshadow the others, but throughout this study I have sought to understand how these issues combined to shape the consciousness of the African American women and men who created the union. The BSCP was not simply a labor union, nor a race organization, nor a political movement, nor was the Auxiliary just a women's group, but an amalgam of all four. Union leaders understood that race, gender, and class were fundamentally political, and their programs reflected that consciousness. As Mrs. Tucker recalled, the founders of the Ladies' Auxiliary proudly proclaimed themselves "members of the first international labor organization of Negro women in the world."

The story of the Brotherhood of Sleeping Car Porters is well-known, but little has been told of the women who fought to organize the union and the Ladies' Auxiliary. Telling the women's side of the tale makes clear how much gender mattered to both the women and the men. Everyday experiences, as African Americans and as working-class people, informed their awareness of gender and sexual differences. Moreover, the meanings attached to gender changed as the decades passed and the BSCP attained political power and social prestige.

The Brotherhood of Sleeping Car Porters made Pullman porters the aristocrats of black labor in the African American community. That admiration derived, in part, from the union's political power. The union initiated the modern civil rights movement in 1941 when union president Randolph organized the March on Washington, the first national nonviolent action to demand an end to job discrimination and race segregation. The march empowered local members to seek political rights. In local communities, BSCP and Auxiliary members directed the earliest campaigns. Economic independence gave Brotherhood and Auxiliary members the power to challenge voting restrictions and racial discrimination.

The desire for respect and class consciousness determined the site of the women's demonstrations. Incivility toward African American women as consumers and as workers reinforced racial subordination and second-class citizenship; civil rights depended on earning the respect of whites. Wielding their husbands' union wages, Auxiliary members sought recognition of their economic status, demanding from store clerks the same courteous treatment given to white women. For Auxiliary women, consumerism was more than a labor strategy: it was also a tactic to obtain civil rights.

The bourgeois notions of domesticity that constrained the leadership activities of President Halena Wilson and Secretary-Treasurer Rosina Tucker still confine African American women today.[2] Interest in trade unionism has declined as many workers identify themselves as middle class regardless of income or occupation. Racial integration as a goal of civil rights remains stalled by white racism and by growing African American rejection of the acculturation of white American values and behaviors it appears to require. The Auxiliary's activism throughout the forgotten years of the civil rights movement provides an opportunity for exploring these themes. Their experiences also illuminate the source of the conflicts over gender, race, and class that still confront us.

Many extraordinary women and men had provided comments on, criticisms of, and critical citations for this work as a dissertation and as a manuscript. I would like to thank Evelyn Brooks-Higginbotham, Carroll Smith-Rosenberg, Joan Hoff, Nancy Hewitt, and Alice Kessler-Harris for reading various drafts. Over the course of many years, I have also benefitted from discussions with Adele Logan Alexander, Elizabeth Alexander, Arlene Avakian, Joyce Berkman, Eileen Boris, John Bracey, Linda Brodkey, Kim Christiansen, Blanche Wiesen Cook, Clare Coss, Robert Engs, V. P. Franklin, Alvia Golden, Sarah Hanley, Sharon Harley, Sylvia Hill, James O. Horton, Mary Hussman, Linda Kerber, Jeff Kerr-Ritchie, Marsha Kinslow, Theresa Kolish, Amy Kratz, Greg LeRoy, Walter Licht, Jeanne McCarty, Genna Rae McNeil, C. Bethune Nugent, E. Pauline Myers, Winn Newman, Phyllis M. Palmer, Ethel Payne, Mindy Shapiro, Deborah Gray White, Linda Faye Williams, Rhonda J. Williams, Francille Rusan Wilson, Komoze Woodard, Linda J. Yanney, and members of the Black Women and Work Seminar at the University of Maryland. La'Tonya Rease Miles, Thembi McWhite, Javonne Paul, Marc Powers, and Krishna Toolsie provided excellent research assistance; I wish them well in their own scholarly pursuits. Finally, this book would not have been completed without the support and encouragement of Mary Frances Berry, who has been my mentor and source of uxorial support these past ten years.

The Brotherhood Story

A union is not only for the men, but also for their wives and families.
—Rosina Corrothers Tucker, "My Life as I Have Lived It"

Organizing the Brotherhood of Sleeping Car Porters was a long, hard journey. The men's story has been told and re-told. The Brotherhood's official version can be found in the proceedings for any union convention, in any member's recollections, in any biography of its president, A. Philip Randolph, and in the annals of African American workers. To professional or lay historians, retired union men and women recite the tale like a lesson well-learned.

The Brotherhood story contains all the essential folklore characters: the Pullman porters, humble and honest African American working men sorely oppressed and exploited by the evil and gigantic Pullman Company. The men are led by their brilliant savior, International President A. Philip Randolph, in battle against the Pullman Company, once presided over by Robert T. Lincoln, the son of the Great Liberator. Their eventual success, despite a failed strike attempt, bankruptcy, and eviction, can be summed up in the Brotherhood's slogan, "A quitter never wins and a winner never quits."

The Brotherhood of Sleeping Car Porters began crafting its history right after its founding. As in many labor unions, the story of the workers' struggle for recognition served as an educational tool, a catechism for union membership. Learning the history instilled in members respect for union leaders and for the power of organized labor. The story drew on familiar themes from the Bible and African American folklore, cultural symbols with which members could easily identify. The central role of men in the Brotherhood story strengthened the importance of black manhood for rank-and-file sleeping car porters.[1]

As folklore, the Brotherhood story is part of the culture of African American railwaymen, of Pullman porters who spent much of their time in boarding houses, train stations, and union halls, telling tales. As the men tell it, theirs was a struggle of epic proportions to free African American working men from the shackles of Pullman slavery. As the story evolved, women became literally anecdotal. In the men's version, a wife threw out her husband when he mortgaged the house for the union, while another found rent money for a new Brotherhood office after the marshall served an eviction notice. The female characters are ephemeral, cast as Sapphire or Mammy. But stereotypes, like folklore, do not provide the real story.[2]

The women of the Brotherhood of Sleeping Car Porters remembered how they helped to organize the union. In later years, they constructed their own stories about the courageous few who fought to keep the Brotherhood going through the dark days of the Depression. Their stories, told by porters' wives, sisters, and daughters, Pullman maids, clubwomen, and union women, speak of sacrifice: a wife who took in laundry when Pullman furloughed her husband, a daughter who put aside dreams of college, and other women who volunteered their time and resources to support the union. Women collected and paid dues, organized secret gatherings and public meetings, lectured crowds, and buttonholed porters about their union membership. As Rosina Corrothers Tucker, one of those who preserved the women's story recalled, "It was the women who made the union."[3]

This is the women's version of the Brotherhood story. The women show their lye-stripped hands and bunion-swollen feet, the sacrifices they made to found the union and enjoy its brilliant triumphs. The International Ladies' Auxiliary Order to the Brotherhood of Sleeping Car Porters, the women claim, was the first international African American women's labor organization. Unnoted at the time or by historians later, Pullman maids also achieved a "first": they were the first African American women to be represented by a railway brotherhood. As wives and as workers, women participated in the creation of the first African American union recognized by a major U.S. corporation.[4]

The role of women in organizing the union is obscured because BSCP historians, both laymen and professionals, have based their accounts on the Brotherhood story. But women's work has also been ignored because the story itself is grounded in the rhetoric of black manhood and the ideology of manhood rights. In that context, women, whether wives or maids, could play only a secondary role, as helpmeets to their men.

Through the Ladies' Auxiliary, African American women constructed an organizational role for themselves in the labor movement, declaring domestic issues as their domain. They praised the Brotherhood because it brought economic security to their families; their husbands' union wages allowed them to become housewives. With thrift and domestic science, union wives produced an American standard of living for their families. Union wages and housewifery also granted African American women respectability and safe-guarded their moral reputations. As a result, they asserted their political power. As respectable union wives, Auxiliary members participated in public debates on labor, social welfare, and civil rights issues. Many became social activists and grassroots political workers in their communities. These race-conscious, trade union women believed they should fight side by side with their husbands in the struggle for "the equal rights of all men, regardless of race, color or creed." Porters' wives, whether housewives or wage-earning women, joined the Auxiliary, claiming the Brotherood as their own.[5]

Pullman maids and other female union members claimed the union too, but were told to join the Auxiliary. This book tells the story of these twentieth-century African American railwaywomen, who faced the racism of railroad companies and the sexism of their Brotherhood. Denied fair representation, Pullman maids worked without seniority rights under the questionable protection of protective labor laws. Diverted into the Auxiliary with a complimentary membership, and too few in number to win elective offices in the union, BSCP officials often treated their concerns as working women casually, while Auxiliary leaders ignored them. The Brotherhood and the Auxiliary agreed, woman's "place" was in the home.[6]

Domesticity offered respectability and the rights of citizenship. To discredit the economic and political demands of African American women, popular culture exploited the stereotypes of Mammy and Sapphire. As a domestic worker, Mammy "loved" her white charges more than her own children. But when she organized as a worker to demand better pay and working conditions, she risked her maternal authority; popular wisdom held that a working mother could not raise her children properly. Citizenship, granted to the mothers of virtuous citizens, was thus also denied. Sapphire was disqualified from citizenship, too, by her refusal to heed male authority; headstrong and ungovernable, she could not be trusted with suffrage. A woman's citizenship rested, then, on her domesticity: the married woman who worked in the home for her family could voice her opinion in public. Her respectability gave her the right to make economic and political demands. The Ladies' Auxiliary drew on female domesticity to claim a role in the Brotherhood.[7]

The Brotherhood's demand for manhood rights supported the Auxiliary's domesticity. In economic terms, manhood meant a living wage, equal pay for equal work without regard to race, and humane working conditions. These were demands other African American workers, male and female, could easily identify with and desire for themselves. In this sense, many saw the BSCP as a civil rights organization focused on workplace issues. This focus differentiated the Brotherhood from other race organizations of the

1920s that preached self-help and racial uplift without mentioning systemic causes. As a rhetorical device, manhood rights invested the unionization of porters and maids with broader concerns, but the term carried specific political meanings for African American men and women and for white working men and women.[8]

African American demands for manhood rights stretched far back into American history. Although they are similar, manhood rights are not synonymous with modern "civil rights." The latter term, as it is currently used, connotes equal rights regardless of race or sex in citizenship, employment, education, housing, public accommodations, and other amenities of ordinary life. In contrast, the Brotherhood's demand for manhood rights evolved from both African American protests and those of white working men. Manhood rights, whether expressed by whites or African Americans, were fundamentally gendered. They were the rights granted by the polity to the head of the patriarchal family. In both European and African political traditions, manhood rights served as the foundation of the nation-state. Slaves, women, and children, by tradition and law, could not possess such rights, even in matrilineal societies. At least since David Walker's 1829 *Appeal,* black manhood has been an essential demand in the rhetoric of race, reflecting the concerns of race leaders, whatever their sex or political alliances. W. E. B. Du Bois, in his Niagara Address of 1906 demanded, "We will not be satisfied to take one jot or tittle less than our full manhood rights. We claim for ourselves every single right that belongs to a freeborn American, political, civil and social." The National Negro Council declared, "Let us unite the Negro Organizations and the friends of Negro freedom on a program for security and manhood rights for the Negroes in America." Occasionally the desire for equal rights was expressed more simply: as one Mississippian, wishing to migrate to Chicago or Philadelphia in 1917 wrote, "don't Care where I Go so long as I go where a man is a man."[9]

To African American men and women, the demand for manhood carried a variety of meanings. In traditional politics, it meant emancipation from slavery, suffrage, equal political rights, and equal pay for equal work. Manhood also signified the right of black men to protect black women and children from white men, and to preserve the family by restoring mothers to the home. In this sense, manhood rights were not for men only.[10]

White laboring men invoked manhood to justify their demands for a family wage and better working conditions, what David Montgomery calls "defiant egalitarianism" toward foremen and fellow (white) workers. Manhood brought men together in the white railroad brotherhoods established after the Civil War, binding the men of the steel rails together in a geographically dispersed industry. Manliness found form in fraternalism, in the contemporary popularity of Masonic and neo-Masonic organizations and protective craft unions. The social aspect of the brotherhoods often commanded more fidelity than their economic functions. Steeped in ritual, secret handshakes, passwords, and special regalia, members pledged sobriety, industry, thrift, honesty, and honor to their fictive brothers. One of the main functions of these craft-based fraternal associations was mutual aid. Railwaymen could turn to their "brothers" when in need. By the turn of the century almost every railway brotherhood offered sickness and death benefits and looked after members and their families.[11]

The railroad brotherhoods admitted only white men to full membership, confining women and men of color to auxiliaries. Sex-segregated auxiliaries for wives and female relatives permitted women's limited participation. These informal women's groups extended help to distressed railroad wives, organized parties for themselves while their husbands were away, and held dances, dinners, and card parties for the whole family when the men returned. The emphasis on charity and sociability supported bourgeois notions of a proper family life, emphasizing women's difference from the male world of labor and politics and sanctioning segregation by sex and race. White laboring men also differentiated themselves from African American men, and defined manhood in racially exclusive terms. Fraternal associations offered a vision of merit-based worker equality to its white male members, as Mary Ann Clawson argues persuasively in *Constructing Brotherhood*. Characterizing themselves as social organizations rather than labor unions, the "Big Four" brotherhoods forbade African Americans from joining by ritual, constitutional provision, or tacit consent. "To admit the Negro to their ranks would be to admit him to social equality," commented early critics. By 1920, the 135,000 African American railroad workers in the south were without representation or belonged to racially segregated "auxiliary" locals, where their white "brothers" could control labor force participation.[12]

These early fraternities served as models for Pullman porters' unsuccessful attempts to unionize in the Progressive Era. Porters followed the customs of white brotherhoods by limiting their membership to African American men, a key factor in gaining control over their job class. The Brotherhood of Sleeping Car Porters did not exclude members by race or sex, but duplicated the gender conventions of the railway brotherhoods by confining women's participation, as workers and as the wives of union men, to the auxiliaries. Membership rituals in the Brotherhood and the Ladies' Auxiliary, patterned after other trade unions and fraternal associations, promoted sex segregation in language and by symbol. Although the BSCP defied the racial traditions of the white railroad unions, its founders endorsed their views on gender and male governance, in order for the union to take its rightful place among the "Big Four" Brotherhoods. The BSCP copied, almost exactly, the organizational structure of the white railroad unions. A constitutionally powerful international executive board determined union policies and directed the activities and programs of its fifty-two local divisions. These divisions, in turn, replicated the office structure of the International and implemented policy and programs as directed. Throughout the BSCP's existence, only African American men held elective offices in the international and division locals.[13]

For Randolph and Brotherhood organizers, black manhood rights meant racial equality in wages and working conditions. When a black man could provide a decent standard of living for his family, just as a white union man did, political, civil, and social equality followed. Racial restrictions that barred porters from promotion to conductor or higher symbolized the second-class citizenship accorded to African Americans. In the early years, Randolph's rhetoric stressed the Brotherhood's goal of "Building Black Manhood." The BSCP was the vanguard in a new manhood movement, Randolph claimed, for "only white men are supposed to organize for power, for justice and freedom." The old porter, the former slave, had passed the way of the wooden Pullman car, and "the new porter has come into being. He is urbanized; he is industrialized, subject to this standardized civilization, and he is thinking through this new medium and it is organized labor."[14]

The new woman, whether white or black, also demanded manhood rights for herself, by organizing for suffrage and equal political rights; in later years, porters' wives wanted to vote in BSCP elections. Pullman maids and other wage-earning women appealed for better working conditions and equal wages in the context of manhood rights. The decision to become a Pullman maid was an assertion of African American women's independence: the choice of a bureaucratized male railroad industry over the individualized female scrutiny of household domestic labor. But when women and men of color demanded manhood, the term's intimate connection to adult white men was destroyed. By invoking manhood rights, to paraphrase Carroll Smith-Rosenberg, Randolph transposed the images and rhetoric of white laboring men into a racialized and gendered reproof. Using similar language, he invested white images with black male political intent, using white myths to repudiate white power, to turn the white labor world upside down.[15]

Randolph's invocation of manhood rights aroused the anger of white labor leaders but won the support of porters' wives. The union's promise to achieve manhood for their husbands would bring the respectability wives desired for themselves. As African American wage-earners, women interpreted the union's demands for manhood as efforts to protect them from harsh working conditions. Housewifery indicated that their husbands earned wages sufficient to support a family, granted them respect and a high standing in the community. Thus, when Brotherhood women discussed manhood, they situated their demands in their domestic situations. Their emancipation as workers and as wives would come with their husbands' union contract.[16]

To support the Brotherood, Randolph organized porters' wives in separate Women's Economic Councils. Although common among white brotherhoods, these auxiliaries also drew on the cultural traditions of gender complementary organizations in the African diaspora. While some union organizers did not think the councils necessary, Randolph insisted that wives were critical to winning the men's support.[17]

The BSCP president was "a new leader," an outsider to the Brotherhood who had never worked as a Pullman porter, although his older brother James had spent a summer with the company. A group of New York porters, many of whom were West Indian, chose Randolph to lead their unionization drive. The very fact that Randolph was not employed by Pullman, they reasoned, would shield him from company reprisals. Randolph, publisher of *The Messenger,* a socialist and street corner orator, had some experience in organizing unions, and had toured the nation speaking against the United States' participation in World War I, during which he was dubbed the "most dangerous Negro in America."[18]

Randolph's connections with Harlem leaders and society, gained mostly through his wife, provided a wealth of other outside contacts that greatly benefitted the nascent union. Only biographer Jervis Anderson touches upon the role of Lucille Campbell Greene Randolph, whose own career as a Walker hair culturist, teacher, social worker, and political activist, financed much of her husband's work. Lucille Randolph was one of the formative influences in the Brotherhood of Sleeping Car Porters, a fact that her husband frequently acknowledged. Lucille Campbell Greene, a widowed Howard University graduate, moved to New York City around 1910, where she enrolled in the new Lelia College of beauty culture. One of its first graduates, she opened a posh Harlem beauty salon on 135th Street and became a frequent guest of her teacher and patron, Madame C. J. Walker. As one of Harlem's "New Negro Women," she took up politics and acting, through which she met A. Philip Randolph, six years her junior. She and "Buddy," her nickname for Randolph, married on their mutual birthday, April 15, in 1913.[19]

She joined the Socialist Party shortly after meeting her husband, and the couple committed themselves to radical politics. They campaigned to elect Morris Hillquit mayor of New York until both quit in disgust over the "Big

Negroes" who controlled the African American vote. From her Walker Salon on 135th Street, she distributed the *Messenger* and used the salon's profits to pay off the magazine's debts on more than one occasion. As William Dufty, columnist for the *New York Post* later wrote: "Lucille Greene Randolph seems entitled to the honor of being called the onetime second most dangerous Negro in America. The title would certainly have once been official if the agents of the U.S. Justice Department had had the initiative and wit to intercept her postal money orders which helped support A. Philip Randolph's 'subversive activities.' "[20]

Thus it seemed natural that in 1925, after being supported by his wife for a dozen years, Randolph would discuss the Brotherhood organizing job with her first. She thought he should accept, and agreed to support the movement. She supported her husband through a decade of union organizing, for Philip Randolph did not receive a regular salary from the BSCP until 1936. Throughout those "dark days," Lucille paid the mortgage for their five-room Dunbar Cooperative apartment. The Brotherhood men knew she supported him; as one porter recalled, "Sister Randolph carried him for years."[21]

Lucille Randolph was a New Negro Woman who, like her husband, believed in the equality of women. Philip Randolph earned his radical reputation, in part, because he endorsed women's suffrage in the inaugural issue of *The Messenger;* other editorials argued in favor of birth control, while columnists wrote favorably on Harlem's early feminist meetings. Perhaps Randolph's first comment on the role of women in the BSCP was his 1926 message at the New York division's second anniversary:

> Negro men are not alone seeking freedom. Negro women are too seeking freedom. Men are not alone the victims of economic exploitation and oppression, women too [are] exploited and oppressed. Organization is not only necessary for the economic emancipation of men, but it is also necessary for the economic emancipation of the women. Recognizing this fact, the wives, relatives, and friends of the porters came together and formed a ladies' auxiliary of the Brotherhood to be known as the Colored Women's Economic Council.
>
> Its program and mission are primarily and fundamentally economic. It is the first of its kind among Negroes in the world. Its plan is to contribute the knowledge of, and develop the interest in, the labor and competitive movements of America in particular and in the world in general, to the Negro women of the country.[22]

Randolph consciously sought women's political and financial support to organize the Brotherhood of Sleeping Car Porters. Through his wife's social circle, he solicited prominent leftist whites and wealthy African Americans to speak in favor of the union and donate money. Lucille Randolph, although not a member of the Women's Economic Council, sought to identify its members as New Negro Women by organizing several "bobbed hair contests" judged by her fellow Walker hair culturists and her good friend A'lelia Walker Robinson. Philip Randolph wanted the women to be taken seriously, not frivolously; as *The Messenger* reminded its readers, "Bobbed Hair is very often attractive and becoming / Bobbed Brains however are a serious handicap to anyone."[23]

Randolph believed women's exploitation was the result of the low wages paid to their husbands. When men earned a living wage, economic necessity would not force women into the labor force. African American wives unable to find decent wages and working conditions would have the freedom to withdraw from the labor force and become full-time housewives. As housewives, they could greet their battle-weary husbands when they returned home from the road. Naomi DesVerney, the wife of BSCP organizer and porter W. H. DesVerney, described the importance of wives in the reproduction of labor (and of the labor movement). Pullman porters spent "their hours of toil in the network of subservience and servility." Wives "feel the reaction in our homes to which our men must return. . . . We know too well their injuries and hardships." Women's great task in the union drive was "to keep inspired, to continue feeding and firing the spirit of endurance in our men." DesVerney called up a "phalanx . . . of real, red-blooded she-women" to inspire the men and women gathered for the union's second anniversary celebration. The Brotherhood struggle, she announced, was for "the very bearing of our men who are fighting for simple manhood rights, a grander manlier tone." Other writers echoed DesVerney's views in *The Messenger*.[24]

The magazine's 1927 forum on "The Negro Woman's Greatest Needs" affirmed the importance of "homelife." The correspondents, most of them clubwomen rather than porters' wives, believed married couples should share domestic responsibilities. This marriage ideal held that wives should concentrate their efforts on domesticity, wrote Christine S. Smith of Detroit, but only so long as homemaking meant more than working as a maid in one's own house. "The building of the home is a partnership in which the father must share as much responsibility as the mother. . . . It is an institution which must have as its foundation, loyal sympathy and understanding. Each of the partners has a contribution to make which cannot be neglected nor ignored. . . . We need the faith and cooperation of men in building a better world."[25] Other clubwomen portrayed wives as marital partners. Vivian Osborn Marsh of Berkeley wrote, "Today true marriage should mean a larger life, a mutual stepping out into the world's wonder house for both participants, and a happy service in performing together the world's needed tasks, which can only be accomplished from contact."[26]

Brotherhood wives felt honored by the invitation to participate in this new economic partnership through the Women's Economic Councils. "Woman's part in the consummation of any work that tends to elevate mankind is of grave importance," wrote Mattie Mae Stafford, president of the Los Angeles Women's Economic Council. "No people need ever despair whose women stand ready and willing to lend assistance for mental, moral and social eleva-tion." The women who led the councils believed that their job was to help the men. As members of the Auxiliary, they put their husbands' jobs first. In later years, some even ceased using their given names, identifying themselves by their husbands' names, such as Mrs. Herman Mitchell of Louisville, Kentucky. Auxiliary members identified themselves as housewives, even when they held paid jobs. Passing references to Auxiliary members' occupations, gleaned from letters and the union newspaper, mention teachers, stenographers, a notary public, a government clerk, and domestic workers. But above all, Auxiliary members identified themselves as porters' wives.[27]

The value women placed on their identity as wives was apparent in the obituaries of fifteen New Orleans women married to rank-and-file Brother-hood porters. The notices provided information about their husbands, their children, their church and social club affiliations, but only two listed possi-ble past employers, the J. C. Penney Company and a caterer. Fourteen were church members from various Christian denominations. Almost every wom-an belonged to a charitable organization; among those listed were Lady Dew-ey's Benevolent Association, Christian Advancement Relief Association, Ladies' Olympian Benevolent Association, Ladies of Love Benevolent Associ-ation, Pilgrim Benevolent Society, and the Rescue Mission Daughters of Allen. Several were active in lodge auxiliaries, such as the Elks and Eastern Star. Ages were not given, but the numerous grandchildren and great-grandchildren indicate they were probably in their forties, fifties, and sixties when active in the BSCP Ladies' Auxiliary.[28]

These rank-and-file porters' wives identified themselves by their organi-zations and as housewives even when they worked for pay. They "did not be-lieve that their presence or their position in the labor force was an accurate reflection of what they were or of how they should be viewed," as Sharon Harley argues. High labor force participation rates for adult African American women between 1930 and 1960 have obscured the fact that more than 40 percent did not earn wages. Among urban, male-headed African American families in 1940, the numbers were even greater: two-thirds of all wives did not work. The presence of children under six made the absence of African American wives from the labor force even more likely. The consistent factor in these figures is the presence of an employed husband, implying economic stability, but other factors influenced the tendency for Auxiliary members to identify themselves as housewives.[29]

The postwar period witnessed the reintroduction of cultural proscriptions against working mothers, white and black, compelling women to obscure their paid employment or to withdraw from the labor force altogether. Functionalist sociological theory suggested that employed mothers undermined family stability, and implied they were to blame for the rise in juvenile delinquency and other social pathologies. Problematizing African American working mothers specifically, sociologist E. Franklin Frazier demonized the black matriarch. In doing so, he shifted the cause of unemployment and underemployment among African American men from race discrimination to female aggression and desire for economic independence. Differences between white and black women's labor force participation rates, female-headed households, and fecundity, reinforced perceptions of racial inferiority; some race scholars implied African Americans would achieve integration and political power when they behaved more like whites.[30]

Of course, "acting white" was gendered. Wives were to appear feminine, attend church, volunteer for charity work, and keep their homes as neat as those pictured in *Good Housekeeping*. Wives' withdrawal from the labor force and conformity to white definitions of gender roles indicated a family's membership in the middle-class and hence, a measure of their respectability. When wives worked, they called their wages "pin money," used for purchasing extras rather than for the family's survival. Adherence to bourgeois gender roles provided evidence of African American civility. Racial segregationists justified second-class citizenship by claiming that African Americans were uncivilized, offering the twin images of the "matriarchal" family and the "black beast rapist" as proof. To destroy those claims, African American women hid their paid labor, identifying themselves as housewives and as church and club members. In the Auxiliary, many thought a marriage license should be required for membership. Such attitudes formed a political subtext, serving as a largely unrecognized tactic in the effort to obtain first-class citizenship.[31]

These gender conventions dictated the role of women in the union. As the definition of the word connotes, the Auxiliary was secondary to the union; in a familial sense, the Auxiliary was the Brotherhood's "wife." DesVerney and Stafford constructed the image of a marital partnership in the 1920s, and leaders later adapted it as ideals of womanhood and marital relations changed. These concepts were significant alterations of the nineteenth-century doctrine of separate spheres. Nonetheless, they sustained the notion of women's particular responsibilities for the home and family while reinforcing the idea that married women should not work. Although Auxiliary officers at times mentioned the predicament of working women, they addressed their members as housewives, not as paid workers. Ada V. Dillon, president of the New York City Auxiliary from 1947 to 1954, was a former Pullman maid, but she never spoke in support of the New York-based Atlantic Coast Line Railroad maids laid-off after a contract dispute. The Auxiliary was silent about the problems female BSCP members faced.[32]

International President Halena Wilson and International Secretary-Treasurer Rosina Corrothers Tucker disagreed on the Auxiliary's role in the labor movement. Wilson believed in the union wife, a woman who enjoyed the domestic security of her husband's union wages and wielded her economic power to advance the labor movement. Tucker believed in the union woman, and would have spoken on behalf of female Brotherhood members. She thought the Auxiliary should be "the big sister" to black women workers everywhere; she wanted to organize trade unions for their own economic advancement. Wilson's defeat of Tucker for the presidency of the International Auxiliary in 1938 signaled the women's orientation in the decades to come. Wilson and Tucker retained their elected offices until the dissolution of the Auxiliary, sparring occasionally over the organization's program. During her tenure as president, Wilson served in several other organizations, including the Executive Board of the Chicago Women's Trade Union League, the National Education Committee for a New Party, and the Mid-West Planning Committee of the American Labor Education Service, Inc. These appointments reflect her position as perhaps the only African American woman to be an international president in the American Federation of Labor. And yet in 1946, writing to the editor of *Labor,* the weekly newspaper published by the standard railroad labor unions, to protest the use of "boy" to refer to an elderly African American taxi driver, Wilson did not use official Auxiliary stationery nor even sign her full name. She wrote in the third person, obliterating her identity and refusing to express a direct opinion. Biographical details reveal a self-effacing personality.[33]

Halena Wilson (1895–1975), a Denver native, became president of the Chicago Ladies' Auxiliary in 1931, succeeding Jessie Bonds, who resigned to join the Chicago police force. Wilson's husband, Benjamin, joined the Brotherhood before 1927 and once served on the local executive board; he died in 1955. For most of their married life, the Wilsons lived in a four-room apartment on Chicago's south side. They had no children. Brought up as a Baptist, Halena Wilson joined the Truth Seekers Liberal Church, established in 1940, described by St. Clair Drake and Horace Cayton as one of the store-front temples of Bronzeville. Founder Ross D. Brown believed "adequate wages, better homes, more stores and factories will do the Race more good than insincere sermons about mansions in the sky." Wilson was also a Worthy Matron of the Eastern Star. Despite attacks of arthritis and perhaps depression for which she was often hospitalized in later years, she presided over both the International and the Chicago Auxiliary until 1956. The International president earned a salary for her labors, but Wilson identified herself as a housewife and a trade unionist, not as a worker.[34]

Rosina Bud Harvey Corrothers Tucker (1881–1987) described herself as a worker in her autobiography, "My Life As I Have Lived It"; she knew that women did not always earn wages for their labor. A native of Washington, D.C., at seventeen she became the third wife of the Harlem Renaissance poet, novelist, and minister, James David Corrothers (1868–1915). They had one child, Henry, and also raised Corrothers's son by his first marriage. In 1918 she married her second husband, Berthea, a Pullman porter on the Broadway Limited. The Tuckers were members of the Fifteenth Street Presbyterian Church. Rosina Tucker challenged its class-conscious minister, the Reverend Francis Grimké, to support the BSCP; she was the first woman to be elected a trustee of this prestigious church. Tucker was also president of her neighborhood civic association and active on several citizen's committees on behalf of children, statehood for the District, and seniors. Widowed in 1963, Tucker remained in her three-bedroom Northeast Washington home near Gallaudet University until her death at the age of 106. Wilson and Tucker received salaries for their work as international officers; other officials volunteered their time and resources to the organization.[35]

Like other officers, Wilson and Tucker shared a commitment to political affairs, their churches, and to trade unionism. Katherine Lassiter held the post of First International Vice-President from 1938 through 1956. Widowed in 1932, Lassiter became president of the New York Auxiliary, but left office in 1946, apparently to devote more time to the Women's Auxiliary of the Republican County Committee of New York. Letitia Murray of Los Angeles served as Fourth Vice-President until 1948, when ill-health forced her to resign. Nora Fant of Jersey City, New Jersey, elected to the International Executive Board in 1948 was also a member of Local No. 25 of the International Ladies' Garment Workers' Union and an elected officer of her local NAACP chapter. Fannie J. Caviness, the Zone Supervisor for the Texas auxiliaries, married into a family of Pullman porters. The Cavinesses were also one of the few elected husband-wife officer teams, her husband having served as secretary-treasurer of the San Antonio BSCP division. Although every Auxiliary member's husband had to belong to the union, not all wives joined the Auxiliary. Yet Randolph and other BSCP officials seemed to expect local officers' wives to work for the union, to collect dues in their husbands' absences, and to help out in the local headquarters. Lucille Randolph and the wives of the BSCP's international officers on the other hand, rarely participated in the Auxiliary; Mrs. Randolph only joined the New York Auxiliary in 1946 when her husband paid her membership dues.[36]

The following chapters explore how the Auxiliary adjusted to shifting definitions of womanhood to maintain its place in the union. In the mid-1920s, the semi-autonomous New Woman organized other women and even men, asserting her political autonomy and economic rights. The Depression checked her independence; the Modern Woman of the New Deal was her husband's partner. She worked with him for the benefit of both, as the Auxiliary worked with the BSCP to win recognition from the Pullman Company in 1936. The Brotherhood's contract affirmed the porters' manhood and altered gender relations in the organization. Institutionalizing a subordinated place in the union, porters' wives founded "the first Ladies' Auxiliary of the first International Negro trade union in the world" in 1938. Building on their new economic power, International President Wilson encouraged labor-conscious consumerism to affirm the economic importance of women. The "Union Wife" had her own sphere of domestic influence, comprised of patronizing cooperative stores, purchasing union label goods, labor education, and political activism. As consumers, these "Soldiers in Aprons" canned, rationed, and conserved the nation's resources during World War II. Auxiliary members also helped out their husbands in Brotherhood-sponsored civil rights protests for equal employment, much like "Rosie the Riveter" substituted for her husband in the factory.[37]

Women's politicization in the March on Washington Movement tested their class consciousness just as passage of the Taft-Hartley Act made their votes crucial to the labor movement. The transition to the suburban house-wife of the 1950s, facilitated by a rising standard of living, encouraged rather than hindered the political activism of the Auxiliary. Using their status as respectable married women, Auxiliary members became involved in civic efforts to improve their neighborhoods, schools, and public facilities. In the midst of the cold war, the National Council of Negro Women initiated a "new crusade" for women's organizations and invited International Secretary-Treasurer Rosina Tucker to participate. "Women," she reported in 1956, "now have a new sense of the destiny of the Negro and are impatient that nothing disturb its progress." Ironically, however, at the ascendancy of the suburban house-wife and the rise of the modern civil rights movement, the Brotherhood dissolved the Auxiliary. Free of the limitations imposed by the union, many impatient women joined new organizations to continue their work.[38]

Many years ago, Alice Kessler-Harris asked, "Where are the organized women workers?" Further research revealed a male union culture that alienated potential female members. This study also examines the male-dominated culture and ideology of the Brotherhood of Sleeping Car Porters, disclosing the indifference union leaders had for wage-earning women. But it also suggests that her question can be approached from another direction, by looking at the ranks of union supporters. In the case of the Brotherhood, the "organized women" were at home. This book, the first on a trade union auxiliary, draws on works in U.S. labor history, African American history, and women's history. The research relies as much on the work of early African American social scientists who wrote extensively on working people's culture as that of the new labor historians. By explicitly employing gender, race, and class as categories of analysis, the ideology and political strategies of African American women and men are illuminated. One crucial strategy was the sexual division of union labor, accomplished through the organization of the Ladies' Auxiliary.[39]

Women's trade union auxiliaries have been largely ignored by historians. Early articles recount the role of auxiliaries in focusing women's activities during strikes. While useful for documenting wives' confrontations with their husbands' employers, these accounts imply that women supported the labor movement only during emergencies. Other scholars emphasize female sociability and charitable works for workingmen and their families. As a result, it is difficult to discern the impact of white women's auxiliaries on the railway brotherhoods, or the extent of their involvement in national groups such as the Women's Trade Union League, the American Federation of Labor, and the Congress of Industrial Organizations. Only in the last few years have feminist labor scholars addressed the organizational symbolism and political role of women's auxiliaries. As Susan Levine notes, auxiliaries gave wives a collective voice in the labor movement and national politics.[40]

But auxiliaries restrained female union members too: by institutionalizing a hierarchy of gender, male unionists merged workingwomen's concerns with those of housewives, frustrating efforts to discuss women's workplace issues. Thus the experiences of Brotherhood maids serve as a mirror, reflecting society's and the union's disinterest in African American women as workers. Neither the Brotherhood nor the Auxiliary took female employment seriously, believing the issues of wage-earning women could be resolved by addressing the problems of African American male workers. Once men earned good wages under decent working conditions, women could withdraw from the labor force. Brotherhood men and Auxiliary women shared these beliefs.

The myriad obstacles African American women faced in the labor force have been examined closely though narrowly by scholars. Published research on black women's labor and political history in the twentieth century remains woefully inadequate. Even a 1995 anthology in black women's history suspends the narrative between 1945 and the Montgomery Bus Boycott of 1956. Studies of African American women workers in this period focus almost exclusively on domestic workers, or analyze the failure of women to form interracial working class alliances. Darlene Clark Hine's study of the integration of the nursing profession testifies to the wealth of political and labor issues that dominated the lives of African American women during the "forgotten years" of the civil rights movement. Yet labor history depicts African American women as unorganized and unorganizable, despite the major union victories scored in the garment industry. The BSCP Auxiliary's activism on political and labor issues between the ratification of the woman's suffrage amendment and *Brown v. Board of Education of Topeka, Kansas,* illuminates the foundations women laid for the modern civil rights movement and reminds us that labor issues were central to those protests.[41]

International BSCP President A. Philip Randolph, the "Dean" of the civil rights movement, fused racial equality with trade unionism during those forgotten years. In telling the story of the union, scholars have focused on several major themes. Randolph's leadership as a union president and as an organizer of civil rights protests is the focus of several biographers; his "charismatic leadership" has produced what William H. Harris calls "the field of A. Philip Randolph studies." The tension between the union's New York headquarters and its local divisions, and the contrasting styles of Randolph and First International Vice-President Milton P. Webster, are other themes in the Brotherhood story.[42]

The prominence of former porters, the status of Brotherhood porters in the African American community, and even the marriage prospects of porters, also attract the interest of the public and historians. Many have called Pullman porters the aristocracy of black labor. Saunders Redding captures the idolization these men enjoyed:

> Pullman porters were of the industrial elite and the economically advantaged among Negroes. They wore uniforms, not overalls; carried valises, not lunch pails. In the Negro social community they stood just below professionals, civil service employees and businessmen. Their rank was important in the community and they were proud of it. . . . The porters . . . had the same considerable though disingenuous identification with the white middle class . . . the same complex relationship between the exploited and the exploiters.[43]

The community's awe of Pullman porters was based in part on the number of successful black men who once worked as porters. Rayford W. Logan and Michael R. Winston's *Dictionary of American Negro Biography* lists an impressive array, among them: Perry Howard, Mississippi Republican and special assistant to the U.S. Attorney General; J. Finley Wilson, Grand Exalted Ruler of the Elks; Frank Crosswaith, International Ladies' Garment Workers' Union organizer, and Rienzi B. Lemus, president of the Brotherhood of Dining Car Employees. Other famous former Pullman porters were Benjamin E. Mays, president of Morehouse College; Melvin Chisum, founder of the National Negro Press Association; novelist Claude McKay, and Pan-Africanist writer Joel A. Rogers.[44]

But the fame of these men resides in their later accomplishments, not in their work as porters. The social prestige of rank-and-file porters was linked to these men, but before unionization many saw themselves trapped in a "blind alley" job. Working as a porter was a step up the ladder, but without promotions there was nowhere else an African American man could go if he remained with Pullman. Porters and maids who spent their lives working for the company were not among this elite. Some, like Robert Turner, were born railroad men and wanted to see the country. Others, such as C. L. Dellums, who once had hopes of a college education, remained with Pullman because they had families to support. They perhaps resented those college students who spent their summers portering but returned to Howard, Fisk, Dartmouth, and Williams each fall. When the BSCP won a contract with the Pullman Company, the occupation itself became prestigious. The pride of working as a porter now came from one's membership in the Brotherhood of Sleeping Car Porters.[45]

The community's esteem for Brotherhood porters arose, too, from their political power, particularly in the South. Unlike other middle-class African Americans who worked as public school teachers or for the U.S. postal service, porters were economically independent; the union protected members from company officials who tried to discipline politically active workers. Unionized porters earned relatively high wages, allowing them to purchase property and pay poll taxes. With their literacy and knowledge of the larger world, porters met southern states' requirements to register to vote.[46]

Unionization made porters' good marital prospects. According to Rosina Tucker, she, like many other women, hesitated to marry a Pullman porter because of the low pay and insecurity of the job. But the Brotherhood gave porters and their wives prestige and political power. "I've had schoolteachers say to me, 'Mrs. Tucker, please get me a Pullman porter for a husband.' So you can see how . . . the union made these porters feel they are somebody." It also made women feel important.[47]

The "all-encompassing identity" of Pullman porters extended to their wives and families. A major theme in the Brotherhood story is the kinship networks of fathers, sons, uncles, and cousins who worked for Pullman, securing their jobs through relatives. As folklorist Jack Santino found, even porters' sisters married porters. Jessie Bonds, former president of the Chicago Ladies' Auxiliary, was the daughter of Pullman porter William and Pullman maid Josephine Puckett, "stalwarts" in the local organizing committee. Porters' wives and female relatives might also work for the company as car cleaners or as laundry workers. The frequency of intermarriage and kinship networks among porters' families was also common among white railroading families, as labor historians have shown.[48]

Brotherhood families recognized that railroads represented the promised land for African Americans, and in their travels porters and maids shared information about distant places to those hoping one day to migrate. Yet the steel rails held specific meanings for men and women, Hazel Carby argues. "The train, which had symbolized freedom and mobility for men in male blues songs, became a contested symbol." In one woman's blues lyric, "The sound of the train fills my heart with misery." Many porters' wives, uncertain of their husbands' return, may have identified with the women's railroad blues. Wives may have been jealous too of Pullman maids who rode the rails, "running wild" from place to place. Women rarely rode the boxcars, but working as a Pullman maid permitted African American women a new mobility. One Chicago woman wanted to get to California, so she took a job as a Pullman maid for the trip to San Francisco and promptly quit. For many maids and porters and their families, railroading was an enviable life promising adventure and an opportunity to meet—if as a servant—the best people.[49]

Service work, however, has been the crux of the African American worker's predicament. To maintain the racial status quo, whites have historically segregated African Americans and other workers of color in service jobs; even white engineers, Eric Arnesen shows, expected locomotive firemen to perform domestic chores for them. Part of historians' fascination with Pullman porters lies in reconciling notions about service with masculinity. Santino interviewed one porter who resolved the disparity this way: "I think you can be a man while being a servant. I think if you have the courage and dignity and respect for yourself, and respect for people, that you can be a man while being a servant."[50] The Brotherhood of Sleeping Car Porters dignified service work, establishing the right of porters and maids to earn a living wage under decent conditions. The women of the Brotherhood, service workers in industry and in their own homes, also earned respect through their participation in the union. In doing so, the BSCP empowered African American women and men in other occupations to seek respect and first-class citizenship.

1

The Case against Pullman

Much has been written about the "Case of the Pullman Porter." Descriptions of his job, his working conditions, his low wages, and his grievances against the Pullman Company testify to the unmanly indignities he suffered before the Brotherhood of Sleeping Car Porters represented him. Indeed, they are essential ingredients in the Brotherhood story. The union and the company contested the question of manhood: the Brotherhood sought the right of porters to exercise personal liberty on the job; Pullman wanted the right to control its black male workers on and off the job. The issue of manhood framed the unionization debate for workers, families, and the company.

"The Case of the Pullman Maid" was never made, even though the conditions under which she labored were as arduous as those of her brother porter. Maids did not articulate a separate set of grievances, despite sexually discriminatory work rules. Female unionists and male union leaders expressed their labor protests in terms of race discrimination and in the language of black manhood rights. This rhetorical emphasis deflected members' awareness of gender inequality, allowing them to focus their attention on gender compatibility.

The wives and families of porters detailed their own grievances against the Pullman Company, supporting the Brotherhood's demand for manhood. Wives protested their husbands' meager wages, which forced them to scrimp on the household budget, forego the education of their children, or forced them into white folks' kitchens. They resented Pullman welfare workers' inspection of their homes, questioning the family's domestic arrangements, spending decisions, and lifestyle. The paternalistic and insulting treatment porters received from white Pullman employees and passengers bred domestic strife, leading one scholar to wonder "how these men, trying to protect their manhood while holding servile positions, treated the women they lived with."[1] Yet the Brotherhood's assertion of porters' manhood allowed African American women to seek their own rights as the wives of honest workingmen.

The demand for manhood by Pullman workers and their families can be traced back to the great strike of 1894, when labor leader Eugene V. Debs denounced Pullman Company paternalism. A. Philip Randolph drew on his rhetoric to formulate the Brotherhood's demands. Debs invested manhood rights with a specific meaning for white Pullman workers. He linked it with individual liberty, arguing the male worker's right to claim the value of his work, to participate in government as an equal citizen, and to raise his family as he saw fit. The manly worker's version of a proper family, however, did not differ substantially from bourgeois versions. African Americans also struggled to achieve this Victorian version of the ideal family, which Randolph believed could be attained with a living wage and better working conditions for the male head of household. While under federal control during World War I, white Pullman workers won bargaining agreements and their manhood from the company. African American workers, however, had not. They remained yoked under the company's racially contextualized paternalism. White railroad workers had won manhood rights; the Brotherhood wanted the same for black railroad workers. One major obstacle lay in founder George M. Pullman's belief that only African Americans possessed the servile attitude that was crucial to providing luxury service on his sleeping cars.[2]

When George Pullman built the "Pioneer," the first sleeping car of the Pullman Palace Car Company in 1865, he envisioned a luxury hotel on wheels. A comfortable bed, good food, and "real service" became his company's trademarks. Servants, stationed in every car, fulfilled passengers' every request. Pullman passengers essentially paid a surcharge for a bed and the personal services of these men and women. According to company lore, the first generation of Pullman servants were recently emancipated African Americans trained to serve their white masters and mistresses. By 1925, the occupation of sleeping car porter became so connected with Pullman that one company logo caricatured the "P" in Pullman as a grinning, white-jacketed, towel-draped African American man.[3]

The "badge of servitude" for African Americans was, of course, a fundamental characteristic of nineteenth-century race relations. Thus George Pullman's belief that black men and women who had worked in white southern households would be ideal porters merely modernized an old relationship. The creation of this occupation and, more generally of Pullman service, at the end of the Civil War signaled the continuance of the old racial order on the railroads, the era's most conspicuous symbol of progress. Pullman cars offered passengers the only first-class long-distance accommodations, allowing the wealthy shelter from the poor. By placing African American men and later African American women in Pullman cars, the company preserved antebellum traditions. It also served to remind African American passengers that their place was the Jim Crow car.[4]

Beginning in the late nineteenth century, railroad segregation laws arranged passengers by both sex and race. White men had smoking cars reserved for their use, but conductors often forced African American men and women to ride in these cars when separate second-class cars were unavailable. Nonsmoking day cars accommodated respectable white women and men. The railroad conductor enforced this hierarchy of passengers by race, sex, and class; he also controlled all operating and non-operating train personnel. Along with the Pullman cars where porters and Pullman conductors worked, long-distance trains offered a dining car, staffed by African American men working under a white maitre d'. By the 1920s, most trains offered lounge cars, where "men naturally gravitate . . . (women, too) to the friendly relaxing atmosphere that makes a man feel very much at home." Pullman hired both Filipinos and African Americans as car attendants. To appeal to businessmen, some Pullman runs included white male barbers for those who had an "important engagement when you arrive" and white "male secretaries . . . available for dictation."[5]

The abundance of men and the difficulty of early long-distance travel made George Pullman especially attentive to the needs of his "lady passengers." There was a decided "lack of protection sufficient to permit the free travel of unescorted women." Lady passengers, whether escorted or not, required different services than male passengers. Ladies often traveled with children who needed someone to care for them while their mothers dined or relaxed; older women also required special assistance, and upper-class women appreciated the services of a hairdresser and manicurist.[6] Like other white men of his day, George Pullman probably did not think it proper for African American men to wait on white lady passengers retiring for the night. To provide these services for his lady passengers, Pullman hired African American women as train maids.

The qualifications for sleeping car maids and porters were demanding, but wages did not not reflect workers' education, experience, or skills, the three quantifiable areas job evaluators used to grade railroad work. Race was the primary prerequisite for Pullman applicants. As late as 1951, the Pullman Company publicly stated "the aspirant must be an American Negro, preferably about 25." Since literacy was necessary, applicants had to have completed grammar school, and by the 1920s, high school. But no more. Benjamin E. Mays, a porter during World War I who later became president of Morehouse College, contended Pullman considered him a union troublemaker because of his college degree. Employment guidelines warned: "Men who have attended colleges or universities are not considered the most desirable material to act as servants; therefore care must be taken in considering them." This restriction, adopted in the mid-1920s, may have reflected company efforts to bar trade union radicals.[7]

Male applicants had to meet age, height, and weight limitations and be clean-shaven. Porters' applications required a complete employment record for the previous five years with references, to be verified by company officials, and a photograph (the only job in the company that did). The photograph, according to union lore, ensured that the applicant met the company's unwritten rule against light-complexioned men. Personnel department memoranda warned against hiring certain "types": "The sheik type, as well as high pressure type, do not make good servants and should not be considered." Finally, Pullman Company investigators made unannounced visits to the homes of all applicants to observe their living conditions and collect neighbors' opinions.[8] The acceptable candidate had to demonstrate that he or she both looked and lived the part of a servant.

The qualifications for maids were also strict, and open only to African American women until 1925. Then, to discourage unionization among Pullman maids, the company began to hire Chinese women for Pacific coast routes. The decision to hire other women of color for the job reflected the company's desire to reinforce the racial status quo of the West. While no personnel memorandum dictated height and weight limitations for maids, the company nonetheless fired at least one woman for being "too large" at five feet, eleven inches, one hundred and seventy pounds. Cosmetics, if used, were to be applied sparingly. Literacy was also required, but without proof of graduation. Pullman eagerly hired trained nurses, since they could provide medical care in an emergency. Despite their college degrees, in their Pullman uniforms, few passengers would take these African American and Chinese women as more than maids. Marital or parental status did not prohibit a candidate from the position of train maid, although the company restricted white married women from holding certain jobs, in the guise of female protection.[9]

In 1926, the Pullman Company employed over ten thousand porters and about two hundred maids. The company assigned one porter per sleeping car; only in exceptional circumstances were relief porters employed. Maids worked on the "de luxe" and limited runs; these trains attracted the very wealthy, such as Mrs. George M. Pullman, who "wintered" in Florida, "summered" in the Berkshires, and relaxed at the spas in Hot Springs, Arkansas. One to two maids ran on the transcontinental trains that took four or five days from Chicago to

Los Angeles; maids were sometimes employed on private cars chartered by various tourist and convention groups. Overseeing their work, the Pullman conductor sold and assigned berths, collected tickets, and ensured the smooth running of the train's Pullman cars.[10]

Porters and maids provided the service Pullman sold to passengers. The first general instruction given in the company rule books stressed, "The employe's [sic] primary duty is to satisfy passengers, giving special attention to those who are ill or infirm and children traveling alone." Manicures, shoe shines, child care, and hairdressing were some of the free services Pullman offered to passengers: "All service is to be performed cheerfully and without thought of gratuities." "The reputation of the service depends as much upon the efficiency of employes [sic] as upon the facilities provided by the Company for the comfort of its patrons," Pullman's general instructions intoned. "It is, therefore, imperative that you be obliging and courteous to passengers, alert to anticipate their wants and diligent and cheerful in executing orders."[11] Service came, literally, before safety in the instruction handbook.

African American women and men performed services for passengers, but their primary responsibility was to ensure safety on the train. The company's instructions to porters, maids, attendants, and bus boys ran over 120 pages. A porter knew how to operate every mechanical and electrical feature of the Pullman car. He regulated lighting, heat, air-conditioning, water, supplies, and of course, he made up the Pullman berths. These beds were heavy and dangerous equipment, the company warned, and porters were sometimes seriously injured when opening and closing them, especially on rough track beds. Porters also knew company and federal safety regulations for railroads as well as food and health laws.[12] If he ran in-charge, performing the Pullman conductor's job, the porter's responsibilities included assigning berths, collecting tickets, and selling better accommodations to passengers when available.

Maids were both ladies' attendants and domestic workers. They kept the restrooms and the ladies' lounges "spotless," tidied up passengers' roomettes, picked up trash, put away baggage, and remade beds. Pullman maids, like porters, offered a variety of personal services to lady and gentleman passengers. The *Pullman News* boasted of these "Hand Maidens for Travelers": "These maids are expert manicurists, they can sew and can care for children, babies and elderly people, particularly when they are obliged to travel alone. Persons taken ill on the trains frequently are cared for by the maids, and sometimes first aid treatment is administered."[13] In promotional photographs, Pullman showed maids attending to lady passengers in a variety of ways: helping a white woman passenger to dress, cleaning her shoes, mending her clothes, fixing her hair, and bringing her breakfast in bed. The maid might also help with showers, and more personal services. "In fact," boasted a 1939 Pullman brochure, "the maid's duties add to the many creature-comforts to be found in Pullman service."[14]

The company did not grant maids the authority to enforce safety and health regulations, but required them to report all dangerous and unlawful situations to the conductor. The maid's most important duty, according to the rule book, was to assist the Pullman conductor in lifting tickets from passengers in the ladies' lounge.

Pullman regarded porters and maids as unskilled service workers and refused to formally acknowledge the safety responsibilities of their work. Job evaluators and passengers alike disregarded the skills, knowledge, and education required to perform these duties. In an industry devoted to standardized wage scales based on job classification schemes, the Pullman Company institutionalized race-based wage discrimination by classifying all African American employees as unskilled workers and paying them less than comparably skilled and lesser skilled white laborers. African American workers were well aware of the company's racism.

Frances Mary Jackson Albrier, a graduate nurse from Howard University, worked as a Pullman maid in the 1920s. Prior to applying to Pullman, she worked for an Oakland obstetrician and volunteered at the Public Welfare League of Alameda County and the county hospital "in the interest of racial patients." Although told by the district manager that as a maid she would look after ill passengers, once hired, she found her main task was to give free manicures, the maid's version of the porter's "complimentary" shoeshine.[15]

The company displayed its racial paternalism explicitly by strictly regulating the deportment of its black sleeping car workers. White Pullman conductors enforced these work rules but were themselves allowed personal autonomy. Porters and maids could not leave their assigned cars except to perform their duties or when directed by the conductor. Maids were forbidden to leave the train at station stops, although male workers might. On the train, no porter or maid could sleep, swear, drink liquor, smoke, chew gum, play cards, or sell any item except the railroad's pillow rental service. "Social conversation or familiarities" with other crew members was prohibited.[16]

The Pullman maid's work was not very different from the domestic servant's work in a private home, but the wages were higher. Except for her service stripes and her brassard, her uniform might have passed for that of any Fifth Avenue domestic worker. At least Miss Ann, like the scenery, kept changing. The Pullman maid had to listen to her lady passenger's tales of woe and show sympathy, while keeping silent about her own worries. How often did Frances Albrier worry about her two young children staying with a neighbor in Oakland?[17]

On the train, the job could be lonely. The maid was often the only female crew member and rules forbade her to socialize with porters. While Pullman conductors and other white crew members slept in Pullman berths, and sometimes their own crew car, the African American crew "rested" in a restroom-lounge. On layovers in foreign terminals Pullman provided low-cost sleeping quarters for porters, while maids spent their nights at the YWCA. Management kept tabs on off-duty maids; it was not uncommon for women who missed YWCA house curfew to be fired or placed on the "extra" board, receiving runs only when the regular maid was unavailable. As a result, maids had little opportunity to partake in the traditional male camaraderie of railroad workers.[18]

In addition to lacking suitable rest periods, racial segregation made restaurant meals hard to find. Before the union, porters bought their own food during station stops, if they could find a store or lunch counter willing to serve them; maids who did not bring their own meals had to rely on a porter for food. Dining car food was expensive, despite an employee discount, and off limits until passengers had been served. Even then, the railroad conductor might refuse service, or force black crew members to eat behind a curtain. "As a result, most porters [and maids] seemed to have chronic indigestion," recalled Rosina Corrothers Tucker.[19]

Sleeping car workers faced long hours on duty; lack of sleep and meals remained major grievances for years. The New York–Chicago run in 1926 was typical. Porters arrived at the New York Pullman Yards at 4:00 P.M. to prepare the cars and then change in to their uniforms. Maids reported at the station, in uniform, by 5:25 P.M. ready for passengers to begin boarding at 5:30 P.M. Pay did not start until the train had left the station at 6:00 P.M. Porters and maids helped passengers find their berths, bagged their hats, hung their coats, stowed their baggage, and familiarized new passengers with the car's safety features.

Between 7:00 and 10:00 P.M. adult passengers went to the lounge and dining cars. Children were often left in the care of the maid, who fed them and put them to bed. Porters broke down the berths: folding down the couches and pulling down the beds, placing mattresses on top, putting linens and blankets on the beds in the special Pullman method, and hanging partition curtains. Car configurations varied greatly, but by the 1920s most had twenty-two berths each; the work had to be done quickly.[20] Passengers began retiring to their berths about 10:00 P.M. and might still be returning from the lounge car after 1:00 A.M. Maids, stationed in the ladies' lounge, helped female passengers prepare for bed and assisted them into their berths. Porters collected and shined all the shoes left by the men; maids sewed, pressed, or spot cleaned any clothing the lady passengers left.

Usually by 2:00 A.M. crew members had a chance to "rest," but rarely were they left undisturbed, and the company forbid them to sleep. They remained in full uniform: porters could not take off their shoes or loosen their ties; maids remained in their dress oxfords and fully fastened undergarments. Porters were also required to call any passengers detraining prior to Chicago. Passengers visited the lounges where porters and maids rested all through the night and, according to Brotherhood lore, drunken white men would sometimes engage the porter in long discussions about their personal problems.[21] Maids could be trapped in similar discussions or spend the night caring for a sick passenger or a frightened, crying child. At 6:00 A.M. porters and maids began helping passengers prepare for their 9:00 arrival in Chicago. Maids could leave the train at 9:10 A.M.; porters left at 10:15 A.M. after gathering all the linens for the laundry and putting away the berths.

After a few hours in Chicago, porters and maids went back to the station by early afternoon for the return trip to New York, where they arrived at 9:30 the next morning. In all, porters had been away from their home stations for 48 hours and 45 minutes, but paid for only the 31.5 hours officially on duty. Maids had been on the cars for 40.5 hours, 24 hours on duty. To work full-time, sleeping car workers needed a minimum of seven round trips each month, spending 341.25 hours on the job, and clocking in over eleven thousand miles. For this, Pullman porters with five years experience earned $76.00 per month; maids with the same years of experience earned $73.50. The New York–Chicago train was considered a short trip; the New York–Miami route required more than twenty-four hours officially on duty each way.[22]

The wages Pullman paid to porters and maids, at first glance, appear high, three times higher than the going rate of one to two dollars per day paid to African American male day laborers and female day workers. Company publicity emphasized the "monopoly" that African Americans held on the job, holding porters out to the public as examples of its benevolence and liberal racial attitudes. The conditions under which porters and maids worked, however, reflected the company's greed and racial paternalism. Pullman President Robert T. Lincoln seemed to endorse the view of Mississippi Senator W. K. Vardaman, "The way to control the [Negro] is . . . never to pay him more wages than is actually necessary to buy food and clothing."[23]

BSCP President Randolph attacked the low wages, unpaid labor, excessive hours, lack of sleep, white conductor-overseers, and particularly the tipping system. Working conditions at Pullman robbed the porter of his manhood, making him a slave. A Pullman official defended the wage rates, telling a federal railroad investigator, "All I can say is that you can get all the men you require to do the work."[24] The color line in labor, Randolph recognized, allowed employers to pay slave wages to African American workers. Higher wages would emancipate porters and maids and break down race segregation.

By almost any standard of comparison, sleeping car workers were poorly paid. The Brotherhood tale never fails to mention that in 1926 a Pullman porter received only $72.50 a month plus tips and had to pay not only all his expenses on the road but even for the polish for passengers' shoes. According to a 1927 study done by the Labor Bureau, Inc., a private economic consulting firm, porters' tips averaged $58.19 per month; occupational expenses amounted to $33.82. Regular porters' annual income of wages plus tips thus amounted to $1,229.76. According to the National Industrial Conference Board's estimate, a minimum of $1,669 was necessary in 1926 for an urban family of four to maintain a decent standard of living; for a family of five in the small town of Marion, Ohio, the Conference Board estimated $1,450 per year was necessary. By comparison, average earnings for full-time white railroad workers were $1,671 in 1926, while full-time earnings for African American workers in domestic service averaged $748.[25] The Brotherhood tale always forgets to note that Pullman maids were paid even less than Pullman porters.

In 1918, before the intervention of the United States Railroad Administration, Pullman maids received a flat rate of $33 per month. As a result of federally ordered wage increases, monthly pay rose to about $50 by the end of World War I. In 1926, maids with less than two years' experience received $70 per month, up to $80.50 per month after fifteen years of service. By comparison, fifteen-year veteran porters running-in-charge (as conductors) received $97.70 per month. The 1929 Pullman Wage Conference granted maids $75 per month, while standard sleeping car porters received a minimum of $77.50. Maids might also receive tips for their services but, if the porters' complaints were reliable, women passengers were mean tippers.[26] It is also likely that then, as now, passengers felt they should pay more for a shoeshine than child care, particularly when the person performing the work was an African American woman.

Maids also had occupational expenses equal to, if not greater than, porters. Maids had to provide all the tools and supplies for passengers' manicures; and if, like Frances Albrier, they did not know how, they paid for their own training. Maids and porters alike paid for their own uniforms and their care. Maids, like porters, had on-the-road expenses of their own. Meals and lodging had to be purchased. Many, such as Albrier, were single heads of households with child care expenses that male heads of households did not bear.[27]

The Brotherhood of Sleeping Car Porters demanded a living wage for porters of $150 per month, the same pay Pullman conductors received. Although the BSCP made no specific wage demands for maids, the parity between men's and women's wages suggests the union recognized that female single heads of households deserved a family wage too. Such a wage would eliminate tipping, and force the Pullman Company to pay for the full wage bill for its porters and maids rather than relying on passengers to pick up the tab. As New York columnist Heywood Broun commented, "The Pullman Company is a pan handler. Some federal police officer should take away the tin can from this corporation and confiscate its pencils. . . . I'm tired of tipping the Pullman Company."[28] Wages and tipping, however, were only the most publicized of the Brotherhood's demands.

Despite Pullman's legendary efficiency in almost every matter, porters' and maids' run assignments seemed to be determined by favoritism rather than planning. Porters and maids favored by Pullman supervisors were more likely to work regularly; many employees, perhaps one third, remained on the extra board, as substitutes.

To have the superintendent's good will did not guarantee an easy job; upon returning from several days out, porters and maids were frequently sent out on the next run, sometimes without enough time to go home, put on clean uniforms, or change personal linen. This "doubling out" and "tripling out" was but one of many grievances against the Pullman Company. Frances Albrier recalled her first year working as a Pullman maid out of San Francisco–Oakland in the mid-twenties:

> The first year I went into the Pullman service, you called it "running wild." That is, wherever there is a need for a maid, you were to go. On the Overland [Limited to Chicago] it may have been the maid was sick and I would have to take her place. If I got into Chicago and there was an emergency for a maid on the Twentieth Century [Limited to New York] I would have to go. In New York, when I got there, they needed the service of a maid who was off, or something happened—going somewhere else—I was to go. They called that "running wild." For a year, then afterwards, you bid on a regular route if there's a vacancy.[29]

The haphazardness of work assignments upset family life; spouses and children did not always know when to expect the return of their mates and parents. Workers who found themselves at distant stations without further assignments had to deadhead home, without pay in unheated cars.

African American workers at Pullman wanted to be treated with dignity and respect on the job. Being "called out of one's name" was one constant slight. Since the early years of the Pullman Company, passengers summoned porters by calling "George." According to one legend, "George" was derived from the practice of referring to porters as George M. Pullman's "boys." To the porters, the name stung because it carried over the antebellum practice of "naming a slave after his master." To force passengers to use their proper names, porters used only their first initials. The porters requested the company supply name cards printed with porters' first initials and last name to be displayed at the front of each car. In October 1926, it granted the request and announced that a porter would not be disciplined if he failed to respond to a passenger's "George" or "Boy" or anything other than their names. The Brotherhood immediately took credit for the policy change, asserting that the union had brought the porters manhood.[30] Train maids never had a common appellation, but conductors often used their first names to call them, and some passengers might have observed the custom of calling female servants by whatever name came to mind.

Randolph, as the president of the Brotherhood of Sleeping Car Porters, enumerated the union's specific demands regarding wages and working conditions in August 1925. Each of these demands had been granted to white Pullman conductors in 1922. Porters and maids wanted the right to sleep at night, in unused berths when available. In place of the mileage rate system, they wanted a 240-hour month, the same as white railroad employees worked. They insisted on pay for all the time they worked, including preparatory time and late arrivals. Meals and lodging in foreign terminals should be paid by the company. Pullman should provide all equipment, including shoe polish, nail polish, and meals; free uniforms should be provided the day of hire, instead of after ten years service. African American workers believed they should have meal privileges and not be forced to eat behind a curtain. They desired to return home between runs to see families and to rest. When porters ran in charge, doing conductors' work, porters should receive conductors' pay. Their wage demands were hardly exorbitant, for even the $1,800 per annum they asked for would have kept them in the bottom quarter of all white railroad men's 1926 earnings.[31] The BSCP believed sleeping car workers were entitled to the same rights and privileges as white railwaymen.

To achieve these demands, the Brotherhood of Sleeping Car Porters fought against both the Pullman Company's paternalistic, anti-labor reputation and the racial and sexual attitudes of company officials. The company had reluctantly signed a contract with the Order of Sleeping Car Conductors effective January 1, 1922. That contract affirmed the right of conductors to supervise and discipline porters and maids, and specified that the job of conductor was reserved for white males. The conductors asserted that "the white traveling public, especially women, were unsafe alone in a car with a Negro porter." Thus their contract, the first Pullman negotiated with an independent union, upheld the racial and sexual hierarchies inherent in the railroad industry.[32]

The apprehensions of Pullman officials about an independent sleeping car porters' union were not based exclusively on fiscal concerns. Higher wages, fewer hours, and better working conditions would have cost money, but the main fear of officials was losing control over its African American workforce. An independent union would destroy the racial subservience that company officials believed essential to good job performance. Even allowing porters to run-in-charge without a Pullman conductor was dangerous because it gave too much authority to black men. To these officials, racial subservience included repressing suggestions of black sexuality, male or female. The Brotherhood's demand for manhood rights, Pullman believed, was a license for black men to accost white women. As paternalistic white men, company officials felt duty-bound to protect white women from such abuses. For this reason, Pullman Company President Edward F. Carry insisted on keeping secret the identities of women who accused porters of sexual misconduct, the company's version of a rape charge.[33]

The sleeping car employee's duties created the potential for sexual and racial misunderstandings. Porters performed their sometimes intimate tasks by relying on the "social distance" behaviors created during slavery and Jim Crow to segregate black men from white women. The rigid rules of segregation forced black male servants to repress any hint of sexuality or even masculinity, rendering them eunuchs to the whites they served. On Pullman cars, social distancing became formalized into work rules. Porters could make up beds for (white) lady passengers, but only white male conductors or African American maids could assist them into upper berths. As one porter recalled, "A black man putting his hands on a white woman, even with the intent to help, was considered out of place in those days." To prevent misunderstandings, work rules specified that porters should only awaken passengers by shaking their curtains, never by touching them.[34] Minor infractions could mean dismissal.

The Messenger reported a representative case in 1925. In this account, a female passenger accused a porter of "hugging" her at 2:00 A.M. while she slept. She claimed she screamed and stuck him with a hat pin, but no one heard her or came to check. She did not report the incident until the following morning. The porter denied having anything to do with the incident, but the conductor wrote up the passenger's report.

Six months later, a grievance committee convened. The accused porter, who had just returned from forty-eight hours on the road, was called in to defend himself on the charge of molesting the female passenger. He pointed out the ridiculousness of the charge and the conditions under which it allegedly occurred. The porter's representative on the grievance committee also tried to defend the porter. He asked that the passenger be called in to state her complaint, but the Pullman Company refused on the grounds that this was an unnecessary inconvenience to her. The porter's representative "pointed out that the Company was doing to the porter what a mob in the South would not do to its victim, namely, it was trying and convicting him without his accuser identifying him." According to the BSCP, Pullman fired the porter and then framed and fired his porter-representative too.[35]

The Brotherhood's diligent defense of African American men's morality did not transfer consistently to protection of African American women workers. Maids faced sexual harassment from train personnel and passengers, but Pullman managers and BSCP officials could do little to protect them. A maid from the Southern District described the treatment she received from a train conductor in 1928 on her regular Miami–Chicago route. At the beginning of the trip, she had had a "bitter and angry" confrontation with the train conductor who "hollered" at her as she performed her duties. She reported the incident to the Pullman inspector onboard, who reprimanded the conductor on his behavior. The conductor retaliated. He

> came to me very roughly, using many curse words and informed me that he stood very strong in Fort Pierce, Florida and that he was going to have me taken off.
>
> I went to bed . . . and had just been in there a little while when the train conductor came in and started to pull the curtain of my berth open. I ran[g] the bell for the porter and the conductor disappeared.

When the Pullman conductor learned of the train conductor's conduct, he suggested "I get up and put my clothes on and go to the rear of the train, inasmuch as the train conductor was determined to take me off at Fort Pierce. . . . I hid in one of the rear cars until we passed through Fort Pierce. . . . However, the sheriff and several of his men and the station master came through the train to [try to] take me off."[36] The maid, a BSCP member, upon Webster's advice, simply requested a transfer from the district. Her letter appears to be the only extant and direct evidence of sexual harassment. Yet the extreme nature of her experience and the willingness of BSCP officials to report it, suggests that the harassment of Pullman maids was not uncommon.

The pulp media of the day encouraged racist attitudes toward African American railway workers. The tabloids portrayed porters as pimps who arranged meetings between male and female passengers. Reinforcing this sexual stereotype was the popular perception that railroad workers generally, and African Americans in particular, were a "syphilis-infested race."[37] The sexual fears of Pullman's white officials encouraged the routine dismissal of any porter or maid accused of impropriety, no matter what the circumstances. The

Brotherhood viewed these dismissals as lynchings, and the accused rarely had due process. But the union did not publicly defend the sexual conduct of African American women workers; when passengers or employees harassed maids, both the Brotherhood and the company seemed to view such male behavior as the woman's fault. Even after the contract formalized hearing procedures, fears and distrust over sexual misconduct remained a consistent factor in the company's relations with the BSCP.[38]

Company paternalism was also evident in the various welfare schemes designed to discourage the formation of independent trade unions. The Employee Representation Plan (ERP) and the Pullman Porters Benefit Association (PPBA), were both developed during World War I in response to the federal government's War Labor Board orders. The PPBA, initiated by porters in 1920, was a fraternal group similar to those established by other railroad workers. The men duplicated their fraternal rituals, secret oaths, and organizational pattern, including their women's auxiliaries. Membership was restricted to "negro male persons of good character and in good general health between ages twenty-one and forty-four inclusive."[39]

The company quickly defused PPBA by presenting the Employee Representation Plan (ERP) in 1920, but allowed the PPBA to continue offering benefits and encouraged porters to join. The company even deposited PPBA funds at the Binga National Bank, the nation's largest African American-owned bank, located in the heart of south Chicago. Jesse Binga, the bank's president and founder, had himself been a Pullman porter.[40] The BSCP's criticisms of the PPBA included the lack of control members themselves had over its assets, and the control Pullman Company officials had in determining benefit eligibility.

The Employee Representation Plan provided for management and porter-representatives to decide work rules and wages for porters and maids in wage conferences held at the company's discretion or upon presentation of a petition signed by a majority of porters and maids (approximately five thousand signatures). The ERP also established hearing procedures for Pullman workers charged with rule infractions by superiors or passengers. Defendants could not use outside representation before the grievance board, which was composed primarily of white male management officials from the Pullman's Industrial Relations Bureau. Hand-picked porter representatives also served on the board, but these men could do little without fear of forfeiting their privileged positions within the company. The United States Railroad Labor Board tacitly recognized the ERP as a union.[41]

Pullman paternalism followed African American workers home. The company sponsored various recreational activities, exclusively for porters, maids, and their families, such as music groups, baseball teams, and talent shows, to showcase African Americans' "natural" musical and athletic talents to the public. Company officials also seemed to believe that they had the right to claim porters' children for themselves. On several occasions, Pullman President Champ Carry referred to a porter's son as a "future Pullman porter." Although many porters had fathers, uncles, sons, and cousins working in the service, Carry's description caused a great deal of resentment, and proved an emotional factor in Brotherhood propaganda. Neither fathers nor mothers wanted to see their children sentenced to a life of Pullman "slavery." It is no wonder that some loyal Brotherhood men and women named their sons and daughters for A. Philip Randolph.[42]

Wives had their own set of grievances against the Pullman Company, which the Brotherhood promised to relieve. Eleven thousand miles per month, one porter reckoned, put him on the road more than twenty days each month. If the union could win the industry standard month of 240 hours, husbands and wives could be home more often. If the union won the $150 per month wages the union demanded, wives might withdraw from the labor force and still have enough money, perhaps, to send their children to college.[43]

"Poor Wages and the Home," a *Messenger* cartoon, illustrated a porter and his wife discussing their daughter's future. The porter's wife promises her daughter she will "work her fingers off" to send her to school next year. The porter complains they cannot live off his tips; his wife urges him to join the Brotherhood, "If organization is good for the white man, it is good for the black man too!" By showing the lifestyle the family might attain with the union wage, the Brotherhood appealed to family members. Many were willing to risk their jobs for that opportunity.[44]

Higher wages would bring a better standard of living to porters' families. Wives would no longer find it necessary to make painful economies with the household budget, and might withdraw from the labor market. This would give them time to volunteer for church and organizational activities, enhancing their standing in the community; children could spend more time in school, increasing their chances for upward mobility. In addition, the family could enjoy better food and material goods, a larger home, and more leisure time. This was the lifestyle many African Americans dreamed of when they came north during the Great Migration.

Fewer financial worries and better working conditions might even make husbands less "cranky." Rosina Tucker described her husband as "grim and sullen and, far from being confiding, to try to glean anything about how he felt or what he was thinking was like pulling teeth." She may have thought the union would make a better husband of him, expanding their married life beyond the rounds of work and home. At a BSCP-sponsored Labor Conference, officers from the Domestic Relations and Juvenile Courts averred that stable wages made for a stable home life. "The experts revealed the fact that 90% of these cases could be corrected if the father made enough money to take care of the family." The Brotherhood's affirmation of the porter's manhood, the union claimed, made for better husbands.[45]

Porters' domestic life and Pullman paternalism were frequent themes in Randolph's *Messenger* editorials. Monthly wages were insufficient to support a family, and the well-being of many porters, Randolph argued, was often due to their wives' industry. Pullman publicized the consumption patterns of porters and their families to undermine union demands for better wages. "The sound of a graphaphone [*sic*] in the porters' home or . . . his wife entering a movie picture show," are signs of their prosperity. "[The newspaper] reporter is . . . not told that the porter's wife is taking in washing or sewing or working out in service. He is not told that the porter's home is packed with lodgers who practically take up all the room, thereby rendering his life less comfortable and health less secure."[46] Randolph no doubt exaggerated the poverty of the domestic lives of porters. On the other hand, the Pullman Company dramatically overstated the prosperity of porters when it claimed that many owned their own homes and automobiles.

Working for the Pullman Company meant leaving one's family, home, and even neighborhood open to company scrutiny. "Pullman Welfare Workers' chief duty is to snoop around and spy upon the unsuspecting and long suffering Pullman porter," Randolph charged. Porter-instructors and welfare workers called at the homes of Pullman employees to determine whether they lived according to some (never specified) standard. Pullman investigators asked neighbors about prospective employees' lifestyles: Did he or she have parties often? Did he or she attend church? Were the children well-behaved? There was, in a sense, no end to the humiliation felt by family members.[47]

Company snooping did not stop after hiring. Welfare workers inquired after veteran workers too. Ostensibly they checked on the family's welfare while the porter or maid was on the road. The union believed these visits had more sinister purposes. Investigators were to look for company property and assess personal possessions in workers' homes. Pullman used a porter's personal property or achievements against him and his family, wrote Rosina Tucker. "Through their informers, they knew that [my husband] Berthea owned his house, that I had a piano, and that I had a son who was in college."[48] Pullman's superintendents "reminded" Brotherhood members that their child's college tuition payment would soon be due to discourage pro-union sentiment. Pullman coerced porters and maids to sign "yellow dog" contracts that forbid them from joining independent trade unions. In Omaha, BSCP organizer

Bennie Smith warned, "The Company is sending some of its stool pigeons to men's houses at 7:30 in the morning with the [contract] and arguing with the men's wives to persuade the husbands to sign."[49]

The battle for the loyalty of porters' wives was sometimes as fierce as that for porters themselves. Randolph and Pullman officials both recognized the influence wives could wield over their husbands. During the struggle for union recognition, Pullman fired pro-union porters and porters whose wives were active in the Brotherhood. At the same time, Randolph made special appeals to wives by emphasizing that the union's demand for a living wage would allow them to withdraw from the labor force and devote themselves to domestic matters. Maids also supported these demands because higher wages for fewer hours would give them more time with their families or for their own leisure. Yet women's activities contradicted Randolph's image of spousal adoration. Their work, so essential to the union's victory, extended women's sphere beyond the reproduction of union labor.

2

"It Was the Women Who Made the Union": Organizing the Brotherhood

The men who founded the International Brotherhood of Sleeping Car Porters and Maids (BSCP) announced their vision for the union in its name: an international organization representing African American men and women in the labor movement. They sought to represent sleeping car workers in the United States, Canada, and Mexico. Similar to the Order of Sleeping Car Conductors, the BSCP avoided using "Pullman," establishing its independence from the company. And in the early years, the organization included women by name.[1]

Despite the explicit inclusion of porters and maids in the union's name, organizers stressed the goal of black manhood. At the Brotherhood's first public meeting on August 25, 1925, leaders announced, "Inaugurating the greatest movement in the History of the Negro. . . . A Call for only red-blooded he-men. . . . Pullman Porters only invited . . . August 25, 1925."[2] Pullman maids were not invited.

President Randolph's gendered rhetoric of race, his demand for black manhood rights, facilitated the construction of specific union roles for women and men. But during the union's early years the precise definition of these roles was ambiguous. While Brotherhood men looked to the "New Negro" as their model of manhood, some women drew on the image of the New Negro Woman, who stood for women's equality in the struggle for racial and economic justice. Drawing on the feminist icons of the Harlem Renaissance, they challenged women's customary work assignments, demanding the right to organize alongside men. They knocked on doors, collected union dues, addressed mass meetings, and argued over members' unfair discharge claims with Pullman management. Many tested traditional divisions of labor, rejecting the notion that women should play feminized roles to complement the brothers' manhood.[3]

The boldness of these New Negro Women made other porters' wives uneasy. Such promiscuous activities risked the respectability they sought to achieve through the Brotherhood. These women preferred to organize among other women, providing distaff support to the men. While they upheld the gendered division of union labor, the Women's Economic Councils successfully enlarged the accepted range of women's activities. With considerable acumen, these early auxiliaries exploited women's traditional role as fundraisers and made themselves essential to the union's financial stability. Their social events raised thousands of dollars for the BSCP and taught other women the benefits of trade unionism. These contradictory definitions of female respectability underlay many of the debates over women's place in the Brotherhood.

During the first years of organizing, the BSCP drew porters and maids, husbands and wives, trade unionists and middle-class reformers into the campaign. Drawing on his experiences as a labor organizer and magazine publisher, Randolph orchestrated a national campaign to raise money, establish local Brotherhood divisions and Women's Economic Councils, and to propagandize the movement, but his primary concern was fundraising. Rather than financing the entire drive from workers' empty pockets, he asked wealthy liberal patrons and progressive organizations for donations, utilizing his networks in the Socialist Party and his wife's networks among Harlem's upper class. A large grant from the American Fund for Public Service allowed Randolph to send "every porter" a six-month subscription of *The Messenger,* which became the union's official paper.[4]

New York porter-organizers Ashley L. Totten, William H. DesVerney, Frank Crosswaith, and Roy Lancaster established contacts with Pullman porters in other cities. Randolph and the men toured the country, whenever money was available, and sometimes when it was not. When money could be raised for a one-way ticket anywhere, one of the men would be on his way. Once there, the Brotherhood held mass meetings and "labor education institutes" or conferences at which local trade unionists, community leaders, and other supporters spoke on trade unionism to the working-class African American audiences. At each stop, organizers set up BSCP locals and Women's Economic Councils to continue organizing porters and wives in the city. After raising additional money through initiation fees, dues, and general appeals, the organizers would leave for the next city.

Brotherhood mass meetings welcomed maids, wives, and other porters' relatives, and substantial numbers of African American working people interested in trade unionism. Union leaders' decision to rely on public mass meetings as a principle organizing strategy served two purposes. Large meetings made it difficult for Pullman Company informants to identify the porters and maids who attended. Equally important, such forums provided labor education to the African American community at large.

Local members arranged these meetings according to Randolph's carefully written instructions, such as those sent to Roy Lancaster for an upcoming labor institute in New York City. Randolph wrote: "I hope you will hit hard at the meetings in New York as I feel they ought to be a huge success if enough energy is put behind them. I would get the cooperation of the Intercollegiate Association from Mrs. Louise Jackson Johnson and Miss [Elizabeth] McDonald [*sic:* MacDougald]. [*Messenger* columnist George] Schuyler knows Miss McDonald. She is quite an active young woman. I would also enlist some of the moving spirits down town."[5] Outside major cities, wives often secured the meeting hall, distributed notices, and contacted porters' families to urge their attendance, while the wife of the local president usually held a dinner party in honor of Randolph and local supporters. With money tight and hotels open to African American guests uncommon, Randolph slept in his hostess's spare room more often than he wanted to recall.[6]

Mass meetings often featured the union's national leaders, who displayed a range of styles. Chicago organizer Milton P. Webster or New York porter-organizer Ashley L. Totten "would rough up the crowd, make people uneasy and agitated." Randolph followed "with the eloquent oratorical style he had honed as a Shakespearian actor: smoothing, other-worldly." The contrasting styles of these men fit perfectly together; as historian Greg LeRoy characterized them, "It was like a hell-fire Baptist preacher bringing on the Pope."[7]

Pullman Company informants also attended these meetings. The Brotherhood's iron-clad oath of secrecy protected members against these spies. Rank-and-file members did not speak about their experiences. Instead, Randolph and community leaders served as the main speakers in order to protect pro-union employees and their families from Pullman retaliation. Sometimes the widow or wife of a Brotherhood porter spoke, explaining the benefits of unionization for families. But this was risky too since the company could revoke the pension she collected.[8]

Other platform guests included the minister of the church where the meeting was held, a spokesperson from organized labor (typically white), and a spokeswoman from a women's club or a social service organization such as a settlement house, the Phyllis Wheatley Club, or Young Women's Christian Association. The broad representation from local officials and organizations gave the union credibility and helped reassure members. Speakers also donated money from their own organizations to the Brotherhood and raised money from the crowd by passing the hat.

The union's mass meetings attracted large numbers of women, both wives and maids, despite the male-only emphasis of the Brotherhood's inaugural meeting. BSCP membership rolls show that maids paid dues from the very beginning. Women joined with the same enthusiasm as the men, and faced the same consequences for their actions. Company service records clearly stated which maids were "disloyal." Ada V. Dillon was fired in 1929 for violating Pullman's loyalty rule. In later years the Brotherhood honored her, along with maids Josephine Puckett of Chicago and Tinie Upton of Los Angeles, among the men who lost their jobs during the union struggle.[9]

Organizing women workers into a predominantly male union posed particular problems for female trade unionists. Frances Albrier described some of the difficulties she had organizing other maids in the mid-1920s:

[Albrier:] The maids joined the union with the brothers, the porters throughout the United States—South, East, and West—that was maids and Pullman porters on the Pullman cars. . . . There weren't many maids out here that sympathized with the union. They weren't brought up under that militancy and they didn't have the background that I had—going through [high] school at Tuskegee and [graduating from] Howard. Our responsibility was trying to educate the black public and the black women on these things. They didn't understand the economics; they only understood the need for the job.

[Interviewer:] You had a privileged job—no question about it. I guess any woman who had it would feel so—would feel that she had a privileged job, especially if she's also supporting a family.

[Albrier]: Yes. A great many maids in the East didn't support the union. They were too busy. Some did. Some gave contributions but they didn't join because they were afraid their names would be known if they had a card belonging to the union. They let the men do it.[10]

Albrier's analysis of maids' attitudes about unionization reveals the competing definitions of female respectability for New Negro Women. Like men, women feared retaliation, a reminder of the lack of decent job opportunities for African American women. Second, she confirms that because of their breadwinning and domestic responsibilities, those who were female heads of households had very little time to participate in labor unions. And third, Albrier suggests that some maids believed unions were for men; women might donate money to the Brotherhood, but only permanent male workers needed a union. The Brotherhood's manhood rhetoric appealed to maids' sense of racial solidarity, affirming their distaste of Pullman paternalism. Although aware that, as women, they had specific problems, they defined their job grievances primarily as racial discrimination.

Albrier believed the Brotherhood could offer women significant benefits and job protection, and from extant membership records in Chicago and Oakland it appears that many other Pullman maids agreed. Furloughs, pay cuts, and the hiring of Asian replacements spurred the women's interest; between 1929 and 1930, twenty-two women paid initiation fees. During the dozen years of the Brotherhood's struggle for recognition, forty-three maids, of about one hundred working in Chicago, paid union dues. The level of women's participation, then, was equal to men's.[11]

Pullman maids had as many different backgrounds as they had reasons for going into service. There was no living male member of Rosa Broyles's family; she was the breadwinner for her family of five generations, including her maternal grandmother of 110 years. A few maids were married to porters; they often continued to work after marriage and after childbirth. Others, like some porters, worked for Pullman only briefly, until they earned enough money to do something else. Perhaps like Albrier, some tired of their old jobs and thought they might see a bit of the world.[12]

A canvass of maids' service record cards provides a glimpse into their lives and Pullman careers. Almost all of these women began working for the Pullman Company between 1920 and 1925. Most were in their late twenties to early thirties; the median age of newly hired maids was thirty-one. Marital status could be determined for about half of the women. Twenty-two married either before or during their Pullman service, two were divorced; only two were given an honorific "Miss." None of the records surveyed indicated children, although other evidence clearly shows that several maids were mothers.[13]

Some women may have hesitated to join the BSCP because of male leaders' antipathy toward their participation. As men, porters embraced the distinctly masculine culture of traveling men and the railroad brotherhoods. On the road, or at home, local Brotherhood headquarters, PPBA lodges, and even crowded Pullman sleeping quarters encouraged fraternization with local and foreign men telling tales, playing cards, and drinking and talking about women. The Oakland BSCP office shared space with a pool hall, owned and managed by local organizer C. L. Dellums. In Chicago, organizer Milton P. Webster, a cigar-chomping, Republican wardheeler, had little use for women, unless they commanded party posts. His "elegant wife" Elizabeth, although active in club and social service, did not belong to the BSCP women's organization because he wanted her to "stay home" raising their three children. Webster's hostility towards women's participation, coupled with the union's rhetorical stress on black manhood, posed barriers to these potential Brotherhood members.[14]

Nonetheless, in the midst of an alienating masculine culture, many African American working women saw the union as a solution to their problems. The participation of Chicago maid Josephine Puckett as well as the prominence of white and African American women trade unionists may have further encouraged their support. For some, the Women's Economic Council may have offered a female-controlled refuge from the male-dominated union hall, even when the council focused on domestic, rather than workplace, concerns.[15]

Tinie Upton, the wife of Los Angeles Brotherhood President Charles L. Upton, joined the union as a Pullman maid, the local's first woman member. She was soon fired. "During the heated campaign for the organization, she worked faithfully and brilliantly in the enrollment of both porters and maids. In fact so successful was her work that the management called her into the office and discharged her for union activities. This move on the part of the management only served to spur her on in her valiant fight for economic freedom."[16] Though dismissed, she exercised her right as a former Pullman worker and remained a Brotherhood member. In 1935 she even ran for a position in the 200-member Los Angeles local, but lost to a younger man.[17]

Porters and maids devised methods to keep their union membership secret. Frances Albrier, running out of San Francisco, paid her dues at the end of the line. "I paid my dues in New Orleans," Albrier recalled. "I didn't pay it out here [in Oakland] because they couldn't see my name on a list. A lot of them did in other cities." The strategy of paying union dues in a foreign city can be confirmed in the Chicago local's rolls. Several of those entries indicate the names of Chicago residents who paid, for example, in New York and Tacoma, Washington.[18]

The Pullman Company used maids as well as porters to spy on the union. The "Porter Growls" column warned of one maid who kept management aware of union activities.

> All hail the power of Miss Capitola Mynard [*sic*] a Pullman maid operating on the Golden Arrow Limited, Penn. Terminal District, who is alleged to be helping the Pullman Company bring distress to the home and families of porters by reporting them to the superintendent because they asked her to join the union. Some who know her while in Chicago wonder if she would be as active for the company, if porters were white men? If the report is true, it would be well to watch the maid.[19]

The "growling" columnist's attack on Minyard linked her support of the company with allegations that she dated white men. Thus Minyard was doubly suspect: disloyal to the economic advancement of the race and disloyal to African American men. Pullman however rewarded Minyard for her loyalty by promoting her to Maid Instructress.[20]

Pullman threatened union maids by hiring Chinese women to work on the Pacific Coast lines. These women tended to be much younger than African American women, hired at age twenty-two. But few remained long in Pullman service, quitting, on average, after eighteen months. The company hired the greatest majority of Chinese women between June 1, 1928, and December 31, 1929, the eighteen months immediately following the Brotherhood's strike threats. At least one African American maid "took exception" to their hiring and promptly quit.[21]

Pullman also used more subtle reprisals to prevent unionization. After the stock market crash in 1928, the company furloughed thousands of employees, including many maids who were indefinitely furloughed. The crew cuts were due, in part, to the changing needs of passengers. Manicurists were expensive incidental luxuries when business travel decreased with the economic downturn. When needed, porters could help mothers traveling with children. Maids had been in more demand when lady passengers needed assistance with their Victorian-era clothing. The only other jobs open to African American women in the Pullman Company were as laundry workers or car cleaners, jobs furloughed maids took willingly as unemployment figures mounted. The company tried to keep only those workers whom it believed were loyal, but many Brotherhood members remained on the job. Conversely, at least four Chicago maids fired for disloyalty could not be located on the local's membership rolls.[22]

In the mid-twenties, while the economy boomed and jobs were plentiful, the Brotherhood's victory seemed imminent. Membership soared, peaking at 4,632 porters and maids by 1928. "The men are flocking in," reported local secretaries all over the country. The New York local grew rapidly under Randolph's direction, drawing together over one thousand sleeping car workers from the region's four railroad terminals and yards. The BSCP represented the first race-controlled labor union, explaining perhaps why membership in Northwestern cities such as Seattle and Spokane, Washington, and Portland, Oregon, remained high, even during the union's "dark years."[23]

In Chicago, the headquarters of the Pullman Company, winning the support of porters and maids was critical to the Brotherhood's success. The city was the heart of the nation's transportation system, with five railroad lines operating out of the city's four stations. More than a third of Pullman's African American passenger car force lived on the city's south side. Under the leadership of Milton P. Webster, membership in Chicago rivaled the New York local, ranging from an estimated 1,150 peak in 1927 to a low of 250 in 1933. To gain the trust of these men and women, the union relied on the efforts of porters and maids, community leaders, trade unionists, religious leaders, and clubwomen.[24]

In Chicago and elsewhere, the Brotherhood drew on the support of many prominent African American clubwomen and white trade union women. These national leaders and neighborhood agitators worked to change black community opinion in favor of the union. Clubwomen provided introductions to male and female leaders, especially ministers, and arranged for Randolph to speak to their organizations, allowing their names to be used in public endorsements.

Ida B. Wells-Barnett, the nation's leading radical Race Woman, endorsed the Brotherhood in December 1925. Randolph gladly accepted Wells-Barnett's invitation to her home to speak to the Woman's Forum. Wells-Barnett also tried to secure the endorsement of the city's African American Republicans, but ran into the Pullman Company. She had originally planned to hold a reception for Randolph at the prestigious Appomattox Club, but its members, who had ties with Pullman, opposed her use of the building. The club's founder and first president, *Conservator* publisher Julius Avendorph, had worked as a messenger to Pullman Company president, Robert Lincoln.[25]

Randolph spoke to the Woman's Forum in December 1925. The club's endorsement of the BSCP introduced Randolph to other prominent Chicago clubwomen, such as Irene McCoy Gaines, then the Industrial Secretary of the Chicago YWCA Negro branch and president of the Illinois Federation of Republican Colored Women's Clubs. Wells-Barnett and Gaines converted "leading society women" to the Brotherhood and worked with the Chicago Citizens' Committee to raise funds and seek new endorsements. Gaines spoke regularly at Brotherhood mass meetings and affairs. Mary Church Terrell of Washington, D.C., former president of the National Association of Colored Women's Clubs, and prominent in Republican circles, announced her support in January 1928; then "she went with Brotherhood officials to call on President [Calvin] Coolidge, at which President Randolph presented the case of the Pullman porters and maids."[26]

In New York, Lucille Randolph seems to have persuaded her good friend A'lelia Walker to donate money to the union. The daughter of Madame C. J. Walker, founder of the black hair care empire, A'lelia was Harlem's leading socialite, with whom Lucille founded the Gothamite Debutantes Association, the first group for introducing young women to Harlem society. Lucille Randolph also organized her fellow Walker salon operators to donate prizes for the Brotherhood's beauty contests. Her 135th Street salon served as a distribution center for *The Messenger,* thus acquainting other Harlem women with the union.[27]

African American trade union women, although few in number, also announced their support for the porters. Gertrude Elise MacDougald Ayers was the vice-principal of P.S. 89, the highest ranking African American woman in the New York City school system and an American Federation of Teachers organizer. Maida Springer [Kemp], another Harlem labor organizer and BSCP supporter, perhaps began her lifelong friendship with Randolph at this time. Randolph editorialized the endorsement of "a capable young woman, Miss Floria Pinkney, graduate of Brookwood Labor College," who became the first African American woman organizer for the International Ladies' Garment Workers' Union. In Chicago, Neva Ryan, founder of the Domestic Workers' Union, endorsed the union as did Irene Goins, who organized Chicago's African American meatpackers and their families.[28] As part of the small world of black labor organizers, these women recognized the need to support each other's work. At the same time, porters' wives often worked in these trades, thus further strengthening the bonds.

White settlement house workers also voiced their support for the African American union. Mary McDowell, head of the Department of Charities at the University of Chicago, former Hull House resident, and Chicago Women's Trade Union League official, was an early proponent. McDowell did her own bit to organize sleeping car workers. She claimed that whenever she rode a Pullman car she "buttonholed" the porter about his Brotherhood membership, encouraging him to join. She continued to support the union and "never missed a Brotherhood mass meeting." Randolph credited McDowell for one of his favorite expressions: "Negroes are beginning to write their own economic contract."[29]

McDowell persuaded her colleagues to support the Brotherhood. Mary Anderson, Director of the U.S. Women's Bureau, accepted Randolph's invitation to speak to the 1929 Brotherhood convention, after McDowell interceded. From that time, Anderson spoke regularly to BSCP women. Lillian Herstein of the Chicago American Federation of Teachers spoke at several meetings; later, as director of the Chicago WPA Worker's Education Program, Herstein developed programs on consumers' cooperatives for the Ladies' Auxiliary.[30]

Among other white progressive and labor women, supporting the Brotherhood appears to have become a trend. In San Francisco, Charlotte Anne Whitney, a prominent socialite turned prodigal socialist, wrote letters on behalf of the union. In New York City, Elizabeth Gurley Flynn of the American Fund for Public Service, veteran leader of both the Lawrence, Massachusetts, and Patterson, New Jersey, textile mill strikes, and chair of the International Labor Defense, appeared at several BSCP mass meetings.[31]

Prominent society women enrolled in the Brotherhood's Citizen's Committees in Oakland, Chicago, New York City, St. Louis, and Boston. Los Angeles Brotherhood organizer and real estate broker George S. Grant wrote that these committees were "formed from among the most prominent individuals in each community who can be persuaded to support the Brotherhood." Committee membership included prominent local and some national leaders; many were also members of the National Association for the Advancement of Colored People. The New York Citizens' Committee of One Hundred in behalf of the Pullman Porters and Maids was chaired by attorney Henry T. Hunt, former member of the United States Railroad Labor Board. The committee pledged to assist in "establishing the right of self-organization [by] Pullman Porters and Maids" and "to stimulate public interest in favor of a living wage for the porters and maids."[32]

Several members of the Citizens' Committees may have endorsed the Brotherhood because they were part of a progressive network of mutually endorsing reformers; the union was another group in the long list of causes they supported. The New York list provides a fascinating glimpse of the networks to which Randolph had access. Socialists, progressives, feminists, and labor leaders all appear on the list, as well as ministers, professors, artists, and philanthropists; of the one hundred listed, twenty-two were women. As a public relations tactic, the Citizens' Committee gave the Brotherhood the stamp of legitimacy and helped to secure foundation funds and other donations.[33]

Yet society leaders and intellectuals did little to convince potential rank-and-file workers to join the BSCP. They may have known that E. R. A. Seligman was a distingushed economics professor at Columbia, but he did not hire Pullman porters; that was for the company to decide. Porters' wives had similar reasons to be skeptical. They perhaps suspected that white women such as Lillian Wald, Frieda Kirchwey, Florence Kelley, Harriot Stanton Blatch, Mary Dreier, Fannie Hurst, Helen Phelps Stokes, and Mary Simkhovitch, socialists though they may be, were more likely to hire African American women for domestic work than join them on the front lines in a struggle for the economic advancement of the race. None of these women was ever a platform guest for a BSCP mass meeting; their politics permitted them to endorse the movement, but their privileges of class and race did not require interaction with its members.

Nor did African American society women regularly attend the BSCP's labor institutes and meetings, except to give advice from "on high." Irene McCoy Gaines, for example, instructed a Chicago women's meeting to "seek culture." Mary Church Terrell did not include the Washington Women's Economic Council in local club activities. Even among the wives of the BSCP national organizers, only Walter (Mrs. C. L.) Dellums actively participated in the Oakland local's activities. Lucille Randolph, Elizabeth Webster, and Hazel Smith had their own circles of social service and club friends and did not belong to their local Women's Economic Councils. Historian Deborah Gray White argues such divisions were "the cost of club work, the price of black feminism," that encouraged class prejudice among African American women. Thus, rather than ally with the traditional leadership class of the African American community, Brotherhood women and men sought partnerships with trade unionists, white and black, in common cause against capital.[34]

The Women's Economic Councils of the BSCP sought to convert the porters' wives and female relatives into dedicated trade unionists. This was no easy task, for, despite intra-racial class prejudice, tradition demanded that African American working women look to clubwomen for leadership. Yet in the 1920s many began to question the dominance of this Republican class, as new political leaders and organizations arose. One example of this new attitude was Marcus Garvey's Universal Negro Improvement Association (UNIA), which attracted thousands of working-class and immigrant African Americans, but there were smaller revolts. In Washington, D.C., for example, Rosina Corrothers Tucker founded the Northeast Women's Club in the early 1920s, "to do something *constructive*" for the community; the club provided clothing, shoes, and carfare to needy students, sent children to summer camp, and lobbied for better city services for the neighborhood.[35]

The Brotherhood of Sleeping Car Porters tapped these sentiments, advocating trade unionism as the solution to the race problem. But Randolph's view of the Brotherhood recognized the need for a distaff organization. Thus, in October 1925, just six weeks after the inaugural meeting of the BSCP, Randolph organized the first Women's Economic Council in New York City. This group, originally called the Hesperus Club, immediately began fundraising, sponsoring the union's first Christmas dance in December 1925 at "the aging but still majestic Rockland Palace (the old Manhattan Casino)." The dance was so popular that it became an annual event. The following year it featured a bobbed hair contest, with entrants from twelve hair culturists, including Madame C. J. Walker's own salon, and judges from the society press.[36]

The Hesperus Club was the first ladies' auxiliary, others soon followed. Wherever Randolph or Ashley Totten organized a Brotherhood local, they also set up a women's group. At the beginning, councils formed under a variety of local names. The Ever Ready Club of Philadelphia announced, "We, the women who are the essential body of everything, are doing our best to make the votes go over big and with huge success." The Chicago Colored Women's Economic Council, founded May 6, 1926, brought together forty-five women, under the leadership of Jessie Bonds, the daughter of Pullman Porter William Puckett and Pullman Maid Josephine Puckett. By 1926, eleven cities boasted women's groups: New York, Chicago, Washington, D.C., Boston, St. Paul,

Minneapolis, Oakland, Los Angeles, Denver, Omaha, and Salt Lake City, the principal northern terminals for Pullman operations.[37]

Any African American woman could join the Economic Council, whether or not she had a relative working for the Pullman Company. Special efforts to recruit porters' wives were made because they might convince their husbands and families to support trade unionism. Randolph also recognized that wives' control of the household budget played a considerable role in whether husbands paid their dues regularly. Council women visited the homes of porters and maids spreading the Brotherhood message, proselytizing, like a band of trade union missionaries. Their tactics fooled company detectives. Sleeping car workers were out for days, sometimes weeks at a time while their families were left to "hold the fort." Pullman did not suspect that a coffee klatsch of wives would gather to discuss unionization. Literature could be left with the family for all members to read. Men could leave their dues for the organizer to collect, or as sometimes happened, the wife would pay her husband's dues without his knowledge. As Rosina Tucker recalled,

> There were some men who were willing to join the organization but who were prevented from doing so by their apprehensive wives. On the other hand, there were many men whose wives were eager for them to join but who balked for fear of losing their jobs. There were some women who put their husbands' names on the rolls and paid their dues for years. If I dare say so, it was the women who made the union in those early days. The men were afraid, though with good reason.[38]

The fear that Pullman would retaliate against union supporters, male or female, required the Brotherhood to extend its oath of secrecy to council members.

Leadership of the Women's Economic Council was a matter of concern to the men. To ensure the continued operation of these groups, Randolph advised: "Success in organizing the council will depend largely upon the character and personality of the individual secured as head or President of the Council. The aims should be to get as strong and popular a woman as possible, provided such person can also be interested enthusiastically in the work of assisting the Brotherhood of Sleeping Car Porters."[39] But Randolph did not require these female leaders to work exclusively with other women, leaving open the possibility that some would attempt to establish a gender-integrated movement. In Los Angeles, the dynamic Mattie Mae Stafford and George Grant worked with porters, maids, family members, and community members, with slight discrimination between the sexes. Grant's proposed "Cooperation Plan," outlining the organizational work of the Brotherhood, demonstrated a remarkable degree of gender integration.[40]

Rosina Tucker challenged sex segregation by working primarily with male union officials as the BSCP's Washington liaison, even though her official title was President of the Women's Economic Council. With President Randolph's consent, she also successfully argued porters' unfair discharge claims to Pullman officials, a task normally reserved for the highest union officials.[41]

Lucy Bledsoe Gilmore, president of the Colored Women's Economic Council, often spoke to Brotherhood mass meetings in St. Louis. In 1927 she spoke to a large audience, where Pullman supervisor-informant J. A. Koupal reported her address to company officials. Two hundred and fifty people, three-fourths of whom were women, attended. "Mrs. Gilmore got up and started out in her usual florid style" which aroused "the baser element," reported Koupal. Her husband, I. C. Gilmore, had been furloughed ten months because he supported the Brotherhood. "If we never have another bite to eat we will still fight for the Brotherhood," said Gilmore. "I am like a rubber ball, the harder you throw me, the higher I bounce."[42]

The $72.50 per month wages her husband had earned was too little to be missed, according to Gilmore, but the principle angered her greatly. "In slave time we could assemble in our own cabins and confer with each other and not be bothered by their masters." According to Koupal, "she became very violent in her denunciation of the officials of the Company" almost creating "a riot right in the church." Attacked, Koupal minced no words, describing Gilmore's betrayal of, and ingratitude toward, the company: "I am sure that the Anarchistic method displayed by . . . Totten, and Mrs. Gilmore, (who is a second Emma Goldman) will [do] more to convince the porters . . . than anything else that has been done."[43] Lucy Gilmore raised money in the same manner that African American religious leaders raised money. She challenged the assembly to give money while BSCP officers passed around the donation basket. Gilmore frequently "took a very active part in the meeting, took up a collection, calling on the men to give a dollar a piece for the good cause."

"That hoorah manner of hers seems to catch the fancy of the men and cause them to respond more liberally to the request for money," reported Pullman's informer. At another meeting, she "wanted . . . eighteen men to have five dollars ready for the collection, said she had two already paid." Gilmore then identified and scolded the Pullman spy: " 'Mr. Koupal keeps hanging around and he must want to do something for us.' She addressed me personally then and said, 'Mr. Koupal, we want five dollars from you.' " Koupal did not say whether he gave her five dollars.[44]

The company retaliated against Mrs. Gilmore. As the widow of one porter and the wife of another, Supervisor A. V. Burr had allowed her to collect insurance premiums at the railroad yard. He revoked her privileges, thus denying her a livelihood. But the BSCP might have also lost its income: it seems likely that Lucy Gilmore used her yard privileges to collect union dues as well as insurance premiums from Brotherhood men and women.

Such subterfuges were not uncommon, according to Greg LeRoy, who found that in Chicago, Milton P. Webster acted as the union's public organizer, while John C. Mills, secretly a member of the BSCP, served as a porter-representative for the Employee Representation Plan. William and Josephine Puckett, a porter and maid, seemed to have split organizing duties, too, with their daughter leading the council. This pattern of organizing appears to have been repeated in other cities. To contact the Louisville, Kentucky, local, Randolph wrote Anna R. Hughes, "the source of information." Rosina Tucker, the wife of a Pullman porter, acted as BSCP's Washington, D.C., secret contact although *The Messenger* listed Peter A. Anthony as the union's organizer. In 1930, "Mrs. Olds" worked as secretary of the St. Paul, Minnesota, division with Frank Boyd.[45] In New Orleans, Oneida M. Brown served as secretary, although whether her membership in the BSCP was based on occupation or family is unclear. It is likely that she also had another Brotherhood member organizing secretly in the city.

Tucker explained how the union's iron-clad oath of secrecy allowed women to play a central role in organizing the Brotherhood:

> Public meetings [in which porters could speak] were out of the question. Any overt involvement by anyone employed by the Pullman Company was suicide. So it devolved upon the wives of the porters to do most of the organizational work.
>
> Fortunately, most of the porters, or so it seemed, had very fine wives who were dedicated as much or more than their husbands to the formation of the union. I was asked to act as liaison between Mr. Randolph and the Washington division. Material was sent to me and I personally disseminate[d] it to the men. I kept in touch with what was going on, because it was dangerous for them to let it be known even to each other that they were members or had expressed any interest in the Brotherhood. One never knew for sure who the informers were. I was responsible for collecting dues and sending them on to New York. I visited the families of the porters and personally explained to them what the union meant and what benefits it could bring. I suppose I visited over three hundred porters in Washington, telling them the advantages of their being members, and letting them know just what progress was being made, what difficulties were being encountered, and how the other men were responding.[46]

Tucker's description of this secret organizing substantiates the pattern discovered in Chicago and that may have been used elsewhere. A BSCP man or wom-

an served as the public representative, while another union supporter operated behind the scenes. The Brotherhood story says that "men were fired for
simply being seen on the same side of the street as a Brotherhood organizer."[47]
By using two organizers, the union misled Pullman Company informants.

Women such as Frances Albrier, Lucy Gilmore, and Rosina Tucker are examples of the New Negro Women who joined the Brotherhood of Sleeping Car
Porters. They plunged into the organizing campaign, convincing both wom-
en and men to join the union. Their activities defied gender stereotypes, demonstrating that women had more to offer the union than their adoring support. And because they were New Negro Women, they believed they could
work in mixed-sex groups and maintain their respectability. Yet many porters'
wives were unwilling to challenge the traditional division of union labor,
maintaining that women should provide the conventional feminine support
that complemented their husbands' quest for manhood. To show their support for the BSCP, these women drew on their experience as fundraisers for
charities and churches.

The Women's Economic Councils proved economically resourceful supporters of the fledgling union. When Brotherhood men recalled women's
contributions, they stressed women's fundraising abilities. This was no small
matter; rents had to be paid, organizers needed to travel, and propaganda must
be printed. Indeed, when Ada V. Dillon and Sara Harper described the New
York City Council's early activities, money was most prominent: "In the early dark days of the Brotherhood, when we did not know where our next dollar was coming from to carry on the work, the women just rolled up their
sleeves and went to work to raise money to help with the organization's expenses. They had dinners at their homes Saturday nights until the Brotherhood could raise enough money to have a place of their own. Mrs. Carrie Love,
then a maid on the Pennsylvania Road, and Mrs. Frank Crosswaith, served
many Saturday night dinners at their homes."[48]

To raise money for the BSCP, the women sponsored public dances and
parties at which they sold refreshments and homemade food. In St. Louis,
Ruth Harris of the Citizens' Committee worked with the council to give a very
successful dance. "Many tickets were bought by people who do not dance, just
to assist and encourage Miss Harris and her co-workers in the splendid work
they were doing for our group." The Chicago women "gave their first monthly entertainment on Saturday . . . at the Barrett Music School where some two
hundred Brotherhood members and wives passed a very enjoyable evening."[49]

Bid whist tournaments, the card game that Pullman porters claim to
have invented, and similar group card parties were also a popular form of
fundraising. Working with the Brotherhood, the women helped to organize

raffles, boat rides, and picnics. The union sponsored a gift book campaign; when the person sold every item in his or her book, "a beautiful and useful gift" awaited.[50]

For a short while, the women even helped pay a mortgage for the BSCP's headquarters at 238 West 136th Street. The house was apparently used for offices, as a recreation hall, and as a boarding house for foreign porters. In Oakland, Walter (Mrs. C. L.) Dellums helped operate a similiar house for foreign porters and maids; while the Los Angeles Council was asked to "assume the responsibility of paying the house rent each month." The wives of Brotherhood officers often ran the local office while their husbands were on the road.[51]

The Brotherhood story venerated the fundraising work of the Women's Economic Councils while ignoring challenges to the sexual division of union labor. This collective history even rewrote women's role in the Brotherhood. Ada Dillon is remembered as a member of the New York Women's Economic Council, even though she lost her job as a Pullman maid due to her union activities. Similarly, the BSCP's official version praises Rosina Tucker for convincing wives to support the union, but neglects her door-to-door organizing work. Grounded in the ideology of black manhood, the Brotherhood story celebrated women whose activities complemented rather than those who challenged sex segregation.

Black manhood encouraged women to guard their respectability. The councils sought respect for their trade union by sponsoring fundraising events similar to African American women's clubs. Other women sought to distinguish themselves from the traditional leadership class, causing tension as they sought to emulate the New Negro Woman. Pullman maids such as Albrier believed trade unionism was respectable. She willingly solicited her fellow workers, male and female, even though she believed herself more effective among the women. Lucy Gilmore collected insurance premiums (and perhaps union dues) in the St. Louis yards, while serving as president of the Women's Economic Council. In New York City however, Katherine Lassiter, a porter's widow, apparently confined herself to organizing women, choosing a traditional role of union wife.

Geography, Albrier and Tucker both contended, made a difference in organizing women and the risks they were willing to take for the union. In the East, wives and maids were too busy to get involved, or too scared, and although eastern women contributed money, it was women on the West Coast who joined and fought. "In the West," Tucker believed, "women had suffrage long before our southern women and were therefore more accustomed to political matters." On the other hand, Albrier thought maids in the West were not as militant as those in the East because they had less exposure to trade unionism. The conflicting perceptions result, in part, from each woman's organizing agenda. Tucker equated women's interest in the union with suffrage and politics, while Albrier described women's interests in the union as economic. Yet they agreed that one could be both a lady and a trade unionist.[52]

Brotherhood wives provided both traditional and nontraditional support to the union. The councils brought women together in common cause to fight for their homes, their families, their men, and their own respectability as wives. They organized and financed Brotherhood activities, planned mass meetings, spoke out at rallies, and then went home to serve dinner to visiting organizers. All of these interests encouraged women to join the movement for economic justice. Their efforts secured the strength of the Brotherhood of Sleeping Car Porters in its struggle for a contract.

3

Striking for the New Manhood Movement

The fight for the Brotherhood of Sleeping Car Porters was a fight for manhood. During their twelve-year struggle, porters and maids battled the company, the state, and labor itself. The union attacked Pullman's tipping system, petitioning the Republican-controlled Interstate Commerce Commission for redress. Simultaneously, Brotherhood men and women prepared to strike assuming, with President A. Philip Randolph, that the National Mediation Board would intervene to prevent a national emergency. To strengthen their bargaining power, BSCP leaders applied for an international charter from the American Federation of Labor. The campaign for unionization contested the meaning of black manhood, and ultimately defined the roles men and women would have in the union.

Nothing went as President Randolph planned. In 1928, Pullman retaliated by furloughing hundreds of sleeping car workers; the ICC and the NMB denied the union's appeals, and the AFL conferred only second-class federal charters to BSCP locals. Herbert Hoover's lily-white campaign strategy for president, the deepening of the Depression, and the defeat of the new manhood movement ushered in the "dark days" of the Brotherhood. Nor did the coming of the New Deal guarantee prosperity for African Americans, a thrice-burned Randolph reasoned. Distrusting any bureaucracy to act in the union's favor, he played the AFL against Congress, the Pullman Company against the AFL, and the National Mediation Board against Pullman.

In 1936, Randolph won: the BSCP became the first independent labor union—of any color—to defeat company unionism, validating the AFL's demand that all workers should be free to form their own collective bargaining units. To acknowledge the victory, the House of Labor granted the Brotherhood an international charter, the first time the AFL recognized an African American-led union as first-class members.

The defeats of the dark days and the victories of the New Deal days recast the meaning of manhood for Brotherhood members. Randolph ceased to speak of the new manhood movement, a trope of the Harlem Renaissance, and in its place fused images of manliness, race, and labor into the Black Worker. Like the New Negro, the image of the Black Worker was masculine. Negroes were men and men were workers; only the addition of "woman" rendered "the black worker" feminine. Thus, when Randolph redefined manhood in the Black Worker, he altered the Brotherhood's hierarchy of gender. Men demanded rights within the organization, institutionalizing male privileges through the union's constitution, and dropping "Maids" from its name. The Women's Economic Councils became subject to President Randolph, their new "Counselor." Sex-segregated auxiliaries exalted the status of wives, allowing porters to assert their manhood through the Brotherhood. The fragile equality asserted by New Negro Women (another trope of the early years) gave way wholly to a gender complementary division of union labor in which female domesticity supported male union activism.[1]

The BSCP's campaign against tipping demonstrates how the rhetoric of black manhood engendered a distaff role for women. In his public relations and legal challenge, Randolph attacked tipping as an assault on the manhood of porters. Frank Crosswaith, the Brotherhood's Special Organizer, linked tipping with masculinity, as "a condition of employment . . . which demanded of [porters] the submersion of their manhood by making public beggars of them." Randolph characterized tipping as immoral. In an open letter to Pullman Company President Carry, Randolph asked, "is it fair for a rich, powerful corporation like the Pullman Company to convert the porters into professional beggars to support their wives and children? No other group of railroad workers is subjected to such an uncertain, as well as demoralizing, practice."[2]

The demeaning nature of tipping encouraged racial prejudice, Randolph continued. Tipping created a "peculiar relation" between the white passenger, "often imbued with a spurious sense of racial superiority" and the porter who "belongs to a race . . . struggling to obtain a recognized social status." "On the one hand we attain a sensation of power and patronage, and on the other we have a possibility of obsequiousness and dependence." A living wage would make tips unnecessary and would eliminate "all the inherent social evils of the tipping system." Randolph argued porters had to grin and shuffle for Ol' Marse Passenger for tips. Pullman porters were "the *monkeys* of the service. They are expected to sing and cut up such capers as are unbecoming to a man." Tipping "is gradually dehumanizing him, converting him to the things that bring a flush of shame to the cheek of more manly men." The BSCP's analysis linked racism with sexism, implying that to maintain the racial status quo, whites subjugated African American male service workers by forcing them into a form of prostitution.[3]

Tipping encouraged the sexual exploitation of women too, but the BSCP was silent on this point, as it was on other issues concerning working women. In the mid-twenties protective labor law advocates opposed the practice of tipping waitresses because of its "potential to reinforce low wages and encourage immorality in women dependent upon male customers for their livelihood." In their eyes, however, tipping endangered only white working women. Anti-tipping proponents, who also advocated the protectionism, did not see tipping as a risk for African American women workers. According to contemporary white stereotypes, women of color were "by nature" immoral and sexually promiscuous. Randolph, also a protectionist on this issue, sought respectability for African American women by promoting black manhood, not by addressing their problems as workers.[4]

Following the lead of other service trade unions, the Brotherhood mounted a legal challenge to eliminate tipping. Prior to World War I, waiters' unions successfully lobbied several state legislatures to pass anti-tipping acts. The BSCP appealed to the Interstate Commerce Commission, which regulated railroad fares. The union's petition, filed in October 1927, argued that tips violated the Interstate Commerce Act because they amounted to a separate, unregulated "excess fare" assessed passengers and further, encouraged porters to discriminate in their services to passengers. Porters possessed police powers to enforce safety and sanitary regulations and prohibitions against gambling and alcohol consumption. Yet Pullman encouraged tipping, the petition argued, thus creating a situation in which porters might be bribed to ignore the law. The commission took the case under advisement.[5]

Meanwhile, union leaders made plans to strike. A year earlier, on behalf of sleeping car porters and maids, Randolph had requested contract negotiations with Pullman President Edward F. Carry. His letter invoked the recently enacted Watson-Parker Railway Labor Act outlining procedures for union disputes. Carry disdained to reply; Pullman refused to recognize the BSCP as the legitimate representative of porters and maids. A second letter to Pullman's president met the same fate. Following procedure, Randolph then appealed to the National Mediation Board, which appointed former Kentucky Governor Edwin P. Morrow to investigate the Brotherhood's claims.

After examining the union's membership rolls, mediator Morrow ruled the Brotherhood's claim valid in June 1927 and called on the company to begin negotiations in good faith. President Carry replied that his company had no dispute with the BSCP since it already had a "contract" with porters and maids in the Employee Representation Plan. Declaring mediation impossible, Morrow asked the presidents to submit to binding arbitration.[6] At this point the limitations of the Watson-Parker Railway Labor Act became inescapably clear to Randolph.

The year before, over the objections of other African American railroad leaders, Randolph had supported passage of the proposed railway labor act because it recognized collective bargaining in the railroad industry. Perhaps Randolph naively believed justice would triumph regardless of race. Reinzi B. Lemus, president of the Dining Car Employees, argued against the bill because he saw that although Watson-Parker gave the National Mediation Board a few new powers, it could not order wage increases, nor force companies to the bargaining table unless a proposed strike threatened a real emergency. Lemus reasoned that a strike by a small African American union could not create a national emergency because it did not possess the numerical or economic strength to shut down railroad transportation across the country.[7]

The leadership of the Brotherhood of Sleeping Car Porters believed their union could threaten to stop the railroads and thus force an emergency board to convene. Pressed by Chicago organizer Milton P. Webster, Randolph announced porters and maids would vote to authorize a national strike in April 1928. Fueled by the Interstate Commerce Commission's March 1928 announcement that it had no authority over the matter of tips, slightly more than six thousand sleeping car workers voted in favor of a strike. Randolph announced a walk-out date of June 8, pending mediator Morrow's negotiations with Pullman. Using a rhetorical ploy, Randolph never promised that porters and maids would actually walk off the job; he only made it appear that such an event was possible. President Carry told the mediator he had thousands of strikebreakers ready and pledged to keep his Pullman cars running.[8]

Throughout these tense four months, the Brotherhood and the Women's Economic Council prepared to strike. In Chicago, Milton P. Webster estimated that 85 percent of the porters would follow loyal Brotherhood men off the cars; in Kansas City, Ashley L. Totten apparently armed himself to fight off strikebreakers. Webster instructed pickets be organized; "These may be composed of porters or porters' wives and children, or citizens generally." In Oakland, C. L. Dellums claimed later he had one thousand volunteers from the University of California prepared to stop the trains, even if it meant putting women and children in front of them.[9]

Women made their own preparations. In St. Paul and Minneapolis, the "women of the Council have begun an active campaign to be of immediate aid to the men in this present crisis, and have been given tasks which will grow according to the enthusiasm expressed in their actions," noting that a recent whist tournament added appreciably to their finances. From Los Angeles, Mattie Mae Stafford reported:

> preparations for a strike are being made. Twenty-five women lieutenants are preparing work among the men with stimulation and moral encouragement and a propaganda committee is at work. A fundraising committee is getting under way for the purpose of raising funds among both white and colored citizens to assist in this fight . . . known as the Citizens' Committee, [it] will give moral support and encouragement and formulate plans for economical and political protest against the unhuman and ruthless attitude of the Pullman Company. The enthusiasm of the women of the Economical Council, under the leadership of Mrs. Lula Slaughter, is very encouraging and gives promise of very splendid results.[10]

Brotherhood women were prepared for a lengthy strike.

Throughout the Brotherhood's strike preparations, the Pullman Company feigned nonchalance. But in management offices serious discussions took place about how to destroy the Brotherhood. For the first time, two African Americans, George Shannon, a porter, and Perry Parker, an official in the Pullman Porters Benefit Association, became members of the Board of Industrial Relations to hear porters' grievances. Under the Employee Representation Plan, the company held an election in 1928 for porter-representatives to confer on wage and working conditions. Pullman maids did not have a representative. Pullman granted an increase of $60 per year, bringing porters to $72.50 and maids to $70.00 per month. Bennie Smith, one of the elected porter representatives, refused to sign the agreement, contending that Pullman granted too little, too late. When the company fired him for complaining, Randolph sent him first to Kansas City to organize with Ashley L. Totten and then to Detroit, where he became president of the local.[11]

Pullman's token gestures to sleeping car workers came with increased scrutiny of their union activities, including those of their wives. Porter-instructors and company welfare workers inspected porters' homes to threaten wives whose husbands were union activists, and fired suspected female members, including New York Pullman maid Ada V. Dillon, for "disloyalty." The company even intercepted copies of Randolph's telegraphed strike instructions to local union leaders. "Dad" Moore, a retired porter who ran Pullman's Oakland quarters for foreign men (two dilapidated sleeping cars) and an ardent union supporter, had his $15 a month pension terminated. Lucy Bledsoe Gilmore, a porter's widow and president of the St. Louis Council, found herself expelled from the Pullman yards, and forbidden to collect insurance premiums there. Brother Kelly Foster of St. Paul was one of the husbands "victimized because of the identification of their wives with the Ladies Auxiliaries or activity in the Brotherhood public meetings." Annie Foster remained loyal, serving as the council's recording secretary until 1939.[12]

Pullman also tried to take Rosina Tucker's husband, Berthea (B. J.), off his run. She did not let the company get away with it.

> I decided that I'm not going to take that, I'm going to the office and see the superintendent. . . . I went to the phone and rang up the superintendent. . . . I identified myself as Mrs. B. J. Tucker. There was a silence. "Wait a minute." Somebody else came to the phone. I said I wanted to speak to the superintendent, calling him by name. This second man told me that the superintendent was "in conference." Now I knew that it was the superintendent to whom I had first spoken and that, when he learned who it was to whom he was speaking, he skipped.

The superintendent stayed "in conference" over the next two days until Brother B. C. Massey advised Tucker to "see the man *over* the superintendent." Finally she called upon the Pullman manager in his office, walking in past the secretary's unattended desk.

> "I came to see about my husband, Mr. B. J. Tucker."
> "What about him?" the official asked.
> "He was taken off his run and the man at the sign-out office told him 'Nothing in hell could take him off that run except your wife's activities in the Brotherhood of Sleeping Car Porters!'"
> "So?"
> Pounding on his desk, I declared, "I want to tell you that nobody has anything to do with what *I* do!"
> "Why are you taking the matter up? Why not Tucker?"
> "Because they brought me into it. Now! You take care of this matter and put my husband back on his run, or else I'll be back."

Her threat worked.

> Well, for a black woman to speak up to a white man like that in those days was considered extraordinary. Naturally, he thought that there was somebody very powerful supporting me. However, Mr. Tucker got his run back immediately.[13]

This confrontation empowered Tucker in her future dealings with Pullman and with Brotherhood men; she believed she now had the right to question their decisions, and to act accordingly.

Other BSCP members, men and women, were not so encouraged, especially after the AFL withdrew its support of the impending strike.

William Green, president of the American Federation of Labor, monitored the Brotherhood's strike preparations. The BSCP's early attempts to join the AFL had been shelved because of disputes over jurisdiction. Randolph however, remained hopeful of an international charter and continued to follow Green's advice. On June 7, the night before the scheduled walk-out, Green telegraphed Randolph advising him to call off the strike. The next morning, Randolph declared he would never give up the struggle but "postponed" the strike until a later date. The National Mediation Board declared no emergency existed.[14]

Brotherhood leaders concluded the board's actions were racially motivated. They noted that it had recently authorized an emergency board to settle a dispute involving only six hundred white railway clerks. In a letter to Webster afterward, Randolph reported his confrontation with the NMB. The board practically admitted that in the railway clerks' case, it had acted on the carriers' and shippers' petitions, a fact that flabbergasted him. Randolph was convinced Pullman played the race card in its appeal to the board. "It is obvious to me that the Pullman Company got a man who was big enough to go to Washington and tell that Mediation Board and perhaps the President himself, that Pullman was not going to stand for any Emergency Board; that it was going to stir up the Negroes of this country and make them cocky, so that they could feel their power and that this would cause the business interests to have trouble with their Negro workers."[15] To Randolph, it seemed clear the Republican Administration would do all that it could to prevent African American men from exercising their rights.

Randolph's dream of the militant New Negro withered in the Brotherhood's contest against the Pullman Company. The strike threat represented a final contest for the new manhood movement. Brotherhood men and women wrote about their preparations as though they planned to avenge the destructive losses suffered in the race riots of 1919. In the worsening racial and economic climate, a strike may well have turned violent. The union's community-wide organizing tactics also meant that other African American workers were probably watching to see whether the Brotherhood would be successful. An African American-led strike might have awakened other black workers to protest for their rights, as the Brotherhood's Labor Institutes had stressed.

Rank-and-file members saw Randolph's decision to postpone the strike as a defeat and began to abandon the union. From a 1928 peak of 4,632 sleeping car workers, membership plummeted to 2,368 in 1929 and continued to career downward through 1932, when a mere 771 paid dues to the national

organization. That *The Messenger,* a repository of African American consciousness during the Harlem Renaissance, ceased publication in June immediately after the strike's postponement signaled the end of the movement.[16]

This episode taught Randolph not to expect the government to fairly administer the law for African Americans. The Pullman Company easily commanded the attention of the pro-big business, Republican Administration,
ensuring that the BSCP's petition to the ICC against tipping and its appeal to
the National Mediation Board would be turned down. Nor could he expect the
American Federation of Labor to act without racial prejudice; trade unions too
preferred the subordination of black workers.

Randolph accepted Green's advice to call off the strike on the condition
that the AFL would approve the BSCP's membership application. The House
of Labor, however, refused to grant the Brotherhood an international charter,
and instead issued federal charters to each of the Brotherhood's sixteen locals.
Federal charters allowed the AFL to administer each local separately, thus
bypassing the union's national officers. AFL officials argued federal charters
were necessary because of the questionable financial practices of Brotherhood
leaders. While denying the accusations, Randolph called a national convention in the fall of 1929 to write a new constitution.[17]

The new constitution duplicated almost every administrative feature of the
standard railway labor organizations. Randolph took the title of International
President. An International Executive Board became the ultimate decision-
making body of the union. Milton P. Webster became chairman of the board,
helping to alleviate a growing power struggle between Randolph and Webster.
Webster, E. J. Bradley, Bennie Smith, and C. L. Dellums became first, second,
third, and fourth vice-presidents, respectively. Significantly, the new constitution retained the word "International" in the union's name, but dropped "and
Maids." At the time, "International" was more of a hope than a reality, signal-
ing both Randolph's continued efforts to obtain an international charter from
the AFL and his plans to organize porters in Canada and Mexico.[18]

The Brotherhood's name and its new constitution omitted any specific
reference to Pullman maids as members of the organization. Membership
qualifications stated plainly that the union did not discriminate on the basis
of race, sex, creed, color, or nationality. However, the purpose of this article
was to challenge the discriminatory language of other union constitutions,
rather than mandate affirmative action in the BSCP itself. As for Pullman
maids, some porters probably thought they were too few in number to matter, while others appear to have considered maids unequal to male union
members. The place for females, the document implied, was the Women's
Economic Council.[19]

The Women's Economic Councils, also known as Ladies' Auxiliaries, reflected the formal segregation of men and women in the organization. The Brotherhood regarded this organization as a body of wives, not workers, even though many worked, and some worked as Pullman maids. The men instructed the councils to help build the Brotherhood. Founder Naomi DesVerney and other members believed this meant bolstering a husband's morale, making him feel like a man, restoring him for the fight. The wife would win vicariously, his victory would be hers.[20] Nothing was said by porters or their wives about uplifting the spirits of Pullman maids.

The Brotherhood reinforced the message of sex segregation in its new official paper, *The Black Worker,* first published in November 1929. While the eight-page newspaper regularly covered news items beyond the narrow confines of the BSCP, it never assumed the cultural significance of *The Messenger.* Unlike that earlier journal, *The Black Worker* reported women's activities on a separate page devoted to the Women's Economic Councils. "One thing in particular, I notice," wrote C. L. Dellums, "is that the porters' wives are reading it. I have talked to quite a number of them lately and I find that they are just now getting a basic understanding of the Brotherhood. And when they are admitted to the meetings, I find them coming out in greater numbers than ever before. They now discuss the Brotherhood with their husbands."[21] With their own page of news, women now had a forum in which to discuss their concerns as union wives.

The Brotherhood divided union labor by sex. In the booming twenties, crucial resources such as money, meeting places, publicity, outside support, and rank-and-file members were ample enough to support the union, and new images of men and women allowed some flexibility in gender roles. But in the dark days, as resources diminished, conventional roles for labor men and women became enmeshed in the organizational structure of the union. The insistence on a complementary role for the sexes carried a political message as well: by duplicating the gender conventions of white trade unions, BSCP leaders signaled that their union would not differ substantially from those of whites.

The BSCP reinforced this hierarchy of gender by writing new national by-laws for the Women's Economic Councils. As Randolph explained, "All of the standard railroad unions have powerful Ladies Auxiliaries that are great factors in the labor movement, and the Porters' Brotherhood will build a similar structure." The BSCP thus copied both the administrative structure and the sexual division of labor of white trade unions.[22]

The councils did not, however, duplicate the political agendas of white railroad auxiliaries. The preamble to the council's new by-laws declared the women would "advance, protect and conserve" the "economic, social, moral and intellectual" interests of its members, and outlined a broad program. The council pledged "to increase and capitalize the purchasing power of our group income" through "cooperative societies, labor unions and all constructive enterprises that promise and make for our group development." Through investigation and study, members would "stimulate, encourage and develop . . . economic organization, education, and agitation."[23]

The aim of this preamble indicated a substantially different role for women than the Brotherhood's constitution suggested. The Women's Economic Councils were not simply "auxiliaries" but the consumer-oriented equivalent to worker-based trade unions. The councils aided in the division of union labor, allowing the women to engage in political and consumer activities beyond the employer-focused scope of trade unions. More than half of the items in the women's plan of action directed their efforts toward economic and racial issues. While the council's immediate task was fundraising for the Brotherhood, "the vanguard of the Negroes economic emancipation," the women also undertook a full educational program on economic matters.[24]

Members were to investigate racial discrimination in employment, housing, and consumer services. The by-laws instructed local councils to form "Economic Vigilance Committees" whose purpose was "to watch out for all forms of economic discrimination against the Negro, such as the replacing of Negro workers by white workers in any field, the paying of Negro workers less than white workers, the barring of Negro workers from certain fields of industry." Trade unions that segregated African American members were a specific target for the committees.[25]

In their local communities, Vigilance Committees were to inspect white merchants for discrimination against Negro customers and to "insist upon their hiring some Negro help." African American business owners "giving the same quality of commodities, service, for the same price given by white enterprises" should be patronized whenever possible. As an alternative, the plan urged members to study the cooperative movement as a method for purchasing food, clothing, and shelter. On housing, members were to protect each other from "the rapacity of conscienceless landlords," encourage homeownership, but also "protect the race against movements calculated to segregate the Negro, thereby depreciating property values."[26]

The council's Economic Vigilance Committees predated the Housewives' Leagues and "Don't Buy Where You Can't Work" boycotts of the 1930s. Membership overlapped in some cities, although the councils had few, if any, middle-class members. Like the leagues, membership in the council was open to any African American woman, thus encouraging broader community support for the BSCP. The council's primary interest in trade unionism however, distinguished it from African American women's clubs, whose leaders were most often concerned with black business development. The council's origins in the labor movement led to occasional conflicts. Members were to patronize union printing shops, even though the printers' union barred African American members, rather than a race-owned nonunion printing business. In short, the integrationist, labor-oriented goals of the Women's Economic Council cut across race lines, while the economic nationalist ideals of the Housewives' Leagues tried to bridge class lines.[27]

The integrationist nature of the council led members to begin interracial cooperation efforts with comparable groups of white women. Delegates attended "conferences or congresses of white women whose purpose it is to discuss problems affecting the economic life of the community or nation." As part of the late 1920s movement to achieve interracial coordination among women's groups, council members agreed to serve as "ambassadors" to white women's labor groups. In Chicago, where the women's trade union movement was strong, the council worked closely with Mary McDowell, "the angel of the stockyards," and formally affiliated with the Women's Trade Union League.[28]

The scope of the Women's Economic Council's political program subverted the idea that women should organize merely to boost the morale of the men. Randolph supported the women's agenda, allowing them flexibility in determining their activities. A few local Brotherhood leaders showed similar tolerance. In Los Angeles, George S. Grant's Cooperation Plan in 1929 called specifically for both men and women to organize the union. The plan's egalitarianism may have arisen from experience: the council held regular joint meetings with the Brotherhood, and Pullman maids actively participated in the local.[29]

Grant proposed dispatching "women lieutenants" to organize porters and maids. Drawn from the Women's Economic Council and the Citizens' Committees, these women were to confer weekly with the Brotherhood. Women lieutenants were to collect dues, secure new members, and make progress reports to headquarters. Given the Brotherhood's desperate financial situation, and its need to zealously guard its fiduciary integrity, the degree of gender integration is significant. The responsibilities assigned to these lieutenants indicate the faith men had in women's organizing abilities.[30]

Men and women did not always cooperate. Some women believed they should take part in union meetings, especially in their husbands' absence, and some Brotherhood members believed they should dictate council activities. Men generally viewed women as useful fundraisers and party hostesses, but even these "decorative jobs" should be controlled by the Brotherhood, with the proceeds going directly to the men. Throughout the existence of the distaff organization, the question of control arose regularly, becoming the main source of dispute between women and men. Randolph advocated women's limited sovereignty: women could do as they wanted under the supervision of their own presidents, provided they did not contravene or undermine the Brotherhood's work.[31]

Randolph wanted to ensure that women members and the BSCP's international officers controlled the councils, not local men. The by-laws for the Women's Economic Council allowed the women to decide locally which issues to pursue and how, but Randolph held all executive authority as counselor. He alone could call conventions and meetings; he was responsible for the council's "general supervision, promotion and development." With the advice of the General Executive Committee, composed of the women presidents and secretaries of the council nationally, he had the "power to suspend or remove any officer for sufficient cause . . . to formulate all policies . . . [and] execute the said policies or cause same to be executed through such subordinate officers as he deems advisable." Randolph supported women's participation in the union but believed some control over their activities necessary. He was unwilling to grant local men this power, preferring to retain authority over the women himself. This policy prevented the councils from becoming political pawns in men's struggles for control of BSCP locals; it also fostered women's independent efforts.[32]

The Brotherhood had planned to hold a national convention of the Women's Economic Councils in 1929, at the same time as the BSCP meeting. The struggle over control of the BSCP, however, and a lack of funds, made the women's meeting inadvisable. The national headquarters distributed constitutions and by-laws for the councils to local divisions, allowing for some conformity among the groups. The council's ambitious political program, however, was only haphazardly implemented in a few cities during the Depression. Nonetheless, the women's group offered an alternative economic program to the more publicized political programs circulated during this period by other race organizations. Its class-conscious, integrationist program addressed the discrimination issues about which African American workers and consumers were concerned. The council's vision for a national organization of working-class African American women allied with the labor movement put it closer, philosophically, to the National Negro Labor Conference and the WTUL than the National Association of Colored Women's Clubs and the NAACP. By their open membership policy, the Women's Economic Councils brought the message of trade unionism to the African American community, transforming the BSCP from an exclusive trade union primarily for Pullman men into a class-conscious race organization of interest to all African American women.[33]

The Women's Economic Council offered an anti-capitalist solution for achieving a racial democracy through an integrated trade union movement. Its ideology was theoretically distinct from other black liberation movements of the era. Garveyism, still strong despite the exile of its leader, advocated black capitalism, and argued against trade unionism, holding that capitalism was "necessary to the progress of the world, and those who unreasonably and wantonly oppose or fight against it are enemies of human advancement." The Housewives' Leagues and their male equivalents, the Negro Business Leagues, also supported capitalism, at times bordering on economic black nationalism, but provided no solution to the masses of African Americans who failed to find work in under-capitalized black enterprises. Randolph, an integrationist and a socialist, held that "black workers should use the same instrumentalities to save themselves as white workers," urging African Americans to form cooperatives and trade unions.[34]

The council addressed members not as "women," but as consumers. Consequently, it proposed a variety of techniques that consumers could use to attack economic problems in the African American community. The program's feminism emanated from its recognition of women's political agency, its insistence that women were essential to the movement for racial democracy and economic justice. Council members argued that women's issues were consumer issues, and thus both economic and racial justice issues. Their consciousness of race guided their understanding of class issues and consumerism: whites oppressed African Americans through economic discrimination, employers paid black workers less than white workers while merchants and landlords charged black consumers more than white consumers. Racial integration was therefore the solution to economic exploitation; the abolition of job segregation and Jim Crow mercantilism would produce racial democracy. Thus while the program of the Women's Economic Council contained elements of communal feminism and womanism, its class-conscious, integrationist intent distinguished the council from other women's groups.

Until Garveyism waned and United Front movements emerged, the council had difficulty convincing women to support its goals. Racial integration and trade unionism were still suspect political goals at the end of the 1920s, as African Americans bickered over political direction in the wake of Herbert Hoover's successful lily-white strategy, which ignored African American political power. The growing Depression sent the entire African American community reeling, felling both the middle class and the working class, and increasing the appeal of alternative political discourses. Until the administration changed, however, the Brotherhood of Sleeping Car Porters faced the "dark days" of organizing, when few supported its goals.[35]

The Brotherhood story between 1929 and 1933 praises the women who "kept the faith," and censures those who abandoned the struggle. The apocryphal nature of this story, and the meager contemporary documents for those dark days, prohibits an appraisal of women's actual activities. Yet the story itself, even its later versions, suggests that gender roles in the Brotherhood crystalized during this period. Men assumed the central role as the union's founders; these union organizers along with a few steadfast porters, fought for manhood rights, consigning women to the status of devoted wives. The story reinforced women's supporting role in its lessons about the faithfulness and the disloyalty of the wives of union leaders. In later years, porters' wives learned their duties to the union through the regular retelling of the Brotherhood story to the Auxiliary.

Storytellers sometimes highlighted Lucille Randolph's support of her husband and her role as the union's most steadfast benefactor. It was she who financed her husband's work during the Depression. At first, her Walker salon provided a substantial income and access to Harlem's elite set. One version of the Brotherhood story says that she was forced to close her shop in 1927 because her patrons did not agree with her husband's radical politics. After that time, she appears to have held a variety of patronage jobs until New York City Mayor Fiorello LaGuardia appointed her a city social worker. Randolph himself did not receive a regular paycheck from the Brotherhood until 1936.[36]

Stories of wives' support for their husbands can be found among the rank and file as well. The daughter of fired Brotherhood Porter William Smallwood of San Antonio drew on these same themes in her description of her family's trials during the Depression:

> I would like to paint a picture for you to visualize, of the struggle of a very frail built woman, of about 118 lbs, and a 15 year old, struggling to get out bundles of laundry in the cold, sometimes, we had to crack ice in our wash tub to wash, after daddy lost his job as a Pullman porter, we had to sell coat hangers and newspapers to buy food, and keep the lights and gas burning so the Porters could have their meeting in our home; we had a very very hard struggle but we kept smiling and striving to help the porters win their rights as working men.[37]

William Smallwood died of "heart break" during the dark days, never knowing the union won recognition. His story became part of the history of the San Antonio Brotherhood.[38]

The Women's Economic Councils showed their faith in the union by continuing to raise money for the Brotherhood. Women sponsored dinners featuring fried chicken, chitterlings, or fish fries. With the Brotherhood they held rent parties, sponsored raffles, bake sales, boat rides, and picnics. After the New York Brotherhood lost its headquarters, Randolph and Ashley Totten rented a series of offices, but each time found themselves evicted. Telling the story of those vagabond years to an Auxiliary convention, Totten recalled:

> I can never forget some of the hard days, the hardest of which fell on Brother Randolph and myself. I remember when we could not pay any rent. I remember one day, there was a brisk breeze blowing up Hudson Street where our offices were located, and a man came in and said, "I am the marshall, you have to get out" and we got out. I sat on the side walk and talked of the Brotherhood. We did not know where to go. And just then a woman came by. She was the wife of a Pullman Porter, and she asked me what was wrong. I said, "What is wrong is that the Brotherhood is in the street, that's what's wrong." She swung around Seventh Avenue, and within an hour she placed Seventy-Five Dollars in my hand, and we rented a place on 140th Street.[39]

Totten remembered another woman "who was a godsend to us in those days. We could always go to Sister [Katherine] Lassiter and she would scratch her head and dig up money from somewhere, and we go back again and pay the bill and have the lights turned back on." The Women's Economic Council's work helped keep the New York office open and bought groceries for Randolph and Totten.[40]

"Unfaithful" wives provided examples as well. Vice-President E. J. Bradley's domestic problems were well-known. To keep the St. Louis local open, Bradley mortgaged his house and kept the BSCP "office" in the trunk of his car. By 1935, "I was flat broke and my wife put me out, and I went to my youngest daughter's home to live." After several years' separation, the BSCP lent Bradley money to divorce his wife. As Randolph wrote to a fellow officer, she "was injured in somebody's home and is unable to work and can't get relief because he is her husband and . . . she has accumulated quite a bill, for which the people with whom she has this bill are planning to sue him." Randolph did not think it was too much for the union to help a member divorce his "unfaithful" wife.[41]

The fortunes of faithful wives and steadfast men began to change for the better in 1933. At the American Federation of Labor convention that year, Randolph pushed through a resolution that porters be included in the Emergency Transportation Act. With prodding from the Railway Labor Executives Association, and strike threats from the AFL and the Big Four Railway Brotherhoods, Congress amended the Watson-Parker Railway Labor Act in June 1934 to specifically include sleeping car companies and non-operating train personnel. The new act removed almost every anti-labor provision of the original 1926 Watson-Parker Act, giving the railroad unions the same bargaining power other unions would later enjoy under Section 7(a) of the Wagner Act. Senator Clarence Dill, who believed only African Americans should be Pullman porters and maids, sponsored the New Deal act. As passed, the Amended Railway Labor Act required companies to negotiate with whichever union represented a majority of a job classification, as determined by secret elections or by other impartial means, held under the auspices of the National Mediation Board. The act extended protection to unions representing non-operating railroad personnel, including Pullman porters, attendants, maids, dining car employees, sleeping car conductors, and similar job classes. Although the Brotherhood of Sleeping Car Porters still had to settle an AFL jurisdictional dispute with the Order of Sleeping Car Conductors, porters and maids could now join the union without fear of losing their jobs. As a result of these developments, Brotherhood membership quadrupled in less than one year.[42]

The Amended Railway Labor Act made sleeping car workers desirable to the trade unions that had previously shunned them. The Pullman Company also moved to secure the support of its nonsupervisory crews, abolishing the Employee Representation Plan to comply, minimally, with the new law. At the company's direction, the Pullman Porters Benefit Association (PPBA) converted from a mutual benefit society to a union, the Pullman Porters' Protective Association (PPPA). Union dues were set at twenty-five cents per month and membership restricted to current employees of the Pullman Company. Under the statute, the PPPA was not a company union, but any examination of its history belies that interpretation. As one scholar calculated, PPPA dues were too little to establish a strike fund or even to engage competent legal representation should a dispute with the Pullman Company arise.[43]

Late in 1934, the Order of Sleeping Car Conductors, which had previously been disinterested and even hostile toward the Brotherhood of Sleeping Car Porters, asked the AFL for jurisdiction over porters and maids. The Order's president, M. S. Warfield, sensed that a BSCP victory might infringe upon his union's territory. His union's constitution explicitly excluded African American members. To counter the BSCP and to prevent porters from demanding the right to hold conductors' jobs, the Order sought to control porters and maids by forcing them into racially segregated "auxiliary" locals. AFL President William Green informed Randolph of his decision to grant jurisdiction to the Order and set up a meeting between Warfield and Randolph. Randolph paid no attention to Green's request for "cooperation and support," and pressed for an international charter for the BSCP at the 1934 AFL convention. The House of Labor approved Green's decision, thereby nullifying the BSCP's charter application. BSCP Vice-President Milton P. Webster was so angry he was ready to walk out of the AFL altogether. Randolph decided to ignore the AFL's decision.[44]

Randolph played a double game. The AFL's vote meant technically that the BSCP was no longer an AFL member, but following the procedure established in the new railway labor act, the Brotherhood president wrote Pullman Company President D. A. Crawford requesting contract talks on behalf of porters and maids. Company officials recommended that Crawford disregard Randolph's authority as president of the BSCP and refuse to grant his request for negotiations. But Crawford thought the BSCP's AFL membership deserved acknowledgment and decided to observe procedure; he may have believed the National Mediation Board would not seek to enforce regulations for an African American union.[45] He did, however, stall for time, reiterating the company's long-standing policy that the Brotherhood did not represent porters and maids.

Continuing to ignore the AFL's jurisdiction ruling, Randolph asked the National Mediation Board to intervene in the Brotherhood's dispute with Pullman. Signed authorization cards submitted by the Brotherhood of Sleeping Car Porters and the Pullman Porters' Protective Association revealed so many duplicates that the board announced an election to determine the legitimate representative. The election, by secret ballot, ran for four weeks, in sixty-six districts and with special provisions for mailing ballots. Polling did not occur on Pullman property (where Brotherhood officials feared company intimidation) but at churches and YMCA buildings where the union had a distinct advantage: many of the polling places had been the site of Brotherhood events.[46]

The Brotherhood of Sleeping Car Porters trounced the Pullman Porters' Protection Association, winning twenty-six of twenty-nine cities, and 71 percent of the eligible votes. Women's Economic Councils throughout the country organized parties to celebrate the victory and to observe the Brotherhood's tenth anniversary. In Chicago, 150 attended the election party on June 27, 1935. "It would be hard to find a happier or more jubilant group of men and women. . . . The assembled were too completely happy to even venture expressions other than their thanks to God and to their noble leaders."[47]

Noticeably, in those cities that had strong Women's Economic Councils, large numbers of men voted for the Brotherhood. In cities where the vote was close, the councils may have helped turn out the winning difference. In San Antonio, Texas, for example, there were eighty-seven eligible voters; forty-eight voted for the BSCP, thirty-four for the Pullman Porters' Protective Association. In that city, the council, led by Fannie J. Caviness and her husband J.B., the Brotherhood Secretary-Treasurer and his father, J.L., formed a united front. To encourage the Brotherhood's support of the council, the women admitted men as honorary members. The Brotherhood lost in only four cities, all of them in the South: Louisville, Houston, Memphis, and Atlanta. There, no councils had been organized and, except for Atlanta, the International Ladies' Auxiliary had difficulty establishing chapters in those cities well into the 1940s.[48]

Randolph won both games. As a result of the BSCP's victory over company unionism, President Green voided the jurisdiction order, and the AFL approved the BSCP's application for an international charter in 1935. The significance of the international charter should be appreciated: the Brotherhood of Sleeping Car Porters was the first trade union led by African Americans to be granted this status. For the first time, the House of Labor admitted black workers as brothers on an equal basis. Although another fifteen years would pass before the lily-white Big Four Railroad Brotherhood presidents conceded Randolph's admission to their ranks, the House of Labor set the precedent.[49]

Trade union victories affirmed the Brotherhood's demand for manhood. Even the company seemed to approve when in 1936 it issued an order to supervisors instructing "that every porter should be treated as a man." Responding to the announcement, Vice-President Webster declared, "This has never happened before [and] is definite evidence that the Brotherhood has accomplished its main objective."[50]

4

The First Ladies' Auxiliary to the
First International Negro Trade Union
in the World

Through the Women's Economic Councils, one group of African American women sought economic justice during the Depression. The renewal of the councils helped the Brotherhood of Sleeping Car Porters achieve victory. The election results forced the Pullman Company to recognize the BSCP as the legitimate representative of porters and maids. More than two years passed before contract negotiations were completed, but on August 25, 1937, exactly twelve years after the union was founded, the Brotherhood of Sleeping Car Porters signed an agreement with the Pullman Company. During those talks, issues of race and sex came to the forefront. How they were resolved and the new contract's provisions for Pullman maids reveals the union's struggle to give black men control over their union, their jobs, and their women. The resulting contract affirmed the manhood of Pullman porters.

When their husbands won manhood, porters' wives believed that they had won respectability and the right to be treated as "ladies." Race underlay their aspirations to ladyhood: the wives of white railway men were "ladies" because their husbands had organized trade unions and proven their manhood. Porters' wives considered themselves ladies, too, prompting them to change the name of the councils to Ladies' Auxiliaries. Although "women's" auxiliaries were customary in the railroad unions, among African Americans, "women" carried negative class and racial connotations that porters' wives wished to avoid.[1]

Yet ladyhood weakened the Auxiliary's independence as an organization, because ladies required male protection. Thus when President A. Philip Randolph called a national meeting to reorganize the Women's Economic Councils, he assured the men that the BSCP would be "the boss" and recommended a separate agenda for the women. In September 1938, delegates from twenty-eight Women's Economic Councils met in Chicago to create the International Ladies' Auxiliary Order to the Brotherhood of Sleeping Car Porters. During the convention, they adopted a new constitution, elected officers, and appointed work committees. As Adolf Hitler moved German troops into Austria and Spanish Nationalists bombed Barcelona, the delegates listened to women speakers discuss the international and domestic situation.

In this setting, Agnes Nestor of the Glovemakers' union, Lillian Herstein of the Chicago teachers' union, Mary McLeod Bethune of the National Youth Administration, Thyra Edwards of the Friends of Spanish Democracy, and a number of Brotherhood women presented diverse ideas about women's role in the labor movement. Herstein, a socialist, and Edwards, who worked with the Communist Party, recommended the delegates to reject "the decorative jobs," and develop a politically active, labor-conscious program. Nestor and Bethune encouraged the women to pursue the helpmeet role that BSCP President A. Philip Randolph advocated.[2]

Throughout the convention, delegates considered the role of "the first international labor organization of Negro women in the world." Rosina Tucker, chairing the constitution committee, made certain that local Auxiliaries would answer only to the international, but delegates rejected her call to organize African American women workers in other industries. During the convention, the women endorsed the views of their new International President Halena Wilson, who anounced, "We are concerned with teaching the power and the effectiveness of mass action, of collective bargaining. . . . We are intent upon arousing in our women a greater realization of the moral and . . . [material] obligations that they owe to a movement of this kind."[3] Although disputes over women's activities and sovereignty occasionally erupted in the locals, the new Ladies' Auxiliary president recognized the Brotherhood as "the boss." Wilson believed wives should nurture their husbands' union.

Wilson had developed her views on the role of women during the dark days of the union. Elected president of the Chicago organization in 1931, Wilson ensured that the Auxiliary differentiated itself from middle-class African American women's clubs through its trade unionist and integrationist orientation. She guided the Auxiliary's interracial efforts, working closely with the Chicago Women's Trade Union League and with other union women during the 1930s. In her fraternal activities, Wilson rose through the degrees of the Eastern Star, the Masonic auxiliary, which reinforced the idea that men's and women's organizational roles should be complementary.[4]

These ideas became apparent as BSCP officials began to renew and reorganize the women's organization as part of the union's election campaign in 1935. Although a few locals had carried on without national supervision during the dark days, most had disbanded. To prepare for the BSCP election, union officials reorganized the women's groups as Ladies' Auxiliaries. New officers implemented, when possible, the 1929 council program.[5]

The installation of officers in the Ladies' Auxiliary represented, in ritual form, the new gender relations of the union. This ceremony became formal and solemn during the 1930s. Often these were evening ceremonies, held in churches or occasionally a labor hall, presided over by officers of the Women's Trade Union League and the Brotherhood. Representatives from other trade unions attended, speaking to the assembled families on their duties to the labor movement. The program included loyalty pledges made by the new officers, a recitation of the Brotherhood's history and the local Auxiliary's history, and often a short sermon by the church pastor.[6]

During the ceremony, members reaffirmed their support for the Brotherhood of Sleeping Car Porters. Los Angeles President Mattie Mae Stafford spoke on the "Privilege of Contributing to Civilization," concluding her address "with a plea to the women to support the movement, stand by worthy leadership, be founders, builders, hand down something to posterity." Elsewhere, auxiliaries adopted other means to display their solidarity with their husbands' union. The Buffalo Auxiliary adopted uniforms, "gray in color and similar to Pullman Maids." The Salt Lake City organization put stripes on their uniforms, "representing the number of years their husbands have worked for the Pullman Company."[7]

The Chicago Auxiliary composed an inspirational candle-lighting service. During the ceremony, similar in arrangement and tone to a religious service, members pledged sisterhood and solidarity to the Auxiliary and the union. At the close of the ceremony, the congregation responded ensemble: "As workers and friends of the Ladies' Auxiliary to the Brotherhood of Sleeping Car Porters, we pledge anew our loyalty to the purpose and object, which is to help the Brotherhood obtain economic justice for the working classes and bring about a better acquaintance between the porters and their families, and consecrate ourselves in service of our master, in helping to interpret to others the Christian Way of Life."[8] The candle-lighting service became an annual event in Chicago, often attended by International Brotherhood officers as well as entire Brotherhood families.[9]

As the prescribed homily for this service implies, the Chicago Auxiliary saw itself as a helpmeet to the Brotherhood. Reorganization in the mid-1930s revived discussions on the role of women. One officer, Mrs. Clarence B. Carter, of Cleveland, Ohio, described herself as "a bit radical, and would like to kick the stuffings out of all who don't support the Brotherhood." She chided her sisters for failing to support the efforts of the Brotherhood.

If every Negro woman knew . . . the [Women's Economic] Council means justice for the Negro in all walks of life . . . I am sure [she] would be more anxious to come out and join. Among the groups of other races, the women have hundreds of organizations and many of their organizations are going to the front this very day, trying to do something for the Negro. . . . Sometimes I wonder what would become of us if we didn't have a few good, clear thinking, smart Negroes in our race to help the better thinking whites to care for that group of us that doesn't care even for themselves.[10]

Mattie Mae Stafford's "Sound Counsel" recommended:

Should any one ask what is the greatest service that the Negro woman can render today, I should answer unhesitatingly, "they can work to rend to the black workers of America a service whose value it is not in my power to express."

There is no woman, certainly no woman in the United States who has more reason to desire, more need to aspire for better working conditions for those of her race who earn their living by the sweat of their brow than the Negro woman. For the problems of the black worker are manifold. They must struggle against the might, power and moss-covered prejudices; they are the last ones hired, the first ones fired. . . . It matters not what we attain personally, the stigma of oppression will be upon us until our masses, our workers are freed from economic bondage.[11]

The president of the Boston Women's Economic Council, Mrs. M. C. Oglesby, also spoke of the new day coming, urging "sleepy men and women . . . to wake up your lazy bones, it is high time you started." The trade union movement promised economic justice; when its goals are achieved, "men and women are enabled to honest labor for honest compensation, resulting in healthy, sane, well-cared for, happy families, whose mental, spiritual and physical possibilities have become freed so as to reach their best." These observers argued that women should organize to support their men's efforts to unionize, believing that trade unionization promised the best means to improve the economic status and political power of the African American community.[12]

Hazel Smith of Detroit, the wife of Brotherhood Vice-President Bennie Smith, agreed that men needed the support of their wives. But she reminded Auxiliary members that the working sisters also needed help. Recognizing the many "firsts" achieved by African American women, she noted that "the great mass of Negro women are still underpaid, under-privileged, and burdened with a multitude of problems. Not only are we handicapped by our own low wages, but doubly handicapped by the meager earnings of our men." The jobs most African American women held were nonunionized and without social security coverage. These problems could be effectively addressed through interracial trade unionism.[13] "The old discriminations of the AF of L still rankle and not without reason. Yet, if there ever was a race that needed organization, it is the Negro. . . . Only solidarity can save the black and white workers of America, and this solidarity must be developed in mixed unions."[14]

All of these women recognized the problems faced by African American women workers and they agreed trade unionism was the appropriate means for ending economic and racial discrimination, yet they differed on the purpose of organization and the appropriate role for women in the labor movement. Smith thought women should be full members of trade unions; she believed women should be organized to demand higher wages and secure their inclusion in the new Social Security Act. Others saw women as auxiliaries to the labor movement, whose purpose was to raise their husbands' wages. They believed a living wage would solve women's problems by making her wage labor unnecessary for the family's economic survival.

Most Brotherhood men held the latter view. One, an admirer of woman's "natural gifts," believed her intuition and finer sensibilities were the perfect complement to the brawn and brain required for union organizing. *Black Worker* columnist A. Sagittarius lauded "the splendid and sustaining physical moral and spiritual support that women have contributed. . . . The long, lonely hours that they have spent at home, waiting and watching for the return of their warriors . . . have supplied that patience, courage and hope engendered by forced action." Yet even this old-fashioned man acknowledged the importance of training African American women in labor issues "if they are to be the intelligent cooperators imperative in this struggle for economic freedom." "We are assured that with them as our aid," he continued, "our Union is safely mothered and will grow in strength and power to be used unselfishly in the interest of workers. The mothers of the race, through oppression, are used to making sacrifices which develops spiritual power."[15]

After the Brotherhood contract was signed, Sagittarius began to emphasize the need to educate women about the economic benefits of the labor movement: "Women, who find themselves of the working class, custodians of families and the resident members of homes, receive valuable and practical lessons in economics. Many are compelled to support large families on small salaries. Consequently any well defined program, possible of achievement that would bring more money into the family through better wages to the husband would with few exceptions, receive their consideration and acceptance, if intelligently presented."[16] At the same time, Sagittarius changed his attitude toward women's role in the labor movement. In this "progressive age, men and women are recognizing the equality of the sexes in civil, economic, and political life and reason and intuition have caught the vision of a world in which a greater share of equity will reign."[17] Sagittarius defined women's "equality" as complementary; the wife made an equal contribution to the family through domestic cooperation, not through wage-earning.

The activities of the Auxiliaries reveal the women's political awareness. Angelo Herndon, an African American Communist facing the death penalty for "inciting Negroes to insurrection" for organizing unemployed workers in Atlanta, addressed the Chicago Auxiliary in July 1935. The women pledged to support his cause. Hulda Flood, the Women's Secretary of Sweden's Social Democratic Party, spoke in Chicago on the trade union movement in her country during a tour of the United States. In Kansas City, Missouri, the council hosted a reception for the city's labor officials. In Los Angeles, local defense committee chairman Carl Echols discussed the political implications of the Scottsboro case.[18]

The Washington women joined the secondary boycotts called by the Women's Trade Union League and the New Negro Alliance of the Sanitary Grocery Company and the Washington *Daily* and *Sunday Star*. President Rosina Tucker and local WTUL Secretary Frieda Jenkinson, helped to organize the Domestic Workers' Union and the Laundry Workers' Union. "Miss Anne Patrick, colored, a laundry worker and expert presser . . . gave a vivid picture of the unsanitary conditions in the plant in which she works, told of the long hours and small wages, and explained the speed-up system." When the plant owner fired Patrick for speaking to the WTUL assembly, "many unions and consumer organizations were so incensed that they staged a demonstration in front of the plant and it is understood that the owner had to go out of business because of his loss of patronage."[19]

In St. Louis, President Nannie Curby brought Mildred Price of the city Labor College to speak on "Women in Industry and the Labor Movement"; Curby in turn addressed the United Steel Workers' Women's Auxiliary. The Auxiliary reported their meetings were "becoming more and more interesting as we continue to study the subject of 'economics' with the result that our membership is increasing monthly." Brotherhood organizer T. D. McNeal regularly spoke, "familiariz[ing] the women with the entire contract between the Pullman Company and the Brotherhood of Sleeping Car Porters." At each meeting he explained the details, rules of pay, seniority, grievance procedures, retirement, and other contract matters. Several council members took additional classes in labor economics from the Adult Education department of the St. Louis public schools.[20]

The St. Louis Auxiliary also sponsored the most active Junior Economic Council, composed of the teenage children of Brotherhood families. Ten "sons and daughters of Pullman Porters" all students at Sumner High School founded this group in September 1935. Nannie Curby hosted the first meeting with her daughter, Evelyn. Special badges distinguished members. Under Mrs. Curby's guidance, the teenagers planned to discuss "trade union problems, craft and industrial unionism, and its development, to study Negro organization and their programs, Elementary Economics, and numerous other problems which face the American Youth and the elders as well." By the end of the school year, the youth group had twenty-five members.[21]

The Junior Auxiliary program taught the principles of trade unionism to BSCP children. "The youngsters should have some understanding of the conditions under which their fathers make the money with which to send them to school, buy food, pay rent, and incidentally, buy toys and pretty things for them," wrote Randolph. "Besides they can help their father and mothers picket in order to inform the public of the justice of the cause of their fathers," he added almost as an afterthought. Mrs. Curby outlined her reasons for organizing Brotherhood youth groups: "We must carry on and enlighten our youth to fight and win ultimate victory of equal rights to all and special privileges to none. . . . We dare not stand still nor will we be turned back on the weary road along which we progressed from slavery conditions, low wages, and long working hours of the past. We shall go forward. We shall choose the road of organized labor. It is the only hope for social justice and economic freedom."[22]

Through the council, Brotherhood children became involved in the national youth movement. Marion Lindsay, president of the St. Louis Council, attended the American Youth Congress in Cleveland in June 1936, where she reported the congress resolved to ask the government "to provide something for the youth after school is finished." Randolph, serving as president of its parent organization, the National Negro Congress, encouraged the youth council's involvement at the time. Two years later, the council participated in the American Youth Congress' meeting in St. Louis and hosted a formal invitational dance for 150 guests.[23]

Among the Sumner High students, the council remained popular for several years, benefiting from the high school craze for social clubs, fraternities, and sororities. The council passed as an exclusive peer group, admitting only children of BSCP members and thus elevating them among their nonunionized cohorts. Class of 1937 senior and council treasurer, Mattie Bowen, was elected Football Queen; another council member ran for Queen of Queens. The council also held a formal affair honoring the graduates. Three members began college the next fall. Others may have followed in their fathers' footsteps, becoming Brotherhood porters.[24]

In Chicago, Auxiliary President Halena Wilson opposed "numerous influential Negro citizens" when she took a job organizing black women workers of the Sopkin's Shops for the International Ladies' Garment Workers' Union (ILGWU). The Sopkin's unionization campaign drew popular support because the garment manufacturer employed primarily African American women who worked under conditions many believed were akin to slavery. Wilson also served on the city-wide Chicago steering committee organizing the 1935 Thursday-Friday meat boycott to protest prices. Later, along with two other Auxiliary members, Adeline Terrell and Mattie Jackson, she joined the Southside Tenants' League to work against the high rents landlords demanded from African Americans. The women endorsed municipal ownership of light and gas companies. Eleanor Rye, "one of our own young women," briefed the council on the efforts of the Chicago fur workers' union. She also worked with the women's auxiliaries of the Congress of Industrial Organizations to organize the wives of Chicago steel workers and joined the National Negro Congress.[25]

A *Black Worker* profile of Ada V. Dillon, a furloughed Pullman maid, provided another example of women's trade union consciousness. Dillon obtained work as a Works Projects Administration sewing teacher with the Board of Adult Education of New York City but encountered many instances of racial discrimination. "For instance if a colored teacher is sent to a white school, she is immediately substituted by a white teacher. The same is done to a white teacher who finds herself in a colored school." In addition, "Many of the colored schools have to hold their classes in cold rooms, they have to apply for cost to heat the places." The school board even dispensed supplies in a biased manner: "the colored have to wait longer than the white." To fight against these conditions, she and other WPA teachers formed their own trade union, the Adult Teachers' Project Union.[26] Clearly, Dillon and others believed trade unionism was the correct approach to fighting racial discrimination.

Throughout the years 1935 through 1938, the Brotherhood held Labor Institutes as part of its workers education program, in the first years in conjunction with regional conferences of the National Negro Congress. The institutes in Philadelphia, Washington, D.C., Chicago, and elsewhere always set aside one session, and sometimes a full day, to discuss labor issues of specific interest to women. In Philadelphia, a three-day Brotherhood Labor Institute in 1935 sought "to awaken the interest of the workers, both Negro and white, and give the Pullman porters a new orientation to working class education." Crystal Bird Fauset of the American Friends Service Committee chaired the women's program, giving a "brilliant address" on "Race Relations and Negro Women in the Labor Movement." A labor skit directed by Frieda Nurenburg, a newsreel on the Camden, New Jersey, strike, and a visit to a new housing project erected by the Kensington Hosiery Workers, completed the women's program.[27]

The Women's Day Program in Washington in December 1936 featured Mary Anderson, director of the Women's Bureau of the U.S. Department of Labor. Sharing the platform with her were Agnes King, president of the Washington Women's Trade Union League and Mary Mason Jones, president of the city's Teacher's Union No. 27. The Boston mass meeting invited former BSCP organizer Frank Crosswaith, now working for the ILGWU; Mary Thompson of the Boston Women's Trade Union League; Margaret Wiseman of the Consumers' League; and Minnie Wright, a woman "outstanding in the fraternal world."[28]

Where possible, the auxiliaries took advantage of the programs offered by the Workers' Education Division of the WPA to develop programs especially for trade union women's auxiliaries. Speakers from the New York Worker's Education Bureau and WPA Workers Education Project came regularly to union and Auxiliary meetings. Harlem educator Gertrude MacDougald Ayers spoke on "Negro Labor and the National Recovery Program." WPA instructor Pauli Murray was another speaker. "She emphasized the need of education of workers to help them understand the social problems which effects them today."[29] Describing those intense days, Murray remembered in her autobiography:

> As I became more involved in workers' education, my conceptions of racial identity and of injustice began to undergo a significant change. . . . The study of economic oppression led me to realize that Negroes were not alone but were part of an unending struggle for human dignity the world over. . . . Seeing the relationship between my personal cause and the universal cause of freedom released me from a sense of isolation, helped me to rid myself of vestiges of shame over my racial history, and gave me an unequivocal understanding that equality of treatment was my birthright and not something to be earned. I would be no less afraid to challenge the system of racial segregation, but the heightened significance of my cause would impel me to act in spite of my fears.[30]

Murray's recollection of interracial trade unionism seems to evoke the spirit of the Brotherhood women who became trade unionists in the 1930s; they left a fragmentary written record, but their activities bespeak a new consciousness.

This political consciousness expanded the significance of the BSCP's struggle for recognition. Through the auxiliaries, Halena Wilson, Eleanor Rye, Mattie Mae Stafford, Ada Dillon, Hazel Smith, and Rosina Tucker became advocates for trade unionism, using its lessons to organize African American women into their own unions. Nannie Curby kept her eyes on children's futures by organizing the Junior Economic Councils. In a period when workers and the unemployed founded trade unions as a means for making political demands, Brotherhood women sought to make the movement accessible to their less powerful sisters. Feeling the power of organization, working-class wives made their own demands on the capitalists they knew: grocers, butchers, merchants, and landlords. Their demands included lower prices, rent control, higher wages, and jobs for their men. Nor were they afraid to confront the government, demanding President Franklin Roosevelt provide for the general welfare, protect civil liberties, and recognize their equality as citizens. But with their husbands, the immediate challenge was forcing the Pullman Company to negotiate a fair contract with the Brotherhood of Sleeping Car Porters.

The Pullman Company was not yet prepared to recognize their husbands' union. President D. A. Crawford stalled talks for more than a year after the National Mediation Board certified the BSCP as the elected representative of the sleeping car porters and maids, using every procedural means at his disposal. Contract negotiations finally began in earnest in April 1937.[31]

Race, consciously and unconsciously, shaped many of the discussions between the Pullman Company and the Brotherhood. Even the minutes taken by company officials show racial contempt toward the African American-led union. Pullman officials and mediator Robert F. Cole were referred to by their appropriate honorifics of "Mr." or "President." President Randolph and other Brotherhood officials did not receive titles. Race was explicitly contested in the company's demand that the contract define appropriate rules of conduct for Pullman porters. Manhood, particularly the gendered rules of race, was at issue.[32]

The company and the Brotherhood agreed porters should be absolutely courteous to all railroad passengers. Pullman wanted to ensure that its white lady passengers could trust Pullman porters; its reputation had been built on porters' gentlemanly services. Pullman believed the contract itself, rather than work rules, should contain language specifically prohibiting porters from indecent behavior. According to minutes kept by Pullman Vice-President Champ Carry, the company wanted the rules to "be kept so clear that no porter could get any idea from them that he can take liberties with passengers, especially women passengers." Carry pressed for a specific statement in the agreement. He wanted the Brotherhood to agree, further, to a provision keeping secret the identities of female passengers who accused porters of misconduct.[33]

The Brotherhood rejected Pullman's demands. In its view, to agree to such a rule was to assent to racial injustice. No other union representing service workers had such contract provisions. The union agreed that passengers should file grievances against porters who acted improperly but porters should have the right to due process. Mediator Cole supported the union, arguing porters "should have the right to interview the complaining passenger and the Brotherhood should have a woman investigator for such purpose." Carry countered, "We will not sign an agreement if this rule was not included." Cole finally forced the company to accept a grievance procedure requiring that complainants (of both sexes) file duly attested affidavits of their charges before they could be admitted as evidence. This, and a guaranteed right to representation by Brotherhood officials, including Brotherhood-hired attorneys before the grievance committee, satisfied the union's demand for due process.[34]

The Brotherhood's opening wage proposals asked for a standard minimum wage for porters of $93.00 per month and $90.00 for maids. They asked that porters receive pay for all hours spent preparing cars, en route and at the terminal at the request of the company; these hours were to be counted toward an industry standard 240-hour month. The Brotherhood also sought separate seniority rosters for each class of porters, attendants, and maids.[35]

The BSCP also claimed to represent attendants who waited on passengers in the club cars, a position filled almost exclusively by Filipino men; after several discussions, Pullman relented. In return, the company requested the exclusion of porters working in Mexico, who were almost exclusively Hispanic, from the agreement; the Brotherhood agreed. The issue of representation for sleeping car porters in Canada, most of whom were Canadian citizens, was left open.[36]

At one point in these discussions, mediator Cole referred to "classes of colored labor," revealing his racial attitudes. His remark provoked a lecture from Randolph, who wanted him to understand "that the work itself was the only thing that mattered, not by whom the work was performed." Unlike Carry, who believed that particular kinds of work were best done by workers of a specific race and sex, Cole perceived, if dimly, the logic of Randolph's argument. He pressed Pullman to accept that "no kind of agreement should give the Negro exclusive rights to any class of work."[37]

Carry felt racial job classifications should also apply to other "classes of colored labor," claiming that Filipino attendants provided better service than African Americans. "Filipinos had generally proved to be much more proficient as attendants than the Negroes." Cole's own proposal to mix the seniority rosters of porters and attendants, Pullman believed, was "full of dynamite" because it would break down heretofore racially exclusive job classes. For this reason, the company fought vehemently to maintain its own definitions of "fitness and ability" and "the right of management to use selected men in certain classes of service." This language served as coded racial messages for supervisors and workers alike.[38]

Pullman claimed management also had the right to use selected women as it saw fit. The issue involved Pullman maids, both African American and Chinese women. Unlike African American porters and Filipino attendants, the maids' job class was not confined to a single race, but railroad companies agreed with Pullman that women of color were the appropriate workers for the job.

By the 1930s, most Pullman maids were actually contract workers. When requested, the company provided maid service to other railroad companies; train maids remained on the Pullman payroll but the railroads reimbursed Pullman for the expense. The Union Pacific, the Southern Pacific, Atlantic Coast Line, and a few other railways regularly contracted for maid service for their sleeping cars. The Brotherhood represented these women.

The Brotherhood's insistence that maids should be assigned based on their seniority, even though a sex-segregated list, was fundamental to keeping African American women in their jobs. Brotherhood Maid (Mrs.) Yetta J. Drye of the Oakland district filed a grievance against the company in February 1937, when she was not allowed to exercise her seniority to bid on the Overland Limited. Drye had twelve years' experience, three years more than any other maid in the district; she wanted a regular run when the SP discontinued her train, the Cascade Limited. Pullman Agent Andrews informed Drye that African American women were not permitted to take the route because the company was using Chinese maids on the Overland. This was in violation of the rules, argued Brotherhood Vice-President C. L. Dellums. The rules provided that a senior employee could bump a junior employee if his or her "fitness and ability [were] sufficient." According to Andrews, the Southern Pacific, which paid the maids' salaries, "demanded that the Chinese maids be retained."[39]

Dellums countered that this was certainly news to everyone since the maids were hired by, trained by, supervised by, and received paychecks from the Pullman Company. Even if the Southern Pacific reimbursed Pullman for the maids' salaries, Dellums continued, the SP recognized the principle of seniority among its own employees, and did not discriminate based on race, creed, or color. The BSCP vice-president added that the union represented both African American and Chinese maids and the case "was solely a case of protecting the rights of all concerned." As Dellums explained to Milton P. Webster, "In this kind of case we have everything to gain and nothing to lose because the Negro maids don't have the jobs now and if we fail to win the case they just maintain their present [furloughed] status; if we win it four or five of them would have jobs."[40]

In its negotiations with the BSCP, the Pullman Company argued that although it employed maids, the railroad companies who paid their wages should have "their wishes in the [racial] designation of the maid personnel be recognized." The Pacific Coast lines preferred to employ Chinese rather than African American maids. Reviewing the proposed language, Pullman's in-house counsel L. M. Greenlaw warned Carry against accepting the BSCP's proposed language because it dictated the assignment of maids in order of seniority. This would eliminate Chinese maids at once, Greenlaw believed, and noted such a situation might cause complications.[41]

Ironing out the seniority and fitness and ability rules were the last issues to be resolved at the meeting of August 25, 1937. To conclude almost two years of negotiations, the Brotherhood agreed "after considerable discussion" to Pullman's demand for an exception regarding maids. The union refused to allow the company to discriminate on the basis of race against porters and attendants, but it condoned sex and race discrimination against African American and Chinese women. The final language of the new contract allowed, "Where the expense for maid service is borne by a railroad company or companies, maids may be, in order to meet the wishes of the roads, assigned without regard to seniority." With that, Champ Carry announced, "Gentleman, the Pullman Company is ready to sign."[42]

The Brotherhood forsook its women members in order to sign the contract. The union abrogated the seniority rights of Drye and other African American train maids, and it specified different wage scales for porters and maids. The newest porter received $89.50 per month at a minimum; a maid with less than two years experience received a basic monthly wage of $87.00. Minimum monthly pay for attendants was set at $102.00, while busboys received a flat monthly rate of $86.40 (see table 1).[43]

Tips were part of the wage calculus. Despite the Brotherhood's stand against the tipping system, porters and maids still expected gratuities from passengers. There is no hard data on the amount of tips collected by sleeping car workers in the 1930s, and industry-wide declines in passenger miles distorts potential comparisons with figures available for 1927 and 1947. However, it seems reasonable to infer that since porters served more passengers than maids, men had greater opportunity to earn tips than women. While the 32-bed sleeper cars porters attended may or may not have been full, maids attended to passengers only when called, decreasing their potential to earn tips. Thus, if a regular porter collected, conservatively, $28.00 per month in tips in 1937 (half the average of monthly tips in 1927), his income increased by more than 30 percent. With fewer passengers to attend, tips raised maids' income probably no more than 10 percent.

Table 1. Minimum Monthly Wage for Maids, Porters, and Busboys, 1915–56

Effective Date	Maids	Porters	Busboys
April 15, 1915	$ 26.00	$ 27.50	n.a.
April 30, 1918	33.00	30.00	n.a.
1926 Wage Conference	70.00	72.50	n.a.
1929 Wage Conference	75.00	77.50	n.a.
October 1, 1937	87.00	89.50	n.a.
December 1, 1941	111.00	113.50	n.a.
February 1, 1943[a]	154.20	156.69	$153.69
January 1, 1946[a]	192.60	195.09	192.09
May 22, 1946[a]	198.60	201.09	198.09
September 1, 1947	235.80	238.29	235.29
February 1, 1951	258.98	259.08	258.98
October 1, 1952	287.68	287.78	287.08
November 1, 1956	345.46	354.56	344.86

a. Hourly wages computed for 240-hour industry standard.
Sources: Brazeal, *Brotherhood,* 210–12, 214, 219; "Agreement between the Pullman Company and Porters, Attendants, Maids and Bus Boys in the Service of the Pullman Company in the United States, represented by the Brotherhood of Sleeping Car Porters," effective October 1, 1937, and supplemental agreements, LC/APR Box 4.

Maids did receive longer rest periods than porters. The Pullman Company granted porters three hours' rest each night but required the men to guard the cars even while asleep. Maids received up to seven hours rest per night. The company was not trying to comply with women's protective labor laws but rather, cutting wages: rest time was unpaid, and did not count toward the standard 240-hour month. But neither maids nor porters won the right to sleep in unused Pullman berths.[44]

Two factors influenced the Brotherhood's decision regarding the rights of maids. As a result of reductions-in-force, there were very few maids employed by the Pullman Company in 1937, although many working and furloughed maids remained union members. By the summer of 1936, Pullman had reduced its maid workforce by half; three years later, only fifty remained. At the same time, the union's and the Auxiliary's attitudes toward women workers undermined any hopes maid Drye and Brotherhood women may have held for better working conditions.[45]

Most Brotherhood and Auxiliary members shared the belief that women should not be permanent members of the labor force. Men and women viewed "women" as wives and mothers "naturally" suited to take care of the home and children. Economic realists in the African American community realized that women needed to work to support themselves, their children, and their husbands. Most however, preferred that married women not work unless their

husbands earned too little to support the family. Thus, the Brotherhood's attacks on race-based wage discrimination should be read as demands for a living wage to support a man and his family. The Auxiliary's reporter from Portland, Oregon, praised the Brotherhood's success in negotiating a living wage
for porters: "Negro men and women should realize that it is the first time in
history that Negroes have massed together in a union; therefore making it a
decisive move in the field of labor to protect homes, wives, and children."[46] A
living wage for husbands protected families, but it also offered protection to
wives who chose to work. When women worked by choice, rather than because of economic necessity, they were freed from wage slavery. This gave African American women some degree of freedom in a labor market that offered
few choices. At the same time, restricting the living wage to male heads of
households strengthened the notion that women worked to supplement family income rather than serve as sole or major breadwinner.

The attitudes toward working women reinforced the Brotherhood's demands for manhood and a living wage. Although the BSCP supported paying
maids a base wage relatively equal to that of porters, they knew that tips did
not add appreciably to the women's wages. Nonetheless, when working full
time, these African American railwaywomen earned more than many southern school teachers, enough to minimally support one adult and two children.
But hardly anyone, including the maids themselves, expected a woman to
continue working when her husband could support her. Thus, after Pullman
fired maid Frances Albrier for union organizing, she soon remarried and began organizing a Ladies' Auxiliary for her husband's union, the Dining Car
Waiters, Local 456. Ada Dillon, recognizing she would never get her job at
Pullman back, took a WPA job and joined the New York Ladies' Auxiliary.[47]

The Brotherhood's victory at the bargaining table affirmed porters' man-
hood rights and affected significantly the position of women in the union.
Although the phrase "manhood rights" fell into disuse in the labor-conscious
New Deal years, gender remained a major concern to union members and the
Pullman Company. The contract validated porters' rights as workers and as
black men. As a result, the women's program assumed a more wifely charac-
ter. An organizational chart placed the Ladies' Auxiliary on the same level as
International Brotherhood committees. The chart linked the BSCP to the
American Federation of Labor and the Auxiliary affiliated with the Women's
Trade Union League.[48]

Even the name of the organization reflected the women's new relationship
to the Brotherhood. The "Women's Economic Council" indicated independence; it did not annex women to the BSCP and implied separate economic
goals. The new name, the Ladies' Auxiliary to the Brotherhood of Sleeping Car

Porters, announced by President Randolph in September 1938, formally "married" the women to the union. The women became an appendage, the dependent, distaff side of the fraternal organization. The struggle over gender literally turned women into ladies and transformed the way members saw themselves.[49]

As part of the transition from "women" to "ladies," Auxiliary members perceived a change in their social status. Irene McCoy Gaines, one of Chicago's prominent African American clubwomen, acknowledged their new status in her address to the Midwestern Regional Conference of the BSCP in 1937. After encouraging the Auxiliary to remain supportive of the labor movement, Gaines told the women to learn to use their new leisure time constructively, remembering the necessity of culture for self and children, and "being careful how we dress for work." Gaines also believed the women's new social and economic status required that husbands and wives adopt deferential gender etiquette. "We should help our men overcome their weaknesses; demand courtesy" from them. Recognizing that some wives might think their elevated status precluded involvement in the labor movement, Lillian Herstein sought to ease their anxieties advising, "Now recently, they have tried to make you believe that it isn't lady-like to be a union woman. . . . I think it is very lady-like to belong to a union. And the next best thing to it is to belong to a union man."[50]

President Randolph called the Brotherhood's first official convention as an international union of the AFL for September 1938 in Chicago. On that date he also announced the founding convention of the Ladies' Auxiliary to the Brotherhood of Sleeping Car Porters. The *Black Worker* announced, "This is a distinctive and unique convention. It is the first national convention of Negro women relatives of an international or national trade union in America or anywhere else." Thirty-eight women and one male proxy, elected delegates from twenty-seven councils, as well as dozens of interested observers assembled for four days to write a constitution consolidating the forty-two established councils.[51]

During the founding convention of the International Ladies' Auxiliary Order to the Brotherhood of Sleeping Car Porters in Chicago in 1938, guest speakers, Brotherhood leaders, and women delegates offered competing definitions for the new Auxiliary. These debates show that some women were not willing to give up their independence as easily as their organization assumed a "married name."

The issue of control over the women's organization remained contentious among Brotherhood men. Some believed the women no longer needed a formal organization once the contract had been signed. Others supported the Ladies' Auxiliary but thought local union men should oversee its affairs. Randolph supported limited sovereignty for the women with supervision coming from international officers. "The question has been raised as to what is the position of the Ladies' Auxiliary. The answer is simple and clear. The Ladies' Auxiliary is subordinate to the Brotherhood. The Brotherhood gave it birth. It is consequent to the Brotherhood. It is the Brotherhood's assistant. It is its helpmeet. The Brotherhood in common parlance is the boss."[52] This doctrine of subordination was written into the Auxiliary's international constitution at its founding.

Calling the Auxiliary convention to order, Temporary Chairman A. Philip Randolph gave the opening address, setting the tone for the meeting. He began with an hour-long review of world affairs in 1938: Hitler had invaded Czechoslovakia while England and France did nothing. "Are we about to witness a Hitler, a fascist dictator, setting about to bestride the world?" The threat of fascism required special efforts on the part of women, he continued.

> My dear sisters, as members of a race and a labor group interested in the preservation of democratic traditions in order that we may fight the more effectively for liberty and social justice, as mothers, wives, sisters and daughters, you cannot be unmindful of the great changes in world affairs that move in kaleidoscopic fashion before you. . . .
>
> Only the organized forces of the workers into trade unions, Ladies Auxiliaries that will fight for progress, freedom and justice against all forms of reaction and tyranny, yes, only organization, aggressive and enlightened organization of the workers, political and economic, of their families and the true friends of liberty, can stay the hands of world Fascism.[53]

Other speakers also addressed the international political situation. Their observations on the rise of fascism were directly related to their views regarding women's role in the labor movement. Thyra Edwards, about to depart for the front in Spain, warned of fascism's rising threat, underscoring the misogyny of its leaders. The Auxiliary must be attentive "because we are a women's group and because the fascist powers immediately dissolve women's groups and send them back to the kitchen, church and cooking. Most women would like to have these things, but certainly as an optional matter. The fascists believe that women have only one purpose and that is to bear children."[54] Lillian Herstein commented, "We must get rid of all these prejudices that divide us. . . . If we can only get the conception that we are all workers, whether we are women or men, whether we are Germans or Austrians, Czechs or Slavs, then we can go forward."[55] The anti-racist, feminist views Edwards and Herstein espoused were farther to the left than most Auxiliary members, who believed firmly in their duties as wives.

At this founding convention, Randolph introduced a new version of the Brotherhood story that set out the principles of manhood and the necessity of conjugal support. The responses of porters' wives to the union figured prominently. Most wives had been ignorant. Many were so worried about their husbands' jobs that they did whatever the Pullman Company and the Pullman Porters' Protective Association told them to do. After all, "it was difficult for the average porter's wife to understand all . . . the plans devised by the Company." Wives did not realize their husband's manhood was at stake, but Randolph allowed, "the women could not be expected to see this when the men as a whole didn't see it." The union, he claimed, could solve the domestic concerns faced by porters' wives.

"Woman, by nature," Randolph declared, "is interested in her children's safety" and thus she is "primarily interested in the security and stability of living conditions." A wife's goal should be "better homes" so that her family might "enjoy the civilizing agencies." A wife should not be concerned with the size of her husband's paycheck but the control he had over his job. "But how can the porter's check be made larger and more continuous? The answer is Organization." The conditions under which her husband worked must be the woman's great concern. Wives "should also want to know if the attitude of the Company insults the manhood of their husbands."[56]

Manhood was insulted when the paycheck did not support the family. Wives, Randolph argued, "must fight for an organization that will increase the income of their husbands."[57] Whether women wanted to work was immaterial; Randolph assumed wives' work was economically unnecessary when their husbands earned a living wage; he assumed women wanted to be housewives. In this new version of the Brotherhood story, he relegated women to a dependent role in the trade union movement and the union family.

The Brotherhood's fight for a living wage was linked intimately with manhood and women's role in the union. Monthly wages sufficient to maintain a family meant Pullman recognized porters as men with wives and children to support. When African American men earned a living wage, they would achieve equality with white working men and this would solve women's economic problems. Randolph offered the women of the Auxiliary a gendered vision of racial equality: through the trade union movement, women could become housewives who need not work for wages. Most porters' wives shared Randolph's vision. They preferred housewifery to paid employment, especially the low-wage, low-status jobs most African American women could obtain. They coveted the cleanliness and respectability of female domesticity. They envied the privileged position of white union wives, whose husbands enforced the racial discrimination against their men.

Randolph's plans for the Ladies' Auxiliary embodied these assumptions. He announced a modest agenda, abandoning the extensive 1929 program, as he described a narrow list of activities for the women. His 1938 plans gave the Auxiliary only two goals: organization and education. He abolished the racial restrictions on members. New members had to be recruited without drawing lines on the basis of race, creed, nationality, or color. Filipino, Mexican, and Chinese women as well as the white wives of Pullman porters should be persuaded to join. Participation in the Auxiliary by non–African American women would encourage men of other races to join the BSCP. Through the Auxiliary, Randolph hoped to broaden the racial composition of the Brotherhood.[58]

Educating "ignorant" wives was to be the Auxiliary's second goal. Women should know why their husbands were Brothers and the importance of paying dues, taxes, and special assessments. The union had achieved so much for the men, Randolph declared, that wives should willingly give "an entire month's check or several, if necessary for the maintenance of the Brotherhood."[59]

Randolph exhorted the Ladies' Auxiliary to organize and educate but to remember the Brotherhood was "the boss." Despite his stance against fascism, he told the women to go home, offering them no opportunity to participate directly in union business or political matters.

Delegate Katherine Lassiter of New York affirmed Randolph's new version of the Brotherhood story and supported his views on women's place. As the widow of a Brotherhood man, she said, "I thought it always my solemn duty to do whatever I could for the Brotherhood of Sleeping Car Porters." Delegate A. Neal of Minneapolis pledged to try hard to make "our Auxiliary better: because the Brotherhood has helped our husbands." Mae Dailey of St. Louis urged the delegates to "follow this [Brotherhood] leadership and pledge ourselves to help them carry on the fight." She thought Randolph's ideas for the Auxiliary "a wonderful program for women. This day is one that I have looked forward to for a long period: the day when Negro women of America would organize in the interest of economic justice. . . . I am going to urge you to continue to be alert and labor-conscious and to work together for the success of the organization."[60] It was the women's duty to support the Brotherhood, said St. Louis delegate Nannie Curby, "As Pullman porters' wives, we have all had experiences during this fight for this contract. Our fight, as women, has not yet begun. We must continue to take part in this great organization of ours. We have opportunity here and if we do not grasp it, I am afraid that we will never get another."[61]

Lillian Herstein arrived at the convention "full of the woman question." She had just returned from the Illinois Federation of Labor meeting, where she had helped to defeat a resolution prohibiting the employment of married women whose husbands already held jobs. She offered an alternative feminist program to the Ladies' Auxiliary. She assumed this group of African American women wanted equality in the labor movement and might desire the independence wage work offered. "Wives want to be equal with their husbands. If they are equal, they must understand how they make their living—the economic implications of the job—but they must do it as equals and understand the position. . . . Certainly a woman—like a man—has the right to do the job that she loves to do."[62]

She did not believe women should be labor's "auxiliaries" and expressed her hope that "we will change that word 'auxiliary' to something that means equal."

> I hope you will realize that [yours] is a trade union auxiliary; it isn't a pink tea and it isn't a lodge and it isn't the kind of job that when the Brotherhood has another convention, they will have a committee to decorate the room.
>   You are going to be an auxiliary of trade union women, and you are going to share the work and responsibilities of the Brotherhood. . . . Don't let them fool you with the decorative jobs. When they can't get rid of the women, they always give them little decorative jobs. All through history, women have shown that they have the courage, ability and stamina to fight for the big things in life. We've got to show the men that we still have that stamina.[63]

Although Herstein and Randolph agreed that women should be educated in labor economics and be prepared to man the picket lines when a strike was called, they differed on women's role in the labor movement. Herstein saw women as equals, recognizing that some wives desired to work, especially when they held good union jobs. But she did not think union work should be divided into tasks for men and women. Randolph saw porters' wives relieved of demeaning jobs in white women's kitchens now that their husbands earned a living wage. He believed in a sexual division of union labor, optimizing women's special talents. With other feminist trade unionists, Herstein insisted that women should have equality in the workplace and the union, predicting that the family wage would preclude equal pay for equal work.[64]

Convention delegates generally supported Randolph's views on the role of women in the labor movement. The few who agreed with Herstein were influential within the Auxiliary; led by Rosina Tucker of Washington, they put up a spirited defense. Tucker's small faction pressed for women's equal participation in the union. "My heart is in the labor movement," Tucker told the convention. Taking inspiration from the Washington Auxiliary's efforts to organize African American laundry and domestic workers, she wanted the Ladies' Auxiliary to become "the big sisters of the labor unions that are to come." She believed the Auxiliary should function as an African American version of the WTUL, organizing black women to support trade unionism as workers and as wives. She found a few allies, who tried to persuade the convention to adopt a more ambitious plan of action similar to the 1929 program, but they failed.[65]

Although she did not obtain delegates' approval for her political agenda, Rosina Tucker chaired the Committee on the Constitution, ensuring that the Auxiliary would have the freedom necessary to determine its own program. The new constitution emphasized women's importance in the Brotherhood family. "The Auxiliary is organized," the preamble read, "To unite the families of the Brotherhood of Sleeping Car Porters." The organization shall "promote and advance [Brotherhood families'] welfare economically, socially, morally, intellectually and to encourage and stimulate their interest in all matters pertaining to the good and progress of the Brotherhood of Sleeping Car Porters." The women pledged "good feeling and clear understanding" between the Auxiliary and the Brotherhood.[66]

"Good feeling and clear understanding," other articles in the constitution made clear, gave final authority to the president of the BSCP, the international counselor of the Ladies' Auxiliary. He could call any one in the Ladies' Auxiliary before the International Executive Board; he could even dissolve the organization "if in its opinion, the Auxiliary is not cooperating with the Brotherhood and is adopting policies not in harmony with or inimical to" union policies.[67] Not only did the international counselor (who would always be President Randolph) hold power externally, he was also an ex officio member of the Auxiliary's International Executive Board. He advised and counseled the organization in harmony with the aims and objectives of the BSCP. Randolph was, in common parlance, "the boss."

The highest authority in the Ladies' Auxiliary rested in the International Brotherhood, and specifically Randolph, but the constitution also forbade local Brotherhood members from interfering with the Auxiliary's "exercise of initiative and freedom . . . in the handling of their own affairs, but shall assist and cooperate in every way with the Auxiliaries." At the same time, the men should "advise [the Ladies' Auxiliaries] against the adoption or expression of anti-Brotherhood or anti-organized labor policies or allying themselves with movements that are not endorsed" by the BSCP.[68]

While the new constitution lacked the overt political statements of the earlier council by-laws, the reports of convention committees indicated that politics were not forsaken. The committees on Workers' Education, Cooperatives and Credit Unions, and Education and Propaganda described activities for the local auxiliaries to undertake. Carrie McWatt of St. Paul, Minnesota, chair of the Committee on Workers' Education, recommended that locals establish committees "to investigate civil liberties in our cities, housing conditions, health problems through our clinics and local health centers." These new economic vigilance committees added family and domestic concerns to the women's work against racial discrimination. The report of the Committee on Cooperatives and Credit Unions, submitted by chair Marion Sappington of Pittsburgh, recommended a substantial reading list for each local to study intensively.[69]

President Randolph had opened the convention by calling attention to the international brinkmanship of the day. The convention concluded its business by passing resolutions on international and national affairs. Significantly, Randolph authored all of the purely political resolutions. In all, twenty-two of forty-one proposed resolutions were Randolph's; the convention approved all of his resolutions but only four of those proposed by delegates.

The First International Convention of the International Auxiliary Order of the Ladies' Auxiliaries to the Brotherhood of Sleeping Car Porters proclaimed "its unalterable condemnation of Fascism and appeal[ed] to all minority groups to unite to preserve the traditions of democracy and the jewel of liberty in the world, by crushing this foe of humanity." In response to Thyra Edwards's appeal (and with Randolph's approval) the women resolved to support the Loyalist government of Spain, and called upon President Roosevelt to lift the arms embargo. Other resolutions demanded Congress amend the Social Security Act to include domestic and agricultural workers and pass the federal anti-lynching bill. The women called for freedom for the Scottsboro Boys; freedom for Tom Mooney and other political prisoners jailed for labor activities; the abolition of lily-white primaries; and continued support for the Works Projects Administration and Public Works Administration relief.[70]

The final resolutions considered by the convention considered the Auxiliary's affiliation with other national organizations and honorary memberships. During her address, Mary McLeod Bethune invited the Ladies' Auxiliary to join the National Council of Negro Women to represent the economic interests of African American women. On Randolph's advice, the Auxiliary respectfully refused Bethune's personal invitation, but extended the NCNW president an honorary membership. Instead, the women voted to join the National Federation [*sic:* Association] of Colored Women's Clubs (NACW), although there is no record of their participation in the organization. The Auxiliary also agreed to affiliate with the Women's Trade Union League, but it did not offer either Agnes Nestor or Lillian Herstein an honorary membership.[71]

The decision to align with the Democratic, but predominantly white and labor-oriented WTUL as well as the Republican-controlled, bourgeois NACW, indicates the Auxiliary's problematic relationship to other women's organizations and political parties. The Auxiliary carefully remained nonaligned with a specific political party. Like the WTUL, Bethune's NCNW, organized as the Democratic alternative to the NACW, was actively pro-Roosevelt, but Auxiliary women wanted to identify themselves as part of the NACW's long record of leadership and public service among African American women. Many also believed the NACW was more socially prestigious than the recently established NCNW.[72] The convention delegates' choice of international officers reflected these conflicting desires.

In the last item of business, convention delegates elected officers for their new organization. Tucker remembered a good deal of politicking throughout the convention, but claimed she herself did not campaign. Delegates nominated Tucker and Halena Wilson, the Convention Chairman and President of the Chicago Auxiliary for International President. Wilson won the election. As consolation, Tucker won the office of secretary-treasurer. The first, second, third and fourth vice-presidents were respectively, Katherine Lassiter of New York City, Mae Dailey of St. Louis, Fannie J. Caviness of San Antonio, Texas, and Letitia Murray of Los Angeles. The husbands of many of these officers were charter members of the BSCP. Eight other delegates, all of whom had participated extensively in the convention, became members of the International Executive Board.[73]

The new name of the Ladies' Auxiliary affirmed the sexual division of union labor. Although presented with a variety of definitions for their new organization, convention delegates agreed ultimately to undertake a program they believed best suited to women: organization and education. While these goals did not confine the Auxiliary to the "decorative jobs" that Herstein had warned them against, the program did restrict their efforts to the field of aiding porters' wives and women relatives, rather than African American women generally.

The international and gendered context of the first Auxiliary convention set the direction for the organization's work during the next two decades. Confirmation of black manhood rights through the BSCP contract assured a new sexual division of union labor and a gendered notion of equality: wives should help in their husbands' struggle for a living wage so that he could support the family. Married women, Randolph and Wilson assumed, would not want to work if their men earned wages equal to those of white union men. This assumption had detrimental results for maid Drye and other railwaywomen. Seniority mattered little when women quit working upon marriage.

During the 1920s, the broad-ranging program of the Women's Economic Council encouraged women to fulfill a variety of roles in the organization. By 1938, however, views on women's role in the labor movement had narrowed. Pullman maids were no longer integral members of the BSCP; their numbers were too small. The men had made their attitude toward working women quite clear when the organization traded women's working rights for men's advancement. The constitution of the Ladies' Auxiliary reaffirmed the women's subordinate status by emphasizing wives' dependence on their union husbands. To participate in the union, maids had to choose between identifying themselves as workers and therefore as "men," or as "ladies" and therefore dependent on men. Most, it seems, compromised by paying their union dues and remaining silent. Thus, the most visible Brotherhood women became the porters' wives of the Ladies' Auxiliary.

International President Halena Wilson (right) works with her secretary, Lucille Edwards [Coward] in the Chicago headquarters, ca. 1945. (From *Twentieth Anniversary Celebration of the Brotherhood of Sleeping Car Porters Souvenir Journal, 1925–1945*, Chicago Division, August 25, 1945. Photographer unknown. RCTP.)

International Secretary-Treasurer Rosina Corrothers Tucker in her Washington, D.C., office surrounded by official tools of her rank. She is holding a copy of her composition, "Marching Together." (Date unknown. Photographer unknown. RCTP.)

Katherine Lassiter
First International Vice-President
Ladies Auxiliary, BSCP

Mae Dailey
2nd Intl. Vice-Pres.
Ladies Auxiliary, BSCP

Fannie J. Caviness
Third International Vice-President
Ladies Auxiliary, BSCP

Carrie E. White
Member International Exec. Board
Ladies Auxiliary, BSCP

Ella McBride
Member International Exec. Board
Ladies Auxiliary, BSCP

Carolyn Lowe McWatt
Member International Exec. Board
Ladies Auxiliary, BSCP

Members of the International Executive Board, Ladies' Auxiliary, 1950. Katherine Lassiter, New York City; Mae Dailey, St. Louis, Mo.; Fannie J. Caviness, San Antonio, Tex.; Ardella Nutall, Oakland, Calif.; Florence Ball-Jones, Pittsburgh, Pa.; Ella Johnson, Tampa, Fla.; Carrie E. White, Kansas City, Mo.; Ella McBride, Den-

Board, Ladies Auxiliary

Ardella Nutall
Fourth International Vice-President
Ladies Auxiliary, BSCP

Florence Ball-Jones
Member International Exec. Board
Ladies Auxiliary, BSCP

Ella Johnson
Member International Exec. Board
Ladies Auxiliary, BSCP

Rosie Taylor
Member International Exec. Board
Ladies Auxiliary, BSCP

Nora O. Fant
Member International Exec. Board
Ladies Auxiliary, BSCP

Velma Coward-King, Montreal, Que.,
Member, International Executive
Board, Ladies' Auxiliary, BSCP

ver, Colo.; Carolyn L. McWatt, St. Paul–Minneapolis, Minn.; Rosie A. Taylor, Cleveland, Ohio; Nora O. Fant, Jersey City, N.J.; Velma Coward-King, Montreal, Que. (From *Silver Jubilee Anniversary and Seventh Biennial Convention, Sept. 10, 1950* [souvenir journal]. RCTP.)

Ada V. Dillon, a New York Central Pullman maid, was fired for union activities. She became president of the New York Ladies' Auxiliary in 1947. (From *Silver Jubilee Anniversary and Seventh Biennial Convention, Sept. 10, 1950* [souvenir journal]. RCTP.)

Dorothy Allison, field organizer, New York Central District, 1950, was the highest ranking woman on the BSCP's organizing staff. (From *Silver Jubilee Anniversary and Seventh Biennial Convention, Sept. 10, 1950* [souvenir journal]. RCTP.)

Lucille Campbell Green Randolph (1883–1963), "the onetime second most dangerous Negro in America," was a prominent Harlem social leader, owner of a Walker Salon, and financed her husband's activities. Active in the American Labor Party and campaign worker for Maida Springer's 1943 candidacy for the state legislature, she joined the Ladies' Auxiliary only after Philip paid her dues. (Courtesy of the Library of Congress.)

Porter and Maid, invitation for the annual Brotherhood Ball, New York Division, 1938. (From *The Black Worker*, Nov. 1938, p. 3.)

"Poor Wages and the Home Under the Employee Representation Plan." BSCP organizing propaganda emphasized the interests of wives and daughters in persuading porters to join the union. (From *The Messenger,* July 1926, pp. 328–29.)

Velmer King, seated second from left, served as president of the Montreal Ladies'
Auxiliary and helped to reestlablish the Canadian League for the Advancement of
Colored People. Helen Sheffield, to her right, was active in the Canadian Consumers' League's campaign to "roll back prices" in 1948. (From *Silver Jubilee Anniversary and Seventh Biennial Convention, Sept. 10, 1950* [souvenir journal]. RCTP.)

Addie Fletcher Booth led the Seattle, Washington, Ladies' Auxiliary during a successful two-year lobbying effort to enact the state's fair employment practice law. (From *Silver Jubilee Anniversary and Seventh Biennial Convention, Sept. 10, 1950* [souvenir journal]. RCTP.)

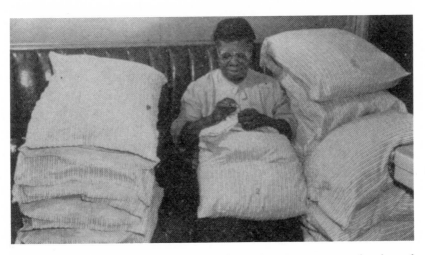

"Fannie Powers" was one of hundreds of African American women who cleaned Pullman cars. (From "This Is the Way We Clean Our Cars," *Pullman News,* Oct. 1946, p. 16.)

PULLMAN SERVICE

PHOTOGRAPHS BY
PULLMAN COMPANY

"Pullman Service" illustrates the personal services provided to "lady passengers" by Pullman Maids. (From *Pullman News* 3 [May 1924]: 2.)

The Pullman News

FRESH FROM THE PULLMAN LAUNDRY . . .
"Cool . . . Crisp . . . Clean linen for all Pullman passengers."
That's the theme song of Pullman Laundries, See Page 5.

July, 1946

"Fresh from the Pullman Laundry." By 1951, all of the African American women employed by the Pullman Company in the Chicago area worked in the laundry or as hourly yard employees. (From "Fresh from the Pullman Laundry," *Pullman News*, July 1946, cover.)

"The Majorette" was a popular symbol of the Ladies' Auxiliary. The Winnipeg, Manitoba, Auxiliary embroidered this figure on its friendship quilt in 1944. (From the back cover of the Auxiliary anthem. Artist unknown. RCTP.)

"At the Other End of His Run." Porter Golden William Smith mowing the lawn of his Los Angeles home, purchased in 1950, as his wife looks on. (From the *Pullman News,* April 1952, p. 14.)

5

"A Bigger and Better Ladies' Auxiliary"

Armed with their new agenda after founding the International Ladies' Auxiliary, convention delegates returned to their local Auxiliaries to organize and educate the wives and female relatives of sleeping car porters. The new International Auxiliary officers moved into offices donated by local Brotherhood divisions in Chicago and Washington. President Halena Wilson ordered stationery from a union printer and Secretary-Treasurer Rosina Tucker sent for a grand register from the American Federation of Labor on which to enroll every Auxiliary member. BSCP International Secretary-Treasurer Ashley L. Totten arranged salaries for Wilson and Tucker. Auxiliary vice-presidents planned tours of their districts to teach the group's program to every Brotherhood wife. BSCP President A. Philip Randolph ordered his vice-presidents and Field Organizer Benjamin F. McLaurin to promote the Auxiliary. The men called meetings asking porters to urge their wives to join the Auxiliary.[1]

Organization became the watchword. The union wanted "more than dues from a member," Randolph declared. "It wants his allegiance, devotion and understanding, which can only come through continuous education, agitation and organization." Leaders maintained that tightly disciplined, loyal regiments of black workers and wives commanded power. "Organization is the only force recognized by the great capitalists of this country," Wilson asserted. The International Auxiliary wanted the complete loyalty of porters' wives, and for that reason, refused to admit women who still belonged to the Ladies' Auxiliary of its old rival, the Pullman Porters' Benefit Association. World War II heightened her conviction, for "these are critical times and in the days that are to come the Negro will need organization and unity as never before." Wives were essential to the movement's might: "To build an invincible Organization, Negro men must have the same loyal support and the same encouragement that women of other races give to their men," for the BSCP "will never reach its full strength until it has at its command all of its potential strength." With its organized power, the Brotherhood and the Auxiliary would fight for all African Americans against racial discrimination and economic injustice.[2]

To secure their commitment to the organization, new members took part in elaborate initiation ties, vowing loyalty with the same solemnity of union men. To educate new and old members, as well as Brotherhood men, local Auxiliaries developed workers' education programs under the direction of the international president. Wilson suggested they study such topics as the BSCP contract, "man, woman and child labor," "labor conditions, social legislation, consumer education, health, housing, all would tend to increase the general knowledge and help build an interesting program for the Auxiliary members." "Each Auxiliary member, to make an effective contribution to the progress of both organizations, should acquaint herself with the aims, and the fundamental principles of the labor movement, since the permanence and the security of the home depends upon this strength and the bargaining power of the labor classes."[3] The ideology of the Auxiliary's workers' education programs reinforced the sexual division of union labor by addressing women as housewives and mothers. Members learned that their domestic roles offered economic power and respectability. Consumer education, the feminine complement to workers' education, instructed wives to use their husbands' paychecks to demand union label goods and courtesy from white merchants. As union wives, these African American women pledged themselves to the labor movement.

But the labor movement was a reluctant bridegroom. The iconography of the period restricted President Wilson's power to construct an identity for black trade union women. Each group was personified by someone Auxiliary members were not. White male industrial workers embodied trade unionism. African American men symbolized the Brotherhood, the race, and the black worker. "Women" meant white women, or in labor circles, white working women. Labor history, as taught in workers' education classes, reinforced these images, as did the leadership of each group. And despite their high labor force participation rates, almost no one honored African American women as workers.[4]

Indeed, African American women workers were more often dishonored by the stereotype of "Mammy" or "Aunt Jemima." This deeply ingrained image of a bandanna-crowned female domestic whose maternal nature derives more satisfaction from caring for her owners' or employers' children than her own, justified the low wages whites paid to black women. Thus, to create a positive image of black women in the labor movement, Wilson drew on black cultural traditions to enthrone a counter-image, the black mother. To render African American women respectable, Wilson declared motherhood the primary duty of African American women, ignoring women as paid workers. Indeed, the African American mother did not work, but devoted her energies to her own family. Wilson updated these "mothers of the race" to reflect the class-conscious times. The Auxiliary president translated the three principles of trade unionism "unity, organization, and cooperation" into an ideology for racial advancement, principles she believed union wives should teach their children. The "Modern Negro Mother" raised her own children (not someone else's), secure in the economic comfort her husband had won for his family through trade unionism.[5]

Wilson did not question wives' economic dependence on their husbands. Indeed, she capitalized on women's fears of male unemployment, which sent their husbands to distant cities for employment, or required wives to find jobs. By protecting the man's job, unions made family life secure, "and as a result thereof, he is in a better position to protect those who are dependent upon him." The Auxiliary offered women the respectability of housewifery and motherhood, reinforcing the gender roles of bourgeois society. Brotherhood men gauged their manhood by their ability to protect their wives from paid labor and the sexual harassment that often came with it. Tensions arose when union men extended those protectionist attitudes to the Ladies' Auxiliary.[6]

Battles for control of the Auxiliary threatened the "harmony" of the organization. Men claimed the Auxiliary was "subordinate" to the BSCP. Women agreed to "cooperate" with the Brotherhood, but refused to let the men interfere in their affairs. President Wilson guarded the financial and programmatic independence of local Auxiliaries, ensuring that the women determined their own direction. Her success at implementing the Ladies' Auxiliary's programs—largely through correspondence—indicates the support the Auxiliary enjoyed among the wives of sleeping car porters. And for the good of the organization, Brotherhood men usually supported their work, particularly when their goals coincided in the union's first major membership drive and its campaign to represent Canadian porters.[7]

The International Ladies' Auxiliary announced an extensive membership drive in 1938, and began to reorganize defunct local divisions and recruit new members. Counsellor Randolph advised the women to use the proven recruitment tactics developed during the Brotherhood's own organizational campaign. Using a method similar to the Cooperation Plan, local Auxiliaries divided into squads, each led by a lieutenant, to canvass every neighborhood in their city. Members visited every porter's home to spread the word of trade unionism. Armed with copies of the *Black Worker,* the trade union mission-

ary had "a heart to heart talk with the women . . . on the value, power, necessity and importance of the Brotherhood and why every woman relative of a
porter should join the Ladies' Auxiliary in order to give their moral, intellectual, and spiritual support to the Brotherhood whose work and fight have
benefitted every Pullman porter whether he is a member or not, or even if he
be a stool-pigeon."[8] If the lady of the house was still not "convinced of the
reason, justice, and common sense" of joining the Ladies' Auxiliary, do not
condemn her. Leave a copy of the *Black Worker* and call again, even if twenty
calls are necessary to win her over. "To spread the gospel of the Brotherhood
among those who will accept or reject it, is itself work of supreme value," Randolph sermonized. "The Auxiliary member should not be embarrassed for she
is on a mission of good will. . . . RIGHT will ultimately prevail."[9]

The squad member was to ask after the husband and other porter-mem-
bers of the household. Was he a Brotherhood man? If so, were his dues and
taxes paid up? "This is most important since the main object of the Auxiliary
is to help build up the Brotherhood, and getting members of the Brotherhood
to pay dues is a fundamental and constructive service." Wives' support determined the Brotherhood's financial security. The BSCP regularly dismissed
members for nonpayment of dues, International Secretary-Treasurer Tucker
warned Auxiliary members, "If these men were married and their wives members of the Auxiliary, they would have known the importance of their husbands paying dues."[10]

Randolph instructed the Brotherhood's international officers to help organize auxiliaries wherever they held meetings for the porters. The membership drive required the cooperation of these men when the Auxiliary realized
it could not afford to send its own officers on tour. Vice-President C. L. Dellums grumbled to fellow officers about the assignment, but agreed to humor
Randolph in his plans for the Auxiliary. One passenger told a porter he was
"surprised to know how well we had organized the women," and as a result,
"the porter came down, paid [his dues] up to date including his tax," reported an impressed Vice-President Bennie Smith.[11]

In the West, Fourth International Vice-President Letitia Murray wrote to
local Auxiliary officers instructing them to attend the upcoming meetings
held by Dellums. Through his assistance and interest, Murray reported, "I am
happy to say that . . . we have been successful in . . . complet[ing] the list of
Auxiliaries in the Pacific Coast Zone and [this] gives us 100 percent organization." With Dellums conducting local meetings in the Pacific Zone, Murray
could boast of 187 members among its six Auxiliaries in 1940; however, only
Los Angeles, Oakland, and Portland had sufficient funds to send delegates to
the International Auxiliary convention in New York City that year.[12]

Milton P. Webster spoke to Brotherhood and Auxiliary meetings throughout the Midwest. Webster's visit to Oklahoma offers an example of the union's conscious efforts to organize men and women. In Oklahoma City, where the Brotherhood division was new, leaders used this gender-complementary strategy to build support for the union from all members of the worker's family. Webster visited the city for three days in the fall of 1939 to officially present the recently organized men their BSCP charter and to hold a series of organizing and solidarity meetings. After a "smoker" exclusively for porters, Webster held a mass meeting the next evening, inviting porters and their families, the CIO Red Caps, and citizens of the city. Lastly, local Brotherhood President Fred Bennet held a joint meeting at his home for union men and their wives. After "Milton Webster spoke on necessity and importance of the Ladies' Auxiliary . . . one was set up with Mrs. Fred Bennet as temporary chair." Webster instructed the women to elect permanent officers and to send $5.00 to International President Wilson to obtain their own charter and seal.[13]

Mrs. Lessie Bennet, the newly elected Auxiliary President, wrote Wilson enclosing the names of other elected officers and the necessary money. To establish personal contact with local women, Wilson wrote welcome letters to each new member in Oklahoma City, reminding them that "The Auxiliary's purpose is to convince other women whether married or single, of their need for organization." Over the years, this small group (which averaged fifteen members) became an active participant in trade union and civil rights movements in the city.[14]

The International BSCP's support for the Auxiliary sent a strong message to local men. In Montgomery, Alabama, local Brotherhood President E. D. Nixon held a joint meeting in his home in early 1941 to organize an Auxiliary. He "spoke of the importance of great cooperation on the part of the division." By 1944, there were fifteen dues-paying Auxiliary members, while the Brotherhood had only thirteen men.[15]

Auxiliary membership grew swiftly. "Since my return from the convention," reported Murray from Los Angeles in 1938, "new interest has been manifested and the membership is steadily increasing. We have been successful in adding eleven members to our roll. Some are new, others who were delinquent, are returning." The vice-president promised Randolph she would "contact every Auxiliary under my supervision and put forth every effort to increase the membership and stimulate interest in this grand work for the progress of the Brotherhood and Auxiliary." International officers from the Auxiliary and the Brotherhood successfully established new auxiliaries even in southern cities such as Atlanta, Memphis, and Houston, where porters had voted against the union just two years before. Local membership drives brought hundreds of members into the International Auxiliary and the BSCP. "A little maid was in here yesterday," Vice-President Webster reported to Dellums in 1939. She "told me that the heat was on; that you couldn't stay out there without a [union] card and she had to have one." By June 1940, paid-up Auxiliary members numbered over 1,163 women; the BSCP's membership for that year was 7,374.[16]

In early 1940, the Brotherhood of Sleeping Car Porters began to unionize sleeping car porters in Canada. Nearly five hundred men, mostly African Canadians and some white, worked as sleeping car porters for the Canadian Pacific Railway (CPR) and Canadian National Railway (CNR). To win a contract for them would be incontrovertible proof that the BSCP was not just a "Negro union." The Canadian organizing campaign was the first of several to expand the union's jurisdiction to represent all job classes of railway porters.[17]

Under their contract with the Pullman Company, the BSCP represented Pullman porters stationed in Montreal and Toronto on southbound trains. But in Canada, the majority of sleeping car porters worked on cars owned and operated by the Dominion's two national railways. During World War II, the government recognized workers' right to organize, and granted labor unions powers similar to those in Britain and the United States. The BSCP used those powers to target the Canadian Pacific Railroad. International Vice-President Bennie Smith, who had lived in Alberta before migrating to Detroit, led the two-year campaign. Relying on the commitment of men and women to unionization, Smith organized Brotherhood and Auxiliary CPR divisions in Montreal, Toronto, Winnipeg, Calgary, and Vancouver.[18]

When the Labour Ministry held an election for union representation in 1944, 470 voted for the BSCP; only seven porters voted for the company union. The Brotherhood's negotiations with the CPR, although marked with the same acrimony as its talks with the Pullman Company eight years earlier, reached a conclusion on May 18, 1945. V. I. Petgrave, president of the Toronto Division and a member of the negotiation team, declared, "The consummation of this contract presents the most victorious precedent ever afforded Negroes in Canada." Canadian members of the BSCP and the Auxiliary became part of the largest African American-led union in the American Federation of Labor and made the organization truly international. The Canadian Auxiliaries, with one hundred members among the five divisions, enthusiastically adopted the women's program.[19]

In Canada and the United States, porters' wives and female relatives formally applied to join the Ladies' Auxiliary, which voted to admit the candidate, so long as she was not a member of the PPBA Auxiliary. Next came an elaborate initiation ceremony. New members learned the catechism of the

Brotherhood story and the purpose of the Auxiliary. In dignified ceremonies, the women pledged their loyalty to the Brotherhood, the Auxiliary, and the labor movement. At the member's first meeting, the sentinel announced each initiate and brought her to the rostrum where she placed her hand on the local Auxiliary's charter while the president spoke on the significance of the document as a symbol of "honesty, service, sacrifice, and unrelenting determination on the part of the pioneer members of this greatly beloved Organization." She reminded the new member of the "constant and relentless struggle" of the trade union movement, asking the pledge "to defend it and its leaders, against all unjust criticism. . . . to serve it to the best of my ability, come what will or may."[20]

The great ritual of Auxiliary ceremonies and meetings, styled after those of other fraternal societies, reiterated members' oath to the organization. Regular Auxiliary meetings required uniform opening and closing ceremonies. The president's appointed officers conducted each step. To enter the meeting, members whispered the password, "A Bigger and Better Auxiliary," to the sentinel; after assembling, the women sang the Brotherhood Marching Song and recited a passage on the mission of the Ladies' Auxiliary: "For each member to do her whole duty nobly, and well being ever mindful of her responsibility for and her obligation to her fellow membership and to the Brotherhood of Sleeping Car Porters." The secretary-treasurer concluded: "The Auxiliary stands for union, strength, love and peace. To this end we strive to develop women in body, mind and spirit." Meetings closed with a prescribed speech by the recording secretary and a prayer led by the chaplain.[21] The Auxiliary's official anthem, with its quick tempo and stirring lyrics, called the women to action.

"Marching Together" composed by Rosina Corrothers Tucker, roused the women to march with their husbands; as its chorus sang: "Together we are marching proudly; / Proudly marching as one pow'rful band. . . . We are determined and won't turn away, / But will steadfastly face the new day; / And courage and unity lead us to victory." The verses of the march decried "all tyranny, reaction, and abuses," for "the union gives us power." "Arise ye women, nothing fear. . . . This battle we will win." Letitia Murray reported, "When we feel discouraged, we sing this song and it peps us up."[22]

Tucker's lyrics to "Marching Together" held a different message for Auxiliary members than Wilson's maternal image. In the anthem, Tucker portrays women as equals, encouraging them to work with their husbands in the "great campaign" for racial equality and economic justice. Tucker usurps the rhetoric of manliness too, describing the "manly hardships" women endured to found the union. The song served as an educational tool, invoking the Brotherhood story and reminding listeners of the role wives played in founding the union.

"An uneducated membership is a weak membership," Randolph declared in his instructions to local Auxiliaries to establish workers' education programs. A small but informed group of women "can do a marvelous piece of work in any community," Wilson told a Montreal officer worried about the size of her local.[23] Ceremonies primed new and old members with an organizational consciousness; educational programs instilled them with the Auxiliary's ideology.

The BSCP and the Ladies' Auxiliary worked continuously to educate its membership. The first lesson taught all members, male and female, was the story of the Brotherhood of Sleeping Car Porters, the union's catechism. Younger members rejected: "this is old stuff and say they're tired of hearing it," Secretary-Treasurer Tucker later acknowledged. "But let me emphasize that this history is precious to us and it must be repeated and sounded forth until everyone understands the miracle wrought thru the suffering of the old porter and his determination to be free." In the Brotherhood story, members learned to respect union leaders for their sacrifices and to appreciate the power organized labor could bestow on African American workers.[24]

The Auxiliary's workers' education program elaborated these lessons. Women (and men) learned labor economics and workers' rights, the fundamentals of trade unionism. Wilson advised, "[It is] only by becoming familiar with the intolerable working conditions . . . and by knowing of the part played by organized labor in correcting those conditions that we may fully appreciate the value of labor organizations. It is only by contrasting the conditions under which our own men now work with those that existed before the signing of their contract with their employer that we may comprehend the far reaching benefits of organized labor."[25] The main text for many workers' education lessons was the BSCP's agreement with the Pullman Company. "Local Auxiliaries should spare no pains in having their members become more fully conscious of the meaning and significance of the wage agreement," Wilson wrote to her presidents. Randolph thought the wife's interest in her husband's paycheck would help to enforce the contract. Women needed to know the nature of the work Pullman required of their husbands, the contract's rules regarding pay, sleeping arrangements, care of uniforms, vacation, sick leave, death benefits, and the porter's right to representation before grievance boards. The power of organized labor gave porters these rights: "for the first time [our men] can say how long they shall work, under what conditions they shall work, and how much they shall receive for the service that they render."[26]

Wives also learned about unresolved contract issues, in order to create pressure for new concessions. The 1938 Agreement, for example, did not settle the issue of pay for preparation time, the two to four unpaid hours each porter spent before the train was due out preparing his car for passengers. As T. T. Patterson, the BSCP's Eastern Zone Supervisor, suggested provocatively to Auxiliary wives: "When a porter leaves his home, going on his own time and works for the Pullman Company 2–3–4 hours before he is due, he robs his wife and children of $1.50 or $1.60. . . . It is up to the women to stop their husbands from going down on the job before the proper time. That is the reason we can't get any more money for you. I want every wife, every sweetheart, every friend to ask, 'What time is your run due out?' Stop him any way that you can. Stop him. You know how."[27] Wives should keep their husbands off the job to win this dispute, thereby protecting them from company abuse.

The workers' education program instructed union members to familiarize themselves with the "principles and program and aims and objects of The Labor Movement" by reading classics from the Wisconsin school of labor history. Randolph also recommended studies on black workers by Charles Wesley, Ira De A. Reid, and Charles L. Franklin; later, he added Herbert Northrup's book. When Brailsford Brazeal published his dissertation on the Brotherhood in 1946, Randolph ordered three hundred copies, which he signed and distributed to each division.[28]

In Los Angeles, the Auxiliary's year-long book review program at the public library in 1939 discussed *Human Exploitation,* by Norman Thomas, *Racial Factors in American Industry,* by Herman Feldman, *The Negro Labor Unionist of New York,* by Charles L. Franklin, *Good Homes with Nice People,* by Josephine Lawrence, and *The Stricklands,* by Edwin Lanham, all emphasizing the importance of labor. Several auxiliaries purchased or borrowed the books recommended in "Labor Library," an AFL-syndicated column run in the *Black Worker.* At each biennial convention, the Education Committee approved reading lists for Auxiliary members' further development. During education meetings, members reported on these books. The Brotherhood headquarters in New York established a library open to all members; the Washington, D.C., division also started a lending bookshelf.[29]

President Wilson relied on these interpretations of labor history and economics to educate readers of the Ladies' Auxiliary page. Her series, "Organized Labor Movement and the Ladies' Auxiliaries," for example, began with workers' protests recorded in the Bible through World War II. To modern readers, her depiction of women's labor history is frustrating, yet accurately reflects the paltry state of that historiography in the mid-twentieth century. More truthfully than she perhaps realized, Wilson wrote: "The various histories of the organized labor movement indicate that there was no intention in the earlier days on the part of the labor organizer to include women in a movement that was intended to be purely masculine in its composition."[30] When labor historians discussed women at all, they wrote of women's auxiliaries, authenticating the sexual division of union labor. Wilson praised the wives of Pennsylvania striking coal miners, who in 1924 proved "beyond a doubt" the worth of Ladies' Auxiliaries. They raised funds, organized food kitchens, paid household bills, and toured the country speaking on their husbands' behalf. "But most important of all," Wilson wrote, "the morale of the strikers remained unimpaired as a result of the attitude displayed by their women folk." Wilson's columns provided local workers' education committees with material for discussion. Other *Black Worker* articles and newspaper clippings "dealing with the general welfare of the workers of this country" could supply further reading "if they are discussed from a purely impersonal point of view." This curriculum emphasized uxorial values, because "the labor movement is made up of the husbands, sons, fathers and brothers of Auxiliary members."[31]

The Brotherhood argued that trade unionism was the only effective solution for correcting the economic and racial problems African Americans faced. Workers' education, however, represented job discrimination and the labor movement as masculine; with organization, men could surmount these problems through the collective bargaining process. The Auxiliary taught the basics of trade unionism, not so that working women could organize their own trade unions, but because husbands needed their wives' moral support. In return, trade unions protected wives and homes by providing increased wages and job security. As Wilson wrote to the president of the Oklahoma City Auxiliary: "Today Brotherhood members do not have to worry about the permanence or the security of their homes nor about the education or the happiness of the children who belong in those homes. Their wives do not have to secure outside work because of the necessity of supplementing the family budget."[32] Members of trade unions and trade union auxiliaries, Wilson insisted, have identical "needs, responsibilities, and problems." Both require the basics of life and protection during crises; "both are at least partly responsible for the environment in which their children are bred." These essentials come through "a regular or permanent income," which "the working classes may [only] hope to obtain . . . through their affiliation with labor organizations." "This is the message which the Brotherhood of Sleeping Car Porters and its Auxiliary are trying not only to write upon the minds of their own members but upon the minds of all persons whose happiness and security depends upon the size, regularity, and permanence of their income."[33]

Wilson highlighted the supportive role of ladies' auxiliaries and the contributions women made to the labor movement. Auxiliaries linked women's interests with men's, disseminating "loyalty, confidence, appreciation, and understanding" in collective bargaining efforts. This gave the organization strength, "Man and woman [must be] united in a common fight for the maintenance of the greatest of human institutions which is the home."[34]

Wives should be aware of their dependence on wage work. "The greatest contribution that the women relatives of men who work for a living can make to the labor movement would be for them to stop deluding themselves," Wilson warned. "They [must] learn that food, shelter, clothing, life insurance premiums, doctor's bills, educational costs, lodge dues, church dues, all social activities are directly dependent upon a regular and adequate pay check and regardless of the importance attached to any or all of these essentials or nonessentials, they are obtainable only with a portion of some one's pay check." Elsewhere, she continued: "For no matter who are their friends, no matter what are their aspirations, the fact remains that they are still dependent upon these men for their livelihood and that their standard of living, their protection, the security and permanence of their homes depends upon the wages received by the man who must sell his labor in an effort to maintain and to perpetuate his family."[35]

Randolph, as counsellor of the International Ladies' Auxiliary also stressed the protection, permanence, and security of porters' homes. Little Rock, Arkansas, President A. D. Napier complained, "The greatest hindrance" to building the Auxiliary "is they cannot spare the time to attend the meetings nor the large amount of eight cents." Randolph's blunt four-page reply reminded the women "that their bread and butter and the maintenance of their homes is dependent upon the [BSCP] which owns the contract that regulates their husband's jobs." It was beyond his understanding how any porter's wife could say she would attend the meetings of other organizations and "hasn't the time to attend meetings of the Ladies' Auxiliary, when the very job of her husband is dependent upon the maintenance and strength of the Brotherhood."[36]

Wilson's and Randolph's references to other organizations suggest that the Auxiliary had difficulty dispelling potential members' negative perceptions of trade unions. Despite the gains made during the New Deal, several factors mitigated against black support for the labor movement. Anti-union attitudes within the African American community, particularly from middle-class male and female leaders, thwarted efforts to make union membership respectable. The racism of white unionists, male and female, and their repudiation of attempts by African American women and men to organize, heightened their doubts. Brotherhood rhetoric convinced some women to reject these prejudices, but the Auxiliaries' extensive and elaborate entertainment schedules, which raised money for various political and charity projects, helped to allay the fears of many more women and men.

Entertaining should carry an educational message. Parties should not be for "the MERE MAKING OF MONEY," Randolph cautioned. Rather, "The entertainment committee should be primarily interested in the LABOR CULTURAL IMPLICATIONS OF ITS ENTERTAINMENTS." The labor content was sometimes disguised, however. The Winnipeg, Manitoba, Auxiliary's St. Patrick's Day Silver Tea of 1945 may have been the social event of the season, bringing together representatives from the city's civic, labor, church, ethnic, fraternal, social, and political organizations. "We are asking every interested person in our community to attend and it is our desire to have every colored ladies organization represented at our table to preside over the tea cups and render selections on our Musicale. Our colored Girl Guides will be assisting us with the serving."[37] Silver teas were especially popular fundraising events, attracting the largest crowds with a wide audience, and with minimum outlay. The Chicago Ladies' Auxiliary's annual tea routinely raised over $1,200 for its educational programs. Silver Teas and Pink Teas may have been scorned by those who preferred more confrontative tactics, but their bourgeois femininity—the formal tea gowns, the decorum, the classical music—gave respectability to members of the Ladies' Auxiliary. Indeed, the Auxiliary declared the Denver Brotherhood's "Womanless Tea" a success.[38]

The prevalence of dinner parties, teas, card parties, dances, and other genteel entertainments, reported in nearly every issue of the *Black Worker,* brought members closer together and bestowed on the Ladies' Auxiliary the respectability other women's clubs enjoyed. As Lillian Herstein had noted during the founding convention, some people wanted women to "believe that it isn't lady-like to be a union woman." Parties made trade unionism appear less threatening, less masculine, and more socially legitimate. And as the porters' standard of living rose and household budgets increased, Auxiliary members realized the Brotherhood's importance to the "security and permanence of their homes" and their own status in the community.[39]

Such respectability, however, required a more important part for women in the union. Confining Auxiliary activities to social affairs did not address the issues faced by modern trade union women. The big "women's issues," as President Wilson saw them, lay in the economic power of housewives and their influence as mothers. As managers of the household economy, wives spent 85 percent of the husband's paycheck. The amount of his check was determined by collective bargaining and guaranteed by the power of trade unions. Women's role in empowering the labor movement should not be confined to bolstering morale, Wilson argued, but in allocating the household budget. Union wages should be spent on union goods and union services. By creating consumer demand for union label goods (and by refusing to purchase non-union products), wives could force manufacturers and shopkeepers to bargain with trade unions. As a result, consumer issues became increasingly prominent in the Auxiliary's educational programs.

Milbrey Sneed, chair of the Chicago Auxiliary's Education Committee, requested the federal Workers' Service Program (WSP) plan a lecture series on consumer issues. The Auxiliary's longtime supporter, Lillian Herstein, now chair of the Illinois State Advisory Committee of the WSP, was responsible for its multi-racial outreach efforts. The WSP's four programs for the Chicago group in the fall of 1941 included lectures on consumer education and Chicago housing problems, a demonstration on the selection of quality products, and films provided by the Household Finance Corporation. Attendance averaged seventy women and men for each meeting. The series was so successful, the Auxiliary requested another WSP series on "how the government agencies affect the workers."[40]

Wives commanded an important role in the trade union movement through their spending power as labor-conscious consumers. But Wilson recognized that Auxiliary members were also mothers concerned for their children's future. As she saw it, the labor movement offered excellent principles with which to guide children's awareness of race issues. The "Modern Negro Mother" should indoctrinate her children with the three principles of trade unionism, "Unity, organization and cooperation." Children who learned this creed would advance the race as adults. "Self-help through collective action is one of the constant utterances of the organization. . . . One race is not justified in asking another to do for it that which it is unwilling to do for itself. As other races band together for development, protection and survival so must the Negro race. . . . If children are taught racial unity and racial pride in their youth they surely will be present in the adult."[41] Wilson told Brotherhood women that the labor movement needed their strength as consumers, as housewives, and as mothers.

Using these domestic roles, Wilson empowered the African American mother, resourcefully creating a place for her in the labor movement. She did not challenge the gendered division of union labor, but sequestered women into a supportive capacity. Yet Wilson's promotion of this maternal figure, who worked for the betterment of the family and race, stigmatized women who worked outside the home. Auxiliary members' aspirations for respectability and Brotherhood men's focus on masculinity prevented the development of a role for women as wage earners. To acknowledge African American women as legitimate and permanent members of the labor force would undermine the Brotherhood's arguments for unionization; respectable families did not depend on the wages of wives. Thus, although Wilson earned a salary for directing the International Ladies' Auxiliary, ironically she did not consider herself a worker; in her mind, her husband was the breadwinner.[42]

Even the explosion of women's paid employment during World War II failed to alter the Auxiliary's uxorial ideology significantly. With men called away to war, women became their substitutes, continuing the complementary partnership established during hard times. Wives might take advantage "to make this good money while it is going around," but they did not plan to join the workforce permanently. Unions reinforced the short-term nature of women's wartime employment by granting only temporary membership; employers such the Pullman Company classified African American women as temporary employees, denying them seniority rights, and thus job security. While the BSCP supported women's efforts to obtain war jobs, union leaders saw those efforts as part of the political strategy for the March on Washington Movement; Auxiliary women could help their fight against race discrimination by demanding jobs employers reserved for white women. But BSCP officials regarded women's war work as temporary.[43]

Wilson recognized job discrimination based on race but did not acknowledge gender bias in the job market. She blamed women workers for their own predicament because they refused to learn skills that would provide job security. "Thus, through [women's] own indifference, they practically sentence themselves to remain economically insecure, even though the statute books are filled to overflowing with laws that were enacted for their protection."[44] Unless women recognized their rights as workers, including the right to receive wages in return for the amount of labor performed, they would likely end up in "a flophouse, a soup kitchen or to even greater degradation where the woman is concerned[!]"[45] Wilson's use of classic human capital arguments failed to address the race and sex discrimination African American women faced from employers and trade unions alike. Her own rhetoric, stressing women's economic dependence on men, discouraged Auxiliary members from thinking of themselves as workers.

A few local Auxiliary leaders did try to speak to African American women as workers. Susanna D. Lester, the "militant leader" of the New Orleans Auxiliary, spoke of the "double harshness" and exploitation of African American women in the job market. Noting the improvements made during the war, she told her female audience that unions were responsible for alleviating some of that harshness. Lester said women's past indifference toward the labor movement would no longer be tolerated. But rather than asking women to join unions representing the trades in which they were employed, she entreated them to join the BSCP Ladies' Auxiliary.[46]

While ideology prevented leaders from discussing the problems of working women, rank-and-file porters' wives used the Brotherhood to secure employment and job protection for themselves. Vice-President Milton Webster, appointed by President Franklin D. Roosevelt to the Fair Employment Practice Committee, received numerous letters from Auxiliary members asking for federal jobs and to complain about race discrimination. In California, dozens of porters' wives wrote Vice-President C. L. Dellums asking him to investigate the status of their employment applications, or to recommend them for jobs. With Dellums's help, Frances Mary Albrier, the former Pullman maid, managed to become one of the first African American women members of the Boilermakers' union at Kaiser Shipyards. These letters suggest that Brotherhood women saw their husbands' union as their own.[47]

Porters' wives thus reinterpreted Wilson's message of female economic dependency. They depended on the Brotherhood for the security and permanence of their homes, and they expected their husband's union to protect their own rights as workers. The masculine composition of the labor movement and the sexual division of union labor encouraged them to think this way. Trade unions dealt with job issues; auxiliaries addressed their domestic needs. Even though the Brotherhood refused to publicly acknowledge the needs of wage-earning women, rank-and-file Auxiliary members forced their leaders, male and female, to address those issues.

Local members forced their Auxiliaries to make other adjustments as well. The war disrupted schedules, compelling new meeting times. Dues payments reached a new high, reflecting increased household incomes, but members did not attend Auxiliary meetings as regularly as they once had. While many took war jobs, not all wives took jobs outside the home. Expanded domestic responsibilities, brought about by rationing and scavenging, appropriated more time from housewives, as did lodging wartime workers. Porters' overtime hours also increased, as the Pullman Company transported hundreds of thousands of troops across the country. These new time constraints made it difficult for wives to attend meetings. The Chicago Auxiliary met twice each month, once in the afternoon, and once at night. When no quorum attended Los Angeles meetings, Letitia Murray reported, members paid their dues and held discussions on the "good and welfare of the Auxiliary."[48]

In Boston, "too many" Auxiliary officers worked, Vice-President Katherine Lassiter complained in 1944, and could not devote time to union matters. In spite of their busy schedules, the Boston Auxiliary "have played hostess each day" staffing the union headquarters daily from 1 P.M. to 5 P.M., "so that our

Brothers may come in and pay their dues and socialize." Wilson suggested their educational programs reflect members' interests, recommending the local develop a series of programs "centered around child health, child delinquency, child labor laws, nutrition, etc. [which] would be very much in accord with the needs of the present times. Women in industry and the laws of the State in so far as they pertain to hours of work and rates of pay are equally as interesting." She also urged study of "the proposed amendment to the existing Social Security Act," extending widows' benefits to nonworkers. This "should be understood by Auxiliary members since their future well being will most likely depend upon the passage of these amendments."[49]

In the New York Auxiliary, employment and geography combined to strain the organization. The Auxiliary held regular meetings on Tuesday nights in Harlem at the Brotherhood headquarters. For members living in Manhattan and the Bronx, commuting to 135th Street was manageable. For those who lived in other boroughs, though, the 9:00 P.M. Harlem meetings created "hardships, particularly in the winter months, [which] are intensified by the traveling expense back and forth and the late hours." Rather than take the long trolley, bus, and subway ride into the city, Brotherhood women in Jamaica, Queens, met informally "keeping the fellowship" each month. This group of perhaps 150 women was organized mainly by domestic workers employed on Long Island, "experiencing the long hours and other hardships attendant on this type of work." They preferred not to spend the last hours of their Tuesdays off in Harlem. To accommodate their needs, New York President Katherine Lassiter attended the Jamaica meetings and allowed members to pay their Auxiliary dues.[50]

President Wilson did not fully comprehend the situation nor New York City geography. She instructed the meetings be abolished because she believed that "feminine physiology" [sic] would lead to divisiveness and split the organization in two. Referring to the traditional geographic rivalries in Chicago, Wilson wrote "The west side of the city [will be] almost unalterably opposed to anything proposed by the women on the south side and women on the south side will more or less look with a feeling of condescension upon most women of the west side." But she suggested the New York Auxiliary could meet in Jamaica occasionally, providing that all members received official notice of the special meeting site. Apparently, this solution was not attempted, indicating Harlem members' reciprocal aversion to the suburban commute.[51]

Unlike the BSCP, the Auxiliary consolidated its locals to include every Brotherhood woman in the area, without concern to her husband's employer or district conditions. Rather than encouraging development of the organization, however, the policy hindered its growth. In eastern Virginia, though intentions were good, problems arose because the "ladies of Norfolk were reluctant to be guests of their Portsmouth sisters once a month." Travel between these Hampton Roads communities took "from one hour to one hour and fifteen minutes to go from one city to the other." Because of bad roads in the African American neighborhoods, "when it rains the water stands on the streets and . . . [if it] happens on one of our meeting days, we can't get from one town to the other so well." Also "because so many ladies work as I do . . . we . . . meet . . . at 7 P.M. and we get out so the ones that have to cross the river will get home before it's too late." Women in Minneapolis and St. Paul, Minnesota, Kansas City, Kansas, and Kansas City, Missouri, and Montreal's CPR and Pullman Auxiliaries faced similar problems.[52]

The Auxiliary responded to these problems by reminding women of their common interests as union wives. Husbands were another obstacle, however. The Norfolk Auxiliary overcame its geographic and occupational difficulties to become "a credit to our organization, yet [they] are handicapped in their efforts and thwarted in their progress because of the attitude of some of their husbands, especially their Counselor," reported International Secretary-Treasurer Rosina Tucker. "I was asked over and over again by this Brother, as to what we do with the 30 cents they give their wives to pay to the International."[53]

There were men who resented the financial and programmatic independence that dues gave to the Auxiliary. Tucker discussed Auxiliary finances with brother J. E. Huntly, the counselor of the Norfolk Auxiliary, which brought peace to Virginia, but elsewhere men's objections to the women's autonomy arose regularly. Vice-President Letitia Murray was furious when the Los Angeles BSCP secretary-treasurer "overstepped his authority" and arbitrarily canceled a workers' education class she had arranged with the school board. Randolph concurred with Murray, outlining the process for the men to object to the women's activities. "If the Los Angeles division objects to this matter, they should first take it up with the Zone Supervisor of the Brotherhood, who would in turn take it up with the Zone Supervisor of the Auxiliary; and if not properly adjusted would refer the matter to the International President of the Auxiliary. Failing to adjust the question, she would then refer the matter to the International President of the Brotherhood."[54] In other words, the local BSCP officers did not have the right to interfere with the local Auxiliary.

A spirited exchange of letters from union members in Winnipeg document the debates between the Ladies' Auxiliary and the Brotherhood over women's role in the labor movement. The men's attempts to control the women, and to require that Auxiliary meetings be held in their union hall, provide a fascinating political subtext to the gender issues of organization. The Winnipeg Auxiliary was one of the Dominion's most promising groups during the war years. Its development and educational activities during the Brotherhood's organizing drive parallel the union's growth in Canada nationally. At the same time, the Auxiliary's success raised questions among Brotherhood men about the women's power.

BSCP Vice-President Bennie Smith organized the Winnipeg Brotherhood and the Ladies' Auxiliary in 1941. The Royal Club donated money for the Auxiliary's charter. Miss Helen Williams, president, led the new group of twenty-three members; Yvonne Blanchette, who served as first vice-president; Alva Mayes, second vice-president; and Helen Iola Hudson, secretary-treasurer. Membership captains quickly recruited neighbors and relatives. Six members lived in the same apartment building, Sutherland Court; Blanchette lived across Selkirk Avenue from Violet Fisher, executive board member; Mayes lived next door to Louise Guilberry, also on Selkirk; and Hudson, the wife of the local Brotherhood president, lived with her mother-in-law Mabel Brown, chairman of the executive board, and was sister to Edith Simmons, another member of the executive board. By the end of 1942, the Auxiliary had twenty-nine members.

By the spring of 1943, disagreements between the Auxiliary and the Brotherhood threatened the future of the organization. The men and women argued ostensibly over minor issues, but their fundamental disagreement was the women's independence. The Brotherhood wanted control over the Auxiliary's treasury, and invited Mabel Brown and her executive board to attend a BSCP meeting to discuss their future relationship with the union. The meeting degenerated into a sharp debate over the Auxiliary's role, with the men presenting several "grievances" against the women. Each side cited its own international constitution, interpreting each document to fit their argument. Brown's feminist appeal to Vice-President Smith showed considerable familiarity with constitutional procedure.

"The first grievance," Brown wrote, "arose over a meeting place." The men said that the constitution required the women to use the Union Hall for Auxiliary meetings; "the ladies feel that this hall is not suitable for many obvious reasons and refuse to go there." Although their reasons are no longer obvious, it seems the men used the hall as a social club, playing cards, gambling, and serving alcoholic beverages, which the women believed tainted the reputation of the place. The Auxiliary rented a room at another club for its meetings. Further, Brown argued, since the brothers only shared temporary office space with four other organizations, the article specifying the location of Auxiliary offices did not apply.[55]

Money was the Brotherhood's second grievance against the Auxiliary. The men "think that we should turn our money over to them," Brown continued. Although the union had not been recognized by the Canadian Pacific Railway, nor acquired permanent office space, nonetheless some of the men thought they should start buying furniture and equipment: "Now we ladies have worked hard to build up our Treasury and will be very happy to assist our Brothers financially when ever they have some sort of project or definite plan outlined, but we do not want to be exploited. We told the[m] that whenever they were ready to let us know and we would gladly cooperate with them but Brother Turner said that it wouldn't be necessary to let us know as 'being wives we ought to know our husbands' needs; therefore we ought to know what the Brotherhood would require and when.'"[56] This debate over the purpose of the Auxiliary's treasury illustrates the tensions between Brotherhood women and men, and women's power. The women attached a different meaning to support, believing they should offer moral, but not necessarily monetary support to the men. Chairman Brown was clearly unwilling to concede, but she confided to Smith: "So much confusion has been caused over the question . . . that some of our ladies now feel that we should turn over our money without further ado. I don't think this is the sole purpose of our money and I would greatly appreciate it if you would please explain to us the actual purposes this money should be spent besides of course, our monthly expenses for operation."[57]

In the "dark days," women's support meant "to help the Brotherhood in raising money with which to continue their work." Under the new International Charter however, the Auxiliary was independent, determining its own program and expenditures separately from the Brotherhood. The men could no longer expect the Auxiliary to automatically hand over its money, especially since union dues receipts were considerably larger than Auxiliary dues. The Winnipeg Auxiliary maintained that the men should apply for the money since a state of coverture, in which a husband possessed the right to his wife's paycheck, no longer existed. Although Brown may not have known all of the Auxiliary's history, she understood the implications for its future.[58]

Brown acknowledged to Smith that the Auxiliary might have made some mistakes during its first three fundraising events. Nonetheless, she contended that the proper forum for discussion was the Auxiliary's executive board, not Brotherhood meetings where Auxiliary members could not defend the organization. "But these Brothers think that they have full jurisdiction over us, that as the International is over them so they are over us. We know we are subordinate to the Brotherhood," Brown admitted, "but jurisdiction and authority is assigned by our International Auxiliary Order . . . and not by the local Brotherhood."[59]

Brown correctly interpreted the Auxiliary's constitution. The disputed article in the Brotherhood's International Constitution stated "The Ladies' Auxiliary to be subordinate to the International Brotherhood of Sleeping Car Porters and its respective Officials." The question centered on whether the phrase "and their respective Officials" included local Brotherhood officers, or referred only to International officers.[60]

"We do not think," she added, "that they [the men] really understand their constitution." "Now we do not want to do anything which is unconstitutional contrary to our International or which will hinder the progress of our men towards their objective, but the ladies feel that we are capable of taking care of our own business without interference. . . . If they had constructive suggestions or recommendations which would actually help us we would be more than happy to comply, but we do not like dictatorship nor the[ir] attitude."[61]

Vice-president of the Winnipeg Brotherhood Joseph Richard Hudson dismissed his mother-in-law's complaints in his letter to Smith. He believed the entire matter was the result of "petty jealousies." "It was woman-like and had it stayed in the Ladies' Auxiliary it would have erased itself in due course," Hudson wrote to Smith. "All very well had we [the Brothers] confined ourselves to a few recommendations to the ladies, but the petty jealousies that lay behind these moves caused many points of order to be ignored and brought about interpretations of the Constitution that I do not believe were intended. Hence, the many appeals to the International. For the good of the cause I will not outline personal instances nor will I say that they did not include myself."[62] The Brotherhood's relationship with the Auxiliary was a "sore spot." He explained that some of the Brothers opined that the Brotherhood's constitution "gives us the power to dictate to our Auxiliary." He erroneously believed the local president had the same authority over the Auxiliary as the International President had over the International Auxiliary. "It was not a very popular interpretation," he conceded to Smith. As far as the Auxiliary's offices were concerned, the constitution applied only to international offices, although "I see no reason why if the men and women are agreed they cannot have the same offices" locally.[63]

Chairman Brown was absolutely within her rights to deny the Brotherhood money, according to the International Auxiliary's constitution and the ruling of International Counselor Randolph. The local Auxiliary answered to the International Auxiliary, and the International Auxiliary to the International Brotherhood. The local Brotherhood answered to the International Brotherhood, which told them not to interfere in Auxiliary matters. The limited sovereignty granted by the Auxiliary constitution called for the brothers to advise the women on proper union policies but gave the women independence to develop their own programs.[64]

Vice-President Smith asked President Wilson for her opinion. While her reply has not been located, her advice in similar situations was for the Auxiliary to cooperate with the BSCP more. Earlier, she counseled all Auxiliary members,

> There are many minds and dispositions in all large organizations, but these individual minds should be made to blend in the common interest of the majority or for the furtherance of the entire organization. Bad faith or contrariness should never be condoned less they jeopardize the home, happiness, and safety of those who stand for what is right. It is my fervent hope that each division will place the well-being of the organization before any other consideration and that each division will prosper and develop during the coming months.[65]

Membership in the Winnipeg Auxiliary dwindled despite a full calendar of social and educational events. Helen Iola Hudson, Mabel Brown's daughter and secretary-treasurer reported in February 1944 that despite two new members, membership had declined to twenty-five, "but only a few . . . are really active and only one with nearly a perfect attendance at the meetings, that member being the Secretary-Treasurer."[66]

The Auxiliary's efforts to build its membership succeeded, even though a few locals were unable to overcome the distractions and disputes of the war years. Between 1939 and 1945, the rolls of the Chicago Auxiliary grew to over 250, of which 145 had paid-up dues. When the International Ladies' Auxiliary convention met in New York City in 1940, thirty-seven Auxiliaries sent representatives, ten more than in 1938. Membership in the International doubled between 1938 and 1946, to 1,360 women in fifty-six locals (see the appendix). Organized and educated, President Wilson prepared to demonstrate the Auxiliary's collective economic and legislative power.[67]

6

"The Duty of Fair Representation": Brotherhood Sisters and Brothers

The entrenched racial segregation of the railroad industry was not haphazard but a product of the progressive convictions and prejudices of the nineteenth century. Railroad barons and company bureaucrats agreed with skilled laborers that their industry should be controlled by white men; the work force reflected the racial and gender order these men felt ideal. Early company bureaucrats devised organizational schemes to control the hiring, assignment, promotion, and wages of thousands of workers. The job classification schedules first implemented by the Pennsylvania Railroad at the turn of the century rationalized discriminatory employment practices, codifying race- and sex-based job segregation and wage discrimination. Railroad carriers and white brotherhoods "plotted together" to keep black workers in the lowest-paying and hardest-laboring jobs, despite and sometimes through, unionization. Almost a century after these immense employee management systems emerged, BSCP President A. Philip Randolph observed accurately, "In every job that Negroes hold on the railroads today, that job is a blind alley job, in the sense that there is no outlet for promotion." As late as 1960, whether he was a redcap, a waiter, a sleeping car porter, or a fireman, brakeman, or switchman, a black man could not advance on the railways. And an African American woman could hardly get a job.[1]

Racial segregation in the railroad industry remained intractable until the civil rights movement forced changes in federal law. Yet the contours of job discrimination underwent significant reshaping prior to that time. In the twentieth century, the carriers began to modernize, adopting new technologies and creating new jobs in response to government regulations and consumer demand. As railroads switched from locomotive to diesel engines, trade unions won agreements from the railroads and the government to protect skilled white male members threatened by technological displacement. To compensate for job losses and to maintain their "psychic wage," white engineers and firemen redefined masculinity from brawn to brain power. Railroad officials experimented with white female service workers, retooling the pattern of subservience from racial to gender hierarchies in their efforts to retain male business passengers increasingly attracted to new commercial airlines. In the process, African American women, classified in the lowest paying and often the most strenuous and dirtiest of women's jobs, were moved into industrial cleaning jobs for which little technology existed to ease the work load. And at the end of World War II, when unionization and higher wages for Pullman's yard workers appeared imminent, supervisors began to hire returning veterans to replace these women.[2]

To mitigate the harsh penalties of modernization and to better their economic circumstances, black railroad workers turned to the Brotherhood of Sleeping Car Porters to represent their interests. Under Randolph's direction, the union's jurisdiction expanded to include thousands of workers in North America. After signing a collective bargaining agreement with the Pullman Company, the BSCP proceeded to win contracts from every passenger carrier, including the Baltimore and Ohio, the Atlantic Coast Line, the Santa Fe, the Louisville and Nashville, the Seaboard Air Line, the Union Pacific, the Southern Pacific, the Rock Island Line, the Canadian National Railway, and the Canadian Pacific Railway. By 1957, the Brotherhood represented non-operative classes such as train and chair car porters, attendants, busboys, maids, barbers, mail porters, non-Pullman sleeping car porters and porterettes, and Pullman's nonclerical storeroom employees, and had attempted to organize Pullman's car cleaners and yard forces. In addition, the union represented the operative classes of locomotive firemen and porter brakemen. All of these classes were racially designated, dead-end jobs. Led by black men, the organization united male and female workers from non-operative and operative job classes, establishing a diverse union of workers "regardless of race, sex, creed, color, or nationality." Then, using traditional trade union principles such as seniority, leaders demanded more job opportunities for African American men and women in the railroad industry.

The BSCP's expansion coincided with the apex of railway union power. Even so, African Americans held less than 4 percent of all transportation jobs in 1943, making the railroads one of the most racially segregated industries in the nation. Randolph exploited every opportunity to abolish Jim Crow on the railroads. As annual convention delegates to the American Federation of Labor conventions, he and First Vice-President Milton P. Webster annually lobbied the House of Labor to prohibit race discrimination by labor unions. Traveling in the south, BSCP officials regularly confronted railroad employees' attempts to enforce the color line. For twenty years, Randolph fought for membership in the lily-white Railway Labor Executives Association so that he could nominate "a black man [to] sit on the National Railroad Adjustment Board." The BSCP organized the Provisional Committee for the Organization of Colored Locomotive Firemen, Switchmen, and Brakemen in 1940 to represent black railwaymens' interests before the courts, employers, and white-controlled labor unions.[3]

The union also fought for African American women denied jobs because of race, but it did not challenge sex segregation. During World War II, when employers denied African American women jobs reserved for white women, Randolph regarded the cause as racism, as did the plaintiffs. The BSCP's International officers received scores of race discrimination complaints from black women who demanded the Fair Employment Practice Committee assist them in entering the "pink collar ghetto." But sex discrimination in the railroad industry remained an unacknowledged obstacle for Brotherhood women and the union did not meet its "duty of fair representation" for women as a class. To obtain its first contract from Pullman, it had bargained away the seniority rights of train maids. Futhermore, Brotherhood organizers did not pursue women members as aggressively as they did men. When Pullman's black female laundry workers asked the BSCP to represent them, Randolph referred their request to another union unfamiliar with the specialized field of railroad labor law. And though the union spent tens of thousands of dollars in litigation expenses on behalf of displaced locomotive firemen, Randolph did not even consider court action on behalf of African American railwaywomen disabled by protective labor laws.

In addition, despite the Brotherhood's efforts to diversify membership and expand its jurisdiction, officials made no attempt to organize white women hired in new passenger service jobs. During the Depression, railroads began to hire hostesses and stewardess-nurses as low-wage substitutes for white male conductors as well as for newly unionized African American waiters, porters, and maids; other carriers hired white women when World War II created a shortage of male workers. Although the postwar nursing shortage forced carriers to suspend the stewardess-nurse job class, they continued to hire hostesses and other white females to perform services for passengers and to capture the attention of male passengers. As competition from the airlines increased, railroad carriers relied on white women workers to modernize their services and image.

Some of these newly hired women performed the same work as railwaymen. Carriers also created new jobs, assigning women workers duties from several male job classes. Pullman Hostess Director Wanda L. Myers, running on the Tennessean from Washington, D.C., to Memphis, assisted porters and conductors by greeting passengers, helping them find their seats and berth assignments, and enforcing safety regulations. The Southern Pacific hired "women passenger aids" while the Union Pacific (UP) created the job of stewardess-nurse, hiring one hundred white women for this position in 1935.[4]

The duties of stewardess-nurses corresponded to those of Pullman maids and porters. "Our first duty as stewardess was chiefly to assist mothers in the care of their children," stated one employee. They also cared for children traveling alone. Elderly passengers "present a pathetic situation [for which] her understanding of these lonely people and her friendship and sympathy are most appreciated." Passengers needing regular medical attention "are grateful for the attention of the nurse" who can help with treatment for diabetes, asthma, and related conditions, especially in using patients' prescribed hypodermic needles. As a graduate nurse and a Pullman maid, Frances Mary Albrier performed all the duties of stewardess-nurse but without the pay or benefits. Because of her race, she could not even apply for the job, even though she was a qualified registered nurse. Even her Pullman uniform of gray cloth with starched white apron, collar and cuffs, marked her from the stewardess-nurse. Their uniforms of "French blue serge . . . worn with a heavy cape of darker blue" patterned after the uniform of visiting nurses, conveyed a message of professional authority; passengers recognized they were not servants, and would not perform the personal grooming services a passenger could ask of a Pullman maid or porter.[5]

Officials from the predominantly white American Nurses' Association (ANA) praised the railroads for "pioneering a new branch of public health and industrial nursing." According to the *American Journal of Nursing,* railroad executives set stringent job qualifications, but one criterion was consistent for railroad hostesses and the newly created job of airline stewardess. "It is essential that each one present an attractive personality and appearance, since these factors determine her first impression on the public."[6] All candidates had to be unmarried and pass a "personality test" and a company physical. In addition, women had to be adults between twenty-five and twenty-eight years of age, and stand between five-feet, three inches and five-feet, seven inches in height with "a corresponding weight of from 125 to 145 pounds."[7]

None of these requirements were essential to job performance, nor did Pullman impose such exacting physical conditions on maids. Rather, the railroad industry employed white female service workers, in part, to modernize its image and to appeal sexually to traveling businessmen. Pullman advertised its deluxe service using pictures of white male passengers directing African American male porters, recalling the old master-slave relationship. The rise of white female office workers, however, changed the preferences of white male businessmen, the elite clientele of the transportation industry. Suzanne Kolm has suggested that commercial airlines hired white women to appeal to these male passengers. The stewardess, in her association with the new air transportation industry, became a modern invention, a phenomemon of twentieth-century culture that linked sex with service and speed. The association of color with women's service work remained powerful, but it was always tinged with the notion of dirt. Modernity dictated clean, white "career girls" with whom the mainly white male passengers might feel more at ease than black men or women.[8]

For its stewardess-nurses, the railroads complied with state protective labor laws, providing these white women with better working conditions and more privileges than all other railroad workers. In addition to liberal layovers and "comfortable sleeping quarters in Pullman Cars . . . the railroad company assumes living expenses incurred away from the home terminal." In fact, train maids should have enjoyed the same protections, but the Union Pacific and other railroad carriers did not always comply with these laws for female workers of color. Nor did the BSCP file complaints with state enforcement authorities or the Fair Employment Practice Committee about these racially distinct employment practices.[9]

Racism on the part of stewardess-nurses, coupled with the trade union movement's ambivalence about working women, forestalled unionization. As non-operating, non-supervisory workers, the BSCP or the African American-led Dining Car Employees could have claimed jurisdiction over stewardess-nurses and hostesses. However, race relations of the period prohibited African American men from speaking for white women. Assumptions about marriage and commitment to the labor force also militated against organizing this group of women. The BSCP shared with other trade unions the belief that women, white and black, did not want to be permanent labor force participants. During the war, government and company officials stressed the temporary assignment of women workers, claiming that when "normal conditions" (i.e., male workers) returned, the women would be furloughed. Bans against married women encouraged rapid employee turnover and allowed union organizers to dismiss hostesses and stewardess-nurses as too impermanent to be worth their efforts. Besides, what husband with an ounce of manhood would allow his wife the independence and freedom of regular overnight road travel?[10]

Nor is it likely that white nurses wanted a predominantly African American male trade union to represent them. Nurses' education stressed their professional status, which was reinforced by their membership in the ANA. To participate in collective bargaining and strikes would be "unprofessional." For train hostesses, their light physical tasks, the comfort and cleanliness of their work, and their gender separated them from the common railwayman; sleeping car porters might hold college degrees, but as male African American service providers they were among the working class. Although stewardess-nurses and hostesses might have fared better with union representation no railway Brotherhood wanted them. Indeed, the unions did not protest the substantial postwar furloughs of women workers, white or black.[11]

Rather than organizing the nurse-stewardesses, the BSCP fought them, justifiably contending they were hired over the seniority rights of Pullman maids. At the AFL convention of 1938, Randolph and Webster sponsored a resolution denouncing the abrogation of train maids' seniority rights in favor of stewardess-nurses. The BSCP delegates asked the convention to "condemn this violation of the principle of Seniority . . . as unfair to a group of maids, regardless of color or race." The proposed resolution directed AFL President William Green "to address a letter of protest to the President of the Union Pacific Railroad and other railway systems, against this outrageous abuse of the Seniority rule which organized labor so dearly prizes." Randolph presented the maids' case in the language of labor, but the House of Labor saw only race. The debate over the resolution became so acrimonious that the convention took the extraordinary step of setting aside the recommendation of the resolutions committee.[12]

The BSCP's convention rhetoric, of course, contradicted its own actions just twelve months earlier when the union allowed Pullman to assign maids on the basis of race. The willingness of trade unions to relinquish women workers' seniority rights, even when male and female employees had separate seniority rosters, seriously abrogated their duty of fair representation. Loss of seniority rights also made it easier for companies to eliminate job classes reserved for women. Exercising that provision, Pullman eliminated train maids by 1948 and threatened men's jobs by hiring white stewardesses to perform porters' and attendants' duties. Ironically, after the war, only the southern carriers continued "to extend southern hospitality" by employing African American maids.[13]

In contrast to their indifference toward women workers, the Brotherhood went beyond its duty of fair representation in its efforts to maintain seniority and promotion rights for locomotive firemen, an elite class of African American railway workers threatened with technological displacement. Classed as operators, these men were outside the BSCP's traditional jurisdiction, but Randolph felt their case represented the racial injustices faced by black male workers in the transportation industry and elsewhere. African American men did not dominate the job of locomotive firemen nationally but were employed almost exclusively by the southern railroads. Recognizing the threat black firemen posed to their jobs, the white Brotherhood of Locomotive Firemen and Enginemen (BLFE) organized them into racially segregated "auxiliary" locals. They then obtained contract provisions from the twenty-one southeastern carriers guaranteeing that only white firemen would be promoted to engineers and served notice that henceforth "only 'promotable,' i.e., white men would be employed as firemen or asssigned to new runs or jobs or permanent vacancies." The Washington Agreement of 1936, as these provisions were called, also restricted African Americans from holding more than 50 percent of the positions in any operative job class. In return, the railroad brotherhoods allowed industry-wide furloughs, provided the carriers offered hefty termination packages for all displaced railwaymen and guaranteed severance payments for as long as five years. In 1941, the National Mediation Board affirmed the legitimacy of this "nonpromotable" class of African American workers when it approved an accord between Class I carriers and the lily-white Railway Labor Executives Association. Two months later, white firemen began to displace black firemen in the locomotive engines on all the southern carriers; the railroads did not give furloughed black workers severance pay.[14]

To fight the Washington Agreement, African American workers founded the Negro Railway Labor Executive Committee (NLRE), and hired Charles Hamilton Houston, dean of Howard Law School, to pursue their race discrimination claims under the Fourteenth Amendment. Houston filed lawsuits on behalf of Bester William Steele and Tom Tunstall against the southern railroads and the BLFE. Then, "like the caboose" to the NLRE's "double heater engines," as Houston described it, Randolph organized the Provisional Committee for the Organization of Colored Locomotive Firemen (PCCLF), with its own Ladies' Auxiliary. Randolph retained Joseph Rauh, author of the Fair Employment Practice Executive Order, as counsel for PCCLF locomotive fireman Leroy Graham's suit against the BLFE.[15]

Race discrimination in the railroad industry, particularly the Washington Agreement, came under scrutiny from the Fair Employment Practice Committee (FEPC) during World War II. During the long-delayed September 1943 hearing, the committee heard testimony from Steele, Tunstall, Graham, and other locomotive firemen and porter brakemen regarding racial bias against African American and Hispanic men; there were no women witnesses. Committee member Milton P. Webster persuaded the FEPC to order the twenty-one railroad companies and seven lily-white unions to dissolve the Washington Agreement. But lacking both subpoena and enforcement powers, the FEPC could not require compliance. Southern railroads continued to replace senior "nonpromotable" black workers with newly hired whites.[16]

Meanwhile, Houston pursued Steele's and Tunstall's cases through the courts, arguing both cases before the Supreme Court in November 1944. Four weeks later, the Court ruled that racially discriminatory union contracts were unconstitutional, finding on behalf of the African American locomotive firemen displaced by "promotable" white firemen. Adopting Houston's argument, Chief Justice Harlan Fiske Stone ruled that under the Fourteenth Amendment, federal laws could not be applied in a discriminatory fashion, even when the statute in question did not specifically prohibit racial discrimination. The Railway Labor Act of 1934 recognized a union elected by a majority as the exclusive bargaining agent for all workers under its jurisdiction or craft. As such, union officials had a statutory and fiduciary duty to represent every member fairly. Workers in segregated auxiliary locals, even though a minority in number, were constitutionally protected from abuse of union bargaining power, since they had no process for redressing grievances under the act. Thus the Brotherhood of Locomotive Firemen and Enginemen must "in collective bargaining and in making contracts with the carrier . . . represent non-union or minority union members of the craft without hostile discrimination, fairly, impartially and in good faith." "The key point," Constitutional scholar Derrick Bell notes, "is that the courts have imposed a duty of fair representation upon the unions in representing employees; that is, the union 'must represent the entire membership of the craft.'"[17]

The Court reaffirmed its opinion in 1949 when it upheld PCCLF member Leroy Graham's seniority rights and ordered the BLFE to assign Graham and all other qualified African American firemen to the diesel engines. In a deliberate effort to prevent job integration, the Locomotive Firemen and the carriers created a new promotion prerequisite for firemen, a written examination. Again, the Provisional Committee filed suit, winning a permanent injunction restraining the railroads from using such spurious tests, as well as damages for the PCCLF plaintiffs.[18]

Racial integration and diesel technology threatened to undermine the ideology of manhood on which the Brotherhood of Locomotive Firemen and Enginemen had been founded. The virile image of the railway labor brotherhoods in the nineteenth century derived from the raw muscle power required to lay track and operate the steam locomotive. With white men engineering the controls, white or African American men stoked the engines, shoveling hundreds of tons of coal over their working lives. Men needed brawn to perform the job, but achieving the proper degree of heat to run the steam engines under diverse track and weather conditions required considerable skill as well.

For this reason, white firemen viewed their jobs as apprenticeships for becoming engineers, a prestigious position that granted power, respect, and authority to run the train. Engineers in the South, however, preferred subservient African American firemen because they could "insist on not just deference from blacks but a far greater range of labor than they usually could exact from whites," Eric Arneson argues. This additional labor provided the white engineer with a "psychic wage" that confirmed his racial superiority. But as push button diesel engines replaced steam locomotives, white firemen changed their definition of manhood to accommodate the decreased physical labor of their jobs. Brain power, rather than muscle power, came to signify the modern concept of manhood. Black men possessed strength, but not intellect, according to popular stereotypes. Once this representational shift occured, the railway brotherhoods could eliminate African American firemen without sacrificing their masculinity or racial superiority.[19]

White railroad unions benefited from occupational segregation by race and by gender because it reinforced members' ideas of manhood and race while protecting them from competing directly against African Americans for jobs. The Brotherhood of Sleeping Car Porters challenged the racial customs of the "Big Four" brotherhoods, highlighting the racial exclusivity of their constitutions; their practice of creating segregated "auxiliary" locals for African American workers; their contract agreements designating jobs and wage rates by race; and their failure to represent every member fairly regardless of race. The BSCP also fought the railroad unions directly by organizing African American workers outside its craft, such as the locomotive firemen and Pullman car cleaners and yard forces.

Witnessing the Brotherhood's success at organizing porters and maids and its fight against racial discrimination, African American workers in the Pullman yards asked the union to represent them. The union also had an interest in organizing car cleaners: Pullman was teaching them how to "make down berths" in the event of a BSCP strike. The company's discriminatory employment policies relegated black workers to a narrow band of job classes, over which the BSCP easily claimed jurisdiction in the AFL. These classes included car cleaners and "helpers"—a euphemism for "nonpromotable" African Americans working in the skilled crafts unions. Nominally represented by the company union, the Independent Pullman Workers Federation, African American male and female workers earned wages that appeared to be set according to their race and sex, rather than by the experience, skills, and training required to perform the work.[20]

Race- and sex-based occupational segregation was especially apparent in the workforce of "The World's Greatest Housekeeper," as Pullman called itself.

The cleaning was actually done by more than fourteen thousand predominantly African American women and men in 232 railroad yards in the United States, Canada, and Mexico, although the racial composition of the yard forces varied by region, as the wartime emergency required thousands of workers to clean and repair Pullman's rolling stock. When a sleeping car arrived in the yard, these women and men stripped and cleaned the entire car inside and out. Then workers disinfected, scrubbed, polished, vacuumed, dusted, and "plushed" all that remained. This "army" constituted the second greatest concentration of African American women in the Pullman Company; Pullman laundry workers employed the largest number of black women.[21]

African American women so personified "The World's Largest Laundry" that the *Pullman News* represented this division as a smiling African American woman holding a pile of freshly laundered Pullman towels. As Pullman employees, these women received railroad workers' benefits, including the wartime security of union recognition. In January 1942, sixty-five "girls"— laundry workers from Pullman's Long Island plant—met with BSCP leaders and asked to affiliate with the Brotherhood. Irritated by the long hours, poor working conditions, and the "southern bosses," these women were ready to sign authorization cards and to organize other laundry workers to join the BSCP. Despite their standing as railroad workers, Randolph declined to represent them. He suggested they approach the Laundry Workers' International Union (AFL), even though it had no experience with railroad labor law.[22]

Randolph did not hesitate to represent Pullman's yard workers, however. With great publicity, he announced in February 1942 the BSCP's campaign to organize these railroad workers. While the BSCP appointed men as organizers, most of the car cleaners who joined the BSCP were African American women who had been deceived by Pullman's advertisements offering high pay and benefits. These women represented the bulk of BSCP supporters. When the Brotherhood presented nearly six thousand union authorization cards to the Pullman Company in 1943, President D. A. Crawford refused to negotiate. He argued that the Independent Pullman Workers' Federation held the contract for yard workers and asked the National Mediation Board to supervise an election. By calling in the NMB, Crawford sought to pit the lily-white Brotherhood of Railroad Carmen and the Brotherhood of Railway and Steamship Clerks against the African American trade union. The United Transportation Service Employees of America (UTSEA) of the CIO was also active in the yards, campaigning hard for an industrial union. Crawford successfully engineered a defeat of independent trade unionism through a free-for-all NMB election.[23]

Faced with so many competing claims, the National Mediation Board "deliberately and arbitrarily" extended the scope of the bargaining unit, according to one historian. The NMB grouped the skilled crafts workers (machinists, blacksmiths, electrical workers, sheet metal workers, carmen, and powerhouse employees) into separate classes, along with their apprentices and helpers. The NMB's decision to combine all yard workers resulted in losses for both the AFL and CIO as Jim Crow divided union supporters by race. The board included nonclerical storeroom employees, a job held by African American men, over which the Steamship Clerks wanted jursidiction. The Brotherhood of Railroad Carmen established "auxiliary" locals for "nonpromotable" African American helpers and car cleaners, reserving full membership for "promotable" skilled whites.[24]

Car cleaners saw through the ruse. "The AFL white man was here to hold a meeting with the day coach cleaners," Minnie Lou Sellers, president of the Miami car cleaners division reported. "Some of my members . . . said that they didint care to go. . . . I told them to or 3 go . . . and tell me what was said because he cant say any thing to upset you be cause you understand. that we are in a Jim Crow State, town, all so a Jim Crow job we do not want a Jim Crow union." BSCP organizer C. D. Miller visited Pullman yards up and down the Mississippi River in 1946, finding the color line almost everywhere. Helpers and car cleaners willingly signed authorization cards for the Brotherhood, but skilled whites working as electricians, mechanics, and upholsterers wanted the segregated carmen. In Texas, the company did not segregate Mexican-Americans by national origin; Miller reported they supported the Independent Pullman Workers Association. "All Mexicans, including the crafts, who are surely and completely connected with the Company Union, to a point where they are even afraid to be seen talking with any one who is connected with the Brotherhood, although I was successful in getting 2 to sign authorization cards."[25] Only in Corpus Christi, Texas, did Miller find a mechanic who "is white and sold on the Brotherhood."[26]

Locally, the problems workers faced were immense, especially in the south. Many women complained of the preferential treatment the "southern bosses" gave to men. From Goldsboro, North Carolina, Mattie Hooks carefully penned a letter requesting "the proper information" from Randolph:

> I want to no, does your union include Pullman Car cleaners, as I am a female cleaner imployed by the Pullman Co and have been in their service since the first of the year. This Co is paying the cleaners 57 cents an hour for 8 hrs straight time, over 8 hr time & half. But since working with other cleaners from other towns and in other towns I learn they get from 62 to 67 cents an hour. And for traveling expences for out of town, I was suppose to get $2.00 a day that was for 3 meals a day, but when I made my first trip

out my forman said the Co had cut on the expence money to $1.75 but the other place they get $2.50 a day for expence money a day. And one more item I wish to explain, when we make these trips we have to dead head back to our destination and our time is suppose to go on untill we get back and sign out, but this forman claims the Co is only paying for 2 and ¾ hours regardless of how long it may take for us to get back.

So I want to no if joining the union would take care and straighten out this matter.[27]

Other African American women and men in the Pullman yards endured similar conditions. Elizabeth Davis organized her fellow workers in Columbia, South Carolina. "Things are so messy up here until I don't know just what to do," she reported. The foreman hired and fired so fast it was almost impossible to keep up with the workers. Four women and five men worked in the Columbia yards, "the youngest femal[es] on the job have been here on the job longer then the oldest male." The foreman promoted a male cleaner with only two months' seniority to head cleaner: "be sure and write me back and tell me where you think I am a wise plan or a mistake. I hope I am not taking the wrong step for we sure do need help of some kind for is we don't get help of some kind soon I don't no what we will do. So please rite me at once and give me some at vise about what to do. I no you no what is better for us to do so this is all for this time."[28]

Minnie Lou Sellers also wanted Randolph's advice on wage discrimination and seniority rights violations against African American women, especially those who supported the BSCP.[29]

Mr Franklin [the yard supervisor] now for spite are going to Pull me off the upholsterer helper job that pay me 76 ct per hour and yet he is keeping all the white men on the job he will pay them 105 cent per hour to do the same work that I doing for 76 ct he ask me if want to clean car day or night. I said to him clean cars no I don't want a night job unless it was paying more money. He said I am going to pull you off. Please do something about this because I don't feel like I should give up what I am earn to them just because they are white I have got to live and pay me bills to.[30]

Sellers endured such working conditions throughout the war, and quietly organized dozens of other female car cleaners in Miami for the BSCP.

Some women confronted the yard supervisor directly when discrimination became apparent. Minnie Rincon, head cleaner in Pullman's Oakland yards, was charged with insubordination and using "vulgar and indecent language unbecoming a Pullman Employe [*sic*]." At a hearing before the company grievance board, Rincon admitted she "blew her top," but countered that the company had violated her seniority rights when it demoted her during a reduction in force. When Rincon questioned the discriminatory action, the assistant foreman said the company "had to do away with some of the head cleaners and also said that later on they were going to take all the women off and put men on." Rincon reminded him she "had 3½ years and [another female cleaner] hasn't had a year yet." She thought, "There is something funny about that." The yard foreman told Rincon she was not qualified to be head cleaner, even though "three and one half years was ample time to test her efficiency." "I understand you say seniority doesn't count," Rincon repeated to Welch, "and he said, 'In this case it doesn't.'"[31]

Rincon confronted Welch, the foreman of the Pullman yards, calling him "a stinker" and adding that "all the supervisors were a crummy bunch and further more a bunch of crooks." When Welch asked her to quiet down, she cursed him and said that "she would say what she wanted to as this was her life." According to one witness, "Rincon used other abusive language, denouncing the supervisors in this yard, but she talked so fast and so loudly that I don't remember it all." Pullman suspended her, still refusing to acknowledge the discriminatory treatment that led to the incident.[32]

Other women expected the BSCP to mediate their disputes with Pullman. "A delegation of women from the Pullman Yards were just in," Dellums reported to Webster in 1945. They complained "that the Company had a lot of Negro women working as mechanic helpers and electrician helpers and the Company was replacing them with white men listed as mechanics." In Washington, D.C., Pullman refused to accept Viola Perry's bid for a helper's job as an upholsterer's apprentice. The manager denied her the promotion because she was "too old." "She is not yet forty," Milton P. Webster informed Randolph, noting Perry and her mother had both worked in the Pullman yards for nineteen years. When Perry went to see the supervisor regarding her bid, he kept her waiting for four hours, until he simply dismissed her complaint at 4:55 P.M., reiterating she was too old to work as an upholsterer's apprentice-helper. Perry wrote to Randolph explaining her situation; the BSCP president agreed that hers was a clear case of racial discrimination and instructed Webster to meet with Pullman officials regarding Perry's complaint. They apparently denied the charge.[33]

Perry's case was one of many complaints Randolph received from African American women after President Roosevelt issued the fair employment Executive Orders. Virtually every woman had the same grievance: racial discrimination kept her from obtaining jobs reserved for white women. The upholster's apprentice-helper job Perry bid for was traditionally a white woman's job; Perry was not trying to end sex discrimination, but rather sought to break down racial barriers in sex-segregated jobs. Like many African American women, she tried to use the Executive Order's prohibition against race discrimination to gain entry to white women's jobs.[34]

Pullman officials fought vociferously against opening new jobs to African American women. When Florie Wellington and (Miss) Reuben Young applied for clerical jobs in the Pullman commissary in 1943, the supervisor admitted that Pullman would not hire them as checkers because of their race; he suggested they apply for work as car cleaners. Wellington and Young, utilizing the new Fair Employment Practice order, filed a race discrimination complaint. In an inter-office memo, Champ Carry told President Crawford there was no question that Wellington and Young met the educational qualifications for the job. "Our men tell me that in some cases these girls are college graduates, although they can't remember the two women in question." Carry said he personally "had no great feeling" against hiring

> colored commissary checkers, but the difficulty comes in the fact that once we do hire them they immediately acquire seniority in the [Brotherhood of Railway Clerks] and there is no telling where they will eventually end up in the organization. Of course we would classify them as temporary employees, [and they] would not acquire seniority and in all probability be let go as soon as the war is over. However in the meantime, regardless of the fact that they do not accumulate seniority we would be up against it just as we are now if there are vacancies and we didn't let them bid in on them so we might as well face the fact that they could appear in almost any office in the company.[35]

When African American women continued to apply for white women's positions such as Pullman telephone operators, Crawford became concerned, fearing "hostility against them [from white operators] . . . will lead to total disruption." He asked Corporate Counsel L. M. Greenlaw if the company could get around the law, since a walkout of a whole group of employees during the war might jeopardize operations. "[Isn't] there some sort of law against this," he wondered, "or is it only the Presidential directive?" Greenlaw replied firmly that the company could not avoid the Executive Order. "As basis for our future hiring policy, there is no question but that we will have colored girls, and probably men, in our clerical forces."[36]

The President's Committee on Fair Employment Practice was not interested in discrimination against African American women in the railroad industry. Regional FEPC offices, as a result of individual complaints such as those filed by Wellington and Young, investigated several cases, causing a flurry of inter-office correspondence at Pullman's headquarters in Chicago, but there was little, if any, fundamental change in occupational segregation. Pullman's foot-dragging illustrates that employers could undermine the Executive Orders through simple procrastination and when that failed, through due process delays, as the southern carriers had done when ordered by the FEPC to cease their discriminatory practices.[37]

Greenlaw's prediction regarding the company's eventual integration proved false. When the Executive Orders expired, no "colored girls" worked in the company's clerical forces. An in-house survey for Pullman's Chicago operations conducted just six years after the war revealed that African American women were employed exclusively as hourly workers in the yards and laundry (see table 2). This pattern of segregating African American women into the narrowest band of job classes existed throughout the railroad industry; as late as 1960, the industry's one million member workforce employed only 3,122 African American women, constituting 0.3 percent of all employees.[38]

The lack of female participation in the railroad industry was mirrored in the elective offices of the brotherhoods, including the Brotherhood of Sleeping Car Porters. African American men held all of the elective positions and almost all of the paid positions, except the (unionized) clerical jobs. As union officers, women were well-represented only in the car cleaners division. In these locals there were female presidents such as Minnie Lou Sellers, and many secretary-treasurers, and first and second vice-presidents. In the New York division, almost all the officers were women: Rosa Warren, president; Annie Outlaw, vice-president and Lovie Russell, secretary-treasurer. Five women and one man served on the executive board. In Jacksonville, Florida, Leslie Oliver, a thirty-year veteran upholsterer-helper, continued serving as secretary-treasurer of the local after retiring. More than half of the "Inside Committee" of the Chicago organization were women. Although men filled most of the elective offices in the Washington local, women were well-represented on the

Table 2. Pullman Company Employees Chicago Area, by Race and Sex, 1951

	Men		Women					
Department	White	Black	White	Black	White	Black	Men	Women
Porters, attendants, and busboys	0	2419	0	0	0	2419	2419	0
Hourly yards	354	369	58	283	412	652	723	341
Calumet shops	617	156	23	0	640	156	773	23
Laundry	12	20	7	114	19	134	32	121
Storerooms	3	77	0	0	3	77	80	0
Commissary	43	1	9	0	52	1	44	9

Source: Adapted from Fair Employment Practices Commission File, Box 335-1, Pullman Company Records, Newberry Library, Chicago, Illinois.

executive board and on the appointed committees. The Washington local was also the largest of all fourteen divisions, with 135 members in 1943. Women also served on the important local grievance committees that represented members to Pullman management. In New York City, Annie Mae Dantzler and Rosa Warren served with four men. Randolph instructed them "to keep an eye on all matters happening in the Yards and to report the same to this Office. Members bringing grievances to your attention should be investigated and brought to the attention of [the zone supervisor] who will assist you in adjusting those grievances." Dantzler was an effective representative; fellow members praised her as an "ardent, dependable, and courageous worker." They elected her secretary-treasurer of the New York local, but her sudden death in March 1947 ended what might have been a promising union career.[39]

Despite the fact that Pullman's car cleaners were predominantly female, the BSCP hired only African American men such as C. D. Miller to organize the yards. Local BSCP President E. D. Nixon, instructed to organize cleaners in Montgomery, Alabama, in 1943, had trouble because, he claimed, "the men seem to be timid about signing [cards] because they really don't know the power of the organization." Nixon's reference to "the men" implies he initially approached male yard workers while ignoring female car cleaners. By 1944, the Montgomery division of eighteen members had two women officers, Ruth E. Jones, vice chair, and Berdie Lee Thomas, secretary-treasurer. Nixon's focus on men also led him to a rather ludicrous effort to organize a Ladies' Auxiliary for the car cleaners' wives.[40]

Although the BSCP could have employed more women organizers in the yard forces campaign, car cleaners nevertheless supported Randolph's efforts to abolish racial discrimination. Detailing her troubles with IPWA and AFL organizers, Minnie Lou Sellers wrote to Randolph, "Don't let none of these things stop me I am fighting but the harder trying to over come. . . . Some how one of the Co. union man told me that he had the Seaboard [Air Line Yard] Force and he has already sent to Chicago for there charter. . . . I am going over hire to see for me self. But [I] told him that he should let the collard force alone and let them join their own unions. . . . You know you don't mean them no good. Why you want to take there money."[41]

The Pullman Yard Forces first election, finally held in November 1946, was a study of contrasts. The "skilled" crafts workers were pitted against the "unskilled" BSCP; the AFL craft unions against the industrial CIO union; the AFL and CIO combined against the IWPA and another company union representing skilled crafts workers. To most white workers, the contest was white versus black. To black workers, the election featured the African American-led UTSEA against the African American-led BSCP. But characterizing the election along race lines alone obscures the complex racial and gender alliances on which the Brotherhood of Sleeping Car Porters relied. As Milton P. Webster noted to C. L. Dellums days before the election: "47% of the car people in the yards are Negroes and 25% of the car people in the shops are Negroes. So you see we have to get some other votes since it is known that we are not going to get all the Negro votes. Many of the Negroes in the shops are pro-CIO. . . . So you see we will have to make quite a stride in order to be able to win the majority."[42] The election came on the heels of widespread furloughs of temporary wartime employees, giving the advantage to company unions. Representation of Pullman's 11,588 workers was divided among four unions; UTSEA received only 837 votes (see table 3).

The election results, certified by the Mediation Board on Christmas Eve 1946, show that each organization won votes from each class of workers. The AFL Railway Employees' Department (RED), a combination of railroad brotherhoods, won 870 votes of a possible 1,683, or 51.7 percent of the eligible votes. The board awarded the International Brotherhood of Electrical Workers (IBEW) representation of Pullman's electrical workers, apprentices, and helpers. The majority of blacksmiths, sheet-metal workers and powerhouse employees voted for the Pullman Car Employees' Association of Repair Shops (PCEARS); the board awarded the company union representation of these classes. The Brotherhood of Sleeping Car Porters beat the Steamship Clerks, winning jurisdiction

Table 3. Election Results, December 1946, National Mediation Board

Job Class	IPWF	PCEARS	RED AFL	UTSEA CIO	BSCP AFL	Void	Eligible Voters	Number Voting
				Unions[a]				
Machinists	7	118	40	59	3	4	238	231
Blacksmiths	5	51	3	25	1	2	89	87
Electrical workers	417	179	870	49	113	10	1,683	1,638
Sheet-metal workers	3	181	64	80	2	0	335	330
Carmen and car cleaners	1,039	1,385	2,040	532	2,228	166	8,233	7,390
Powerhouse employees	8	129	15	51	5	8	244	216
Storeroom nonclericals	50	67	136	41	347	17	766	658
Total votes	1,529	2,110	3,168	837	2,699	207	11,588	10,550

a. IPWF = Independent Pullman Workers Federation; PCEARS = Pullman Car Employees' Association of Repair Shops; RED = Railway Employees Department, AFL; UTSEA = United Transportation Service Employees, CIO; BSCP = Brotherhood of Sleeping Car Porters, AFL.

Source: Adapted from Representation of Employees of the Pullman Company, Case No. R-1625, Certification Dec. 24, 1946, National Mediation Board, Washington, D.C.

over an entirely different job class than it had originally sought to represent, the nonclerical storeroom employees. The BSCP also won a plurality (27 percent) of carmen and car cleaners, with the RED winning the second largest number of votes (24.7 percent). But since no organization won a majority, "the Company union will continue to represent or rather mis-represent" as Randolph called it, the carmen and cleaners. Sellers was angry. "I know that the car cleaners here voted for the BSCP and if I knew of one or ones that other wise I'd wring there ears for them. I think its dirty shame and a disgrace to my race."[43]

The racism of the white railway brotherhoods was a major reason for the defeat of independent unionism. As a matter of policy, the AFL normally forbid two white unions to run against each other; hence the emergence of the AFL's Railway Employees' Department, allowing different groups of workers to vote for the AFL in an multi-class election. But the RED refused to accept the BSCP as a railway union, forcing the African American-led union to compete against white unions for the votes of male and female workers of all races. The 1946 election results, as well as a subsequent election in 1948, seem to indicate that had the AFL members joined forces, they might have won a majority of carmen and car cleaners. But to have combined their efforts would have meant the abolition of racial segregation, an action the white railway unions refused to consider.[44]

The war had little effect on occupational segregation by race and gender in the railroad industry. While Perry and other African American women attempted to break down color bars that prevented them from holding white women's jobs, other women obtained jobs normally reserved for African American men. During the war, railroads hired African American women as engine washers, freight and baggage handlers, section gang "men," and in other unskilled and semi-skilled "men's jobs." The railroad brotherhoods opposed women's employment; as an RED spokesman told federal officials in 1943, "we are only trying to protect them from the very heavy work women have been doing for generations in Europe." State labor officials, however, granted wartime industries special exemptions from protective labor laws to allow them to hire women for these positions. Special exemptions ended with World War II, and women workers found themselves quickly demobilized, or prohibited from performing their normal duties. The women employed as porterettes by the Baltimore and Ohio Railroad won equal treatment in 1944, only to lose equal employment opportunities when company officials invoked protective labor laws to prevent women from exercising their seniority rights. Like Pullman maids and other African American women workers, porterettes did not benefit from the protections extended to women, but rather found themselves disabled by such laws.[45]

Porterettes did the same work as porters, except that their job title was feminized. With minor alterations, they also wore the same uniforms as porters: jacket, white shirt, cap and pants. More importantly, porterettes earned the same wages as porters. Porters and porterettes were on the same seniority list and bid against each other in their district for run assignments. As BSCP organizer T. T. Patterson commented after successfully negotiating a contract for these workers in 1944, "The porterettes are . . . considered porters." The Seaboard Air Line classified its porterettes as temporary wartime workers and placed them alongside train maids; SAL furloughed its porterettes with demobilization, while maids remained on the job. The B&O hired porterettes as permanent employees, with full seniority rights; many remained working until retiring in the early 1960s.[46]

Wartime exemptions from protective labor laws permitted porterettes to handle passengers' baggage, but this duty was performed incidentally, not regularly. According to Ohio's protective labor law, female workers could not lift weights over 25 pounds. Although the State of Ohio did not threaten to prosecute violators, in 1946 the B&O suddenly decided to abide the law and promptly terminated two of its oldest porterettes. Gertrude Milner and Lucy Price, both members of the Brotherhood of Sleeping Car Porters, filed protests.[47]

T. D. McNeal, one of the few Brotherhood officials to consistently fight for wider employment opportunities for African American women, convinced the union to defend the porterettes. "As I see it," he wrote, "even if there is such a law the B&O is violating the seniority rights of these women by permitting two younger women to continue operating while older people on the same roster are not working." But BSCP leaders may have been more persuaded by threats to their territory. The United Transportation workers was attempting to raid the Brotherhood by appealing to women members. According to McNeal, the CIO union was "spreading a rumor that the Brotherhood . . . decided to get rid of our women members." The union's decision to employ its full resources on behalf of Milner and Price suggests that some porterettes responded favorably to UTSEA's claims to better represent the women's concerns.[48]

Brotherhood attorney Henry Epstein advised President Randolph that restrictions on women's employment would be upheld by the Ohio court now that the emergency was over. The union, he wrote, should have recognized that protective labor laws could be revived and understood that their contract did not protect the porterettes' seniority "against the illegal employment of women in certain types of heavy work." Epstein concluded, "State laws safeguarding health of women . . . are clearly valid and enforcible [sic]. . . . These women, doing porters' work, would be barred in Ohio from such labor." The only way to rectify the problem, he noted, was to ask the B&O to join the union in a lawsuit challenging the constitutionality of protective labor laws. Instead, in contract negotiations the following year, the BSCP and the carrier agreed to reassign porterettes to routes that did not run through Ohio; Randolph refused, however, to relinquish the porterettes' seniority rights. But Milner and Price were not rehired.[49]

Eight years later, the problems posed by protective labor laws reemerged when porterette Edna Comedy bid for a run through Cincinnati. Again, the B&O cited the Ohio law prohibiting women from performing manual labor and refused to assign her. Again, the union asserted that the carrier violated the seniority rule. This time, however, BSCP attorney Joseph L. Rauh Jr. decided to challenge the constitutionality of Ohio's law, on the grounds that it imposed an undue burden on interstate commerce. Through protective labor laws, Rauh argued, the State of Ohio prescribed "the qualifications, character, age, sex, and other characteristics of employees on interstate carriers" thereby impeding "the free and efficient operation of the roads." If other states enacted their own employee specifications "the added expense and confusion . . . could be multiplied many fold." National uniformity in state laws governing transportation should be favored. Moreover, the state's prohibition against employing women in jobs requiring "frequent or repeated" 25 pound weights would "not preclude the employment of porterettes." The statute specifically forbid women from "operating freight or baggage elevators, in baggage handling, freight handling and trucking of any kind," occupations that required the frequent and repeated lifting of heavy weights or those that required occasional lifting. "While porterettes may handle baggage, this is but an incidental part of their duties and their occupation cannot fairly be classified with such employment as baggage handling or freight handling. Furthermore, we understand that there are no runs employing porterettes which do not also employ porters and that the porters handle the heavier articles of baggage."[50] Rauh asked the Baltimore and Ohio Railroad to join in the BSCP's lawsuit challenging the statute's constitutionality. The B&O's counsel replied he had "no objection but under the circumstances I do not see how the railroad company could be considered as a necessary party." The railroad had no compelling financial or political reason to keep women, who earned wages equal to men, employed as porterettes.[51]

Nor did the Brotherhood have the financial resources to pursue such a suit on behalf of a few women workers. Rauh's interpretation of the statute was as sound as the B&O's; depending on the politics and the judge, the court might have decided either way. To ensure a favorable outcome in her case, Comedy needed the 1964 Civil Rights Act. Under Title VII, the courts struck down women's protective labor laws as an undue burden on interstate commerce. But by then Comedy had retired.[52]

The Supreme Court's decision in *Steele*—that labor unions had a duty of fair representation to all workers within their bargaining class—covered only race discrimination; the court did not impose a similar duty in sex discrimination cases. Similarly, the Brotherhood of Sleeping Car Porters exceeded its duty to represent African American railwaymen, but women members fared less well. When the war created labor shortages, the union did not push the Pullman Company to re-hire furloughed maids, nor did BSCP organizers attempt to unionize stewardess-nurses and hostesses who had displaced the maids. In addition, the Brotherhood did not include Pullman laundry workers in their efforts to organize Pullman yard forces. The equality promised porterettes in their B&O contract proved to be temporary when companies invoked protective labor laws to limit their choice of runs.[53]

For African American women such as Viola Perry, Florie Wellington, Reuben Young, Frances Mary Albrier, Gertrude Milner, Lucy Price, and Minnie Lou Sellers, job opportunities during World War II proved temporary and rare. The U.S. Women's Bureau might boast of one African American woman who worked as a train announcer, but several thousands of African American women found war work racially segregated. The records of the Fair Employment Practice Committee and the Pullman Company recount the persistent efforts of black women to obtain jobs held by white women. Those records also show that exemptions from protective labor laws allowed employers to substitute black women for black men in race-specific jobs that often required heavy physical labor. When governments forced compliance with protective labor laws, railroad carriers showed a preference for white women.

Carriers and labor unions used technology to displace African American railwaymen in the name of modernization. White men refused to shovel coal into locomotive steam engines unless it was part of an apprenticeship for engineering positions, but when the diesel engines with their pushbutton operation arrived they sought to eliminate black men from engine cabs. To keep white women off the trains, white union and railroad officials fought more surreptitiously, reasserting the efficacy of protective labor laws and denying them seniority rights. They relegated African American men and African American women to dirty, back-breaking, low-technology jobs. Taking these jobs because they needed the work, black railroad workers fought for better wages and working conditions.

In demanding their rights as workers, the Brotherhood's female members shared with porters' wives a desire for respectability. Their quest proved elusive. Even when they held sex-segregated jobs, working women did not have the respect of their union brothers. Women's wage-earning challenged the Brotherhood's ideology of a gender complementary division of labor. Domestic work reciprocated male economic activities; as housewives, women should "work" in the marketplace. Through labor-conscious consumption, women could enhance the power of the labor movement. In the Ladies' Auxiliary, Brotherhood women used their role as union wives to win the respect of the trade union movement.

7

Union Wives, Union Homes

A man does not make a good union member unless he has a union home.
—Halena Wilson, *The Black Worker*

The sexual division of labor within the Brotherhood of Sleeping Car Porters prescribed a distaff role for the Ladies' Auxiliary. The union attended to the business of workers while the Auxiliary looked after affairs at home. This allocation of responsibilities recognized both sides of the paycheck, the problems of earning it and the problems of spending it, implicitly joining the point of production to the point of consumption. Union wages made the porters men. Union wives made the union home.

Auxiliary members recognized the economic significance of housework long before "the reproduction of labor" became a colloquialism among socialist-feminists. The housewife created a harmonious home and family life to reinvigorate her husband for his return to work, but this was only one of her responsibilities. The union wife used her position to expand the power of the trade union movement. She understood that the household budget came from union labor, and returned that money to labor. To make the home comfortable, she purchased union-made commodities; to counter the corporate influence on education, she taught her children the value of work. And to protect her husband's job, the union wife made sure he paid his union dues. The housewife's "cooperation" with the labor movement enhanced domestic life, literally bringing home the benefits of trade unionism to the workingman's family.[1]

The consequences of this gender ideology did little to improve working conditions for wage-earning women, as previously demonstrated. The Auxiliary, to which the BSCP assigned female unionists, saw its members as unpaid household laborers, whose separate sphere complemented, rather than competed with, working men. In this female sphere, women were responsible for the purchase of domestic commodities; government surveys showed that wives spent 85 percent of the household income. Yet Pullman maids and other

138

Brotherhood women "consumed" like others responsible for the care of their homes. Indeed, it was in the commodity market that the Auxiliary addressed the needs of both wage-earning and unwaged women. By operating consumer cooperatives and providing advice on "better buymanship" and other consumer issues, the Auxiliary politicized the spending habits of all union women and raised members' living standards.[2]

Unionization brought a significant rise in the standard of living for porters, maids, and their families. Brotherhood-won wage increases and job benefits brought sleeping car workers into the upper quartile of income earned among the African American population, an "undreamed of" gain. Higher wages allowed porters' wives to become housewives, a privileged status for African American women in the 1940s and 1950s. Some wives, particularly those who held professional positions, continued to work because they derived personal satisfaction from their jobs; others held paid jobs because the additional household income allowed them to achieve the standard of living they desired. However, many women, especially those without high-demand skills, chose to withdraw from the labor force, even when there were no children requiring care. For these women, a higher standard of living meant the "leisure" to stay home like "Miss Ann," devoting their time to family and domestic concerns. As housewives, they produced an American standard of living for Brotherhood families.[3]

Efforts to raise the standard of living also heightened class consciousness, but not in the socialist sense of the term. The labor movement remained a point of reference for Auxiliary members, and the Brotherhood a point of pride. At the same time, steady wages brought porters' families solidly into the African American middle class. Thus, while porters and maids were members of the working class among white trade unionists, they were simultaneously members of the middle class among African Americans. This tension over class position eventually undermined the ability of older, trade union-oriented members to recruit younger, civil rights-oriented women. The former group, to which the Auxiliary's leadership belonged, believed strongly in housewifery and labor-conscious consumerism.[4]

During the Auxiliary's heyday, this domestic ideology shaped the collective identity of Brotherhood wives, endowing their housework with economic importance and respectability. International Ladies' Auxiliary President Halena Wilson encouraged women's activism on domestic issues, stressing a program of "Education, Cooperation, and Organization." Leaders appealed for women's participation by reminding them of the labor movement's achievements on behalf of family life. As Mattie Owens, president of the Minneapolis Ladies' Auxiliary, declared:

Every conscientious sister sees the need of building a strong organization whereby our struggle for economic justice, improved working conditions, job security, and other high standards of living might be accomplished. We, the wives and female relatives can no longer sit by and see our men toil and struggle for existence; join the Ladies' Auxiliary and thus prove to them that you realize that through their struggles, progress has been made and that you are willing to help them in an organized way.[5]

Through organization and cooperation, conscientious sisters would improve the conditions for workers on the shop floor and in the home. Cooperation between spouses brought harmony to the family, just as coordination between the Brotherhood and the Auxiliary brought order to the labor movement.

The housewife's role as consumer could do more potentially for the labor movement than enlisting one million men in one thousand industries, Wilson argued. If the wages of those million men were spent on union-made goods, consumer demand would create many millions more union jobs in thousands of industries. The goal of trade union auxiliaries was to teach wives that valuable lesson. "The task of raising people's standard of living, of increasing their family income and of giving protection to that income once it is obtained, requires undivided and unremitting vigilance. . . . The program of building, of educating and of convincing the housewife of her need to participate in such activities goes on not only on special occasions but from day to day . . . with the conviction that a responsive chord will be struck somewhere along the way."[6] Politicizing wives' spending habits was not an easy task. But the Auxiliary had struck a responsive chord with the Economic Vigilance Committees in the union's early years. These groups introduced the widespread consumer activism of the Depression. Milk prices were a major issue. Shortages, caused by farmers' milk dumping, drivers' strikes, high prices, and lack of refrigeration, caused chaos in several cities. When philanthropists' drives failed to deliver enough milk to working-class neighborhoods, consumers turned to cooperatives, such as the interracial milk cooperative in the Philadelphia region. Milk prices in Washington, D.C., were among the highest anywhere in the nation. In 1938 and again in 1940, Rosina Tucker and the Washington Auxiliary joined with the Women's Trade Union League to lobby Congress for milk price-control legislation for the District.[7]

The Depression accustomed wives to "making do." The emphasis on home economics encouraged Auxiliary members to study better budgeting and home management. The Detroit Auxiliary reported, "We now buy articles that give us the most usage." A demonstration on "the qualities and cuts of meat most advantageous to the consumer" generated praise, as did talks on the Federal Trade Commission's suit for false advertising against *Good Housekeep-*

ing and on the new Food and Drug Act. The Chicago reporter claimed five hundred people attended a showing of the film "Getting Your Money's Worth." The Washington women appreciated a guest speaker from the Tuberculosis Association who "stressed the need for frequent chest x-rays for the detection of T.B." and a film, "Goodbye, Mr. Germ." In Tampa, the Colored Locomotive Firemen's Ladies' Auxiliary heard Eva Williams, president of the Good Housekeeping Club, give an "interesting talk." A round table discussion on "Nutritions and their Values" drew many Pittsburgh members. The *Black Worker* also carried tips from the Consumers' Union on topics ranging from diet fads to carpet beetles.[8]

Consumer education and confrontations with merchants led Auxiliary members to investigate more comprehensive methods of directly controlling consumption. Consumers' cooperatives offered one means of spending wages to reflect trade union power. "The Auxiliary being of the opinion," Wilson wrote, "that it is equally as necessary to organize at the consumer level as it is to organize at the wage level. That is if the purchasing power of the worker is to be protected." Trade unionists and socialists since the nineteenth century had advocated producer and consumer cooperatives as a "second line of defense" in the labor movement, and Brotherhood President A. Philip Randolph endorsed cooperatives in his earliest *Messenger* articles. The cooperative movement gained leverage as various WPA programs encouraged new ventures, ranging from credit unions and housing to childcare and food co-ops. The American Federation of Labor also extolled the virtues of cooperatives "to protect the workers in their relations with the merchants . . . in the same sense that the trade union movement protects them from their employers."[9]

To many African Americans however, cooperatives were as dubious as trade unions. In the South, producer cooperatives formed by white populist farmers barred black members. In the urban North, the scanty array of goods sold in cooperative stores failed to gratify consumers mesmerized by the abundance offered in department stores and grocery markets. Convincing Auxiliary and BSCP members to support cooperatives required affirmation of their anti-racist potential. Casting aside earlier ideological distinctions between the Housewives' Leagues and the Auxiliary, Wilson hinted at economic black nationalism. "I just read an article in a local daily newspaper that I found very interesting," she noted. "This article points out that there are around 300,000 Negroes in this city [Chicago] with an income of about $70,000,000.00 yet we are so disorganized that practically none of that huge sum remains in the Negro race."[10] "The pooling of resources in one form or another has helped solve the problems of other groups almost since the beginning of time and it is only logical to conclude that the same principle can be made to help solve the problems of our own racial group. . . . The cooperative movement stands out as the one great avenue through which the Negro race may eventually accumulate great wealth, great influence, and even greater independence."[11] Wilson's rhetoric probably appealed to members familiar with Garveyism, but despite her rhetoric, neither she nor Randolph believed economic black nationalism was a sound solution in a racial democracy.

Black trade unionists also endorsed consumer cooperatives as an alternative to the overpriced, low-quality goods sold by stores in racially segregated neighborhoods. Layle Lane, vice-president of the New York American Federation of Teachers and a socialist, graphically depicted the economic stranglehold South Street merchants held over working-class blacks in Philadelphia for the *Black Worker:*

> The shops, small and usually dirty and bad smelling, carry a very cheap grade of merchandise and sell for as high a price—sometimes more than that for a high grade of goods. People buy in small quantities—one half pound of sugar—a pound of flour—5c worth of lard, 10c worth of pigs' feet— 59 and 98 cents dresses and trousers. Here is exploitation of the worst kind. Negro leaders decry it, but have not been able to do very much about it, mainly because they have not tackled the problem from the economic side, but usually from a racial one. . . . Until our leaders omit altogether the color problem and concentrate on the economics involved, we are not likely to change the situation.[12]

Lane criticized African American leaders who fought racism without regard to its economics, believing cooperatives would eliminate profiteering from racial discrimination. "The cooperative movement offers a solution for many of our economic ills. It is a solution too that is immediate, for it does not depend on enlisting the aid of some well-meaning wealthy friend or on working for the 'coming revolution' (whenever that may be). It is based on the needs of its members for consumers' goods and on the honesty, vision and sincerity of its leaders."[13]

Cooperatives provided a lasting method for surmounting economic injustices, preferable to the temporary boycotts called by black community and trade union leaders. African Americans might not buy where they could not work, but one sales job did not mean control over profits. The BSCP was sympathetic to the "Don't Buy Where You Can't Work" campaigns of the 1930s, but cooperatives and credit unions, which African Americans capitalized, managed, and controlled, offered more economic power. By the time Japan bombed Pearl Harbor, these arguments and a booming wartime economy made members receptive to cooperatives; the racial consciousness arising from the March on Washington and later the establishment of the Office of Price Administration eventually committed the Auxiliary to such ventures.[14]

The Chicago Ladies' Auxiliary formed several study groups on consumers' cooperatives in the early 1940s. Auxiliaries in Denver, St. Louis, Minneapolis–St. Paul, Detroit, Indianapolis, Washington, D.C., New Orleans, Omaha, Oklahoma City, Los Angeles, Seattle, Montgomery, Pittsburgh, Montreal, Buffalo, Jersey City, and elsewhere also formed study groups, devoting at least one meeting per month to discussing cooperatives. Wilson's articles on the Women's Page of the *Black Worker,* as well as contributions from semantics professor S. I. Hayakawa, the chairman of the Chicago Cooperative Union; Helen Norton and Mark Starr of the ILGWU; the Central States Cooperatives; and economics professor Mary Allen of Sophie Newcomb College provided reading material. Auxiliaries also obtained literature from various cooperative organizations; some subscribed to *Consumers' Union* and *Consumers' Guide.* Representatives from local cooperative projects lectured and where possible, sponsored group tours of stores, credit unions, and housing projects. "Miss Mollie Yard representing the Cooperative League" spoke to the Washington, D.C., Auxiliary, and several of its members attended a six-day course offered at Howard in the summer of 1943.[15]

President Wilson favored the Rochdale Principles, an interpretation of Owenism developed in Lancashire, England, in 1843. These principles insisted on democratic control, Wilson wrote. Membership was unlimited and open to all without exclusion. Unlike capitalist ventures in which one share equaled one vote, cooperatives allowed only one vote per member, no matter how many shares of stock he or she owned. She also detailed cooperatives' profit-sharing plans, their educational missions, their rules regarding "Neutrality in politics, religion and equal rights for women," and their fair treatment of labor.[16]

Two Auxiliaries established their own cooperatives. Denver established a Buying Club that distributed groceries bought wholesale directly to members. In Chicago, with the encouragement of Lillian Herstein and the WPA Workers' Study Program, the local opened its own cooperative store. Following "the true Rochdale Principles, membership is not confined to the Brotherhood nor Auxiliary members but includes some men and women who are in neither organization." Organized in February 1941, the club set the joining fee at $1 and priced each share at $10; the women set a minimum goal of three hundred shares before renting a storefront. Although one porter bought fifty shares of stock, most invested much smaller amounts. The Brotherhood Cooperative was one of several operated by African Americans on the South Side, such as the Ida B. Wells Cooperative, but perhaps the only one founded and controlled by African American women. All of its founding officers but one were women, and all were active Auxiliary members; the only man resigned from the board when he became secretary-treasurer of the Chicago Brotherhood. As Wilson recalled, "some members actually laughed, but that was to be expected because the program was new and not too well understood. Few believed women would cooperate and go into the movement for all that it was worth."[17]

By midsummer of 1942, founder Agnes Thornton reported that the Brotherhood Community Cooperative Study Club had "reached the bookkeeping stage and hopes to start the buying club in the fall." The study group grew rapidly, splitting into two neighborhood clubs, one in the Woodlawn District and the other in the 43rd Street District, to accommodate members. In an outreach effort to housewives, co-op representatives spoke to local PTA groups in Woodlawn. "In the winter of 1942, a group of seven women and one man met, and began to talk about a cooperative. It was a slow and steady movement but these women were zealous and determined to prove that this great principle was a means of self-help. Slowly but surely the idea crystallized, until today [1948] there are well over 250 persons paying shares into our coop. It is a Democratic organization, one member, one vote."[18] In the fall of 1943, the Buying Club joined the Central States Cooperative Wholesale from which it obtained goods.[19]

The Brotherhood store opened in November 1943, selling groceries on Saturday afternoons. Soon the store moved to the Brotherhood headquarters at 3456 South State Street, with weekday and Saturday hours to encourage more shoppers. "Wives are reminded to make out a shopping list and the Brothers are requested when they are in headquarters to 'stop and shop.'" The store's stock of canned and dry goods was wholesome, if basic: "Corn, tomatoes, peas, vinegar, salad dressing, evaporated milk, baking powder, table salt, black pepper, baking soda, oats, coffee, pancake flour, egg noodles, macaroni, flour, white beans, red kidney beans, tomato juice, grapefruit juice, pineapple juice, bottle bleach, kitchen cleanser, paper towels, wax paper, laundry soap, corn flakes."[20]

The store's location in Brotherhood headquarters posed as many problems as it solved. The brownstone-style building housed the offices of BSCP International Vice-President Milton P. Webster and other division officials, an auditorium for union meetings, as well as sleeping quarters and recreational areas for off-duty porters. It was male territory, explaining the co-op organizers' appeal for husbands to buy groceries when they stopped in to pay dues and meet friends. Perhaps wives felt less welcome, even though they too used the space; Halena Wilson's office was in the building, and the Chicago Ladies'

Auxiliary held its regular business meetings there. For the BSCP's women members, the store provided a neat solution, allowing them to "cross over" from male union space into female domestic space. But shoppers, male and female, could not buy everything they needed at the Brotherhood Cooperative; additional stops at the greengrocer's, the butcher's, and the baker's had to be made to complete the grocery list. Nor was the building close to members' homes; many lived more than ten blocks away and thus needed carfare to get to the South Side business district. Nonetheless, during the war, while government rationing and price controls of scarce food products remained in effect, the co-op did well. According to its financial statement for the quarter ending March 31, 1947, the Brotherhood Community Cooperative Buying Club had a balance of almost $3,800.[21]

A principle purpose of the cooperative movement was to teach wise buying habits. As the war effort mounted, the federal government also stressed consumer education to lessen the impact of rationing and conservation. International Vice-President Letitia Murray told the delegates to the Auxiliary's 1942 convention of "the part that women as consumers play in this world emergency."

> If [civilized men] are to give their time, their efforts and even their lives to preserve our democratic way of life . . . it is our responsibility to know how to control prices, how to conserve, be willing to ration, and eager to salvage. Our most strategic weapon of defense . . . is . . . how to buy, what to buy, how to use, how to save and how to repair. In gaining this knowledge as consumers, we aid in keeping the cost of living down, we maintain our living standards, maintain our morale and prevent postwar inflation. In our consumer knowledge, properly used, we have a collective buying power to supplement the bargaining power of the trade unions. It is in the home that the basic health and efficiency of the nation must be protected.[22]

Agnes Thornton, secretary-treasurer of the Chicago Auxiliary, spoke on "Better Buymanship." The housewife's responsibility is to keep her home "cheerful, clean, inviting and above all, the highest standard of health must be maintained. . . . The housewife must exercise greater care and judgment in selecting a well balanced diet that is wholesome, nutritious and essential." Better buymanship, finding quality as well as quantity, was the housewife's responsibility. As she described the work of household management,

> They must buy wisely on a market that has been curtailed by the war effort, at a price that is higher than they have been accustomed to paying. Yet they must save at least ten percent of the gross income to buy war bonds

and stamps. Income taxes will be much higher next year and will include practically all brackets of incomes, therefore, in order to make a limited budget cover all phases of her household very careful planning is required. . . .

[The] wise buyer . . . knows in order to get the best "buys" she much "shop" at different stores and be on the alert for sales and week-end specials and buy where she can get the most for her money. . . . Such items as clothing, fuel, utilities, insurance, doctor and dental care, school expense, rent or home payments, taxes and many other necessities must be worked into the budget. This as everyone knows cannot be done haphazardly, there must be forethought and planning.[23]

In addition to shopping wisely, the patriotic housewife must also donate money and time to the community, for "there must always be an effort to raise the standard of living in our own community."[24]

"Mrs. America Is Willing," responded Nannie Wells, president of the Denver Auxiliary.

She's not the type to join the WACs or be a Red Cross nurse . . . she has her hands full cooking 3 meals a day for the family, washing, mending, and performing other mundane, but necessary household duties. She is just as patriotic as the next one.

The housewife is one of the most important instruments used in winning the war. Victory is sure because of her knowledge of nutrition, that is the vitamins, A, B, C, D, and B^2.[25]

Summing up the panelists' remarks, Letitia Murray compared the "soldiers in aprons" to the soldiers in uniform. "By living up to these ideals, the women in the home are emulating the gallant boys on the firing line, and are doing their bit for victory and for the preservation of our precious way of life in order that we might build a firmer and more permanent future."[26]

The Office of Price Administration (OPA) relied on women's work as consumers to enforce price controls during the war. Consumerism became patriotism, as Auxiliary members volunteered to monitor prices for their local ration boards. "Do your part to help prevent a catastrophe," Wilson asked *Black Worker* readers. "Refuse to pay more than ceiling price. Help OPA help your community—Enlist as a volunteer to work on your Price Control Board." Mary Flournoy, chair of the price control section of the Chicago Auxiliary's OPA program, provided "an anti-inflation shopping list to be used by members when reporting overcharges made by their neighborhood grocers." Jacksonville formed a Cost of Living Committee to report all violations of ceiling prices. Education chairs presented programs on point rationing, the best use of limited grocery items, and canning methods. In Washington, D.C., an expert from the Office of Price Administration demonstrated food canning and preservation methods to the Ladies' Auxiliary.[27]

Auxiliary representatives attended OPA-sponsored conferences to gather information, where government officials and participants alike commented positively on the efforts to include African Americans. OPA's policy that War Price and Rationing Boards "represent the community as a whole" encouraged the inclusion of "a housewife and members from labor, agriculture, business, the professions and consumers, and various minority and racial groups." A 1945 analysis of "volunteer manpower" concluded, however, that "there is a recruitment job to be done" to better utilize African American women; less than .5 percent of all board members nationally were African Americans, and of these, men outnumbered women three to one. The high participation rates of Auxiliary members is one indication of the BSCP's visibility in the community.[28]

The Consumers' Interest Committee of the Office of Civilian Defense copied OPA's principle of affirmative action when it sponsored Consumers' Town Meetings in St. Louis. "The Ladies' Auxiliary to the BSCP had the largest number of members of any of the many groups present at this meeting which was very interesting, educational, and informative." Henry Von Avery, "the only Negro working out of the OPA offices in St. Louis, [spoke] to us on price control, rent control and the role of the Negro in the reconversion period." The Denver Auxiliary reported on their adjustment to rationing. "We are ever aware of the problems arising with the new rationing system and do not fail to take time out at our meetings to discuss these problems. We also discuss consumer programs as they relate to proper foods and clothing for our families."[29] The OPA recognized the work of Denver women as Price Panel Assistants in the district, and rewarded Auxiliary members Nannie Wells, Thelma Freeman, and Minnie Hamilton with War Service Awards.[30]

> No women in the city are better informed or more cooperative than these women. . . . They have had complete control of the surveys of grocery stores, drug stores, restaurants, and rent surveys. A committee of from ten to twelve women have checked 75 stores regularly and no complaints have been received as to their checking. It has been 100% in volume and accuracy.
>
> Concluding a report, Mrs. Wells says, "We feel that our group have done a great part in winning the war. The work has been of educational value as well as an important responsibility as citizens, housewives, consumers and labor members."[31]

In St. Louis, Auxiliary members Josie Scott and Selma Burroughs also received OPA commendations for their rent surveys.[32]

Housing was a particular concern for Chicago Auxiliary members, as hundreds of thousands of African Americans crowded into the racially segregated wards during the war. As Wilson described the situation for Chicago Mayor Edward J. Kelly,

> It is the hope of the auxiliary that [you] will take into consideration the exorbitant rents already being paid by Negro tenants especially on the South Side where the most ordinary steam-heated apartments here range in rental from ten to fifteen dollars per room per month and in many instances even more and this from a group whose income seldom exceeds or averages more than one hundred dollars a month. It is common knowledge that one-half to three-fourths of the monthly family income of Negroes in this area is expended for rent which as you can readily see causes the visitation of many hardships, poor health and other evils.[33]

A pre-war rent survey by the Chicago Auxiliary documented not only inflation but also the race-based differences in rents. In September 1941, whites paid an average $28.83 rent per month for a five-bedroom apartment, while African Americans living in the same apartment complex paid $54.37. Higher rents did not mean better buildings or a higher standard of living. Describing her own 24-unit building, Wilson wrote "porches and fences are allowed to fall down—laundries become so foul that they are not fit for use and careless or indifferent janitor service is condoned to a point that is almost appalling, while tenants requesting cleaner surroundings are classified as trouble makers."[34]

Housing costs took a larger percentage of African Americans' earnings than whites, not only because rents were higher, but also because household incomes were lower. Budget surveys conducted by the Bureau of Labor Statistics and the Conference Board might claim that workers spent less than a quarter of their incomes on housing, but the statistics for black and white railroad families show a different story. The minimum wage for Pullman Porters in 1941 was approximately $1,362 without tips; according to the housing survey, rent devoured 47.9 percent of that income. A white railroad man with a comparable union job earned about $1,872; if he lived in one of the surveyed apartments, rent consumed only 18.4 percent of his yearly income. The housing squeeze during the war exacerbated these disparities.[35]

Rent control alleviated part of the problem by preventing spiraling inflation from wiping out higher wages. Renting spare rooms to war workers, encouraged by the National Housing Agency, also helped some families to pay the landlord. The urgent problems in south Chicago, East St. Louis, Harlem, West Oakland, northeast Washington, Watts, and Roxbury were housing segregation, race discrimination, and redlining. Union members complained that the Federal Housing Administration refused to guarantee mortgages to them because of their race. The Auxiliary condemned these discriminatory practices, demanding that Congress fund a national housing program "to establish a national housing objective" providing for slum clearance. International Secretary- Treasurer Rosina Tucker, chair of the Legislative Committee, asked Auxiliary members to write their Congressmen, reminding them that a national housing act was "especially needed because returning soldiers are crowding in with in-laws and families." When Dixiecrat senators threatened filibusters of the Taft-Ellender-Wagner bill the resulting act "was so amended and weakened that it will be of little service to low income groups," Tucker charged. The Legislative Committee urged Auxiliary members "to vote and to work for the election of candidates and the passage of improved legislation in the interest of all labor."[36]

High meat and grocery prices aroused housewives' anger after the war, too. Robert Stanford of the CIO's Council for Cooperative Development vividly described the issue at the 1946 Auxiliary convention. "I say ladies, and I say that knowing that today it is mighty hard to be a lady especially when you go shopping and try to get something and put in on the table for pop and the kids. We go into a store and instead of groceries we get a lot of lip and some sass. Maybe we happen to be a friend of the clerk and we get a few groceries from underneath the counter. Meat—ha—possibly if you raise your own you get it and maybe then you are not sure."[37] In 1947, led by the St. Louis Consumers' Federation, the council and the WTUL "sponsored a community wide effort to boycott pork and beef selling for more than 60 cents a pound. The housewives were asked to stop buying to force meat prices down."[38]

The St. Louis Auxiliary's work with the Consumers' Federation became a key element in the local's anti-inflation activities during the postwar period. Eva Swait, chairman of the Auxiliary's Consumer Committee, arranged talks on price controls for food; "Consumer's responsibility in a buyer's market"; the "Need for Constructive Action in [Infant] Mortality"; "Freedom from Margarine Taxes"; and report on the local bread situation. Other educational forums on "the wide discrepancy between Retail and Farm prices" elicited great interest, as did "a picnic with an international flavor." The St. Louis Auxiliary's legislative efforts included lobbying for a clean bakery bill and for compulsory enrichment of all flour.[39]

When Congress considered phasing out the Office of Price Administration at the end of the war, the Auxiliary joined the protests of other trade unionists. The elimination of OPA, they believed, was a threat to their economic well-being. St. Louis Auxiliary President Lela M. Lee was part of a delegation that visited Congressman Louis E. Miller, asking him to support the price control and stabilization bills. The Chicago Auxiliary sent letters to Congress and other government officials demanding retention of current price control orders. Although she spoke off the record, Edith Christiansen of the OPA Labor Relations Division apparently condemned the government's efforts to eliminate price controls and asked the Ladies' Auxiliary to write letters of protest. The International passed convention resolutions in 1948 and 1950 calling for the restoration of price and rent controls.[40]

Canadian Prime Minister Mackenzie King's postwar economic policies placed strict limits on imports, exacerbating the cost-of-living and forcing housewives to do without. Lucille Edwards Coward, Halena Wilson's personal secretary until her marriage to Victor Coward, secretary-treasurer of the Montreal Brotherhood, longed for the foods of home during the winter of 1947–48. "When I read about the fresh strawberries, sweet peas, string beans, lettuce, tomatoes, etc. I really do get homesick since the only vegetables one can purchase at present are turnips, very old carrots and a bit of cabbage. Perhaps during the summer months we will have more. I hope Canada will have saved enough dollars by this winter so she can resume her exchange with the States."[41] Helen Sheffield attended the Canadian Consumers League's two "Roll Back Prices" conferences in Montreal and Ottawa as the Auxiliary's representative in 1948. The Montreal Auxiliary added the names of their twenty-three members to the one million signatures collected by the Consumers' League to protest the high cost of living. When their petitions reached Ottawa, however, the Liberal Prime Minister repudiated the group, denouncing members for their "communistic affiliations." The Conservative Party's rise to power in late 1948 brought new discussions of "the housing shortage and use of margarine," as Auxiliary members found new ways to adjust to the economic crisis.[42]

Careful savings plans were as essential to budgeting as wise buying habits. The *Black Worker* exhorted members to open savings accounts and establish good credit. Even those who lost their entire savings in Depression-era bank failures, such as Rosina Tucker, reopened accounts. Throughout the war, while jobs were plentiful and wages high, BSCP members were told to save and to buy war bonds and stamps to protect themselves during the reconversion period. Postwar inflation would deplete those accounts before savings bonds matured, President Randolph warned.[43]

The Montreal division responded by organizing its own credit union. The Walker Credit Union Limited was the first "American" credit union in Quebec; it was also one of three institutions founded by African Canadians. President William P. Lee had been a Pullman porter and a former vice-president of the Montreal BSCP, and "most of the charter members were Brotherhood men and their relatives." Brother and sister Victor and Velmer Coward served as vice-president and secretary, respectively; each held posts in the Brotherhood and Auxiliary. Velmer Coward also served as manager of the Quebec Credit Union League, which monitored "legislation, taxation, and any other matters which may affect the interest of the Canadian Credit Unionists."[44]

The Ladies' Auxiliary's experiments with cooperation exposed members to alternative economic policies and the potential power of housewives. However, their development depended on government advice and support, most notably from the WPA Workers' Education Program. Postwar anti-communism fervor cast suspicion on such vaguely socialist projects. As Republicans cast aside Keynesian economic policies, consumers' demands for price controls appeared undemocratic. Similar reevaluations occurred in public education, where conservatives sought to control the curriculum and school faculty. The struggle for the loyality of youth became acute.[45]

President Wilson editorialized against the introduction of Junior Achievement (JA) programs in public schools. Calling it "the most subtle long range anti-labor campaign ever conducted in America," Halena Wilson condemned the program sponsored by the National Association of Manufacturers (NAM). Its aim, "is to recruit three million boys and girls from 14 to 21 years of age in an attempt to preserve what NAM terms 'American Business' and the system of free enterprise." Noting "the crusade against what the NAM term a violent swing toward some form of socialism," Wilson asserted its "aim is to follow the Hitlerian pattern of working with the minds of the youth of the country." In sharp contrast to the Auxiliary's cooperative program,

> The JA movement . . . instructs its youthful members how to "raise capital by selling stocks and bonds, how to vote dividends, how to make, advertise and sell their merchandise," [it] also teaches them how to circumvent "existing labor laws and how to oppose organized labor." . . . The more disturbing phase of Junior Achievement is that its program is being introduced into the "public schools under the pretext of teaching the pupils business management."[46]

Junior Achievement, Wilson believed, "is being used as an opening wedge to a serious conflict between labor and business, via the youth of the present age."[47]

A well-planned national youth program, modeled upon the successful Junior Economic Council in St. Louis, was the only effective counterbalance to this insidious maneuver. Although Wilson, Randolph, and the Auxiliary's International Executive Board drafted a constitution and program for a Junior Auxiliary in the mid-1940s, this program proved difficult to implement. Interesting workers' children in trade unionism was part of the labor movement's larger agenda in its fight against business in the mid-twentieth century. Unlike the 1930s, however, mass media influenced the rise of a new peer culture among teenagers that the BSCP Ladies' Auxiliary could not counter. The relative affluence of Brotherhood families also weakened their influence; mothers and fathers wanted their children to become professionals, not proletarians.[48]

Economic prosperity, after almost two decades of circumscribed consumerism, also undermined the appeal of consumer cooperatives. The abundance of goods filling grocery and department stores in the United States made the basic groceries offered by the Brotherhood Cooperative look paltry. To renew interest in the co-op and raise an additional $1,500 in assets, President Randolph headed a special membership drive in 1948. Unlike the mostly female original members, the postwar drive attracted a large number of men. About "150 Brotherhood members, not including their wives [bought shares]. . . . giving as much of their time and resources as possible to help us [women] put this great project over." The board of directors underwent a similar sex change, starting with four women and one man; by 1949 five new men joined the original four women on the board. This burst of interest in the Brotherhood Cooperative generated another study group that decided a credit union should be the next step, as many other cooperatives and trade unions had done. Randolph immediately squelched the idea, believing it was far too large a commitment for the union to shoulder.[49]

"The Auxiliary's Cooperative Buying Club isn't doing so well at present," noted the Chicago Auxiliary's annual report for 1949. Efforts to revive the cooperative proved unsuccessful. New supermarkets opened in South Side residential areas so that sales fell, despite new memberships. In addition, several consumer cooperatives in the Chicago area consolidated to form one large store that could better compete with the new chain stores. But when Wilson, with some misgivings, presented to Randolph the suggestion to merge with the other co-ops, the Auxiliary counselor refused to endorse the plan. Similarly, Randolph rejected an invitation to join the Council for Cooperative Development, suggesting that the $500 membership fee could be better spent for a full-time employee for six months. In July 1949, Wilson wrote Randolph explaining that the credit union was suggested as a "last attempt to save the Co-op Buying Club." "As for my part, I am satisfied with the efforts that were made to develop a Co-op program. It just happened that the opposition is too strong and too powerful to surmount. I am content to bow out gracefully and forget the whole thing, since I am not the first person who has tried and failed."[50] She believed the co-op failed because too few women were "fully imbued in the ideals of cooperation." Randolph tried to console her, writing, "You can feel that your efforts have been fruitful because you have planted the seed of cooperation among the women." In January 1950, the Brotherhood Cooperative Buying Club disbanded, returning the "full amount of share deposits . . . to each member."[51]

The Chicago Auxiliary continued to participate in consumer cooperatives after its own buying club closed. In the fall of 1951, Wilson helped found the Chicago "Union Cooperative Optical Center." This joint effort, in which many AFL unions participated, made more than sixty thousand trade union families eligible for low-cost eye care. "Our purpose," wrote Auxiliary President Wilson, "is to give our people absolute assurance that they are getting trust-worthy and reliable eye care at prices they can afford to pay. . . . We have been able to bring about this program because of the interest of forward-looking labor unions in the health and well-being of the membership. After we have succeeded in the Union Eye Care Center it may well be that we shall consider further steps in providing medical care and treatment under joint union spon-sorship."[52] The cost to join was only 30 cents per month. Members needing eye care or glasses could "obtain the very best of care at a very nominal cost, for instance the same eye examination for which a Specialist charges $25 is obtainable at the Eye Center for $2. Glasses that cost $30 and $40 elsewhere are supplied Auxiliary members at about half this price and even less."[53]

Consumer cooperatives were only one means of controlling the distribu-tion of union wages. Union label buying was another, which the Brotherhood and the Ladies' Auxiliary promoted. The *Black Worker* regularly ran the AFL's "We Don't Patronize" list of unfair businesses, and instructed readers to hon-or picket lines. The Brotherhood also found union label buying an effective tool against the Pullman Company. Porters and maids were required to pur-chase their uniforms from company-designated suppliers. In response, the BSCP told its members to ask for union label uniforms.[54]

When the clerical staff at the BSCP's international and divisional offices organized, secretaries typed their "oeiu" union label on each piece of union correspondence. Printers' "bugs" appeared on all union literature, following orders from both the Brotherhood and the Auxiliary to use union printing shops. For African American trade unionists, this issue highlighted the ten-sion between the labor movement and race issues.

An Auxiliary should never go to a printer unless he has a trade union label, since the label is a symbol of the organized labor movement. When
having an invitation or a pamphlet or bulletin . . . printed, it must be done
by a union printer. The question has been raised—union printers do segregate Negro printers. Negroes in most instances are not allowed into such
unions. That is something that will have to be broken down with education in those groups, the same as we are educating our people to go all out
for trade unionism.[55]

In Houston, the International's directive led to a prolonged, internecine battle between the local Brotherhood and the Auxiliary. The BSCP president
wanted to patronize an African American operated shop, owned by "the father of his son's wife." When the Auxiliary president (who was also the wife
of the BSCP secretary-treasurer) ordered tickets from a union printer, lines
were drawn. "The Women's organization was ordered not to give any sort of
affair until he [the BSCP president] decided to permit them." It took visits from
both the BSCP and the Auxiliary zone supervisors to reconcile everyone to the
use of union printers.[56]

The priority of the labor movement over race issues arose in other consumption issues as well. Besides advising members where and what to buy, the
Ladies' Auxiliary offered "Union Maid" cosmetics, which were presumably
manufactured in union shops. These products were sold in a manner similar
to other fundraising products in which the seller received a small commission
on each unit. The Chicago and Kansas City Auxiliaries reported some financial success from these sales. Yet Auxiliary members may have preferred cosmetics and hair care products marketed by African American women's beauty culture entrepreneurs. While the data is incomplete, consumption patterns
in this industry as well as apparel purchases made by members of the Ladies'
Auxiliary can provide clues about the way they constructed their class, race,
and gender identity.[57]

Beauty culture helped launch the BSCP; hair culturist Madame C. J. Walker
and many of her students, including Lucille Randolph, provided financial
support to the union by sponsoring bobbed hair contests. During the March
on Washington Movement, a national association of African American wom-
en salon owners donated a large check, a sign of their long relationship with
the union. In New York City and elsewhere, local auxiliaries held annual fashion shows to raise money for their programs. Photographs of Auxiliary gatherings reveal close attention to contemporary style and fashion. At an open
house in Detroit in 1955, Auxiliary members toured "in autumn's latest fash-
ions, with furs and corsages." Although the *Black Worker* did not provide fashion tips, published reports from local auxiliaries reveal a consistent awareness

about women's attire. Failure to dress appropriately was not taken lightly; Mrs. Tillery, president of the Kansas City Auxiliary, tendered her resignation after being criticized by members for not purchasing a new evening gown for their annual tea. Through the creation of a fashionable and cultured image, Auxiliary members sought the respectability conferred to bourgeois and working-class whites. Their values were not uncommon; market studies conducted in the 1930s show that urban African Americans purchased proportionately more clothing, beauty products, and other commodities than whites. "Historically, clothing," Vance Packard noted in his 1959 best-seller, *The Status Seekers,* "has been one of the most convenient, and visible, vehicles known for drawing class distinctions." African American women and men, believing that class could triumph over race, wore better apparel to disguise their financial status with the hope of being accepted by whites. Appearance served, then, as a protective strategy, shielding the well-attired African American person from a blatant display of racism. But not necessarily from whites' patronizing attitudes. At a national meeting on price control, OPA official Frances Williams praised Auxiliary representative Rosina Tucker for making "a splendid appearance; she was neatly dressed and made a worth while contribution."[58]

Considerations for personal appearance and a middle-class lifestyle vied with postwar consumerism. For the Auxiliary, the challenge lay in transforming acquisitive North American culture into a political and economic weapon for union families. Flush with wartime earnings and a pent-up desire for new consumer goods, wives could protect their husbands' jobs by buying union label goods. Brotherhood women shopped for clothing in better department stores where they could find a good selection of ILGWU and ACTW-made goods. The *Black Worker* advised them to buy furniture and household appliances from reputable merchants in cash, and to avoid the over-priced neighborhood stores that offered installment credit. In Auxiliary rhetoric, the housewife's consumption patterns became a labor conscious, and thus political, act.[59]

But housewives, even those loyal to the Brotherhood, still had to budget carefully to make ends meet. The war raised wages but prices also rose; real earnings for BSCP members increased but never became comparable to white railroad workers' wages. For every wage increase granted BSCP members, the railways granted proportionately higher increases to white workers. During World War II, the white brotherhoods realized a demand of the First World War, a living wage. In 1920, the Brotherhood of Railroad Trainmen petitioned the United States Railway Labor Board (USRLB) for a living wage. The Trainmen insisted: "that for those services a man has to sell, he not only should be able to live and educate his family, but he should be able to lay up a competency for his old age, when he is no longer a wage earner, and that living wage should be measured by the American standard of living. . . . The wage ought to be fixed for a man so that it would be an incentive to a higher standard of citizenship, a higher standard of home life."[60] The USLRB did not raise the trainmen's wages, but it did grant a "comparable worth" increase to sleeping car porters before returning control to the Pullman Company. As a result, porters and maids earned $60 per month in 1920, approximately equal to the wages earned by white office boys and messengers in the Brotherhood of Railway Clerks. The case of the Pullman porter argued that the men deserved a living wage of $150 per month in 1926. This amount would not only support a family, it would also make the porter a man.[61]

A decade later, the BSCP contract effective on October 1, 1937, established a minimum monthly wage of $89.50 for the lowest-ranked sleeping car porter. A Brotherhood economist consulted in 1934–35 determined that porters' tips averaged $21.88 per month, while occupational expenses amounted to $21.47 per month. Even after the raise negotiated by the Brotherhood, most porters probably just broke even in 1938 with a yearly income of $1,075, assuming that passengers' tips remained flat during the Depression. Union wages for Pullman porters and maids compared favorably to African American professionals whose incomes ranged between $1,250 and $1,750 in that period. Yet porters and maids earned only 42 percent of the $2,529 annual wage earned by assistant road passenger conductors and ticket collectors, an exclusively white male job class comparable to porters.[62]

Wage increases, the Trainmen had argued in 1920, should not simply keep pace with inflation, since this method maintained preexisting pay inequities. Over the next twenty-five years, through contract agreements backed by tough federal railway labor legislation, the transportation brotherhoods won every feature of a living wage. By 1946, all unionized railroad workers received time and a half for Saturdays; double time for Sundays and holidays; two weeks paid annual vacation for workers with five years of service; railroad retirement pensions, unemployment insurance, and other social welfare benefits. A study of African American railroad workers, written under the supervision of Herbert Northrup, contended that wages in the railroad industry tended toward "equalization": the real wages of non-operating and low-skilled workers increased while operating workers' decreased. Members of the Brotherhood of Sleeping Car Porters benefited from this trend, but despite real wage increases remained locked into the very disparities once condemned by the Trainmen.[63]

The wages of Brotherhood porters gained on other railroad workers during the war but never reached parity. Effective January 1, 1946, the Brotherhood negotiated a minimum wage for sleeping car porters of $0.8129 an hour per 240-hour month; $0.15 more per hour over the 1943 contract. White road passenger baggagemen earned an industry-wide average of $1.751 per hour, working a mean of 45.4 hours per week. One year later, porters' pay was about two-thirds of baggagemen's pay. Baggagemen, represented incidentally by the Brotherhood of Railroad Trainmen, now enjoyed a living wage.[64]

A living wage was different than a family wage, although both had gendered meanings. In its twentieth-century definition, the family wage theoretically supported the male-headed household, his nonworking wife, and two or more children in "sufficient comfort." Through various pretexts, African American men had historically been denied a family wage, forcing the household to rely on the combined contributions of wives, children, and extended kinship networks. Union wages allowed Brotherhood families to live in "sufficient comfort," perhaps even according to "the American standard of living." Yet political disfranchisement prevented African American families from obtaining the "higher standard of citizenship, and of home life" that a living wage was supposed to provide.[65]

The federal income tax return filed by James T. and Emma Catlett Lowe of New Orleans in 1947 reveals the standard of living for a Pullman porter's family in a postwar southern city. That year J. T. Lowe reported a gross income of $2,519.33 with tips; his earnings were $265 higher than the national average for Pullman porters. A porter with twenty-five years' experience with the Pullman Company, Lowe ran thirty round-trips to Los Angeles in 1947, spending over 150 days on the road and logging 2,450 hours; he averaged about $10 in tips for each round trip. Emma Lowe was a housewife.[66]

Mr. and Mrs. J. T. Lowe, members respectively of the Brotherhood of Sleeping Car Porters and the Ladies' Auxiliary, appear to have led modest and devout lives. In 1947 their five children were all young adults who probably lived on their own; the couple had fifteen grandchildren by 1960. He spent his leisure time at baseball games, which he attended regularly, and in his church, Trinity Methodist Episcopal; he also attended church when in Los Angeles. Mrs. Lowe went to mass every Sunday at the Holy Ghost Church and also attended Tuesday evenings. Both gave generously to their respective churches, putting money in the poor box and subscribing $100 to Trinity's remodeling fund, reporting total donations of $250. Mr. Lowe also made several one-dollar donations to the Red Cross, the March of Dimes, and $10.00 to the National Association for the Advancement of Colored People.[67]

Comparing the Lowes's spending patterns with the Department of Labor's budget for city workers in New Orleans that same year provides a measure of their living standards and consumption patterns. The government's panel of economists, home economists, health experts, and union officials estimated the total cost of goods, services, taxes, insurance, and occupational expenses necessary to maintain an "American Standard of Living" for a New Orleans family of four. The fictional Standard family consisted of an unskilled or semi-skilled working husband, implicitly a white union member, a housewife, a boy of thirteen, and a girl of eight. "To provide family health, worker efficiency, nurture of children, and social participation by all members of the family," the Standards needed $3,004 in New Orleans in 1947. The Lowes lived on $484 less; however, since they had no dependents, they "needed" only $1,952 to keep up with the Standards. Yet while their five children were at home, the Lowes must have "f[ou]nd it harder and harder to economize, being unable to shift extensively to cheaper commodities and therefore forced to 'do without.'"[68]

The Lowes lived on a budget of about $110 per month, after deductions for federal income taxes ($10.72), union dues ($3.00), occupational expenses (fifteen days at $4.50 per day), and Railroad Retirement ($10.72). They economized on housing, paying $18 rent each month for their house, including utilities and a telephone; these accounted for 24 percent of their monthly budget. The Standards' budget allocated one third of the father's net income for a five-room, rented dwelling with indoor plumbing, with gas and electricity. The Standards did not have a telephone (remember Dewey's "election"); the Lowes paid $3.75 per month for this "luxury." Mrs. Standard's grocery list was based on both nutritionists' recommendations for worker efficiency and actual eating habits. She spent $20 a week for a diet high in red meat, eggs, starches, lard, oil, and some fruit and vegetables. Mrs. Lowe did not economize on food; she spent perhaps $15 a week on food for herself and her husband, who ate at home only nineteen days each month.[69]

An older couple, the Lowes spent 10 percent of their monthly income on doctor bills and various insurance policies. The remaining $45 per month went to clothing, sundries, transportation expenses, and, of course, admission to baseball games. The Standards' expenses for "recreation, education, personal care, tobacco and communications" were minutely described:

> The family owns a small radio, buys one daily newspaper, including a Sunday edition, and 32 copies of some popular-priced magazine in a year. Movies are attended by the husband, wife and daughter once in 3 weeks, and the son once in 2 weeks. A small sum is allocated for children's toys and games, pets, camera supplies, and dues to social and recreational clubs, such as the Boy Scouts and women's civic organizations. . . . The husband has a haircut about once every 3 weeks, the son every 5 weeks, and the wife and daughter every 3 months. Toilet soap, tooth paste, shaving supplies

for the husband, and inexpensive cosmetics for the wife are specified. . . . An average of 3 local calls are made each week [by pay phone]. Stationery and stamps are included to provide for about one letter a week.[70]

With grown children, the Lowes could allocate their budget differently. Mr.
and Mrs. Lowe gave an enormous 20 percent to charity, tithing themselves for
their churches and community organizations. If they followed the government's recommended budget, each month they would have spent $6.25 for
"Christmas and birthday presents to persons outside the family and donations
to community welfare." The panel did not specify donations to church, but
it did budget for poll taxes. The budget nonetheless limited the Standards'
political power; while they could hear issues discussed on their radio, and
follow the editorials in a single newspaper, they did not have funds to send
letters to their representatives, or carfare to attend political events.[71]

The Standards' budget did allow for occasional indulgences. "The place of
'other consumer products' [is] justified on the grounds that families will sacrifice food, housing, and medical care . . . in order that the family may go to
the movies, the husband may have his tobacco and an occasional glass of beer,
or the wife may have a permanent wave." The Lowes' spending patterns for
similar extras is unknown, although they likely attended annual BSCP and
NAACP fundraising affairs, which required expenditures for both tickets and
appropriate attire. Mrs. Lowe probably had her hair done more than four times
a year. However, the Lowes gave $315 more than the Standards to religious
institutions, accounting for much of their "extra" funds.[72]

The Standards owned an automobile but used it only for family leisure;
according to the budget, the cost of owning an automobile in New Orleans was
$314 in 1947. Mrs. Standard and the children walked, Mr. Standard used pub-
lic transportation. For pleasure travel, the Standards took "a trip out of town
every 3 or 4 years for a vacation or to visit relatives." The Lowes owned a car,
which was probably not new. However, their car represented a measure of freedom unaccounted for by government experts. Mr. Standard could ignore Jim
Crow public transportation, but Mr. Lowe could not. To avoid overt racial discrimination, the Lowes used their automobile more extensively than the Standards. Mr. Lowe might drive to work. Mrs. Lowe may have used the car to shop,
to attend church and Ladies' Auxiliary meetings. When the Lowes visited her
kin in Mississippi, they probably drove to avoid the Jim Crow car, even though
Mr. Lowe, as a railroad man, was entitled to free passes. The Lowes' use of their
car, although considered a luxury, was essential to maintaining a higher standard of living and citizenship.[73]

The Lowes lived more comfortably than many African Americans in New

Orleans, though their income was well below that of white railwaymen's families. In 1947, the mean national income for white families was $3,697; for African American families, $1,986, or 54 percent of white family income. Within the railway industry, J. T. Lowe's wages were lower than those paid to white men and women; he earned 69 cents to every dollar earned by white assistant passenger conductors, whose income averaged $3,653. He also earned 81.6 percent less than the white female stenographers and typists represented by the Brotherhood of Railway Clerks. Even though the cost of living in New Orleans was lower than in northern cities, the Lowes obviously could not afford the Garden District.[74]

By 1956, through contract negotiations and federal laws guaranteeing union shops in the railroad industry, the minimum wages Brotherhood members received from the Pullman Company rose to $345.56 per 205-hour month. Porters' income was 81.6 percent of the industry average of $5,080 for that year. Although still below the standard of living enjoyed by white railwaymen, BSCP members' income was well above the mean for African American families in the mid-1950s. Brotherhood families were now firmly entrenched in the African American middle class. As Venzie P. Witt of the Denver Auxiliary praised the Brotherhood: "Our husband's pay now has been increased and it has given us better homes to live in. It has given us a better chance to educate our boys and girls. It also have given us higher standards of living in every way."[75] These gains were over and beyond the early family wage proposal. They were "an incentive to a higher standard of citizenship, a higher standard of home life" for Brotherhood men and women.

The frequent reports of new home purchases in the *Black Worker,* particularly in the 1950s, are one clear measure of the economic stability of BSCP families. In Detroit, the Auxiliary held an open house "at the newly purchased and beautiful home of Brother and Sister Aurthur Hill of 3015 Carter Street." The secretary-treasurer of the Salt Lake City Auxiliary, "Sister Otha Warren and her husband have purchased a new home in the Rosa Park area. . . . They have also bought a new automobile." Mrs. Herman Mitchell held a party for the Auxiliary on "the beautiful and spacious lawn" of her newly purchased home in Louisville in the fall of 1951.[76] Material comfort created a new class consciousness.

Consumerism and cooperation expanded the earlier definitions of women's role in the labor movement. At its founding, Auxiliary members debated several roles for women's auxiliaries, but accepted their subordination to the Brotherhood and to their husbands. In creating the Auxiliary's program, Wilson built on women's domestic labor. This gendered, race-, and class-conscious choice acclaimed women as household economists, but easily encompassed their familial roles as wives and mothers; Wilson refused to place Mammy on a pedestal.

Wartime propaganda created a gallant image of Mrs. America, painting her domestic sacrifices red, white, and blue. In studying the impact of World War II on women in the United States, historians have focused on the rapid increase of working women, the iconography of Rosie the Riveter, and the emerging discourse on motherhood. The activities of the BSCP Ladies' Auxiliary demonstrate another role for women. The government used their skills as housewives and consumers to lessen the war's domestic impact. Auxiliary women construed their economic decisions and housework as acts of patriotism.[77]

"Mrs. America" was a career housewife, knowledgeable in nutrition, household buying, sewing and clothing maintenance, salvaging and conservation, food preservation and preparation, home medical care, child psychology, and community development. By glorifying the housewife's diverse duties and emphasizing cooperation, Auxiliary women turned their subordinate status into an economic partnership. As Wilson wrote, "Building the economic structure of a people is not for man or woman alone, but for both working earnestly and sincerely together."[78]

That partnership could also mean contributing one's wages to the household budget. It appears that many Auxiliary women held paid employment, but they did not discuss their work. This dissonance suggests that Brotherhood wives did not define themselves by their jobs but by their marital-household status and organizational affiliations. They were union wives because of their husbands' trade union membership. As African American women, they were pleased to identify themselves as housewives, a title many desired, but only a minority attained. The Brotherhood had made that title possible; for that reason, the Auxiliary recognized its obligations to "the Boss." Yet by emphasizing "cooperation," a system of mutual obligations between husband and wife, union and Auxiliary, the women surmounted conservative arguments against their participation in the labor movement. Cooperation could also advance the race, by insisting on solidarity and the elevation of all, rather than the talented few.[79]

A skit, written and performed by members of the Chicago Auxiliary in 1951, embodies these themes. Two housewives, complaining about the high cost of food, persuade another of the value of the Auxiliary in the labor movement.

> "It didn't take me long to see the value of the Auxiliary once I became a member; for since unions affect the home and welfare of their members and their families, I felt definitely that it was my duty to become part of such an organization." . . .

"I learned that no home is secure as long as the job is insecure." ...

"This is all very true, but I still don't see where the housewife fits into the picture."

"Husbands and wives are partners aren't they? Isn't one just as responsible as the other for the success of the home? How is a wife to share her part of the responsibility unless she understands the problems and the obstacles that threaten her husband's job and as a result threatens her own home?" ...

"That's the stuff, let's not waste any more time, these high prices and other conditions will soon have us all done. I have a feeling that it is much later than most of us think."[80]

This interpretation of the housewife's role gave the International Auxiliary the right to develop a legislative program. The best way to retain price controls, defeat the Taft-Hartley Act, and guarantee their children's future, AFL leaders reasoned, was to double labor's vote. That could be accomplished by developing the political power of the union wife. But in reality, the labor movement's political strategy was limited to white women who confined their activism to voting, petitioning, and good government organizations. African American women could not enter electoral politics without challenges to their authority and citizenship. Despite improvements in their material condition, BSCP members had not been granted a higher standard of citizenship.

8

"We Talked of Democracy and Learned It Can Be Made to Work": Politics

Americans talked much of democracy in 1941. President Franklin Roosevelt's Four Freedoms, freedom of speech and worship, freedom from want and fear, represented the era's finest expression of democracy in the United States. But for African Americans, democracy also stood for racial equality; freedom from discrimination was the fifth freedom. Throughout the 1940s and into the 1950s, the women of the Brotherhood "talked of Democracy." They believed a racially democratic society could be attained through politics. Having achieved a higher standard of living, they felt empowered to work for a higher standard of citizenship.

As they worked in democratic and consumer movements, the Ladies' Auxiliary gained experience in the legislative process. Their outlook as African American trade union women facilitated the Auxiliary's entry into a multitude of fields from bread and butter labor policies to international policy issues. They completed their political apprenticeship after the March on Washington Movement (MOWM), when President Halena Wilson announced the International Auxiliary's new political program. The multifaceted agenda of trade union, civil rights, women's, international, and domestic issues came on the eve of the Taft-Hartley Act. Although not yet promoted to the master rank, under Randolph's guidance, the political journeywork of the Ladies' Auxiliary created a foundation for their children's entry into the civil rights movement.

When founded in 1938, Article 21 of the Auxiliary Constitution explicitly forbade members from using their "influence or sympathy . . . either for or against any political or religious organization. No local division Auxiliary shall be permitted to engage in any political activities." The Ladies' Auxiliary was, of course, never apolitical; speakers and discussions on a broad range of international, national, and local "current issues" were regular meeting features. These programs, however, were considered educational, not "political" activities. Similarly, the Auxiliary justified its participation in consumer movements as the housewife's domain, a method of cooperating with union demands for higher wages and better working conditions. At every convention, the Auxiliary passed resolutions on national and international issues. Despite resolutions decrying poll taxes, the Equal Rights Amendment, and nuclear weapons, for example, the Auxiliary Constitution prohibited members from joining political movements on these issues as representatives of the organization.[1]

The March on Washington in 1941, sponsored by the BSCP, became the first exception to this constitutional rule. In January 1941, Randolph publicly discussed plans for a march on Washington to demand jobs for African Americans in the burgeoning defense industry. It was the union's first experience with a national political movement of its own making. March organizers insisted on a new definition of democracy and citizenship. In his "Call to March on Washington," Randolph defined the stakes for African Americans in World War II:

> We believe in national unity which recognizes equal opportunity of black and white citizens to jobs in national defense and the armed forces and in all other institutions and endeavors in America. We condemn all dictatorships, Fascist, Nazi and Communist. We are loyal, patriotic Americans, all.
>
> But if American democracy will not defend its defenders; if American democracy will not protect its protectors; if American democracy will not insure equality of opportunity, freedom and justice to its citizens, black and white, it is a hollow mockery and belies the principles for which it is supposed to stand.[2]

Leading Randolph's list of demands was first-class citizenship for all African Americans, a demand that originated in his earlier pursuit of black manhood rights and a living wage. Those wages were about to be realized; it was now time for a higher standard of citizenship. Echoing abolitionist and statesman Frederick Douglass, Randolph demanded, "We want the full works of citizenship with no reservations. We will accept nothing less." The march actualized the "Double V" campaign: "Victory over our enemies at home and victory over our enemies on the battlefields abroad." "Winning Democracy for the Negro is Winning the War for Democracy," was the motto of the March on Washington Movement.[3]

The demand for first-class citizenship came during the "forgotten years" of the civil rights movement, 1941 to 1949. In that period the March on Washington spawned the major protest demonstrations for racial equality. The "Call to March" demanded that the president prohibit discrimination in the defense industry and in defense training courses; required that the United States Employment Service supply workers without regard to race; and called on Congress to amend the NLRA to forbid coverage to unions that imposed racial restrictions on their memberships. Finally, the march called for "A Free Africa and A Free Caribbean" and a pan-African conference of "Free Negroes" to negotiate for independence and for the free exercise of self-government.[4]

To obtain these demands, Randolph declared that ten thousand African Americans would walk down Pennsylvania Avenue on July 1, 1941. By choosing the nation's capital, Randolph sought to expose racial intolerance in "the symbol of democracy and America." Joining the Brotherhood of Sleeping Car Porters, the Ladies' Auxiliary mobilized men and women to march. In Washington, the BSCP and Auxiliary rented space in the center of the African American business district at 7th and T Streets, N.W. In addition to office space, the building's "third floor was reserved to house marchers who should be unable to find other accommodations."[5] By May 1941, when Randolph realized the extent of interracial support the march was receiving, he raised the number of marchers to 100,000. Fearful of the impact so many African Americans might have on the segregated city, the administration sent representatives to ask Randolph to cancel the march. "Mrs. Bethune fought me like a dog on the March," remembered E. Pauline Myers, executive secretary of the MOWM, of her private battle with Mary McLeod Bethune, a member of FDR's black cabinet and friend of Eleanor Roosevelt. Randolph refused to compromise until President Roosevelt agreed to sign an Executive Order prohibiting discrimination on the basis of "race, color, religion, or national origin" by defense contractors. Executive Order 8802, issued June 25, 1941, also established the Fair Employment Practice Committee (FEPC) to oversee the enforcement of the ban.[6]

To African Americans, the Executive Order symbolized the president's willingness to act on issues of racial justice. Assessing the impact of the FEPC, Louis Ruchames wrote, "The committee was far more than an agency securing jobs for members of minority groups. FEPC concentrated in itself the dreams and hopes of millions of people who had never before been given the opportunity of sharing in the processes of American Democracy. . . . FEPC changed all that. It brought hope and a new confidence into their lives. It gave them cause to believe in democracy in America."[7] The FEPC may have symbolized equality, but the agency lacked power: lacking subpoena powers, it could not force contractors to provide evidence; and lacking enforcement authority, it could not revoke federal contracts even when it found blatant cases of discrimination against African Americans. Six months after the Executive Order, the bombing of Pearl Harbor and the United States' entry into World War II heightened awareness of racial discrimination. Yet a February 1942 survey of defense industry managers found that employment policies had not changed; more than half of the 282,245 newly created positions were reserved for whites. Factories begging for workers announced, "The Negro will be considered only as janitors and in other similar capacities."[8]

The disparity between the promise of the Executive Order and the weakness of the FEPC, and the still unmet demands of the call to march, maintained the momentum of the movement. Still spoiling for a showdown, march organizers planned "monster rallies" in New York, Chicago, St. Louis, and Washington. Brotherhood men and women did the grassroots organizing, speaking on street corners, passing out handbills, staffing offices, and on the night of the rally, serving as ushers. Thousands attended the Madison Square Garden rally on June 16, 1942. All of Harlem blacked out its outdoor lights from sundown to 10 P.M. that Tuesday night to show solidarity with the movement. Ellen Tarry, assigned by the *Amsterdam News* "to cover the women's angle," remembered "Harlem was like a deserted village. Every man, woman and child who had carfare was in Madison Square Garden." Randolph, scheduled to make the keynote address, was escorted to the platform by 150 uniformed BSCP porters and maids. "Many of Harlem's prominent women served as ushers and guides," Tarry reported. Mrs. Bessye Bearden, "one of Harlem's outstanding civic leaders" and head of the Harlem Housewives' League, introduced the publicly supportive Mary McLeod Bethune as "Negro America's First Lady." The "meeting represented the most unified mass demonstration I have ever witnessed," Tarry wrote a dozen years later.[9]

"The giant demonstration of last Friday evening is still the marvel of the day and is being widely discussed, not only by the Negro, but by the whites as well," wrote Wilson, extolling the success of the Chicago Mass Meeting on June 26th. Twelve thousand people attended the Chicago Coliseum event, while businesses and homes on the South Side turned out their lights to show their support. The rally in St. Louis, held August 14th, drew nine thousand, proportionately more people than the New York and Chicago events, but organizers shortened the blackout to fifteen minutes. The rally planned for Washington, D.C., on September 4, failed to materialize, in part because of the difficulty of finding a suitable site in the racially segregated city. Momentum for the rallies declined as the war emergency grew, personality clashes between male and female organizers sharpened, and other racial issues took the spotlight.[10]

In the midst of these demonstrations, however, union members followed closely another drama that reached its grim conclusion in Pittsylvania County, Virginia. An all-white, all-male jury convicted an African American share-cropper, Odell Waller, for murdering his white landlord, who had appropriated his tenant's share of the wheat crop. Mrs. Waller, accompanied by Workers' Defense League member Pauli Murray, toured the country speaking about her son's case. The *Black Worker* devoted feature articles to Waller. The BSCP and Auxiliary sponsored public meetings in Chicago and Los Angeles for Mrs. Waller and to condemn the poll tax that prevented African Americans from serving on the jury. A national appeal to Governor Colgate W. Darden failed to win a commutation of Waller's death sentence, and he died at 8:30 A.M., July 2, 1942. Halena Wilson, who had closely followed events, believed that though "the gallant fight to save Odell Waller was lost . . . the fight was not in vain since it like the March on Washington Movement is a definite indication that the Negroes are being aroused and determined to fight their own battles." Ethel Payne, organizer of the Chicago demonstration concurred, "I feel now more than ever we must redouble our efforts to make democracy work."[11]

The injustice of Waller's execution and the ongoing organizing for the March on Washington spurred in the formation of several single-issue organizations. The "We Are Americans, Too" conference held in Chicago over Fourth of July weekend in 1943 served as the founding convention for the March on Washington Movement; its delegates were largely BSCP and Auxiliary members. The MOWM, a membership organization with annual dues of ten cents, was both popular and controversial because only African Americans could belong. In Canada, the MOWM inspired Brotherhood women and men to establish the Canadian League for the Advancement of Colored People. The National Non-Partisan Conference, which convened in Chicago in 1944 three months after the Supreme Court ruled the Texas white primary unconstitutional, encouraged African Americans to vote for whichever candidates agreed to support full citizenship rights, regardless of political party. The National Council for a Permanent FEPC, headed by Anna Arnold Hedgeman, brought together local chapters to lobby for an independent agency to enforce federal fair employment legislation. The Committee to End Jim Crow in the Armed Services and Training, organized in 1945, successfully challenged military segregation and passage of Truman's Universal Military Training bill.[12]

Women participated substantially in all of these movements, contending with the same sexist attitudes women endured in other organizations. Vice-President Milton P. Webster characterized the "We Are Americans, Too" conference as "the biggest piece of bunk that has happened around here," in part because there were "too many bossy dames." Neva Ryan, the "official office manager, whatever that means" of the Chicago rally committee, believed that men quickly dismissed women's complaints as "personalities"—a slang term to describe a "difficult" woman. She warned Randolph against ignoring the disagreements over the role women should have in the MOWM. "Because women have done most of the complaining perhaps the mistake was made in emphasizing personality difficulties." Rosina Tucker ignored the paternalistic instructions of men in the Washington unit to speak on street corners and in theaters to raise public awareness of the movement.[13]

The day-to-day jobs—postering and leafleting, arranging housing and meals, ushering, typing, and answering telephones—were women's work, often done by local Auxiliary members. The MOWM relied solely on the volunteer labor of African American men and women from all segments of the community. A list of sixty Indianapolis donors illustrates the grassroots support. No one gave more than $2.00, most gave but $1.00. Husbands and wives, parents and children joined, giving their occupations as YMCA staff, photographer, Pullman porter, housewife, beautician, barber, red cap, "Eli Lilly," undertaker, chiropractor, chauffeur, cleaner, stenographer, dining car employee, reverend, doctor, attorney, and professor.[14]

The racial exclusivity of the March on Washington Movement aroused controversy. Randolph ostensibly wanted to prevent the Communist Party from taking over the movement, as had happened three years earlier in the National Negro Congress. But African American communists were hardly a rarity, even after the 1939 Hitler-Stalin pact; further, Randolph claimed the MOWM "did not shun" their membership. Rather, Randolph was skeptical that white-dominated organizations established to promote racial integration, such as the NAACP, could truly express African American opinion. The BSCP was race-led and race-controlled, so too should the MOWM be, especially if its purpose was to set the political agenda for African Americans. And by relying on the resources and abilities of the community, African Americans would discover they could work independently, as a later generation would discover for itself.

> The essential value of an All-Negro movement such as the March on Washington Movement is that it helps to create faith by Negroes in Negroes. It develops a sense of self-reliance with Negroes depending on Negroes in vital matters. It helps to break down the slave psychology and inferiority complex in Negroes which comes and is nourished with Negroes relying on white people for direction and support. This inevitably happens in mixed organizations that are supposed to be in the interest of the Negro.[15]

But composed exclusively of African Americans, the MOWM had less political power. Denied the right to vote in many states, and ignored by most elected officials when they possessed suffrage, the organization could not rely solely on traditional politics. MOWM members thus turned to nontraditional methods to register their protests against second-class citizenship.

The MOWM tested the effectiveness of nonviolent protest. E. Pauline Myers, author of the MOWM's handbook on nonviolence, explained the necessity of employing new protest tactics in 1943: "The old method of round-table discussions, pink teas, luncheons and Black Cabinets has been exploded," she began. "The need is for mass organization with an action program aggressive, bold and challenging in spirit, but non-violent in character." She defined the principle of nonviolence as "Matching one's ability to suffer against an opponent's ability to inflict suffering. It is not resignation; it is not submission; it is bold, aggressive, revolutionary. It invites attack, meeting it with a stubborn and non-violent resistance that seeks to recondition the mind and weaken the will of the oppressor."[16] Myers claims it was she who encouraged Randolph to adopt nonviolent protest tactics. The "We Are Americans, Too" conference endorsed the use of nonviolent direct action to break down racial segregation. The conference encouraged its urban delegates to use traditional political methods where they could, directing them to register, to vote, and to lobby legislators for federal supervision of elections for those denied voting rights. After the conference, Montgomery, Alabama BSCP President E. D. Nixon began attending meetings of the local Voters League. The following June he led a two-day protest on the steps of the state capital, bringing "750 Negroes to register as voters under Montgomery Voters League."[17]

Elsewhere, MOWM members employed nonviolent methods to open jobs to African Americans. Randolph described to conference delegate Blanche Lee, a member of the Washington Ladies' Auxiliary, the various actions around the country:

> The New York MOWM is waging a war against the Metropolitan Life Insurance Company for its Jim Crow policy refusing to employ Negroes. The St. Louis MOWM is waging a strenuous campaign to get Negroes integrated into all the public utilities including the street cars. In Denver, the MOWM is working to the end of having a committee set up by the governor and the mayor for the purpose of trying to get Negroes integrated into public utilities. The Denver group is also breaking down barriers against Negroes in places of public accommodation such as restaurants and theaters. . . . The Chicago Division is working with the Congress of Racial Equality to break down barriers in places of public accommodation and is going to begin a campaign against the Metropolitan Life Insurance Company there.[18]

Randolph urged the Washington Auxiliary and BSCP to support the Capital Transit demonstrations, organized to protest the private company's refusal to hire African American motormen and platform workers. Nearly three years of agitation however, failed to integrate the company, and showed how powerless the FEPC was against recalcitrant employers.[19]

The most successful Brotherhood demonstrations occurred in St. Louis. T. D. McNeal, the BSCP's zone supervisor and his wife, Thelma McNeal, organized a movement that mobilized "a true cross-section of the St. Louis Negro community," in repeated demonstrations against discriminatory ordinance, aircraft, and communications industries. The McNeals led pickets in front of Southwestern Bell Telephone to draw public attention to the company's refusal to hire African American women operators. According to the MOWM's "Statement of Facts," the company admitted it needed "additional help particularly operators. It repeatedly runs large ads for operators in the daily papers." The company refused to hire the African American men and women who applied for these positions. "We sought a conference with the Telephone Company to discuss the feasibility of using some of the well-trained Negro women and men who are citizens of the Community. We were not even given the courtesy of a reply." Picketers' placards emphasized the "Double V" campaign. "How Can We Die Freely for Democracy Abroad If We Can't Work Equally for Democracy at Home?" "Let's Practice Democracy as We Preach It!" By the spring of 1943, McNeal recalled, the St. Louis MOWM gained almost eight thousand jobs for African American men and women.[20]

Throughout the summer of 1944, the St. Louis MOWM organized some of the first sit-ins against segregated public facilities. Pearl S. Maddox, chair of the Civil Rights Committee, led dozens of African American and white women to protest Jim Crow lunch counters in the city's department stores, the Grand Leader, Famous-Barr, Scruggs-Vandervoort-Barney, Stix, Baer & Fuller, and Katz Drug Store. The first demonstration in May, held at the Grand Leader, established the pattern used in other sit-ins. "Three young American pretty brown college girls . . . each got a stool at the counter, and shortly after they were seated, one of the waitresses, nervously approached and informed them that they did not serve Colored. The girls wanted to know the reason why, which she stammered and tried to answer but it was done incoherently."[21] An observer did not hear "one single angry word" from other patrons in the dining area. "There were only three persons who seemed ill at ease and they were the waitress, the floorwalker and the manager." The manager persuaded Miss Vora Thompson to confer with him in his office. When she left her seat, "a white friend got it and he bought a sandwich and a soda and was given a glass of water. He gave the refreshments to Miss Shermine Smith and Miss Ruth

Mattie Wheeler, which they ate leisurely unmolested." Later the same day, during a sit-in at Katz Drug Store, the women were prevented from protesting peacefully. "Miss Shermine Smith gave a demonstration of poise, culture and training when the manager . . . lifted her from her seat and took a half-eaten sandwich from her hand, and she never resisted or uttered one word. Miss Smith deserves a badge of honor."[22]

The demonstrators claimed their citizenship rights by publicizing their contributions to the war. At lunch counter demonstrations in the other downtown stores, Mrs. Hattie Duvall carried a sign reading "I Invested Five Sons in Invasion"; Ruth Mattie Wheeler's sign read, "My Mother Serves, My Brother Serves, May I be Served." Vora Thomspon told the manager of the Grand Leader that it was "time to begin training Americans to respect Americans. Our brothers, and our sweethearts are suffering and dying all over the world, to destroy Fascism and you and I must get rid of it at home." Protesters won the support of customers, but management refused to desegregate the lunch counters.[23]

Less than a year after founding the MOWM, the integrated "Save the FEPC Conference" organized the National Council for a Permanent FEPC. Anna Arnold Hedgeman ran the Washington office of the interracial, interfaith organization. The council's nineteen-member executive committee brought together the leaders of a dozen national groups, creating a formidable coalition for civil rights. Local councils, established by BSCP and MOWM members, worked with the national council's field representatives to build grassroots political support, to send local delegates to lobby Congress, and to raise funds for the national office.[24]

In many cities, the Brotherhood and Auxiliary were the backbone of the FEPC councils. Nora Fant, president of the Jersey City, New Jersey, Auxiliary and a member of ILGWU Local No. 25, buttonholed First Lady Eleanor Roosevelt about the FEPC when her Hudson Shore Summer Labor School class visited Hyde Park. Thelma Freeman chaired Denver's FEPC council. In a single drive, she recruited thirty-three new members who contributed $300 to the national office. Mattie Owens of Minneapolis and Milbrey Sneed of Chicago suggested FEPC stamps, "to create favorable reaction to Negro Servicemen" and to raise money for the FEPC. The stamps, similar to Christmas Seals, "should hearten the Negro soldier as well as keep his plight before the country. . . . The sale of these seals would be helping the United States and pleading the cause of the Negro at the same time." By February 1945, the New Orleans division sold 100,000 FEPC stamps, with the assistance of local unions and churches. At the 1946 Auxiliary convention, twelve locals reported contributions to the cause. The Fort Worth Auxiliary worked with civic and fraternal groups on two fundraising drives that netted over $1,000. In Louisville, president Anna R. Hughes reported that 250 tickets were sold ("but the Ladies' Auxiliary sold most of the tickets") to the banquet honoring Randolph's FEPC tour, sponsored jointly with the BSCP. And Addie Fletcher Booth, a Seattle Auxiliary member, spent two years persuading legislators in Olympia to enact a fair employment statute in Washington State. She succeeded.[25]

The civil rights activism of these "forgotten years" was not limited to the United States. In Canada, Brotherhood women and men also demanded the elimination of racial barriers. The president of the Montreal Auxiliary, Velmer Coward, committed herself to work for democracy after attending the MOWM's "We Are Americans, Too" Conference in 1943. "If only we can put the [conference] proposal into operation, the dawn of a brighter day for the Negro is not far distant. If the delegates have returned to their respective homes enthused and fired as I have been, then the harvest will be an abundant one, and the Negro in winning democracy for the Negro will have aided her white brother to practice true democracy in the sense of the word."[26] Coward was responsible for reviving the Canadian League for the Advancement of Colored People (CLACP). Writing to Randolph in late 1942, she asked for his advice "by return mail."

> We have been advised recently of several specific cases of open discrimination in this City, and we are determined to do everything in our power to stop and stamp it out. We shall of course solicit the aid of the Local Jewish Congress, in eradicating these unpleasant occurrences, but we feel that if we became members of an International organized group such as the NAACP that we could command greater respect, accomplish more, and learn ways and means whereby we can combat these common forces of evil which if allowed to germinate will grow in enormous proportion too great for solution in the Post War period.[27]

Randolph replied promptly, concurring with Coward about the expediency of such a move and agreeing to address an open forum on the value of "such a group in . . . preserving a reasonable standard of life and its maintenance." Halena Wilson also supported Coward's efforts to form a group to fight racial discrimination.[28]

Coward believed the Canadian civil rights organization should adopt the goals of the MOWM; she even asked Randolph to serve as honorary chairman. "In the meantime," Coward reported, "I have canvassed 35 of our local groups in order to secure the names and addresses of those who will lend their wholehearted support. To date we have been able to get over a hundred names, and expect to get many more. The Negro populace being so scattered it is difficult to bring before them the actual conditions that exist, and why the urgent need for unified action."[29] Although a Canadian version of the NAACP was organized in 1924, it had never formally affiliated with the U.S. group. Confined to Ontario, by 1940 the Canadian League for the Advancement of Colored People was regarded as a local charity group. Coward received word from NAACP Executive Director Walter White agreeing to help revive the CLACP, but he soon withdrew support, feeling the U.S. organization could not bear the responsibility and expense of organizing Canadian branches. Coward then offered the CLACP the assistance of the Brotherhood of Sleeping Car Porters to organize new chapters and create a Dominion-wide organization. Under her guidance, the CLACP worked for fair employment legislation and civil rights protections for African Canadians.[30]

The Montreal chapter, formed in mid-1943, drew its members largely from the ranks of the BSCP, the Ladies' Auxiliary, and their associates. Coward became secretary; her brother Victor Coward, president. Less than a year later, Coward reported a "membership of about 80, and about 60 attending our regular meetings." A canvassing committee was to begin another membership drive soon, and "we are hoping to double this number in the near future." A town hall meeting, in October 1944, with Randolph and Bernard Rose, K.C., as keynote speakers, attracted dozens of new members.[31]

During Randolph's 1945 tour of Canada to celebrate the BSCP's recent contract with the Canadian Pacific Railway, new chapters of the league were established in each of the Brotherhood's five divisions. At an "overflowing" mass meeting in Vancouver, Randolph set up that city's branch of the league, later named the British Columbia Association for the Advancement of Colored People. Its officers were drawn largely from the union men and women; Frank Collins served as president of both organizations. In Winnipeg, Randolph established another CLACP organization with union officials and clergy elected as officers. In the Calgary division, Willa Sneed, vice-president of the Auxiliary, forced the *Herald* to retract racially derogatory remarks about the BSCP international president and other African Canadians. The Montreal chapter sent telegrams to the colonial government of Nigeria to protest the arrest of trade union leaders.[32]

The league's major accomplishment was the enactment of federal and provincial fair employment practices legislation during the postwar period. Although the BSCP received credit for this legislation, Coward and Randolph credited the community-based CLACP. The Vancouver organization began researching a fair employment statute in 1949, but did not begin lobbying until the mid-1950s. The publicity given to race discrimination by the CLACP created a climate favorable to obtaining the BSCP's goals. The Canadian National Railway and the Canadian Pacific Railway both eliminated racial restrictions on promotions, giving porters the right to bid for conductor openings and other supervisory positions. For the first time, the railroad industry had lifted the color bar on jobs.[33]

In the United States, the climate to integrate the military was also favorable. The March on Washington Movement relied on the efforts of the Winifred Lynn Committee to Abolish Segregation in the Armed Services until April 1945, when the groups established the Committee to End Jim Crow in the Armed Services. The committee used both legislative and nonviolent tactics: working for legislation to outlaw segregation and, through the League for Non-Violent Civil Disobedience against Military Segregation, calling for African American and white youth to resist the draft as conscientious objectors to racial segregation. The BSCP Auxiliary took special interest in the Women's Army Auxiliary Corps and Navy Reserves, advocating these units be integrated. Double jeopardy restricted the training opportunities given African American women in the WAVES. According to Secretary of the Navy Frank Knox, the purpose of the program was to "release male officers and enlisted men." White women could take over a variety of jobs, but until the 1960s the only position African American men held in the Navy was that of messmen. Therefore, he concluded, "There is no occasion to replace Negro enlisted personnel by Negro women enlisted in the Women's Reserve" except of course as food service workers.[34]

African Americans already serving did not receive equal treatment, arousing sympathy and anger. Presidents Wilson and Randolph joined Mabel K. Staupers of the National Association of Colored Graduate Nurses in protesting the treatment of Second Lieutenant Norma Green by the Montgomery police. Green, a registered nurse, was attached to the hospital unit of 99th Pursuit Squadron of Tuskegee, Alabama, the Tuskegee Airmen. While off-duty but in uniform, Green visited Montgomery, where an altercation with a bus driver apparently occurred. The bus driver called police to arrest Green for failing to board through the rear door. When taken into custody, the army officer was "brutally beaten and robbed by a white policeman." Green's treatment spurred calls by the Auxiliary for passage of the G.I. Assault Bill, which imposed federal criminal penalties on anyone assaulting a member of the Armed Forces.[35]

The Auxiliary could not support the Committee to End Jim Crow the same way that men did, since women did not have the same stake in military service. Rather, like the lunch counter protesters in St. Louis, Brotherhood women identified themselves as the mothers of soldiers to demand military desegregation. Randolph also appealed for women's support by using motherhood rhetoric. Soliciting for donations to the committee from the Auxiliaries he wrote, "This question involves the sons and daughters of all Negro women of this country. . . . I am sure that our Negro women will be happy to help this fight to break down segregation in the armed forces." The 1942 Auxiliary convention sent a letter to President Roosevelt depicting themselves "as women with husbands, sons, brothers, etc. who are likely to be lost" and implored the president "to decry and deplore the treatment being accorded" uniformed African American soldiers. "Do your utmost to protect them and to spare them the humiliating experience of being denied food while traveling about the country and to prevent their being mobbed, shot, and otherwise man-handled while fitting themselves to help in the defense of their country as well as to help perpetuate that very illusive thing called 'democracy.'"[36]

Auxiliary women used their status as mothers to assert their rights as citizens and to demand racial justice. Mattie Mae Stafford, former president of the Los Angeles Women's Economic Council, used this identity to articulate the concerns of African American women in her 1944 protest letter to the president. Writing on behalf of the Frederick Douglass Unit of the Women's Political Study Club of California, Stafford considered it the president's duty "as Commander in Chief to see that Americans are not discriminated against because of race or color, especially when they are fighting and dying for their country." "In the name of justice and fair play," the president should "issue an edict that will stop discrimination in the armed forces. Not a temporary decree, but one that will make discrimination impossible in peace time and in war."[37]

The goals of the Committee to End Jim Crow expanded when President Harry Truman proposed Universal Military Training (U.M.T.), which would require all young men to receive training in the armed forces in segregated units. Outraged by the plan's implicit endorsement of racial discrimination, the committee renewed political pressure by organizing mass resistance to the draft. Truman still refused to act until the 1948 Democratic National Convention drew near. Then the president, facing a right-wing bolt of Dixiecrats led by Senator Strom Thurmond, and a left-wing exit led by Progressive presidential candidate Henry A. Wallace, appealed to African American voters crucial to his election. On July 26 he issued Executive Orders 9980 and 9981, abolishing segregation in the civil service and in the armed services, respectively.[38]

When seventy-two-year-old Mrs. Emma Clarissa Clement became the first African American woman chosen American Mother of the Year in 1946, Randolph exploited her award in his fight against Universal Military Training. Mrs. Clement was the mother of Abby Jackson of the Louisville Ladies' Auxiliary and Dr. Rufus E. Clement, the president of Atlanta University, and coincidentally a member of the Committee to End Jim Crow. Mrs. Clement's 1947 Christmas statement, released and written by the committee, used motherhood to attack segregated compulsory defense training.

> To us who have lost sons in the last war, nothing could be more of a betrayal of the ideals for which they fought. To mothers who for the first time would see their sons dragged off in peacetime and exposed to various types of discrimination, this piece of legislation is Public Enemy No. 1.
>
> Fortunately, we are not helpless. Our demands can be heard and can be effective. . . . It is up to us to let our congressmen, senators and President Truman know that we as mothers oppose a bill which would betray our sons and the best interests of our nation. The time is short, and I call upon all mothers and all other decent-minded citizens to use the Christmas holidays and the early part of January to force this issue out into the open. If we do not act now, it may be too late a few weeks from now.[39]

Mothers of soldiers could demand citizenship rights because they had patriotically sacrificed their sons for the war. This category of citizenship was available to women without regard to color, even in a segregated military.

Mothers and other female relatives of American soldiers also deserved equal employment rights in the defense industries, argued Sallie Parham of the National Council of Business and Professional Women of the YWCA, at the St. Louis March on Washington rally. "We must fight to work—against discrimination in defense industries where our men and women are to work. . . . We must replace those men who have to fight for democracy. . . . We fight for those who are gone for Victory, now, that they may have victory here, too when they return."[40] Parham and President Wilson invoked maternalist arguments, using the language of democracy to appeal to women's sense of racial and economic justice. Asking members to send letters to Congress in support of a Permanent FEPC, Wilson wrote: "Fair Employment Practice Committee is right and just in a democracy and such opportunities must eventually be made to apply to all persons who are willing and able to work. The Auxiliary which is composed of the wives and mothers of the race must continue to fight to help bring job security and job opportunities to the Negro workers of the world."[41] By describing women as "the wives and mothers of the race," Wilson drew on the traditions of republican motherhood, claiming their rights as citizens to participate in the decisions of government. Yet neither she nor Parham indicated that wives might have equal employment rights after the war, unless they were war widows. While women might have developed a feminist outlook as a result of their World War II experiences, the ideology promoted by the Auxiliary mitigated their radicalism on gender issues. A wife was her husband's partner; "Rosie the Riveter" substituted for him in the factory during the war, holding his place until his return.

This maternalistic ideology affected women's participation in the March on Washington movements. Randolph's appointment of Pauline Myers and Anna Hedgeman to national leadership positions recognized their organizing capabilities and encouraged other women to participate. Yet as Ethel Payne noted, Myers and Hedgeman were executive secretaries, not executive directors. Local MOWM units and FEPC councils also relied on women's leadership and volunteer labor. Velmer Coward's work with the Canadian League for the Advancement of Colored People seems to have been an exception; yet she too was the organization's secretary-treasurer, not its president. The lack of male respect for female political workers meant indifference about their pay, forcing staff at the National Council for a Permanent FEPC to become involuntary volunteers. "Sometimes we are not sure that they will get their pay when pay day comes," Randolph admitted. Despite women's involvement, decisions about national strategies were made, almost exclusively, by Randolph, Walter White of the NAACP, Charles Wesley Burton, Allan Knight Chalmers, and other male members of the executive committees. When women gave directions, steering committee members often complained. Indeed, at one point, Milton P. Webster threw up his hands to Randolph, declaring "there are just too many women involved in this thing." In the National Council for a Permanent FEPC, the executive committee fired Hedgeman and her entire staff on the grounds they were not doing their jobs, then hired Elmer Henderson as executive director at a higher salary.[42]

The Auxiliary's experiences in the March on Washington Movement demonstrated the need for a separate political program for women. Auxiliary members supported Randolph fully and volunteered many hours to "putting over" his political goals. But several factors limited their participation. The twin pressures of greater housework caused by the emergency and increased paid employment opportunities left little time for wives with war jobs. Many already had difficulty attending Auxiliary meetings. Yet time was not the major obstacle. Ironically, the very objectives of the BSCP, black manhood and female respectability, restricted women's participation.

Nor did Brotherhood men generally support women's entry into politics, a traditionally male territory. They rationalized that wives could help to organize trade unions for their husbands in order to protect the well-being of the family. In electoral politics, woman suffragists had offered the same rationale, arguing that wives would vote with their husbands to protect the family's interests. Male-dominated political organizations such as the MOWM relied on women's support work, but scorned women's leadership, while concern for female respectability prevented Auxiliary members from engaging in confrontational protest. Like their husbands, they believed aggressive political behavior would undermine, rather than advance, the civil rights cause. When African American women asserted their rights through sit-ins and other forms of nonviolent protest, they were careful to present a respectable image demonstrating their "poise, culture and training." Through their proper behavior, Auxiliary women hoped to earn the respect of whites, an essential step toward first-class citizenship for African Americans.[43]

Respectability and political authority were particularly elusive when whites generally perceived African Americans as their inferiors. Popular stereotypes and social scientists reinforced these beliefs. The weekly radio and television series "Amos and Andy" broadcast the stereotypes of Sapphire and Kingfish, who figured as satirical political images in popular culture. The Sapphire stereotype is a "hands-on-hip, finger-pointing" woman, "noted for telling people off, and spouting her opinion in a loud manner." "Her sheer existence," K. Sue Jewell argues, "is predicated on the presence of the corrupt African American male whose lack of integrity, and use of cunning and trickery provides her with an opportunity to emasculate him through the use of verbal put-downs." In "Amos and Andy," Sapphire is not taken seriously by her husband Kingfish, who dismisses her ideas by saying "You're always running your mouth."[44] Kingfish is a modern version of the illiterate, former slave elected to public office during Reconstruction, an image created to nullify the Fourteenth Amendment.[45] Sapphire did not appear until after ratification of the women's suffrage amendment, validating the disfranchisement of African American women. The black matriarch of social science literature could be Sapphire or Mammy or a combination of both, depending on the author. In E. Franklin Frazier's classic, *The Negro Family in the United States,* the fiercely independent Sapphire ran the father of her children off, but if she worked, she appeared as Mammy who cared more for white children than her own. In either case, her "disorganized" household was not under male control, and thus "matriarchal." She is immoral and unfit for citizenship, and should be denied suffrage. In the process, she also loses her right to train her sons for citizenship and they become juvenile delinquents. Republican motherhood was reserved for the virtuous married woman.[46]

To disprove these stereotypes, Auxiliary women carefully observed the gender conventions of middle-class white women, especially personal appearance, housekeeping, church attendance, charity, and civic work. Ladylike behavior was thus part of a subliminal strategy of the early civil rights movement. The war for democracy and the MOWM heightened racial consciousness, permitting women to use nonviolent protest tactics; but the conservative backlash of the postwar period discouraged confrontation and restrained the political activism of the Ladies' Auxiliary. Letter-writing, telegrams, petitions, voting, and visiting elected officials were appropriate citizenship activities, but civil disobedience was not.

This construction of ladyhood did not prevent women from participating in every Brotherhood-sponsored political movement between 1941 and 1956. Employing many of the same strategies he used to organize the BSCP, Randolph relied on women in grassroots groups as well as the highest national steering committees. The women who assumed prominence in these campaigns were rarely members of the Ladies' Auxiliary. Pauli Murray of the Workers' Defense League; E. Pauline Myers and Anna Arnold Hedgeman of the Young Women's Christian Association; Mabel K. Staupers of the National Association of Colored Graduate Nurses; Layle Lane, a socialist and member of the American Federation of Teachers; Neva Ryan, founding president of the Domestic Workers' Association; Maida Springer of the International Ladies' Garment Workers' Union; and Ethel Payne, Chicago *Defender* journalist and daughter of a BSCP porter, had separate political bases, freeing them from Brotherhood control. As career women without husbands or children, they avoided the Sapphire stereotype even though they were vulnerable to others.

Auxiliary members in these political movements performed the support tasks necessary to every movement. Through that participation, the Auxiliary found its political voice. Yet Brotherhood women were not content with performing merely the "decorative jobs." Their exclusion from discussions about policy and strategy provoked a rethinking of women's roles. At the end of the war, President Halena Wilson developed a legislative program for the Ladies' Auxiliary in cooperation with, but independent of, the BSCP's program. Wilson announced that the International Auxiliary would monitor the status of labor bills and lobby Congress and state legislatures for their passage; their success depended on efforts of all members. The Auxiliary's tactics included letter-writing, voting, and lobbying. Regular bulletins and special letters informed the membership and instructed them to send telegrams and letters to Congress or other elected officials. Rosina Tucker monitored legislation and occasionally lobbied Congress members. Halena Wilson lobbied the Illinois legislature as part of her work with the Women's Trade Union League. Elsewhere, Auxiliary members visited with elected officials in their local offices. The diverse agenda represented their political interests as African American trade union women.

To work on "trade union issues," "race issues," and "women's issues" the Auxiliary endorsed several organizations. As an affiliate of the Women's Trade Union League, the Auxiliary lobbied for domestic social reforms such as national housing, price controls, and protective labor laws. The voter registration drives of the American Federation of Women's Auxiliaries to Labor (AFWAL) specifically targeted the wives of union men; the BSCP Auxiliary reinforced AFWAL's message through its letter-writing campaign for a permanent FEPC. Attempts to work with the National Council of Negro Women, however, ultimately failed because the Auxiliary believed Mary McLeod Bethune's organization did not address economic issues sufficiently. During the postwar years, the Auxiliary, founded with an international consciousness, drew members into issues of world peace, the United Nations, human rights, and the independence of African and Caribbean nations. For Auxiliary members, as for other African Americans, the war for democracy took place at home and abroad.[47]

Many Brotherhood women learned the meaning of democracy at summer labor schools. The Auxiliary's labor school scholarship program was one of its most popular educational projects. Mamie Willis, a seamstress and president of the Toronto Canadian Pacific Railway BSCP Auxiliary, attended the Hudson Shore School for Women Workers run by former Bryn Mawr professor Hilda Smith. Willis reported in 1946, "It was here that we were taught to live as people all over the world should be doing in spite of their race, color or creed. By working and playing together we gained fuller understanding of the social and economic problems which are tending to bring about the crisis today. We talked of democracy and learned that it can be made to work."[48] Willis and perhaps fifty other women attended summer labor schools held at Hudson Shore and the University of Wisconsin at Madison between 1944 and 1952; in California, a few women used their own money to attend the Pacific Coast Labor School. The curricula of these two-week institutes stressed public speaking, labor economics, government, labor history, cooperatives, and other subjects as they applied to labor organizing. "In our English class," wrote one student, "we were taught under the subject of properganda and improperganda [sic], a very deep seated subject." But most cherished by Auxiliary members was the "true spirit of democracy."[49]

Few of these African American and African Canadian women had lived in a racial democracy. They were therefore startled by the warm welcome given to them by fellow students, instructors, and townspeople. One woman from Jacksonville, Florida, attending the school at Madison could scarcely believe that she could walk into a local restaurant, sit at a table, and order a meal. Another was overcome upon her arrival at Hudson Shore when a young white woman carried her suitcase for her. To Auxiliary members, the two weeks constituted a real education in democracy. Each had praise. Lela Jackson explained, "After such an interesting two weeks together of all races, these are the thoughts that ran through my mind, as we left . . . why can't we still live together, discuss our problems together be happy together in this so called Free America."⁵⁰ Julia Burwell, a member of the Jacksonville Auxiliary, attended in 1947. She claimed she would "never forget my stay at Hudson Shore. There you see democracy in action. All races study, work and play together, and it was evidenced that all people can get along and live together regardless of race, creed, color, or nationality." Classmate Evelyn Ford, a housewife and member of the Jersey City Auxiliary, concurred, "Many nationalities, races, and religions were represented . . . but we were taught how to live with each other harmoniously and how to become more useful citizens. We saw in practice what we would like to see all over the world. People working eating, sleeping and playing together. A real Democracy." Their sentiments, repeated by other scholarship students, gave Auxiliary members a new understanding of the United States and Canadian governments and their own role in them.⁵¹

The major lesson of the war for democracy was the necessity of participating in the legislative process. In announcing the Auxiliary's legislative program, Wilson noted the unprecedented promulgation of federal regulations during World War II and African American efforts to enact civil rights measures. The "desperate struggles" of "professional States' Rightists" to block federal laws

> have convinced the Auxiliary . . . that if a Federal Fair Employment Practice Commission is to be created . . . if the poll tax, Jim Crowism, Rankinism, and Bilboism are to be repudiated and abolished . . . the answer again is legislation. . . . If this legislative power can be used for restrictive and repressive purposes then it also can be used for constructive and progressive purposes. Hence, the Auxiliary's decision to raise its collective voice in regard to all legislative measures that come for consideration before the various legislative bodies.⁵²

To justify women's entry into politics, Wilson used economic arguments, rather than motherhood. By the millions of dollars in war bonds, income taxes, and lives given for the country,

> Negro America . . . has earned the right to say how the affairs of its country are to be conducted, how and for what purposes the material wealth of this country is to be used, and by whom it is to be used. . . . It is the Auxiliary's belief that all [government-owned property] should be made available to the American public and not to the monopolists who are trying to get a monopoly on these surpluses. Since the American public contributed the money for their purchase the American Negro should be among those to say so.⁵³

Wilson could not reverse Auxiliary policy with such strong words without Randolph's endorsement of the program. Under the constitution, the international president consulted the international counselor for advice on Auxiliary policies to keep the men and women's organizations "in harmony." A handpicked legislative committee, composed of senior Auxiliary officers, ensured that the women would not challenge Randolph. President Wilson submitted legislative bulletins, convention resolutions, general letters, and her speeches to Randolph for his approval. Wilson announced the citizenship duties of Brotherhood women, but it was Randolph who defined those duties. Thus, the International Auxiliary's stance on some issues perhaps more closely reflects Randolph's political agenda than the women's.[54]

The Ladies' Auxiliary's agenda on trade union issues was nearly identical to the Brotherhood's. To a great degree, it also reflected the opinions of the Women's Trade Union League. At its conventions, the International routinely passed resolutions on popular labor issues: raising the federal minimum wage, endorsing union shop agreements, using union labels, boycotts of non-union goods, and merging of the American Federation of Labor and Congress of Industrial Organizations. Like all good unionists, the BSCP women were outraged when Congress overrode Truman's veto of the Taft-Hartley Act in June 1947.[55]

Wilson's analysis of Taft-Hartley and the postwar labor movement supported the position taken by Randolph and Agnes Nestor of the Chicago WTUL. "The wave of strikes that swooped down on upon the country in the months following the end of hostilities," Wilson averred, were the result of huge profits drawn by manufacturers while thousands were fired, hours reduced, and employers refused to negotiate contracts. Rosina Tucker characterized Taft-Hartley as the "Slave Bill" and declared it "so intricate its authors don't agree on its interpretation so I won't dare discuss it other than to say that all of labor is against it." Tucker told delegates at the 1948 convention what the Auxiliary expected of them. "You are asked to use your power of sufferance against this bill, by so doing you will unshackle labor. A discussion of this bill will continue in our labor columns until election time when everyone who can vote will do so in the interest of those who have to work."[56]

The American Federation of Labor reassessed women's suffrage after passage of the Taft-Hartley Act. They realized that when union wives voted labor, labor's political power doubled. During the presidential elections of 1948, the labor movement's get-out-the-vote drive, combined with heavy African American turnout after desegregation of the military, provided Truman with a narrow margin for victory and returned the Democrats to power on the Hill, despite the absence of telephones in working-class homes. But the Eighty-First

Congress could not unseat the senior southerners who held key committee posts. Taft-Hartley was not repealed, nor was fair employment legislation enacted. By 1950, Taft-Hartley seemed a moot issue; neither Wilson nor Tucker mentioned it during the Auxiliary's convention. Railway labor leaders found that rank-and-file workers believed it had not affected them, especially in the railroad brotherhoods, where separate laws governed many labor practices. But civil rights and citizenship remained issues.[57]

President Halena Wilson also encouraged members to use the ballot box to further trade unionism and civil rights. The International Ladies' Auxiliary took strong stands on poll taxes, white primaries, and voting rights, although it expressly cautioned locals not to endorse any political party or candidate. Washington, D.C., residents held a plebiscite in 1945 to demand voting rights; Rosina Tucker had charge of two polling districts. The Chicago Auxiliary boasted having the "highest percentage of registered votes of any other group whose membership was investigated." Maida Springer, business agent of the ILGWU, drew a round of applause when she told the 1950 Auxiliary convention: "Your job is knowing your congressman, your senator, and calling your friends together and to politic with them a little bit. It is your life you throw away if you do not do it. It does not require any education or any degrees. It requires common sense and the ability to talk to the person next to us."[58] Randolph spoke emphatically of the need for voter registration, recommending that the Auxiliary begin a block-to-block, door-to-door campaign "where doorbells are rung and families are brought together and you sit down and talk with them about what registration and voting means to them in terms of bread and freedom and peace." These calls to political activism redefined the role of the union wife in the postwar period. The union home was more than a house filled with union-made goods, it also meant a family that voted labor.[59]

The Auxiliary worked more closely with the WTUL than the American Federation of Women's Auxiliaries to Labor. The "per capita plus" formula for membership dues in the AFL organization was too high for the International Auxiliary's budget. Dues to WTUL affiliates in the major cities were borne by local Auxiliaries, which, with their large memberships, were affordable. Auxiliaries in Chicago, New York, Boston, and Washington, D.C., worked with their local Women's Trade Union Leagues on legislative matters. Halena Wilson became a member of the executive board of the Chicago Women's Trade Union League in 1943. She journeyed regularly to Springfield to attend WTUL lobbying conferences in the state capital. Chicago members Hettie McLendon, Augusta Wilson, Czerda Blackburn, and Bertha Batson attended the WTUL's tri-state conferences on legislative affairs. Although the WTUL and the Auxiliary agreed on most labor issues, Wilson also criticized the group for neglecting the needs of the "non-working woman."[60]

The Equal Rights Amendment threatened both working and nonworking women according to advocates of protective labor laws. When Congress reintroduced the E.R.A. in 1946, the WTUL, the BSCP Ladies' Auxiliary, and other labor advocates joined the campaign against its ratification. Agnes Nestor charged, "If that amendment is adopted it will destroy the separate protection labor laws for women." Wilson, with typical rhetoric, attacked the "professional and highly skilled and trained women" who believed women should be equal to men. If the E.R.A. was ratified, wives would lose their right to the protection and security of their husbands. "That means . . . a husband would not be responsible for the light bills, for their children's health, or for the home, because a national law [*sic*] would declare that woman is a man's equal, that she can go out and make her own living and take care of herself and her family the same as he does."[61] Wilson told the Auxiliaries to write Congress, stating "that as women of a working group who are dependent upon their husband's wages, that we are opposed to such a law." Reminding her audience that Eleanor Roosevelt was opposed to the E.R.A., she finally threw in the spurious argument that women would no longer be entitled to separate restrooms and "other sanitary provisions."[62]

There was no irony, however, in the Auxiliary's simultaneous demand for equal pay for equal work. Trade union women wanted women workers to receive the same pay as men, so that men would not lose their jobs to underpaid women. Women who worked for wages should have the same employment rights as men, since some may "be compelled to remain on the job as the head of the family due to the failure on the part of the rightful head of the family to return from this present horrible world conflict." As for the "the male worker [who] persists as a result of his present shortsightedness to encourage such discrimination," Wilson warned, "the time may come . . . when he will find himself faced with the unpleasant task of defending his own wage standard against the one his own indifference helped to create for the female worker." Despite these concerns, the Auxiliary believed men were the "rightful" breadwinners of the family and that women should be housewives enjoying the benefits of a living wage.[63]

The Auxiliary did not address the concerns of the Baltimore and Ohio Train Porterettes fighting against protective legislation. Nor did it comment on the porterettes' case. Maggie Hudson told a reporter she wanted to keep her job after the war. "She feels that this avenue of employment should remain open not on the basis of sex, but on the basis of the ability to do the job." Porterette Hudson, like plaintiff porterette Edna Comedy, could do the work, and kept her B&O job until retirement. But Hudson, Comedy, and the rest of the porterettes did not have equal employment rights with porters; the company prohibited women from bidding on certain runs because of state-imposed weight lifting limitations for women workers. As legal scholars have noted, the interstate commerce clause offered the constitutional power to abolish protective labor laws that denied women equal employment, even without the E.R.A., but no labor leader was willing to pursue such litigation.[64]

To protect African American workers who had little hope of unionizing, the International Auxiliary vigorously supported federal social welfare programs. They advocated the extension of the Social Security Act to cover "domestic and agricultural workers who constitute practically the majority of the working class population of the nation, among whom are numbered hundreds of thousands of Negro workers." They endorsed a compulsory national health program and child health measures, financed by the federal government, which the Auxiliary believed essential to eliminating racial differences in the mortality rate. President Wilson defined child health holistically, as "housing, education, environment, moral and spiritual problems [that] contribute to a healthful or unhealthful mental and physical growth of America's future men and women." Tucker forcefully argued for slum clearance programs. "It is a national disgrace that the National Housing Program has not been established." She cited the problems caused by the housing shortage: children's diseases, tuberculosis, "12 people of mixed sexes sleeping in one bedroom," juvenile delinquency, "separations, divorces and a diminishing of family responsibility." Housing legislation, she believed, would "eliminate slums and blighted areas," allowing for "a decent home and a suitable living environment for every American Family and to develop and re-develop communities so as to advance the growth and wealth of the Nation." The Auxiliary's definition of health demonstrates a concern for the African American community, not just the individual; their demand to address the environmental causes of social problems rejected contemporary analyses that laid blame on personal failings. Nonetheless, Tucker acknowledged that "we have a duty to help these people, a difficult task I admit, but something must be done to deter these from literally tearing down the property they rent." Her solution was education and training programs in home repair and housekeeping.[65]

In Washington, D.C., Rosina Tucker demonstrated her concern for the community through civic work. In 1942, as result of her activities in the Northeast Women's Club, she was approached to reorganize the Public Interest Civic Association, which represented residents in her neighborhood east of the railroad tracks and north of Union Station. Elected president at its first meeting, Tucker also became the organization's delegate to the city-wide Federation of Civic Associations (FCA). Near the end of the war, the association and other civic groups were caught by surprise when the District of Columbia's public parks and recreation board formally adopted a segregation policy, even though recreational facilities in the city under the National Park Service were integrated in 1940 by order of the Secretary of the Interior, Harold Ickes. Despite broad appeals from white and African American residents, including BSCP Division President W. S. Anderson, the board refused to revoke its policy. That decision, coming on the loss of the Capital Transit protests, had wide repercussions, effectively launching the modern civil rights movement in Washington.[66]

Tucker participated in that movement through the FCA, as chair of the Social Service Committee. She surveyed segregated public welfare institutions and schools in the city, and lobbied Congress and the Board of Commissioners for funds to equalize facilities. In her efforts to create a "suitable living environment" for children, Tucker represented the "Working Mothers of the District of Columbia" in efforts to extend federal funding of daycare centers "that are so much needed by the Negro Working Mother." In late 1950, Tucker was the only African American woman appointed by the Board of Public Welfare to investigate its Children's Services division, including the National Training School for Girls and the Industrial Home for Boys. The conditions at both institutions, publicized in a series of newspaper articles, created such outrage that Congress raised the district's appropriation so that new facilities could be constructed within five years. Juvenile delinquency in the District of Columbia, exacerbated by segregation of the local boys' clubs and the public parks, also became a public issue in the early 1950s, as crime rates in both African American and white neighborhoods climbed. Tucker believed juvenile delinquency arose from the lack of employment and educational opportunities for both teenagers and their parents, rather than broken homes, poor supervision, and working mothers, as some charged. To combat "the boy gang" problem, Tucker served on the citizens' board of the Youth Council of the District's Board of Commissioners to develop recreational programs for youth. The Washington chapter of the NAACP recognized her efforts in 1955 with the presentation of its Silver Cup Award for distinguished civic work.[67]

Tucker was not an anomaly. Having attained a position of respect in their communities, Auxiliary women regularly worked on civic matters and social service projects, raising money and ensuring that public officials heard the opinions of African Americans. In Atlanta, President Gertrude Ross and the Auxiliary "contributed to Brother [E. D.] Nixon [and the Montgomery Improvement Association] and annually to the Community Chest, the Boys' Club, the NAACP, the YWCA and YMCA, and Heart and Cancer funds." Zone

Supervisor Katherine Lassiter reported in 1956, "Our locals in the South have dramatically shown where the real struggle for human rights and democracy is for the next decade. It is in the South that a new and creative approach for that struggle has electrified the world."[68]

Between 1941 and 1956 the women of the Brotherhood participated in a variety of movements to gain first-class citizenship rights. Their definition of democracy was grounded in the conviction that racial equality was the best way of ensuring the rights of all citizens, regardless of race, sex, creed, or national origin. Because they worked mostly at the grassroots level, performing the daily tasks necessary to keeping a movement growing and improving their communities, the Ladies' Auxiliary's activities were less noticeable than those of the BSCP.

As they worked, their perspective changed. In the early years of the BSCP, support for feminism and trade unionism encouraged African American women to become involved in new political organizations such as the Women's Economic Council and the BSCP Ladies' Auxiliary. The postwar political shift toward anti-communism and civil rights necessitated a reevaluation of their activities. The restrictions against political activism in the Taft-Hartley Act made trade unionism a less practical vehicle for achieving civil rights for the majority of African Americans, especially after the defeat of proposed permanent FEPC legislation. Then too, during the 1950s, the rise of new civil rights organizations such as the Congress of Racial Equality, and new leaders, such as the Reverend Martin Luther King Jr., rendered the BSCP and A. Philip Randolph movement veterans.

The emerging discourse on civil rights displaced trade unionism. The Auxiliary, caught between politicized members interested in the civil rights movement and those enjoying the status of a high standard of living, failed to attract new members. Other organizations seemed to better address African American women's concerns.

9

"Disharmony within the Official Family": Dissolution of the International Ladies' Auxiliary, 1956–57

The Railroad Age ended with World War II. Postwar transportation policy promoted private automobiles, with an attendant emphasis on highway construction. With federal home loan programs and increases in real wages, suburban housing became affordable for trade union families, including Brotherhood families. Bennie Smith reported that ten BSCP porters purchased new homes in 1950, adding, "the great majority of Detroit Brotherhood men are home owners or are in the process of owning their own homes." In business, many executives found commercial airlines faster, easier, and eager to please; even BSCP officers used the airlines for union business. Vacationing families traveled by car, where they could control their itinerary, their children, and possibly avoid the slap of racial prejudice.[1]

The Pullman Company tried to accommodate these new tastes. Railroad fans hailed the new sleeping cars, featuring private roomettes and other new technology such as air conditioning, but passenger miles did not increase significantly. The major railways that contracted for Pullman services also suffered severe financial losses, forcing schedule cuts and the slashing and elimination of routes. In Montgomery, Alabama, the company reduced E. D. Nixon's district to two-and-one-half men. Finally, in 1954 the Federal Trade Commission determined that the Pullman Company operated a monopoly because it both built and operated sleeping car services. Ordered to divest in one or the other, the company chose to suspend its sleeping car service. Pullman porters and maids became employees of the passenger railroads, such as the Union Pacific and the Atlantic Coast Line Railroad.[2]

The Atlantic Coast Line (ACL), one of the last railroads to employ African American women on passenger trains, furloughed its train maids in November 1951. Maid service had been a tradition on its luxury trains running from New York to Jacksonville and Tampa, Florida, for the winter season since

George Pullman himself had sent a maid along to see to his wife's needs. The ACL had maintained this tradition of southern hospitality for its lady passengers, contracting for maids from Pullman, and then in 1939 employing them directly. The BSCP won jurisdiction over the ACL porters, attendants, and maids in 1941, as the union expanded its coverage of racially designated railroad service jobs. Then, after a decade of representation, the ACL laid off the last seventeen maids in what the company insisted was a cost-saving measure.[3]

"To what extent the wages of these maids will save the Atlantic Coast Line Railroad from bankruptcy is not clear," responded the Brotherhood. The union challenged the furloughs, believing it had a better chance of success while the railroads were under federal control. The maids' petition to the National Railway Labor Board contended the furloughs were retaliatory. The BSCP had recently won a judgment against the ACL for violating the loss of sleep rule, which allowed train maids to have two five-hour sleep periods in the ladies' lounge. The Atlantic Coast Line, however, instructed the women to sleep upright in the chair cars. Two weeks after maid Gertrude Payne won $120.02 in back pay, the ACL discharged all its maids. The ACL never reinstated the women, but based on the rule violations, the BSCP won a total of $2,844.43 in back pay for them.[4]

The case of the ACL maids illustrates the obstacles the African American union faced in the railroad industry. Even as the BSCP won recognition from the Pullman Company in 1937, members complained about increasing competition from the airlines and automobiles. Mrs. E. D. Nixon, who often collected union dues in her husband's absence, became so concerned about the declining Brotherhood membership that she wrote Randolph for the first time in 1951.

> I want to tell you this, a Porter came here the other day told me to tell Mr. Nixon, he just could not pay his dues as he had only seven hour for that payday, and some of these men have been furloughed and call back so often until some of them can hardly find an extra job. Brother Randolph, I am a Porter wife and a house wife I no what it take to keep a house these days, Brother Randolph, I no most of these men are scabs or I may say new members of the organization, but in the name of a good Samaritan for the benefit of these suffering Mothers and childrens won't you see if you can give Montgomery Porters some relief, they all feel that you can if you will.[5]

Randolph could only offer the Montgomery men transfers to other districts. "Good business conditions alone create new lines," he wrote Mrs. Nixon, and business was bad.[6]

The airline industry was good, however. The BSCP had occasional opportunities to organize airline service workers, but chose not to. In 1960, for example, Congresswoman Martha W. Griffiths of Michigan asked Randolph to help obtain an international AFL charter for the embryonic airline stewardesses' organization, then a sex-segregated female auxiliary of the Airline Pilots' Association (ALPA). Iris Peterson, who led the organizing effort, also requested Randolph's assistance in his capacity as member of the AFL-CIO Executive Council. Randolph declined, politely. The BSCP president might have traded his influence for Peterson's promise to help open flight attendant positions and other airline service jobs to African American men and women. The same fears that prevented the BSCP president from organizing white railroad hostesses and service workers during World War II still prevailed in 1960. A partnership between African American men and white women would have figuratively suggested miscegenation in a joint fight against the indigenous race and sex discrimination of their respective industries.[7]

The BSCP Ladies' Auxiliary faced similar declines in membership and revenues. At its height in 1945, the International claimed just over 1,500 members; that same year, the BSCP had as many as ten thousand members. Regular membership drives and dues dispensations after the war brought in new and former adherents, but not enough to sustain membership as Pullman furloughed wartime hires and the founding generation of porters and their wives retired (see the appendix).[8]

Local Auxiliary growth and maintenance depended almost entirely on strong local leaders, female and male. That so many divisions prospered despite irregular personal contact from International officers reveals the organizational loyalty of these members. Baltimore, typical of the small locals, sustained a membership of approximately a dozen women throughout its history. The resignation or death of a respected member might devastate the Auxiliary. After Katherine Lassiter's resignation as president in 1946, membership in the New York division declined to thirty members. As members grew older, speakers at the Auxiliary's international conventions discussed the effects of retirement on the family, and memorial services for deceased members grew longer.[9]

Auxiliary members' dues and special taxes paid the rent, office expenses, convention costs, occasional visits to troubled locals, and small donations to various political, charity, and civic concerns, as well as the Auxiliary's membership fees in the Women's Trade Union League and the American Federation of Women's Auxiliaries to Labor. Dues and taxes were sometimes difficult to collect, perhaps because members had to find the money in the household budget or ask their husbands for it; some husbands wanted to know what the International did with the 25 cents their wives paid each month to belong to the Auxiliary. Members whose husbands had regular work increasingly financed the Auxiliary, while widows and the wives of furloughed and retired porters were exempt from dues.[10]

Contact with local Auxiliaries depended on letters; the costs of long-distance telephone calls and telegrams were prohibitive. As Tucker noted in 1954, "I find that our Auxiliaries are not only needing but hungering for knowledge of our work and longing for information and desperately in need of the personal touch of our officials." Unless International officers secured railroad passes through their husbands and stayed with local officers, there was no travel money. The International Executive Board, the Auxiliary's governing body, met every two or three years during the International convention, but these meetings were too infrequent to allow coordinated oversight and programming. Local officers sometimes failed to reply to officers' letters for weeks, even months at a time. When after a year or two of repeated attempts to contact a local failed, the Auxiliary was declared inactive. Wilson only reluctantly asked local Brotherhood officers for news of the Auxiliary, calling on the BSCP as a last resort to retrieve the Auxiliary's charter and account books.[11]

Some membership losses can be traced to poor communication between the BSCP and the Auxiliary. The union failed to inform Auxiliary leaders when it abolished locals and reassigned workers to other cities. When President Halena Wilson inquired about the status of the Tucson Auxiliary, which she had not heard from for more than a year, BSCP Zone Supervisor C. L. Dellums informed her: "There is no more Tucson division of the Brotherhood. The Tucson Division was abolished by being consolidated with Los Angeles. . . . the Tucson Porters [transferred] to Los Angeles. They are now members of our Los Angeles Division and their wives are, or should be members of the Los Angeles Auxiliary. Sorry that we never thought of calling this directly to [the Auxiliary's zone supervisor's] attention so that you could be notified."[12] Wilson repeatedly pleaded for cooperation from the BSCP officers, local and international. "If the branches of the Brotherhood family are so set up that they remain aloof from each other to the extent that the aloofness prevents the development of a feeling of closeness . . . and . . . of oneness within the group, then it would seem that the Brotherhood is overlooking its strongest bid for organizational strength and for organizational unity." But the men seem to have lost interest in the Auxiliary, particularly after the railroad brotherhoods won union shop agreements in 1951. Ironically, stronger union men meant fewer Auxiliary women.[13]

Membership losses meant the International Auxiliary increasingly depended on the Brotherhood for financial subsidies. These loans of less than $1,500 per year caused friction between the BSCP International Executive

Board and the Auxiliary, as the men demanded to see the results of their out-
lays. Milton P. Webster, the chairman of the executive board, was particularly adamant about conserving BSCP funds. Halena Wilson defended the Auxiliary's efforts, arguing that while the Auxiliary might not be as large as it could
be, its well-trained, dedicated membership could do more than a larger organization that was uneducated and disloyal. The International's greatest handicap had always been its shoestring budget. The Brotherhood's subsidy covered small salaries for Wilson and Tucker and part-time secretaries for each
official. These subsidies reflected the Brotherhood's ideas about women's
wages. In 1951, International President Wilson earned $1,440; Rosina Tucker
earned $1,200. That year, the BSCP contract granted newly hired porters over
$3,000 annually, while Randolph, Webster, and other BSCP officers earned
over $4,000. Even though their salaries were among the lowest earned by any
AFL labor official, BSCP officials still considered the women's salaries "pin
money," since their porter-husbands earned union wages.[14]

One reason for the Auxiliary's decline, according to Wilson and Tucker,
was the men's attitude toward the women's organization. International Auxiliary Counselor Randolph truly supported the Auxiliary, but other male officers, at both the international and local level, were indifferent, especially after the union won a closed shop agreement. Local counselors allowed the
Auxiliaries to succeed or fail as they may. Other Brotherhood men participated in Auxiliary meetings to the point that they dictated program development
and affairs. After an extensive tour of the Eastern Zone in 1954, Tucker reported: "I find that many men are antagonistic to the Auxiliary and are a hindrance
to the progress of their Auxiliaries. I find that many men do not know what it
is all about and don't want to learn. The men in this category wherever they
may be found in our set-up must be taught the value that Organized Labor
places on its women."[15] Or perhaps, Brotherhood men understood the dis-
repect organized labor had for women.

In too few cases did local Auxiliaries develop a rapport with the Brotherhood, Tucker concluded.

> In Portland and Jacksonville for instance, where there is a fine working re-
> lationship between the Brotherhood and their Auxiliary, the morale is
> high. In my opinion, Auxiliaries everywhere will grow and become a great
> asset if this relationship can be cultivated. Just what the International
> Brotherhood can or will do in this direction is yet to be seen. We can only
> hope for greater support in the future. As it is, most Auxiliaries are just
> about being ignored out of existence, when a little help at the right time
> and right place would be of tremendous value.[16]

President Wilson was particularly critical of class-conscious "lady free riders," porters' wives who refused to join the Auxiliary. Rather than supporting the labor movement, she claimed, they preferred "riding in fine Cadillac cars and mink coats and fine homes." The International Auxiliary officers simply wanted more cooperation from the BSCP.[17]

But BSCP officials dashed Wilson's and Tucker's hopes for continued support when they voted to dissolve the International Auxiliary. Just three days before the 1956 convention, the Brotherhood decided the Auxiliary was no longer viable. Despite financial support, the women's organization had declined. In view of these problems, the International Executive Board voted to abolish the International and pension Wilson and Tucker. The proposed reorganization did not disband the local Auxiliaries, only the International structure.[18]

"The Sisters were mad," Randolph admitted to the 1956 Auxiliary convention. But he believed the Brotherhood was only trying to rebuild the Auxiliary, not abolish it. The executive board was "definitely friendly to the Ladies' Auxiliary. The men have their own ideas about organization. They feel that the best test of an organization is increase in membership, and consequently if membership is not increasing where members are available, in their opinion, the methods employed are not effective, and the criticism is that the Ladies' Auxiliary is not growing and expanding."[19] The board had the right to do this, Randolph reminded the convention, "since the Auxiliary is a creature of the Brotherhood"; the BSCP was, after all, "the Boss."[20]

International Secretary-Treasurer Rosina Tucker, however, refused to allow the BSCP to abolish the Auxiliary so arbitrarily. During the Brotherhood's session she marched a delegation of women to the convention floor to protest the executive board's decision, demanding reconsideration. "I have come to this convention from time to time and I have felt inadequate because there was nothing to fight for," she began. "But today I think there is something for women to fight for." BSCP officials considered her remarks so unwarranted that they ordered them expunged from the official record of the convention. But the men listened. If Tucker and members of the Auxiliary would apologize for being "too drastic and too severe and too bitter in your attack," Randolph would ask the board to reconsider.[21]

Tucker apologized before the entire convention. However, she did not forgive the Brotherhood for suggesting reorganization. "It was known over the country, so to speak, and we felt—I felt, speaking for myself, that in order to get this thing where it should be, we had to be strong and militant about it and I felt Brother Randolph, if I hadn't been militant, these men wouldn't have taken that position you finally got them to take."[22] Webster and BSCP board members accused Randolph of retreating in the face of the women's anger, but agreed finally to withdraw the resolution to dissolve the International until "such time as the Board deems it advisable."

Ella Johnson, secretary-treasurer of the Tampa Auxiliary, thought Tucker did the right thing. "Everything seems to have been fouled [?] up . . . and then Bro. Randolph dismissing us. but was sorry of the stand he took. And 'you' took a stand and saved the Int'l officers from being dismissed. I don't care what any one says, it is had not been for you there wouldn't have been any Int'l for the next three years, I am sure."[23]

Tucker wrote to Randolph to thank him personally for supporting the Auxiliary during the convention. "I was not contending myself, but for the faithful, sincere and devoted members of the local Auxiliaries who had struggled against the odds to discharge extra obligations to the International and for the delegates and friends who had made sacrifices to attend the convention. Your decision to take the leadership in programming for study and action will crystallize the purpose of the entire set-up—men and women."[24] The BSCP executive board gave the Auxiliary another year before deciding its fate.

Although the International Auxiliary survived, President Wilson, recently widowed and in poor health, took a leave of absence at the close of the 1956 convention. Randolph took on her duties, in addition to his steadily growing civil rights activities. The "Dean" of the civil rights movement, at the invitation of Kwame Nkrumah, was on his way to Ghana to celebrate its independence from Britain with Adam Clayton Powell, Ralph Bunche, Mrs. Louis Armstrong, Norman Manley (the future prime minister of the West Indian Federation) and Martin Luther King Jr. Along with his new responsibilities as vice-president of the AFL-CIO, Randolph hardly had time for the BSCP Ladies' Auxiliary.[25]

In July 1957, the BSCP executive board met to reconsider the reorganization plan. The men approved the resolution and authorized Randolph to implement it. With other board members, Randolph visited Wilson in the hospital to discuss her health. "She voluntarily suggested her interest in retiring inasmuch as she needed additional income and was unable to function because of her illness." In a letter to Tucker, he reminded her that she had once expressed interest in retiring as International secretary-treasurer. "I never commented on it at the time but your suggestion is timely," and with her consent, relieved her of her duties.[26]

Tucker's resignation letter, which she sent each local Auxiliary, looked back at the history of the organization and toward its future:

Today, all of us have a broader viewpoint and devotion to organized labor and the people in general have also. Our younger porters' wives however, do not the see the necessity of joining the auxiliaries in their cities because they are doing well, and as the older members retire, there are few replacements. For this reason, and Sister Wilson's illness . . . the International Ladies' Auxiliary [will] be dis-established. . . .

I hope that all your members will remain loyal to the Brotherhood in every respect ever remembering what it has done for your husbands in the line of increased wages, better working conditions and pensions for husband, wife and children. Whatever the future set-up, it is my hope and prayer that all of you will always cooperate with the spirit and fervor exercised by all strong labor unions.[27]

In retirement, the BSCP paid Wilson and Tucker their full salaries (so long as they did not remarry) in addition to the Railroad Retirement benefits to which they were entitled as union officials. Wilson's secretary "married and went away"; Virginia Harris, who had worked as Tucker's secretary since 1947, needed a new job. Randolph placed her, as a typist, at the AFL-CIO headquarters in Washington.[28]

During Randolph's presidency of the Auxiliary, membership did not increase. Although some local Auxiliaries continued meeting until 1971, and worked with the newly merged AFL-CIO Auxiliaries, the BSCP Auxiliary's international structure was never reestablished.

Several factors contributed to the demise of the International Ladies' Auxiliary. The generation gap between the women who organized the Brotherhood of Sleeping Car Porters and the Auxiliary and the younger wives of recently hired porters would have been difficult for any organization to bridge. In addition, Auxiliary officials believed Brotherhood men were not as supportive as they should have been.[29] But blaming husbands or generational differences ignores the organizational problems Wilson dealt with daily. Lack of financial resources hampered the Auxiliary's outreach efforts. Many of the organizing techniques that BSCP officials could undertake without much consideration were too costly for the Auxiliary. Even its best organizing tool, the *Black Worker,* was literally addressed to the BSCP member, not the Auxiliary member. It is not too much to suppose that in some households the husband's paper was not touched until he read it.[30]

All of these circumstances underscore the dependency women had on men, a dependency that became more pronounced over the years. Wilson required Randolph's frequent advice; the International Auxiliary relied on the International Brotherhood for financing; and the local Auxiliaries required the local Brotherhood counselor to cooperate at best, or in the least, an independent woman leader and benign indifference from the men. The constitutional limits the Brotherhood placed on the Auxiliary's independence encouraged women's dependency on men. Several Auxiliary leaders chafed at the control the men exercised, demanding more autonomy and independence in developing a women's program. Tucker exemplified this group. Her work in organizing Pullman porters in the dark days before union recognition and her continued involvement in trade union organizing on behalf of domestic and laundry workers in the 1930s exhibited one version of women's trade unionism. Her major disagreement with the Washington BSCP division was the men's refusal to allow her to participate in union meetings when she felt they violated the union's constitution.[31]

B. J. Tucker refused to support his wife's union work or civic activities, telling her to quit because he felt she was too busy to attend to his needs. Instead Tucker adjusted her work schedule to fit his runs. When this strategy failed, she took extended "vacations" (separations), some lasting two years, living with women friends. In her unpublished autobiography, Tucker spoke against Women's Liberation. She thought "the man should be the head of the household—if he has the ability to do so." Her husband, she continued, did not have the ability. She believed in protectionism, and supported trade unionism because it worked for family and home security.[32]

Halena Wilson shared Tucker's belief in trade unionism; this was one of the few areas of agreement between the two. However, Wilson did not apparently possess Tucker's physical or emotional strength. The International president believed husbands should protect their wives and children through secure unionized jobs. Her class-conscious ideal of housewifery appealed to many African American women in the mid-twentieth century. For a generation of women born to the families of southern migrants and urban poverty, the standard of living union wages permitted was "undreamed of." Even if their material circumstances sometimes belied the definition of a (white) middle-class lifestyle, women of the Brotherhood knew their situation was better than others around them.

Yet this very materialism undermined the future of the Ladies' Auxiliary. Younger wives and BSCP children who came of age after the first contract, as Tucker noted, did not appreciate the very real changes the union had achieved. This new class status also brought porters' wives into contact with other organizations. Tucker complained in 1954, "In some districts, there were members of the Brotherhood and Auxiliary who are neglecting their meetings but spending much time actually meeting with and working for the NAACP and secret [fraternal] organizations and taking part in and contributing to many church activities while they could not attend Brotherhood or Auxiliary meetings once or twice a month."[33] Tucker herself was active in her church, the NAACP, and several civic groups. Wilson was a Worthy Matron in the Order of the Eastern Star, the Masonic Ladies' Auxiliary. Other Auxiliary members were similarly involved, but too few, according to Wilson and Tucker, made the Auxiliary a priority in their lives. Membership in other organizations did not preclude participation in the Brotherhood Auxiliary, but perhaps influenced the women's consciousness of class and social status. "I found, especially among our women, that some consider themselves better than others to the extent that they refuse to join the Auxiliary," observed Tucker.[34]

The children of Brotherhood families reaped the benefits of the union's activism and the material benefits union wages provided. Growing up in comfortable circumstances, they could concentrate on their educations; their families could afford college tuition, making professional careers possible. Many participated in the modern civil rights movement. In Little Rock, Arkansas, Jefferson Thomas, one of the nine African American students to integrate Central High, was the son of a former Pullman porter. Looking for a way to transport the students to school, his father found T. L. Bouleware, a member of the local BSCP. "He was and continues to be happy to assist these children," wrote a member of the support committee to Randolph. "When Mr. Bouleware is out of town, his wife drives the children to school." As these Brotherhood children became adults, the movement forced open doors to educational and employment opportunities their parents never had. New members of the African American professional class could trace their gains to unionized workers, and many prominent leaders grew up in Brotherhood homes.[35]

The modern civil rights movement, arising in a time of prosperity, focused on segregation in public accommodations, although the employment of African Americans remained an issue for demonstrators. For politically minded women of the Brotherhood, the movement offered many opportunities. Randolph himself devoted much of his time to the new civil rights movement, leading new marches on Washington in the summers of 1957, 1958, 1959, and 1963. Auxiliary women were part of these pilgrimages and youth marches, as they were in the first March on Washington. In this way they continued the legacy of activism that had begun in Harlem on August 25, 1925.[36]

Appendix:
BSCP Ladies' Auxiliary Membership, 1940–56

	1940	1944	1945	1946	1947	1948	1949	1950	1951	1952	1953	1956
Eastern Zone												
Albany	12	13	11	12	10	10	—	—	—	—	—	14
Asheville	12	16	17	13	14	12	11	11	13	13	13	19
Atlanta	18	23	—	32	21	6	32	28	29	22	18	19
Augusta	—	11	8	8	—	5	—	—	—	—	—	—
Baltimore	18	16	15	16	13	11	11	15	1	11	12	14
Birmingham	—	—	—	—	—	10	—	—	—	18	9	—
Boston	26	20	6	0	15	9	12	14	13	15	18	15
Buffalo	16	17	5	12	8	9	7	—	25	28	19	—
Charleston	—	15	7	—	—	—	—	—	—	—	—	—
Charlotte	—	—	—	—	—	—	—	—	—	—	15	20
Florence	—	—	—	—	—	—	—	41	16	25	20	14
Jacksonville	24	90	76	75	60	54	49	58	56	54	49	61
Jersey City	31	22	18	19	14	16	18	20	21	23	24	—
Montgomery	—	15	9	7	—	—	—	—	—	—	13	—
New York City	77	66	51	65	43	47	41	55	37	39	32	30
Norfolk	7	—	—	—	0	—	—	0	12	—	—	—
Philadelphia	19	21	15	24	19	25	18	25	29	29	27	26
Richmond	12	13	14	14	8	11	3	2	1	—	8	20
Tampa	14	12	9	11	9	10	9	9	12	—	20	11
Savannah	—	—	—	—	—	—	—	—	8	—	—	—
Washington, D.C.	62	60	57	44	38	31	25	19	—	16	19	—
Detroit Zone												
Cincinnati	26	12	0	4	—	—	—	0	—	—	—	17
Cleveland	27	41	33	39	43	33	28	35	30	26	29	26
Columbus	—	12	12	8	7	9	7	8	7	8	—	—
Detroit	16	—	26	29	29	31	34	33	27	35	38	29
Indianapolis	—	—	8	15	8	9	20	16	15	14	17	17
Louisville	9	—	—	10	0	—	22	23	24	23	—	16
Nashville	—	33	22	32	15	13	12	15	18	21	20	—
Pittsburgh	15	34	20	22	—	—	33	38	40	8	—	42
Calgary	—	—	13	—	—	—	12	8	13	—	—	—
Montreal	—	25	—	6	17	21	24	9	29	—	—	—
Toronto (CPR)	17	33	33	23	26	26	18	14	13	—	—	—
Toronto Pullman	—	6	9	9	12	14	—	6	—	10	13	—
Vancouver	—	9	4	10	8	8	9	6	6	—	—	—
Winnipeg	—	20	11	7	8	—	6	—	9	—	—	—

	1940	1944	1945	1946	1947	1948	1949	1950	1951	1952	1953	1956
Midwestern Zone												
Chicago	134	155	124	129	117	139	111	162	40	110	138	110
Denver	48	79	53	67	30	36	43	57	41	37	29	29
Kansas City[a]	51	—	26	37	34	32	22	25	31	27	29	26
Minneapolis	28	21	23	38	15	18	15	13	16	7	18	18
Omaha	32	36	34	39	35	32	33	—	27	28	31	24
Parson-Denison	—	14	0	13	11	8	7	7	17	13	9	—
St. Paul	34	35	34	45	29	28	19	17	23	26	10	12
Southwestern Zone												
Dallas	16	—	—	16	14	19	13	26	22	39	25	42
Fort Worth	28	45	16	29	39	35	18	—	—	—	—	—
Houston	41	32	27	36	23	16	9	11	6	11	10	16
Little Rock	10	7	—	—	—	—	—	—	—	—	—	—
Memphis	10	20	24	30	15	16	23	22	20	22	19	20
New Orleans	37	—	18	33	25	28	23	28	16	25	24	27
Oklahoma City	14	10	15	11	19	41	20	16	8	17	20	—
Shreveport	—	23	—	12	—	—	9	13	0	—	—	—
St. Louis	27	95	90	79	81	76	62	84	70	80	71	55
San Antonio	46	33	18	14	26	20	9	11	5	6	14	10
Pacific Coast Zone												
Albuquerque	—	—	—	—	—	—	—	—	—	—	12	—
El Paso	—	—	—	—	24	20	13	16	8	18	12	12
Los Angeles	36	51	43	41	29	57	57	30	59	60	91	62
San Francisco	39	24	21	34	37	41	41	51	41	36	47	46
Portland	35	35	28	29	—	44	38	42	42	46	42	39
Salt Lake City	11	8	—	—	—	13	12	9	10	11	13	11
Seattle	13	16	14	11	—	9	8	8	8	—	10	13
Spokane	13	—	—	—	—	—	—	—	—	—	—	—
Tucson	—	16	8	9	6	—	—	—	—	—	—	—
Totals	1163	1402	1136	1360	1071	1129	1099	1257	1008	1185	1102	1058

a. Kansas City, Kansas, and Kansas City, Missouri, combined membership for 1940.

Notes

ACL	Atlantic Coast Line Railroad Company
AFWAL	American Federation of Women's Auxiliaries to Labor
AHR	*American Historical Review*
ALT	Ashley L. Totten
ANYLH	*Afro-Americans in New York Life and History*
APR	A. Philip Randolph
BSCP	Brotherhood of Sleeping Car Porters
CHS/BSCP	Brotherhood of Sleeping Car Porters Papers, Chicago Historical Society, Chicago, Illinois
CLD	C. L. Dellums
CNR	Canadian National Railway
CPR	Canadian Pacific Railway
EJB	E. J. Bradley
FEPC	Fair Employment Practice Committee
FS	*Feminist Studies*
G&H	*Gender & History*
GHQ	*Georgia Historical Quarterly*
GMA	George Meany Memorial Archives, Silver Spring, Maryland
HW	Halena Wilson
IEB	International Executive Board
JAH	*Journal of American History*
JNE	*Journal of Negro Education*
JNH	*Journal of Negro History*
JSoH	*Journal of Social History*
JSH	*Journal of Southern History*
LC/APR	A. Philip Randolph Papers, Manuscript Division, Library of Congress, Washington, D.C.
LC/BSCP	Brotherhood of Sleeping Car Porters Papers, Manuscript Division, Library of Congress, Washington, D.C.
LC/JLR	Joseph L. Rauh Papers, Manuscript Division, Library of Congress, Washington, D.C.
MLR	*Monthly Labor Review*
MOWM	March on Washington Movement
MPW	Milton P. Webster
MSRR	Moorland-Spingarn Reading Room, Howard University, Washington, D.C.

NARA/W   National Archives and Records Administration, Records of the
            Women's Bureau of the U.S. Department of Labor, Record Group
NCNW   Mary McLeod Bethune Museum and Black Women's History Ar-
            chives, Washington, D.C., National Council of Negro Women Papers
NMB   National Mediation Board, Washington, D.C.
NNC   National Negro Congress
PCOP   Pullman Company Records, Newberry Library, Chicago, Illinois
PPBA   Pullman Porters Benefit Association
RCT   Rosina Corrothers Tucker
RCTP   Rosina Corrothers Tucker Papers, Leadership Conference on Civil
            Rights, Washington, D.C.
RHR   *Radical History Review*
SCH/BFM   Benjamin F. McLaurin Papers, Schomburg Center for Black Cul-
            ture, New York, New York
SCH/BSCP   Brotherhood of Sleeping Car Porters Papers, Schomburg Center for
            Black Culture, New York, New York
SCH/RCT   Rosina Corrothers Tucker Papers, Schomburg Center for Black Cul-
            ture, New York, New York
SI/NMAH   Smithsonian Institution Archives, National Museum of American
            History, Washington, D.C.
SI/OFP   Smithsonian Institution, Office of Folklife Programs, Washington,
            D.C.
TTP   Thomas T. Patterson
UCB/BSCP   Brotherhood of Sleeping Car Porters Papers, The Bancroft Library,
            University of California, Berkeley, California
UCB/CLD   C. L. Dellums Papers, The Bancroft Library, University of Califor-
            nia, Berkeley, California
UP   Union Pacific Railroad Company

Preface

1. Rosina Corrothers Tucker, "Marching Together" (n.p., 1939), RCTP.
2. See, for example, Linda Faye Williams, "Power and Gender: A Glass Ceiling Limits the Role of Black Women in the Civil Rights Community," *Emerge* 6 (Dec./ Jan. 1995) 3: 63–65; Myrlie Evers Williams's recent inauguration as Chair of the Board of the NAACP was held on Mother's Day 1995.

Introduction

1. "A Brief History of the Organizing of the Brotherhood of Sleeping Car Por-ters, an International Union" [mimeo], n.d., SCH/BSCP Box 87-53, was considered the union's official version; Brailsford Brazeal, *The Brotherhood of Sleeping Car Por-ters: Its Origin and Development* (New York: Harper and Brothers, 1946), 211ff., iden-tifies T. T. Patterson as author. Other versions include: "President Randolph's Third National Report to the BSCP," n.d. [1928], LC/APR Box 10; "Fifteenth Anniversa-

ry and First Biennial Convention of the Brotherhood of Sleeping Car Porters, Souvenir Program," Sept. 15, 1940, RCTP; APR to B. F. McLaurin, May 25, 1944, LC/APR Box 7; V. I. Petgrave, "A Saga of the Sleeping Car Porters of the Canadian Pacific Railway Company," *Black Worker* (May 1945): 3; untitled film script, ca. April 1948, and film strip script, "Brotherhood of Sleeping Car Porters," Nov. 1949, UCB/CLD Box 4; EJB, "Some of My Early Experiences Organizing Pullman Porters in St. Louis," n.d.; "The Brotherhood of Sleeping Car Porters," n.d. [ca. 1965], both LC/APR Box 10; RCT to BSCP International Program Committee, May 10, 1954, LC/BSCP Box 75. Local versions include: "Thirty-Sixth Anniversary Celebration, Chicago Division, BSCP," Aug. 21–25, 1961, LC/APR Box 10; "History of Train and Mail Porters Local #6 Richmond, Va.," n.d. [ca. 1975], LC/APR Box 10; "Los Angeles, California," n.d., UCB/CLD Box 24. Joseph F. Wilson, *Tearing Down the Color Bar: An Analysis and Documentary History of the Brotherhood of Sleeping Car Porters* (New York: Columbia University Press, 1989), apparently took the story as truth, 19–26; for stories told at BSCP functions see 114, 119–21, 148–50.

2. Compare, for example, Brazeal, *The Brotherhood,* with Jack Santino, *Miles of Smiles, Years of Struggle: Stories of Black Pullman Porters* (Urbana: University of Illinois Press, 1989). Brazeal uses "porters and maids" routinely and discusses the role of the BSCP Ladies' Auxiliary. Santino's study of porters' folklore discusses the men and one porter's wife, International Ladies' Auxiliary Secretary-Treasurer Rosina Corrothers Tucker. Pullman maids are absent, as though the job never existed. EJB, "Some of My Early Experiences"; Ashley L. Totten, *Report of the Proceedings of the Seventh Biennial Convention of the Ladies Auxiliary . . . , 1950,* 156–57; K. Sue Jewell, *From Mammy to Miss America and Beyond: Cultural Images and the Shaping of U.S. Social Policy* (New York: Routledge, 1993), 37–45; Patricia Morton, *Disfigured Images: The Historical Assault on Afro-American Women* (Westport, Conn.: Greenwood Press, 1991), 1–16, 87–97; Barbara Christian, *Black Feminist Criticism: Perspectives on Black Women Writers* (New York: Pergamon Press, 1985), 1–30; Hazel V. Carby, *Reconstructing Womanhood: The Emergence of the Afro-American Woman Novelist* (New York: Oxford University Press, 1987).

3. J. W. Stanley to CLD, April 2, 1940, and CLD to C. Beridon, Feb. 18, 1939, UCB/CLD Box 6. For the Auxiliary's history, see "Declaration of the Object, Principles and Aims of the Ladies' Auxiliary to the Brotherhood of Sleeping Car Porters," n.d. but marked "1942," CHS/BSCP Box 28; another version, dated 1951, CHS/BSCP Box 33; W. B. Holland to APR, Dec. 10, 1939, UCB/CLD Box 5; HW to Mrs. Velmer King, Apr. 1, 1948, CHS/BSCP Box 31; LC/BSCP Box 75; "A Brief History of the Ladies' Auxiliary to the BSCP," Oct. 22, 1954, RCTP. The history of the Auxiliary and of the BSCP was regularly told during union meetings, as reports from local groups in the *Black Worker* from 1935 onward reveal. RCT, "My Life As I Have Lived It," [ca. 1980], RCTP. President Wilson made a special appeal for all local auxiliaries to write articles detailing their history: HW to all Auxiliaries, n.d. but ca. June 1951, CHS/BSCP Box 33.

4. Among U.S. trade unions, the BSCP Auxiliary was the largest composed of African American women almost exclusively. While the other African American railway brotherhoods had auxiliaries, none had chapters outside the United States; the BSCP Auxiliary had five Canadian divisions.

5. Sharon Harley, "When Your Work Is Not Who You Are: The Development

of a Working-Class Consciousness among Afro-American Women," in Noralee Frankel and Nancy S. Dye, eds., *Gender, Race, and Class in the Progressive Era* (Lexington: University Press of Kentucky, 1991), 42–55; Evelyn Brooks-Higginbotham, *Righteous Discontent: The Women's Movement in the Black Baptist Church, 1880–1920* (Cambridge, Mass.: Harvard University Press, 1993), 185–229; Elizabeth Faue, *Community of Suffering and Struggle: Women, Men and the Labor Movement in Minneapolis, 1915–1945* (Chapel Hill: University of North Carolina Press, 1991), 47–68; *Black Worker* (Aug. 1945): 3; see also Angela Y. Davis, "Reflections on the Black Woman's Role in the Community of Slaves," *Black Scholar* 3 (Dec. 1971): 2–15.

6. International Ladies' Auxiliary Bulletin, Oct. 10, 1940, LC/BSCP Box 74; Carl Degler, *At Odds: Women and the Family in America from the Revolution to the Present* (New York: Oxford University Press, 1980), 401–5; Alice Kessler-Harris, *Out to Work: A History of Wage-Earning Women* (New York: Oxford University Press, 1982), 180–214; Lynn Y. Weiner, *From Working Girl to Working Mother: The Female Labor Force in the United States, 1820–1980* (Chapel Hill: University of North Carolina Press, 1985), 68–78; Joan Hoff, *Law, Gender and Justice: A Legal History of U.S. Women* (New York: New York University Press, 1991), 197–206; Karen Tucker Anderson, "Last Hired, First Fired: Black Women Workers during World War II," *JAH* 69 (June 1982): 82–97; Patricia Cooper, "The Faces of Gender: Sex Segregation and Work Relations at Philco, 1928–1938," in Ava Baron, ed., *Work Engendered: Toward a New History of American Labor* (Ithaca: Cornell University Press, 1991), 320–50; Mary H. Blewett, *Men, Women, and Work: Class, Gender, and Protest in the New England Shoe Industry, 1780–1910* (Urbana: University of Illinois Press, 1988), 275–76, 288–91; Maurine Weiner Greenwald, *Women, War and Work: The Impact of World War I on Women Workers in the United States* (1980; reprint, Ithaca: Cornell Paperbacks, 1990), 87–138; Nancy F. Gabin, *Feminism and the Labor Movement: Women and the United Auto Workers, 1935–1975* (Ithaca: Cornell University Press, 1990), 42–46, 111–42; Ruth Milkman, *Gender at Work: The Dynamics of Job Segregation by Sex during World War II* (Urbana: University of Illinois Press, 1987); Susan Levine, *Labor's True Woman: Carpet Weavers, Industrialization, and Labor Reform in the Gilded Age* (Philadelphia: Temple University Press, 1984), 103–28; Cheryl Townsend Gilkes, "'Liberated to Work Like Dogs!': Labeling Black Women and Their Work," in Nia Lane Chester and Hildy Grossman, eds., *The Experience and Meaning of Work for Women* (Hillsdale, N.J.: Lawrence Earlbaun Assoc., 1989), 165–88.

7. Jewell, *From Mammy to Miss America,* 37–45; Morton, *Disfigured Images,* 1–16, 87–97; Barbara Bair, "True Women, Real Men: Gender, Ideology, and Social Roles in the Garvey Movement," in Dorothy O. Helly and Susan M. Reverby, eds., *Gendered Domains: Rethinking Public and Private in Women's History* (Ithaca: Cornell University Press, 1992), 109–21; Ruth Feldstein, "'I Wanted the Whole World to See': Race, Gender, and Constructions of Motherhood in the Death of Emmett Till," in Linda Meyerowitz, ed., *Not June Cleaver: Women and Gender in Postwar America, 1945–1960* (Philadelphia: Temple University Press, 1994), 263–303; Linda Gordon, "Putting Children First: Women, Maternalism, and Welfare in the Early Twentieth Century," in Linda K. Kerber et al., eds., *U.S. History as Women's History: New Feminist Essays* (Chapel Hill: University of North Carolina Press, 1994), 63–88; Linda K. Kerber, *Women of the Republic: Intellect and Ideology in Revolution-*

ary America (Chapel Hill: University of North Carolina Press, 1980), 283–87; Susan Miller Okin, *Women in Western Political Thought* (Princeton, N.J.: Princeton University Press, 1979), 227–29, 238–45.

8. Mary Frances Berry and John W. Blassingame, *Long Memory: The Black Experience in America* (New York: Oxford University Press, 1982), 172–76, 409–15; Bair, "True Women, Real Men"; Henry Louis Gates Jr., "The Trope of the New Negro and the Reconstruction of the Image of the Black," *Representations* 24 (Fall 1988): 129–54; Wilfred D. Samuels, "Hubert H. Harrison and 'The New Negro Manhood Movement,'" *ANYLH* 5 (Jan. 1981): 28–40; Mindy Thompson, "The National Negro Labor Council: A History," Occasional Paper No. 27 (New York: American Institute for Marxist Studies, 1978).

9. David Walker and Henry Highland Garnet, *Walker's Appeal in Four Articles . . . And also Garnet's Address to the Slaves of the United States of America* (1829, 1848; reprint, New York: Arno Press, 1969); Frederick Engels, *The Origin of the Family, Private Property and the State,* ed. Eleanor Burke Leacock (New York: International Publishers, 1972); Okin, *Women in Western Political Thought;* Peggy Reeves Sanday, *Female Power and Male Dominance: On the Origins of Sexual Inequality* (New York: Cambridge University Press, 1981); Kamen Okonjo, "Women's Political Participation in Nigeria," in *The Black Woman Cross-Culturally,* ed. Filomena Chioma Steady (Boston: Schenkman, 1981), 79–106; Barbara J. Fields, "Ideology and Race in American History," in J. Morgan Kousser and James M. McPherson, eds., *Region, Race, and Reconstruction: Essays in Honor of C. Vann Woodward* (New York: Oxford University Press, 1982), 143–77; W. E. B. Du Bois, "The Niagara Movement," in *W. E. B. Du Bois Speaks: Speeches and Address, 1890–1919,* ed. Philip S. Foner (New York: Pathfinder Press, 1970), 170; letterhead, East Bay Council of the National Negro Congress, n.d., UCB/CLD Box 23; E. Franklin Frazier, *The Negro Family in the United States* (Chicago: University of Chicago Press, 1939; reprint, 1966), 227.

10. Earle Thorpe, *The Central Theme of Black History* (Durham, N.C.: Seeman Printery, 1969), 3–17; Gail Bederman, "Civilization, the Decline of Middle-Class Manliness, and Ida B. Wells' Anti-Lynching Campaign (1892–94)," in Barbara Melosh, ed., *Gender and American History since 1890* (New York: Routledge, 1993), 207–39; Kevin Gaines, "De-Naturalizing Race and Patriarchy: Black Women and Black-Class 'Uplift' Ideology," unpublished paper, copy in author's possession.

11. David Montgomery, *Workers' Control in America* (New York: Cambridge University Press, 1988), 12–14; Paula Baker, *The Moral Frameworks of Public Life: Gender, Politics, and the State in Rural New York, 1870–1930* (New York: Oxford University Press, 1991), 28–32; David R. Roediger, *The Wages of Whiteness: Race and the Making of the American Working Class* (New York: Verso, 1991), 11–13; Eileen Boris, "'A Man's Dwelling House Is His Castle': Tenement House Cigarmaking and the Judicial Imperative," in Baron, ed., *Work Engendered,* 114–41; Steven Maynard, "Rough Work and Rugged Man: The Social Construction of Masculinity in Working Class History," *Labour/LeTravail* 23 (Spring 1989): 159–69; James H. Ducker, *Men of the Steel Rails: Workers on the Atchison, Topeka & Santa Fe Railroad, 1869–1900* (Lincoln: University of Nebraska Press, 1983), 104–25; Paul M. Taillon, "'By Every Tradition and Every Right': Fraternalism and Racism in the Railway Brotherhoods, 1880–1910," paper presented at the American Studies Association Annual Meeting, Baltimore, Maryland, Nov. 1, 1991; William H. Harris, *Keeping the Faith: A. Philip*

Randolph, Milton P. Webster, and the Brotherhood of Sleeping Car Porters, 1925-37 (Urbana: University of Illinois Press, 1977, 1991), 14; Howard W. Risher Jr., *The Negro in the Railroad Industry,* Report No. 16 (Philadelphia: Wharton School of Finance and Commerce, University of Pennsylvania, 1971), 459, 164-65; see also Nick Salvatore, *Eugene V. Debs: Citizen and Socialist* (Bloomington: Indiana University Press, 1982), 171, 228-30.

12. Ducker, *Men of the Steel Rails,* 129-33; Sterling D. Spero and Abram L. Harris, *The Black Worker: The Negro and the Labor Movement* (1931; reprint, New York: Antheneum, 1969), 284-315 (quote, p. 288); Herbert R. Northrup, *Organized Labor and the Negro* (New York: Harper & Brothers, 1944), 1-8; David Gordon, Richard Edwards, and Michael Reich, *Segmented Work, Divided Workers: The Historical Transformation of Labor in the United States* (Cambridge: Cambridge University Press, 1982); Mary Ann Clawson, *Constructing Brotherhood: Class, Gender, and Fraternalism* (Princeton, N.J.: Princeton University Press, 1989), 136-44; and "Nineteenth Century Women's Auxiliaries and Fraternal Orders," *Signs* 12 (Winter 1986): 40-61.

13. Jervis B. Anderson, *A. Philip Randolph: A Biographical Portrait* (1973; reprint, Berkeley: University of California Press, 1986), 9; Greg LeRoy, "The Founding Heart of A. Philip Randolph's Union: Milton P. Webster and Chicago's Pullman Porters Organize, 1925-1927," *Labor's Heritage* 3:3 (1991): 34-35; "Oath," n.d., UCB/CLD Box 24; "National Convention," press release, n.d. (ca. 1929), UCB/CLD Box 10; "Opening Local Divisions," n.d. (ca. July 2, 1952), UCB/CLD Box 6; see also invitation, "Thirteenth Annual Winter Dance [New York Division]," 1938, UCB/CLD Box 24; ALT to CLD, Oct. 21, 1939, UCB/CLD Box 3; CLD to C. L. Upton, Nov. 6, 1939, UCB/CLD Box 30; APR and CLD were Masons, while HW and other Auxiliary women were members of the order of the Eastern Star.

I identified only three women Brotherhood officials: Mrs. Oneida M. Brown served as secretary of the New Orleans local from early 1926 through at least 1929; "Mrs. Olds" served as secretary under President Frank Boyd of St. Paul in 1930; Mrs. Anna R. Hughes served as acting secretary-treasurer of the Louisville local until 1940. Hughes was appointed apparently because she was also secretary-treasurer of the Ladies' Auxiliary. Note that all of these married women were secretaries, a possibly ambiguous term. For perhaps ten years, Dorothy Allison collected dues at New York's Mott Haven Yards, *Black Worker* (Jan. 1948): 4; Edith Childs was managing editor of the *Black Worker* during World War II; Ashley Totten to "Secretary-Treasurers," May 12, 1942, CHS/BSCP Box 7.

14. Robin Winks, *The Blacks in Canada: A History* (Montreal: McGill-Queen's University Press, and New Haven: Yale University Press, 1971), 426; Samuels, "Hubert H. Harrison"; *Messenger* 9 (1926): 325.

15. Elizabeth Clark-Lewis, *Living In, Living Out: African American Domestics in Washington, D.C., 1910-1940* (Washington, D.C.: Smithsonian Institute Press, 1995), 147-72; CLD to C. Beridon, Feb. 18, 1939; CLD to Charles Upton, July 19, 1939, UCB/CLD Box 5; Carroll Smith-Rosenberg, "The New Woman as Androgyne: Social Disorder and Gender Crisis, 1870-1936," in *Disorderly Conduct: Visions of Gender in Victorian America* (New York: Oxford University Press, 1985), 246.

16. *Messenger* 10 (1927): 204; see also Carole Pateman, *The Sexual Contract* (Cambridge, England: Polity Press, 1988).

17. Sanday, *Female Power,* 28–33, passim; Niara Sudarkasa, "'The Status of Women' in Indigeneous African Societies," and Rosalyn Terborg-Penn, "African Feminism: A Theoretical Approach to the History of Women in the African Diaspora," in Terborg-Penn et al., eds., *Women in Africa and the African Diaspora* (Washington, D.C.: Howard University Press, 1987), 25–42, 43–64; Cheryl Townsend Gilkes, "'Together and in Harness': Women's Traditions in the Sanctified Church," in Micheline R. Malson et al., eds., *Black Women in America: Social Science Perspectives* (Chicago: University of Chicago Press, 1990), 223–44.

18. [Patterson], "Brief History"; Santino, *Miles of Smiles,* 33–60; *The Pullman Porter* (New York: Brotherhood of Sleeping Car Porters, 1927), 6; Anderson, *A. Philip Randolph,* 83, 140–41, 154–55; APR, "The Case of the Pullman Porter," *Messenger* 8 (1925): 254–55.

19. Anderson, *A. Philip Randolph,* 69–73. Lucille Randolph's career has been misrepresented by her husband's biographers. Her death certificate, LC/APR Box 1, and Paula F. Pfeffer, *A. Philip Randolph, Pioneer of the Civil Rights Movement* (Baton Rouge: Louisiana State University Press, 1990), describe her as a school teacher, but she retired in 1910 and spent the next fifty-three years in a variety of jobs and civic work. Theodore Kornweibel, *No Crystal Stair: Black Life and the Messenger, 1917–1928* (Westport, Conn.: Greenwood Press, 1975), 30, 53, describes Lucille Randolph as New York City's first black social worker. Peter Wallenstein offers new early details, but erroneously states she spent her later years working with porters' wives, "Lucille Campbell Green Randolph," s.v., *Black Women in America,* ed. Darlene Clark Hine (Brooklyn, N.Y.: Carlson Publishing Co., 1993). She is listed as a member of the New York City Board of Education in the *Black Worker* (Oct. 1947): 2; Philip Randolph mentions her activities in the American Labor Party and her work to elect Maida Springer [Kemp] to Congress, APR to Mrs. George Phillips, Mar. 3, 1943, LC/BSCP Box 73; Anderson, *A. Philip Randolph,* 18–20, 69–73, 78, 82.

20. William Dufty to Editor, *New York Times,* Apr. 16, 1963, copy in LC/BSCP Box 11.

21. [APR], "BSCP" Outline, n.d., LC/APR Box 10; Rayford W. Logan, "Ashley L. Totten," s.v., *Dictionary of American Negro Biography;* David Levering Lewis, *When Harlem Was in Vogue* (1979; reprint, New York: Oxford University Press, 1981), 217–18; Anderson, *A. Philip Randolph,* 17, 153–55, 175; Patricia McKissack and Fredrick McKissack, *A Long Hard Journey: The Story of the Pullman Porter* (New York: Walker, 1989), 56, 83.

22. *Messenger* 1 (1917): 6; *Messenger* 11 (1928): 5; Kornweibel, *No Crystal Stair,* 79; Program for Second Anniversary Ball [1926], LC/BSCP Box 54. See also APR, "The Negro and the New Social Order," *Messenger* 2 (1918): 9; APR, "The New Negro: What Is He?" *Messenger* 2 (1920): 73.

23. "Winners in Bobbed Hair Contest Held at Manhattan Casino . . . Dec. 3, 1926," and A. Sagittarius, "Bobbed Hair Contest," *Messsenger* 9 (1927): 29; "Dressed Head Contest," in "Souvenir Program, Third Annual Ball of the Brotherhood of Sleeping Car Porters, Dec. 17, 1928," LC/APR Box 54; "Bobbed Hair and Bobbed Brains," *Messenger* 8 (1926): 112. Randolph's partner, Chandler Owen, railed against "Bobbed Hair": "This feminine revolt . . . against masculine tyranny . . . has proceeded beyond necessary limits. . . . All in all the bobbed hair craze seems to be but a reflection of the general tendency of the women to become more masculine

and the men to become more feminine. . . . The feminine women will like the masculine men, while the masculine men will like the feminine women." *Messenger* 8 (1925): 139–40.

24. Program for Second Anniversary Ball [1926], LC/BSCP Box 54; Naomi DesVerney, "Speech Made at Second Anniversary in New York City," *Messenger* 9 (1926): 40, 45; Alice Kessler-Harris, *Out to Work: A History of Wage-Earning Women in the United States* (New York: Oxford University Press, 1982), 189–91. Incidents of sexual harassment by union members of female BSCP office workers were dealt with immediately and harshly by officials: see for example, MPW to APR, Sept. 3, 1926, CHS/BSCP Box 1; Chas. Upton to CLD, April 25, [1939?], UCB/CLD Box 5.

25. Christine S. Smith, "Negro Womanhood's Greatest Needs," *Messenger* 10 (1927): 198. Dorothy M. Brown, *Setting a Course: American Women in the 1920s* (Boston: Twayne Publishers, 1987), 42, discusses this issue of the *Messenger* but ignores the conflict of opinion between Randolph and clubwomen.

26. Smith, "Negro Womanhood's Greatest Needs," *Messenger* 10 (1927): 272, 285, 288. See also columns by Alice Dunbar-Nelson, "Woman's Most Serious Problem," *Messenger* 10 (1927): 73; and "The Negro Woman and the Ballot," ibid., 111.

27. Mattie Mae Stafford, "Colored Women's Economic Council of Los Angeles," *Messenger* 11 (1928): 15; Philip S. Foner, *Women and the American Labor Movement: From the First Trade Unions to the Present* (New York: The Free Press, 1982), 294n, refers to Stafford as "Hatford"; *Black Worker* (Oct. 1951): 7.

28. Henry Epstein to APR, May 9, 1952, LC/BSCP Box 57; New Orleans Public Library, Louisiana Division, New Orleans, Lousiana, Louisiana Biography and Obituary Index.

29. Harley, "When Your Work Is Not Who You Are," 42; Bureau of the Census, *Population: Families; Types of Families, Size of Family and Age of Head, Employment Status, and Family Wage or Salary Income in 1939* (Washington, D.C.: Government Printing Office, 1943), table 14; Stephanie Coontz, *The Way We Never Were: American Families and the Nostalgia Trap* (New York: Basic Books, 1992), 241–46; Evelyn Brooks-Higginbotham, "Beyond the Sound of Silence: Afro-American Women's History," *G&H* 1 (1989): 50–67.

30. Representative social science literature on "Negro Pathology," begins with E. Franklin Frazier, *The Negro Family in the United States* (Chicago: University of Chicago Press, 1948, 1966); see also Office of Policy Planning and Research, U.S. Dept. of Labor [Daniel Patrick Moynihan], "The Negro Family: The Case for National Action" (Washington, D.C.: Government Printing Office, Mar. 1965); Washington, D.C., trade unionist and public school teacher Mary Mason Jones repeated Frazier's thesis in "The Negro Woman as a Factor in the Economic Life of America," *Black Worker* (Aug. 1938): 2. Critiques abound; among them: Hortense Powdermaker, *After Freedom* (1939; reprint, Madison: University of Wisconsin Press, 1993); Gunnar Myrdal et al., "The Negro Family," *An American Dilemma: The Negro Problem and Modern Democracy* (New York: Harper & Bros, 1944), 927–35; Melville Herskovits, *The Myth of the Negro Past* (New York: Harper & Row, 1941); Frantz Fanon, *Black Skin, White Masks* (1952; New York: Grove Press, 1967), 83–108; Andrew Billingsley, *Black Families in White America* (Englewood Cliffs, N.J.: Prentice-Hall, Inc., 1968); William H. Grier and Price M. Cobbs, *Black Rage* (New York: Bantam Books, 1968); Davis, "Reflections on the Black Woman's Role"; Robert Sta-

ples, "The Myth of the Black Matriarchy," *Black Scholar* 2:1 (Jan./Feb. 1970): 8–16; Joyce A. Ladner, *Tomorrow's Tomorrow: The Black Woman* (Garden City, N.Y.: Anchor Press, 1971); see also John Bracey et al., eds., *The Black Sociologists: The First Half Century* (Belmont, Calif.: Wadsworth Publishing Co., 1971), and *Black Matriarchy: Myth or Reality?* (Belmont, Calif.: Wadsworth Publishing Co., 1971); Carol B. Stack, *All Our Kin: Strategies for Survival in a Black Community* (New York: Harper and Row, 1974); Christine Farnham, "Sapphire?: The Issue of Dominance in the Slave Family, 1830–1865," in Carol Groneman and Mary Beth Norton, eds., *"To Toil the Livelong Day": America's Women at Work, 1780–1980: Essays from the Sixth Berkshire Conference on the History of Women* (Ithaca: Cornell University Press, 1987), 68–83; Okin, *Women in Western Political Thought,* 238–46.

31. Harley, "When Your Work Is Not Who You Are"; Brooks-Higginbotham, "African-American Women's History and the Metalanguage of Race," and Elsa Barkley Brown, "'What Has Happened Here': The Politics of Difference in Women's History and Feminist Politics," in Darlene Clark Hine et al., eds., *"We Specialize in the Wholly Impossible": A Reader in Black Women's History* (Brooklyn, N.Y.: Carlson Publishing, 1995), 3–24, 39–56; Delores Janiewski, "Learning to Live 'Just Like White Folks': Gender, Ethnicity, and the State in the Inland Northwest," in Groneman and Norton, eds., *"To Toil the Livelong Day,"* 167–80; Peggy Pascoe, "Gender Systems in Conflict: The Marriages of Mission-Educated Chinese American Women, 1874–1939," and George J. Sanchez, "'Go After the Women': Americanization and the Mexican Immigrant Woman, 1915–1929," in Ellen Carol DuBois, and Vicki L. Ruiz, eds., *Unequal Sisters: A Multi-Cultural Reader in U.S. Women's History* (New York: Routledge, Chapman & Hall, Inc., 1990), 139–56, 284–97; Sarah Deutsch, *No Separate Refuge: Culture, Class, and Gender on an Anglo-Hispanic Frontier in the American Southwest, 1880–1940* (New York: Oxford University Press, 1987); Morton, *Disfigured Images,* 87–97; Jewell, *From Mammy to Miss America,* 142–61; Susan Willis, "I Shop Therefore I Am: Is there a Place for Afro-American Culture in Commodity Culture?" in Cheryl A. Wall, ed., *Changing Our Own Words: Essays on Criticism, Theory, and Writing by Black Women* (New Brunswick, N.J.: Rutgers University Press, 1989), 173–82; Carole Turbin, "Reconceptualizing Family, Work, and Labor Organizing: Working Women in Troy, 1860–1890," *Review of Radical Political Economics* 16 (1984): 1–16; Wilson Jeremiah Moses, *The Golden Age of Black Nationalism, 1850–1925* (New York: Oxford University Press, 1978, 1988), 103–31; Diane K. Lewis, "Response to Inequality: Black Women, Racism, and Sexism"; Bonnie Thornton Dill, "The Dialectics of Black Womanhood"; Sharon Harley, "'For the Good of Family and Race': Gender, Work and Domestic Roles in the Black Community, 1880–1930"; Deborah K. King, "Multiple Jeopardy, Multiple Consciousness: The Context of Black Feminist Ideology"; Patricia Hill Collins, "The Social Construction of Black Feminist Thought," all in Malson et al., eds., *Black Women in America,* 41–64, 65–78, 159–72, 265–96, 297–325; David T. Wellman, *Portraits of White Racism,* 2d. ed. (New York: Cambridge University Press, 1993); CLD to MPW, Mar. 29, 1939, UCB/CLD Box 4; Chas. Upton to CLD, Oct. 15, 1939, and Chas. Upton to CLD, Nov. 12, 1939, both in UCB/CLD Box 5; Edw. Melton to CLD, Jan. 13, 1944, UCB/CLD Box 33; Amanda Riley to CLD, April 3, 1945, UCB/CLD Box 7; Anthony Smith to CLD, Oct. 12, 1949, and Edw. Melton to CLD, Feb. 27, 1951, UCB/CLD Box 6; J. J. Johnson and J. W. Strong to APR, June 2, 1943, CHS/

BSCP Box 7; HW to Bennie Smith, July 11, 1951, CHS/BSCP Box 33; HW to CLD, Nov. 30, 1954, UCB/CLD Box 9.

32. Carroll Smith-Rosenberg, "The Female World of Love and Ritual," *Signs* 1 (1975): 1–42; Nancy F. Cott, *The Bonds of Womanhood: "Women's Sphere" in New England, 1780–1835* (New Haven: Yale University Press, 1977); Linda Kerber, "Separate Spheres, Female Worlds, Woman's Place: The Rhetoric of Women's History," *JAH* 75 (1988): 9–39; Nancy Hewitt, "Beyond the Search for Sisterhood: Women's History in the 1980s," *JSoH* 10 (1985): 299–321; Karen Offen, "Defining Feminism: A Comparative Historical Perspective," *Signs* 14 (1988): 119–57; Cheryl Townsend Gilkes, "Black Women's Work as Deviance: Social Sources of Racial Antagonism within Contemporary Feminism," Working Paper No. 66 (Wellesley, Mass.: Wellesley College Center for Research on Women, 1979).

33. Rosina Tucker, *Report of the Proceedings of the First National Convention of the Ladies Auxiliary, 1938,* 28; "H. Wilson" to Editor of *Labor,* Oct. 31, 1946, CHS/BSCP Box 5.

34. *Black Worker* (Mar. 1938): 2; St. Clair Drake and Horace Cayton, *Black Metropolis: A Study of Negro Life in a Northern City,* rev. and enl. ed. (1945; reprint, New York: Harcourt, Brace, and World, Inc., 1962), 641–42; "A. P. Randolph to Speak at Truth Seeker: Spingarn Award Winner on 2nd Anniversary Program," unidentified clipping, n.d. (ca. Mar. 28, 1942), in CHS/BSCP FEPC Scrapbook; "Souvenir Program, Brotherhood of Sleeping Car Porters Silver Jubilee Anniversary and Seventh Biennial Convention," Sept. 10, 1950, RCTP; HW to Lucille Coward, Sept. 18, 1951; HW to M. L. Stillerman, Mar. 11, 1952, both in CHS/BSCP Box 33; Auxiliary members questioned Wilson's and Tucker's salaries, an indication that they, too, did not see the International officers as workers, see CLD to APR, Mar. 28, 1939, UCB/CLD Box 4.

35. RCT, "My Life"; Santino, *Miles of Smiles,* misspells Tucker's name as "Coruthers." Richard Yarborough, "James D. Corrothers," s.v., *Dictionary of Literary Biography* 50 (Detroit, Mich.: Gale Research Co., 1984); Kevin Gaines, "Assimilationist Minstrelsy as Racial Uplift Ideology: James D. Corrothers's Literary Quest for Black Leadership," *American Quarterly* 45 (Sept. 1993): 341–69; and Gaines, "De-Naturalizing Race and Patriarchy." RCT often recited Corrothers's poetry, particularly "At the Closed Gates of Justice," at Auxiliary events (see misc. speeches, RCTP).

36. APR to Mrs. Brooklyn Lassiter, May 12, 1932, CHS/BSCP Box 4; MPW to CLD, July 14, 1939, UCB/CLD Box 4; APR to CLD, Feb. 14, 1940, UCB/CLD Box 4; Mrs. E. D. Nixon to APR, Dec. 19, 1951, LC/BSCP Box 85; Cora Stewart to CLD, Feb. 12, 1953, UCB/CLD Box 8; May [Mrs. Preston] Davie to Katherine Lassiter, Nov. 19, 1946, CHS/BSCP Box 30; "Meet the Family of Porter J. L. Caviness," *Pullman News* (Oct. 1948): 34–35; APR to Mrs. William [Nora] Fant, telegram, May 29 [1949?], LC/BSCP Box 73; MPW to APR, Mar. 9, 1928, CHS/BSCP Box 3; APR to Sara Harper, Sept. 2, 1946, LC/BSCP Box 74.

37. On shifting definitions of womanhood, see William H. Chafe, *Women and Equality: Changing Patterns in American Culture* (New York: Oxford University Press, 1977); Elise Johnson MacDougald, "The Task of Negro Womanhood," in Alain Locke, ed., *The New Negro* (1925; reprint, New York: Atheneum, 1969), 369–84; Smith-Rosenberg, "The New Woman as Androgyne"; Dorothy M. Brown, *Setting a Course: American Women in the 1920s* (Boston: Twayne Publishers, 1987); Nancy

Cott, *The Grounding of Modern Feminism* (New Haven: Yale University Press, 1987);
Blanche Weisen Cook, *Eleanor Roosevelt*, vol. 1 (New York: Viking, 1992); Jesse M.
Rodrique, "The Black Community and the Birth-Control Movement," in DuBois
and Ruiz, eds., *Unequal Sisters*, 333–44; Jacquelyn Dowd Hall, *Revolt against Chiv-
alry: Jessie Daniel Ames and the Women's Campaign against Lynching* (New York:
Columbia University Press, 1979). On the Depression: Julia Kirk Blackwelder, *Wom-
en of the Depression: Caste and Culture in San Antonio, 1929–1939* (College Station:
Texas A & M Press, 1984); Lois Scharf, *To Work and to Wed: Female Employment, Feminism, and the Great Depression* (Westport, Conn.: Greenwood Press, 1981); Winifred Wandersee, "The Economics of Middle-Income Family Life: Working Wom-
en during the Great Depression," in Lois Scharf and Joan M. Jensen, eds., *Decades
of Discontent: The Women's Movement, 1920–1940*, 2d ed. (Boston: Northeastern
University Press, 1983, 1987), 45–58; Susan Ware, *Beyond Suffrage: Women in the New
Deal* (Cambridge: Harvard University Press, 1981), and *Holding Their Own: American Women in the 1930s* (Boston: Twayne Publishers, 1982); Sharon Hartman Strom,
"Challenging 'Woman's Place': Feminism, the Left, and Industrial Unionism in the
1930s," *Feminist Studies* 9 (Summer 1983): 359–86. On World War II, see Karen
Anderson, *Wartime Women: Sex Roles, Family Relations, and the Status of Women
during World War II* (Westport, Conn.: Greenwood Press, 1981); Margaret Randolph
Higonnet et al., eds., *Behind the Lines: Gender and the Two World Wars* (New Haven:
Yale University Press, 1987); Maureen Honey, *Creating Rosie the Riveter: Class, Gen-
der, and Propaganda during World War II* (Amherst: University of Massachusetts
Press, 1984); Milkman, *Gender at Work;* Nancy Gabin, "They Have Placed a Penal-
ty on Womanhood: The Protest Actions of Women Auto Workers in Detroit-Area
UAW Locals, 1945–1947," *Feminist Studies* 8 (Summer 1982): 373–98. On consum-
erism, see Darlene Clark Hine, "The Housewives' League of Detroit: Black Women
and Economic Nationalism," in Nancy Hewitt and Suzanne Lebsock, eds., *Visible
Women: New Essays on American History* (Urbana: University of Illinois Press, 1993),
199–222; Rayna Rapp and Ellen Ross, "The 1920s: Feminism, Consumerism and
Political Backlash," in Judith Friedlander et al., eds., *Women in Culture and Politics:
A Century of Change* (Bloomington: Indiana University Press, 1986), 52–61; Ron
Rothbart, "'Homes Are What Any Strike is About': Immigrant Labor the Family
Wage," *JSoH* (Winter 1989): 267–84; Dana Frank, "Housewives, Socialists, and the
Politics of Food: The 1917 New York Cost-of-Living Protests," *Feminist Studies* 11
(Summer 1985): 255–85; "'Food Wins All Struggles': Seattle Labor and the Politi-
cization of Consumption," *Radical History Review* (Fall 1991): 65–89, and *Purchas-
ing Power: Consumer Organizing, Gender, and the Seattle Labor Movement, 1919–1929*
(New York: Cambridge University Press, 1994).

    38. Joanne Meyerowitz, "Women and Gender in Postwar America, 1945–
1960," Susan M. Hartmann, "Women's Employment and the Domestic Ideal in the
Early Cold War Years," and Margaret Rose, "Gender and Civic Activism in Mexican American Barrios in California: The Community Service Organization, 1947–
1962," in Meyerowitz, ed., *Not June Cleaver*, 1–18, 84–101, 177–200; Amy Swerdlow,
Women Strike for Peace: Traditional Motherhood and Radical Politics in the 1960s (Chicago: University of Chicago Press, 1993); Eugenia Kaledin, *Mothers and More: American Women in the 1950s* (Boston: Twayne Publishers, 1984); Wini Breines, "Dom-
ineering Mothers in the 1950s: Image and Reality," *Women's Studies International*

Forum 8 (1985): 601–8; Earl Lewis, "Black School Teachers and Equal Pay," paper presented at the symposium, "The Equal Pay Act of 1963 and Its Legacy," Nov. 21–22, 1993, George Meany Archives, Silver Spring, Maryland, copy in author's possession; Paula Giddings, *When and Where I Enter: The Impact of Black Women on Race and Sex in America* (New York: William Morrow and Co., 1984), 231–60; Jacqueline Jones, *Labor of Love, Labor of Sorrow: Black Women, Work and the Family from Slavery to the Present* (New York: Basic Books, 1985), 232–74; Glenna Matthews, *"Just a Housewife": The Rise and Fall of Domesticity in America* (New York: Oxford University Press, 1987), 197–222; Coontz, *The Way We Never Were;* Elaine Tyler May, *Homeward Bound: American Families in the Cold War Era* (New York: Basic Books, 1988); Betty Friedan, *The Feminine Mystique* (New York: Dell, 1963); RCT, "Visits," Sept. 4, 1956, RCTP.

39. Kessler-Harris, "Where are the Organized Women Workers?"; recent literature is neatly summarized by Ava Baron, "Gender and Labor History: Learning from the Past, Looking to the Future," in Baron, ed., *Work Engendered,* 1–46. The male culture of the labor movement has been studied in great detail, but historians have only recently examined how notions of gender hierarchy structured unions and how these arrangements affected the (male) union's relationship to its female workers and auxiliaries. Walter Licht's *Working for the Railroad: The Organization of Work in the Nineteenth Century* (Princeton, N.J.: Princeton University Press, 1983), for example, is replete with rich descriptions of male union culture but he does not analyze how this may have influenced trade unionists' perceptions of women. Jerrold Hirsch raises a similar question in his review of Santino's book, *Miles of Smiles,* in the *JSH* 57 (1991): 347–49. See also Ava Baron, "An 'Other' Side of Gender Antagonism at Work: Men, Boys, and the Remasculinization of Printers' Work, 1830–1920"; Mary Blewett, "Manhood and the Market: The Politics of Gender and Class among the Textile Workers of Fall River, Massachusetts, 1870–1880"; and Nancy A. Hewitt, " 'The Voice of Virile Labor': Labor Militancy, Community Solidarity, and Gender Identity among Tampa's Latin Workers, 1880–1921," all in Baron, ed., *Work Engendered,* 47–69, 92–113, 142–67. Alice Kessler-Harris's essay "Where Are the Organized Women Workers?" *FS* 3 (1975): 92–110, argues that male culture prevented women workers from joining the labor movement. However, she is more concerned with workingwomen than with wives of workingmen. See also Joan Wallach Scott's critique of E. P. Thompson, "Women in the *Making of the English Working Class,*" in *Gender and the Politics of History* (New York: Columbia University Press, 1988), 68–90, and "Gender: A Useful Category of Analysis," *AHR* 91 (1986): 1053–75.

40. Theresa Wolfson, "Trade Union Activities of Women," *Annals* 63 (1929): 120–31; Mrs. R. J. Lowther, "The Typographical Woman's International Auxiliary," *American Federationist* 36 (1929): 980–83; Jean E. Rosinos, "Marching Women of Illinois," *Labor Age* 21 (Nov. 1932): 6–7. Major discussions of auxiliaries may be found in Majorie Penn Lasky, " 'Where I Was a Person': The Ladies' Auxiliary in the 1934 Minneapolis Teamsters' Strikes," in Ruth Milkman, ed., *Women, Work, and Protest: A Century of Women's Labor History* (Boston: Routledge & Kegan Paul, 1985), 181–205; Lisbeth Haas, "Mexican Women in the California Agricultural Strikes, 1933–1936," paper presented at the Organization of American Historians Conference, Washington, D.C., 1990, copy in author's possession; Elizabeth Faue, "Paths

of Unionization: Community, Bureaucracy, and Gender in the Minneapolis Labor Movement of the 1930s," in Baron, ed., *Work Engendered,* 296–319; Gabin, *Feminism and the Labor Movement,* 42–46; Lorraine Gray, dir., *With Babies and Banners: The Story of the Women's Emergency Brigade,* prod. Anne Bohlen et al., New Day Films, 1977; Barbara Kingsolver, *Holding the Line: Women in the Great Arizona Mine Strike of 1983* (Ithaca, N.Y.: ILR Press, 1989); Kathryn J. Oberdeck, " 'Not Pink Teas': The Seattle Working-Class Women's Movement, 1905–1918," *Labor History* 32 (Spring 1991): 193–230; Sharon Hartman Strom, "Challenging 'Woman's Place': Feminism, the Left, and Industrial Unionism in the 1930s," *FS* 9 (Summer 1983): 359–86; Margaret Rose, " 'From the Fields to the Picket Line: Huelga Women and the Boycott, 1965–1975," *Labor History* 32 (Summer 1991): 271–93. Susan Levine's "Workers' Wives: Gender, Class and Consumerism in the 1920s United States," *G&H* 3 (1991): 45–64, discusses the views of women contributors to *The Messenger,* but mistakenly identifies them as members of the Brotherhood's Ladies' Auxiliary, which had not yet been organized.

41. Hine et al., eds., *"We Specialize in the Wholly Impossible";* Ruth Milkman, "Women Workers: A Continuing Process," in Milkman, ed., *Women, Work, and Protest,* 139–55; Gerda Lerner, *Black Women in White America: A Documentary History* (New York: Random House, 1972), chap. 4; Jones, *Labor of Love,* chaps. 6 and 7; Bettina Aptheker, "Domestic Labor: Patterns in Black and White," in *Woman's Legacy: Essays on Race, Sex and Class* (Amherst: University of Massachusetts Press, 1982), 111–28; Clark-Lewis, *Living In, Living Out;* Phyllis Palmer, *Domesticity and Dirt: Housewives and Domestic Servants in the United States, 1920–1945* (Philadelphia: Temple University Press, 1989); Brenda Clegg Gray, *Black Female Domestics during the Depression in New York City* (Hamden, Conn.: Garland Publishing, 1993); Dolores Janiewski, *Sisterhood Denied: Race, Gender, and Class in a New South Community* (Philadelphia: Temple University Press, 1984). Documentary sources on the garment industry include Elizabeth Balanoff, "Interview with Maida Springer Kemp," in *The Black Women Oral History Project,* ed. Ruth Edmonds Hill, vol. 7 (1978; reprint, Westport, Conn.: Meckler, 1991), 39–157; Philip S. Foner and Ronald L. Lewis, eds., *The Era of Post-War Prosperity and the Great Depression, 1920–1936,* vol. 6 (Philadelphia: Temple University Press, 1981), 138–86; Giddings, *When and Where I Enter;* Darlene Clark Hine, *Black Women in White: Racial Conflict and Cooperation in the Nursing Profession, 1890–1950* (Bloomington: Indiana University Press, 1989); Richard M. Dalfiume, "The Forgotten Years of the Negro Revolution," *JAH* 55 (1968): 90–106.

42. Anderson, *A. Philip Randolph;* Harris, *Keeping the Faith;* "A. Philip Randolph as a Charismatic Leader, 1925–1941," *JNH* 64 (1979): 301–15; and "A. Philip Randolph, Black Workers and the Labor Movement," in *Labor Leaders in America,* ed. Dubofsky and Van Tine, 258–79; Pfeffer, *A. Philip Randolph;* Benjamin Quarles, "A. Philip Randolph: Labor Leader at Large," in *Black Leaders of the Twentieth Century,* ed. John Hope Franklin and August Meier (Urbana: University of Illinois Press, 1982), 139–66; Santino, *Miles of Smiles;* Brazeal, *The Brotherhood;* John H. Bracey Jr. and August Meier, "Allies or Adversaries?: The NAACP, A. Philip Randolph, and the 1941 March on Washington," *Georgia Historical Quarterly* 75 (1991): 1–17; Daniel S. Davis, *Mr. Black Labor: The Story of A. Philip Randolph, Father of the Civil Rights Movement* (New York: E. P. Dutton, 1972); Kornweibel, *No Crystal Stair;* LeRoy,

"Founding Heart"; Edgar Edgerton Tucker, "The Brotherhood of Sleeping Car Porters, 1945–1961," M.A. diss., Howard University, 1963; Wilson, *Tearing Down the Color Bar; FBI File on A. Philip Randolph* (Wilmington, Del.: Scholarly Resources, [1990?]); *Guide to the Microfilm Edition of the FBI File on A. Philip Randolph* (Wilmington, Del.: Scholarly Resources, n.d.).

43. Harris, *Keeping the Faith,* 15; Saunders Redding, *The Lonesome Road: A Narrative History of the Black American Experience* (1958; reprint, Anchor Books, 1973), 236; see also William H. Harris, *The Harder We Run: Black Workers since the Civil War* (New York: Oxford University Press, 1982), 78.

44. Rayford W. Logan and Michael R. Winston, eds., *Dictionary of American Negro Biography* (New York: W. W. Norton & Co., 1982); Kornweibel, *No Crystal Stair,* 59, 68.

45. Robert E. Turner, *Memories of a Retired Pullman Porter* (New York: Exposition Press, 1954); Santino, *Miles of Smiles,* 17–18; C. [Cottrell] L. [Lawrence] Dellums, *International President of the Brotherhood of Sleeping Car Porters and Civil Rights Leader,* interview by Joyce Henderson (Berkeley: Earl Warren Oral History Program, Bancroft Library, University of California, Berkeley, 1973). Pullman ceased hiring college students for summer work in the late 1920s and began recruiting recently arrived southern migrants less familiar with trade unions (APR to CLD, Sept. 18, 1929, UCB/BSCP Box 363).

46. Bureau of the Census, *The Social and Economic Status of the Black Population in the United States: An Historical View: 1790–1978* (Washington, D.C.: Government Printing Office, n.d.), 30; Drake and Cayton, *Black Metropolis,* 526–63.

47. Santino, *Miles of Smiles,* 56–57; RCT, "My Life," RCPT; MacKissack, *Long Hard Journey,* 16, 35.

48. Santino, *Miles of Smiles,* 10, 20; obituary, Jessie Bonds, *Black Worker* (May 1939): 2; Ducker, *Men of the Steel Rails,* 72–78; Licht, *Working for the Railroad,* 59, 115, 156.

49. Hazel V. Carby, " 'It Jus Be's Dat Way Sometime': The Sexual Politics of Women's Blues," in DuBois and Ruiz, eds., *Unequal Sisters,* 241–43; Santino, *Miles of Smiles,* 115–30; Maids' Service Records Box, PCOP; Pauli Murray, *Song in a Weary Throat: An American Pilgrimage* (New York: Harper and Row, 1987), 79–81.

50. Eric Arneson, " 'Like Banquo's Ghost, It Will Not Down': The Race Question and the American Railroad Brotherhoods, 1880–1920," *AHR* 99 (Dec. 1994): 1601–33; Clark-Lewis, *Living In, Living Out;* Palmer, *Domesticity and Dirt,* 137–51; Mary Romero, *Maid in the U.S.A.* (New York: Routledge, 1992), 71–97; Elsa M. Chaney and Mary Garcia Castro, eds., *Muchachas No More: Household Workers in Latin America and the Caribbean* (Philadelphia: Temple University Press, 1989); Judith Rollins, *Between Women: Domestics and Thier Employers* (Philadelphia: Temple University Press, 1985); Evelyn Nakano Glenn, "From Servitude to Service Work: Historical Continuities in the Racial Division of Paid Reproductive Labor," in DuBois and Ruiz, eds., *Unequal Sisters,* 405–35; Tera W. Hunter, "Domination and Resistance: The Politics of Wage Household Labor in New South Atlanta," in Hine et al., eds., *"We Specialize in the Wholly Impossible,"* 343–58; Bettina Aptheker, "Domestic Labor: Patterns in Black and White," in *Woman's Legacy,* 111–28; see also Alice Childress, *Like One of the Family: Conversations from a Domestic's Life* (1956; reprint, Boston: Beacon Press, 1986); Santino, *Miles of Smiles,* 111.

Chapter 1: The Case against Pullman

1. Jerrold Hirsh, review of Jack Santino, *Miles of Smiles* in *JSH* 57 (1991): 348; Corlann Gee Bush, "'He Isn't Half So Cranky as He Used to Be': Agricultural Mechanization, Comparable Worth, and the Changing Farm Family," in Carol Groneman and Mary Beth Norton, eds., *"To Toil the Livelong Day": America's Women at Work, 1780–1980* (Ithaca: Cornell University Press, 1987), 213–29.

2. Nick Salvatore, *Eugene V. Debs: Citizen and Socialist* (Bloomington: Indiana University Press, 1982), 171, 228–30; see also Eugene V. Debs to Editors, *The Messenger* 5 (May 1923): 714; Eileen Boris, "'A Man's Dwelling House Is His Castle': Tenement House Cigarmaking and the Judicial Imperative," in Ava Baron, ed., *Work Engendered: Toward a New History of American Labor* (Ithaca: Cornell University Press, 1991), 114–41; Susan E. Hirsch, "Rethinking the Sexual Division of Labor: Pullman Repair Shops, 1900–1969," *Radical History Review* 35 (April 1986): 26–48.

3. Joseph Husband, *The Story of the Pullman Car* (Chicago: A. C. McClurg, 1917; reprint, New York: Arno Press and the New York Times Company, 1972), 29–48, 155; Paul Wagner, dir., *Miles of Smiles, Years of Struggle: The Untold Story of the Black Pullman Porter,* Jack Santino and Paul Wagner, producers, narrated by Rosina Tucker (Briarcliff Manor: Benchmark Films, 1982).

4. The rules of racial segregation varied considerably, sometimes at the whim of ticket agents and Pullman conductors. By the turn of the century, African American passengers in the South were universally restricted to the Jim Crow car. However, when Pullman introduced the "roomette" car, basically separate cubicles with seating that turned into beds and their own bathrooms, African Americans were generally allowed to purchase these accomodations. At the same time, dining cars remained racially segregated, preventing African American passengers from enjoying full run of the train.

5. "Life on a Pullman," booklet (Chicago: Rand McNally Co., 1939), n.p., copy in C. L. Dellums Papers, Bancroft Library, University of California, Berkeley, Container 37.

6. Husband, *Story of the Pullman Car,* 135; *Pullman News* (Mar. 1931): 436.

7. "The Pullman Porter," July 6, 1951, SI/NMAH Series 5, Box 3; Benjamin E. Mays, *Born to Rebel: An Autobiography* (New York: Charles Scribner's Sons, 1971), 61–63. By 1941, perhaps reflecting their numbers in the BSCP, the Pullman Company also barred West Indians.

8. Robert E. Turner, *Memories of a Retired Pullman Porter* (New York: Exposition Press, 1954), 100–101; "Memo of features to be considered in the employment of new porters," Jan. 27, 1951, Fair Employment Practice Committee File, June 19, 1943 to July 20, 1951 (hereinafter, FEPC File), PCOP Box 335-1.

9. Frances Mary Albrier, *Frances Mary Albrier: Determined Advocate for Racial Equality,* interview conducted by Malca Chall, Women in Politics Oral History Project (Berkeley: Regional Oral History Office, Bancroft Library, University of California, 1979), 81–82; Maids Service Records Box, PCOP. The company used separate height and weight requirements for porters' and attendants' jobs to prevent Filipinos from becoming porters, and vice versa, FEPC File, PCOP; Susan E. Hirsch, "Rethinking the Sexual Division of Labor: Pullman Repair Shops, 1900–

1969," *RHR* 35 (1986): 26–48. In a sample of fifty-six maids' service records, twenty-two were married either before or during their Pullman service, two were divorced, and two were listed as "Miss."

10. *The Pullman Porter* (New York: Brotherhood of Sleeping Car Porters, 1927), 7, 15; Florence Lowden Miller, "The Pullmans of Prairie Avenue: A Domestic Portrait from Letters and Diaries," *Chicago History* 1 (1971): 142–55; for one example of crew composition, see "Travelers on the N.E.L.A. Red Special Praise Pullman Crew," *Pullman News* 9 (Sept. 1930): 197.

11. Pullman Company, *Instructions to Porters, Attendants, and Bus Boys* ([Chicago]: The Pullman Company, 1952), iii; ACL, "General Instructions for Chair Car Attendants and Train Maids," Dec. 13, 1948, LC/BSCP Box 80.

12. Pullman Company, *Instructions to Porters,* 49–127.

13. "Hand Maidens for Travelers," *Pullman News* (Jan. 1923): 291.

14. "Pullman Service," *Pullman News* (1924): 2; "The New Pullman Single Car Room," *Pullman News* (1927): 419; *Life on a Pullman* [promotional brochure] (n.p.: Rand McNally & Co., 1939), UCB/CLD Box 37.

15. *Pullman News* (Nov. 1926): 241. Raised in Tuskegee, Alabama, Albrier graduated from Howard in 1920 and moved to Berkeley, California, where she joined the Black Nurse Corps of the Universal Negro Improvement Association. Albrier, *Determined Advocate,* xiv–vi.

16. ACL, "General Instructions"; ACL "Duties Performed by Maids on the ACL," [ca. 1951], LC/APR Box 13.

17. The Pullman maid's uniform consisted of a long-sleeved dress, six inches below the knee in length, of grey cotton or black wool, depending on the season. Black shoes or boots and black hose were required; the hose to be worn with a garter belt; rolled stockings were forbidden. Undergarments were to be either white or black. A starched white apron with scallops, kerchief collar, cuffs, and head bow completed the uniform. A sweater might be worn with the proper emblem sewn on the sleeve. On the left sleeve, maids, like the rest of the crew, wore brassards indicating their trains. Pullman awarded maids and porters one stripe for every five years of service. [Name withheld] reprimanded for wearing a pink slip, Maids Service Records Box, PCOP; "Graduating Florida Limited Class," *Pullman News* (Jan. 1924): 288; Stanley Nelson, *Freedom Bags,* produced by Stanley Nelson and Elizabeth Clark-Lewis (New York: Filmmakers Library, 1990).

18. Maids were frequently reprimanded for taking too much time in the ladies' room, thus closing it off to passengers. Maids Service Records Box, PCOP; ACL, "General Instructions" LC/BSCP Box 80; *Pullman Porter,* 7.

19. Maids Service Records Box, PCOP; Turner, *Memories,* 109–21; Albrier, *Determined Advocate,* 280–81; Santino, *Miles of Smiles,* 11–13; RCT, "My Life As I Have Lived It," [ca. 1980], RCTP.

20. A Pullman bed used three sheets, the third was used in the place of a coverlet, over the blanket, *Instructions to Porters,* 104–6; Santino, *Miles of Smiles,* 32.

21. Santino, *Miles of Smiles,* 82–84. Speaking to the Ladies' Auxiliary Convention, Ernest E. Schwartztrauber, head of the Madison School for Workers, claimed he knew the problems of porters because he often talked to the men at night "when their duties were done." *Report of Proceedings of the Sixth Biennial Convention of the Ladies' Auxiliary . . . Held at Detroit, Mich., Sept. 13 to 15, 1948,* 44, CHS/BSCP Box 30.

22. Brazeal, *The Brotherhood*, 212; D. LaRoche, "Report of the Fact-Finding Committee of the Brotherhood of Sleeping Car Porters," n.d. (ca. 1926), LC/APR Box 4; see also Part 2 of Report of Fact Finding Committee, appointed Feb. 20, 1939, CHS/BSCP Box 6.

23. W. J. Cash, *The Mind of the South* (New York: Alfred A. Knopf, 1941, 1991), 248.

24. Brazeal, *The Brotherhood*, 209.

25. Ibid., 208–16; Harris, *Keeping the Faith*, 211; Paul H. Douglas, *Wages and the Family* (Chicago: University of Chicago Press, 1925), 3–10; "Average Annual Earnings Per Full-Time Employee, by Industry, 1900–1970," *Historical Statistics of the United States, Colonial Times to 1970* (Washington, D.C.: Government Printing Office, 1975), 166–67. Note that these annual incomes are for all service workers, private household, and commercial establishments, and are not calculated by race and sex, for which there are no government employment statistics for 1926. In 1930, railroad workers on Class I roads, an almost 100 percent male work force, averaged $1,717. In domestic services, the average 1930 earnings for full-time workers (64 percent female) was $676. The U.S. Census Bureau however, classified "steam railroad porters" as domestic and personal service workers (of which there were 27,647 males and 1 female in 1930). Wage data, calculated by the Bureau of Labor Statistics, is classified by industry, not by occupation. Bureau of the Census, *Abstract of the Fifteenth Census of the United States* (Washington, D.C.: Government Printing Office, 1933; reprint, New York: Arno Press, 1976).

26. Brazeal, *The Brotherhood*, 211; Patricia and Fredrick McKissack, *Long, Hard Journey: The Story of the Pullman Porter* (New York: Walker, 1989), 21.

27. Albrier, *Determined Advocate*, 81–82.

28. *Pullman Porter*, 14; Petitioner's Brief on Motion to Dismiss, *Brotherhood of Sleeping Car Porters v. The Pullman Company*, before the Interstate Commerce Commission; Docket No. 20,007; Oct. 20, 1927, MSRR; Brazeal, *The Brotherhood*, 75.

29. Albrier, *Determined Advocate*, 77.

30. Brazeal, *The Brotherhood*, 25; Santino, *Miles of Smiles*, 31, 51; Harris, *Keeping the Faith*, 83–84. Not until the 1950s did Pullman Maids win the right to use their initials.

31. APR, "The Case of the Pullman Porter," *Messenger* 8 (1925): 254; *The Pullman Porter*, 8–11.

32. Harris, *Keeping the Faith*, 79; Brazeal, *The Brotherhood*, 12; Santino, *Miles of Smiles*, 91.

33. Pullman Company, Minutes, Apr. 7, 1937; and L. M. Greenlaw, File Memo, July 19, 1937, in "Principle File, Porters' Agreement of Oct. 1, 1937," PCOP Box 267. Disputes over releasing the names of women passengers to the union continued. See Memo, Milton P. Webster Jr. to BSCP, Nov. 20, 1952, LC/BSCP Box 78, and "Memorandum of Understanding Concerning Molestation Cases Nov. 25, 1952," LC/APR Box 53; and Eldridge case file in LC/BSCP Box 76.

34. Brazeal, *The Brotherhood*, 6; Harris, *Keeping the Faith*, 2; Lillian Smith, *Killers of the Dream*, rev. and enl. ed. (New York: W. W. Norton, 1961), 146; McKissack, *Long, Hard Journey*, 21; Pullman Company, *Instructions to Porters*, 46–47.

35. "Porters' Word Regarded of No Value," *Messenger* 7 (1925): 314.

36. "Maid Southern District" to R. J. Ruddy, Mar. 31, 1928, CHS/BSCP Box 3.

37. Allan Brandt, *No Magic Bullet* (New York: Oxford University Press, 1987), 245–46.

38. Marie Ann Evans, "Sex on Wheels," unidentified newspaper clipping, LC/APR Box 54; Edward Swift and Charles Boyd, "A Pullman Porter Looks at Life," *Psychoanalytical Review* 15 (1928): 393–416.

39. PPBA, "Constitution and By-Laws," Feb. 1, 1921, LC/APR Box 54.

40. Harris, *Keeping the Faith,* 47; Carl R. Osthaus, "Jesse Binga," s.v., Rayford W. Logan and Michael R. Winston, eds., *Dictionary of American Negro Biography* (New York, W. W. Norton & Co., 1982).

41. Harris, *Keeping the Faith,* 17–19; Brazeal, *The Brotherhood,* 27, 32–33.

42. Sterling D. Spero and Abram L. Harris, *The Black Worker: The Negro and the Labor Movement* (New York: Columbia University Press, 1931; reprint, New York: Antheneum, 1969), 440–45; *Pullman Porter,* 12–15. See almost any issue of the *Pullman News* between 1923 and 1936 for descriptions of extra-curricular activities. ALT, "An Expose of the Pullman Porters Benefit Association," *Messenger* 9 (1926): 270, and 11 (1928): 91.

43. Letter to the Editor, *Messenger* 10 (1927): 206; Ann Lawrence, "Mandy Jones on the Pullman Porters," *Messenger* 10 (1927): 241; "Wife of a Porter, Oakland to Randolph," *Messenger* 9 (1926): 121; Sharon Harley, "Beyond the Classroom: The Organizational Lives of Black Female Educators in the District of Columbia, 1890–1930," *JNE* 51:3 (1982): 254–65. Conversely, some wives enjoyed their husbands' absences, RCT, "My Life," RCTP.

44. "Poor Wages and the Home under the Employee Representation Plan," *Messenger* 9 (1926): 328–29.

45. RCT, "My Life," RCTP; Charles Upton to CLD, Oct. 15, 1939, UCB/CLD Box 5; Harris, *Keeping the Faith,* 79–80; Jerrold Hirsh, "Review of *Miles of Smiles, Years of Struggle,* by Jack Santino," *JSH* 57 (May 1991): 347–49; MPW, "The National Negro Labor Conference," n.d., but ca. Feb. 10, 1931, article in the Victor A. Olaner Papers, copy in CHS/BSCP Box 4.

46. "Welfareism," *Black Worker* (Dec. 1929): 4.

47. "Instructions to hiring personnel," PCOP Box 267.

48. "Transcript of Testimony Taken at Formal Hearing . . . Relative Dismissal of Former Maid Dolly Salazar," Oct. 11, 1946, UCB/CLD Box 12; RCT, "My Life," RCTP.

49. *Messenger* 11 (1928): 16.

Chapter 2: "It Was the Women Who Made the Union"

1. William H. Harris, *Keeping the Faith: A. Philip Randolph, Milton P. Webster, and the Brotherhood of Sleeping Car Porters, 1925–37* (Urbana: University of Illinois Press, 1977, 1991), 35; CLD to Mike Patino, Feb. 18, 1937, UCB/CLD Box 6. In their 1937 contract talks the BSCP agreed it would not represent porters in Mexico. Unionization of the Canadian porters began in 1941 (see chapter 5.)

2. Handbill, n.d. in "Propaganda: Bills, Poster, Stickers, etc.," PCOP Box 267.

3. Amy Jacques Garvey coined the term New Negro Woman. See Mark D.

Mathews, "'Our Women and What They Think': Amy Jacques Garvey and *The Negro World*," *Black Scholar* (May/June 1979): 5.

4. Harris, *Keeping the Faith*, 36–38; Brailsford Brazeal, *The Brotherhood of Sleeping Car Porters: Its Origin and Development* (New York: Harper and Brothers, 1946), 19–20.

5. APR to Lancaster, Aug. 3, 1927, LC/APR Box 7; Pauli Murray, *Song in a Weary Throat: An American Pilgrimage* (New York: Harper & Row, 1987), 85–86; "Activities of the Month," *Messenger* 11 (1928): 40.

6. RCT, "My Life As I Have Lived It," [ca. 1980], RCTP; MPW to CLD, Sept. 5, 1941, UCB/CLD Box 3.

7. Greg LeRoy, "The Founding Heart of A. Philip Randolph's Union: Milton P. Webster and Chicago's Pullman Porters Organize, 1925–1927," *Labor's Heritage* 3 (July 1991): 37.

8. Harris, *Keeping the Faith*, 55–56; RCT, "My Life," RCPT.

9. Maids Service Records Box, PCOP; *Black Worker* (Jan. 1938): 3; (Sept. 1938): suppl. 4; (Aug. 1936): 8.

10. Frances Mary Albrier, *Frances Mary Albrier: Determined Advocate for Racial Equality*, interview conducted by Malca Chall. Women in Politics Oral History Project (Berkeley: Regional Oral History Office, Bancroft Library, University of California, 1979), 80–81.

11. Brazeal, *The Brotherhood*, 221–23; Chicago Membership Rolls, CHS/BSCP Box 44A.

12. "Five Generations, Eldest 110, in Pullman Maid's Family" *Pullman News* 5 (August 1926): 112.

13. In looking for clues about marital status I did not use honorific titles alone, since Pullman did not always show maids this respect. When an employee, for example, requested leave to care for an injured husband, I assumed she was married. A total of 620 service cards for 573 African American maids and 47 Chinese maids were located at the Newberry Library. Cards providing the most data on African American workers were pulled, for a total of fifty-seven records. Of these, twenty-eight were from the five Chicago districts; five from Pennsylvania Terminal; five from New York districts; eleven from San Francisco and Los Angeles combined; and seven altogether from Boston, Washington, D.C., New Orleans, and Memphis.

14. Santino, *Miles of Smiles*, 131–41; Harold F. Gosnell, *Negro Politicians: The Rise of Negro Politics in Chicago* (Chicago: University of Chicago Press, 1935; reprint, 1967), 204; LeRoy, "Founding Heart," 22–25. According to a fellow unionist, Oscar Soares, president of the Los Angeles BSCP Division also forbid his wife from participating in the union (see Charles Upton to CLD, Oct. 15, 1939, UCB/CLD Box 5); Dellums instructed that a reception for Randolph have "no women whatever," CLD to W. B. Holland, Nov. 6, 1939, UCB/CLD Box 30; also ALT to CLD Oct. 21, 1939, UCB/CLD Box 3; RCT, "My Life," reported similar attitudes among rank-and-file union men. On the other hand, the invitation to the Thirteenth Annual Winter Dance in New York read, "Two fellows always waiting to dance with one girl," and pictured a porter and maid holding hands, UCB/CLD Box 24.

15. Alice Kessler-Harris, "Where Are the Organized Women Workers?" *FS* 3

(1975): 92–110. Cleanliness and women's use of the union hall was frequently an issue, see for example, Charles Upton to CLD, Mar. 17, 1939, and Charles Upton to CLD, June 20, 1939, UCB/CLD Box 5; Ardella Nutall, Elma Patrick, Lucilla (?) S. Shaw, and Willa B. Parker, to CLD, Feb. 25, 1949, UCB/CLD Box 8.

16. *Black Worker* (Aug. 1936): 7.

17. Ibid.; Brazeal, *The Brotherhood*, 222. In 1939, Upton became a charter member of the Los Angeles Ladies' Auxiliary and served on the Auxiliary Executive Board. The BSCP pensioned her in 1941, CLD to APR, Feb. 2, 1942 and Feb. 24, 1942, all in LC/APR Box 61; Charles Upton to CLD, June 26, 1936, UCB/CLD Box 30; Letitia Murray to CLD, July 1, 1939, UCB/CLD Box 5.

18. Albrier, *Determined Advocate*, 80–81; membership list, Oakland BSCP Division, n.d., but ca. June 1928, UCB/CLD Box 23; Chicago Brotherhood Division Membership Book, CHS/BSCP Box 44; see also EJB, "Some of the Hardships Encountered by the BSCP in the St. Louis District in the Early Days of Organizational Program by the then Field Organizer, E. J. Bradley," Jan. 2, 1947, CHS/BSCP Box 10.

19. "Porter Growls," *Black Worker* (June 1930): 3.

20. Maids Service Records. Minyard was hired by the ACL in December 1939 as a maid from the New York district. She joined the BSCP in 1951 when the railroads became a closed shop industry. That same year, the Atlantic Coast Line suspended its maid service; Minyard joined the class grievance filed by the BSCP on the maids' behalf. See chapter 10, and Randolph's correspondence with the ACL LC/APR Box 13, and miscellaneous materials in LC/BSCP Box 80.

21. The service records of all forty-seven Chinese maids were studied. Eleven worked less than two months, while one worked for twelve years. [Name withheld] of the San Francisco district resigned January 15, 1929, after five years of service on the Overland Limited, PCOP, Maids Box; see also "Records of Grievance of Maid Y. J. Drye," UCB/CLD, Container 12.

22. EJB, "Some of My Early Experiences Organizing Pullman Porters in St. Louis," n.d. (ca. 1949–50), LC/APR Box 10; Brotherhood Membership books, CHS/BSCP. The two "disloyal" maids were from the St. Louis and San Francisco districts, where membership records are not extant. No employment record was located for Upton.

23. William H. Harris, "Federal Intervention into Racial Discrimination: The Fair Employment Practice Committee and the West Coast Shipping Yards during World War II," *Labor History* 22 (1981): 325–47. BSCP membership in Seattle remained high even in 1933, when nationally the union had lost 85 percent of its members in five years (Brazeal, *The Brotherhood*, 221–22); see also "Minutes," Ladies Auxiliary, Seattle, Oct. 21, 1937, UCB/CLD Box 9.

24. "Souvenir Program, BSCP Silver Jubilee Anniversary and Seventh Biennial Convention," Sept. 10, 1950, RCTP; St. Clair Drake and Horace R. Cayton, *Black Metropolis: A Study of Negro Life in A Northern City*, rev. and enl. ed. (New York: Harcourt, Brace, and World, 1962), 235–36. The Chicago local had 2,496 members in 1943 (Brazeal, *The Brotherhood*, 222).

25. This group consisted of "teachers, business and professional women whose purpose is to study and discuss the important questions of the day and their relation to our particular group," "S.W.O., Monday, Dec. 21, 1925," LC/APR Box 7; see

also MPW to APR, Mar. 5, 1928, and MPW to APR, Mar. 9, 1928, both in CHS/BSCP Box 3. LeRoy, "Founding Heart," 25, notes Avendorph's role in the club. However, Allan G. Spear, *Black Chicago: The Making of a Negro Ghetto, 1890–1920* (Chicago: University of Chicago Press, 1967), gives Avendorph (who died in 1912) as the founder of the *Conservator,* not the *Defender.* Spear also promotes Avendorph to Lincoln's assistant, rather than his more probable job as messenger.

26. "The Truth About the BSCP," *Messenger* 9 (1926): 37; MPW to APR, Jan. 4, 1928; Program, BSCP Labor Conference, Jan. 23, 1928; BSCP to "Friend," Feb. 2–5, 1928, all in CHS/BSCP Box 3; Program, "Towards Greater Economic Security for the Negro Worker," Mar. 21, 1932, CHS/BSCP Box 4; "Negro Women Turn Attention to Problems of Labor," *Black Worker* (Mar. 1932), in LC/APR Box 54; *Messenger* 10 (1927): 358.

27. Souvenir Program, First Annual Brotherhood Ball, Dec. 3, 1926, LC/APR Box 54; A. Sagitarrius, "Bobbed Hair Contest," *The Messenger* 10 (Jan. 1927): 29; "Activities of the Brotherhood," *Messenger* 11 (1928): 64; "Concerning the New York Citizens' Committee of One Hundred," n.d. (ca. 1927), LC/APR Box 54.

28. Kemp interviewed Randolph for the Columbia University Oral History Project, 1965; "Colored Women Dressmakers Organizing," *The Black Worker* 1 (Dec. 15, 1930): 3; *Domestic Worker* 1:1 (May 1938): 1; LC/APR Box 54; Phyllis Palmer, *Domesticity and Dirt: Housewives and Domestic Servants in the United States, 1920–1945* (Philadelphia: Temple University Press, 1989); James R. Barrett, *Work and Community in the Jungle: Chicago's Packinghouse Workers, 1894–1922* (Urbana: University of Illinois Press, 1987).

29. MPW, "Sidelights on the National Negro Labor Conference," *Black Worker* (Mar. 1930): 1; *Messenger* 8 (1926): 370; APR to MPW, Mar. 7, 1928, and Program, Second Annual Negro Labor Conference, Feb. 3–5, 1929, both in CHS/BSCP Box 3; Program, National Negro Labor Conference, Second Annual Session, Jan. 19–23, 1931, CHS/BSCP Box 4; Barrett, *Work and Community,* 85–86, 141–45, 222–23.

30. Lillian Herstein, *Report of the Proceedings of the First National Convention of the Ladies Auxiliary . . . Held at Chicago, Ill., Sept. 24 to 27, 1938,* 39–43, CHS/BSCP Box 27; "Miss Mary Anderson to Address National Negro Confab," press release, Nov. 15, 1929, UCB/CLD Box 23; MPW to Mary Anderson, Feb. 5, 1930; RCT to Mary Anderson, Nov. 19, 1936; Program, BSCP Labor Mass Meeting, Dec. 6–11, 1936, Washington, D.C.; all in NARA/W Box 52.

31. Charlotte Anne Whitney to D. J. Jones, Oct. 22, 1927, UCB/BSCP Box 393; "Brotherhood Anniversary," *Messenger* 9 (1926): 265; Helen C. Camp, "Elizabeth Gurley Flynn," s.v., *Notable American Women.* Flynn joined the Communist Party in 1926, before Randolph broke with it over the National Negro Labor Congress. In 1948, Flynn's name (along with Irene McCoy Gaines and Charlotte Hawkins Brown) on a Hull House program to "Salute to Chicago's Women Citizens," brought Randolph's strictest "suggestion" that Ladies Auxiliary International President Halena Wilson not participate (APR to HW, Jan. 26, 1948, LC/BSCP Box 75).

32. "Citizens Committee," *Messenger* 11 (1928): 90; "Concerning the New York Citizens Committee."

33. "Concerning the New York Citizens Committee." Among those listed were Rev. Lloyd Imes, William H. Baldwin, Morris Hillquit, Mary Simkhovitch, Arthur B. Spingarn, Dr. Norman Thomas, Prof. Franz Boas, Dr. W. E. B. Du Bois,

Harriot Stanton Blatch, Heywood Broun, Dr. Henry Sloane Coffin, Prof. John Dewey, Mary E. Dreier, Fannie Hurst, Freda Kirchwey, Eugene O'Neill, William L. Patterson, Anita L. Pollitzer, Rev. A. Clayton Powell Sr., Paul Robeson, Ernestine Rose, Prof. E. R. A. Seligman, Helen Phelps Stokes, Samuel Untermyer, Oswald Garrison Villard, Lillian Wald, Walter White, and Leo Wolman (Harris, *Keeping the Faith*, 35–38).

34. Deborah Gray White, "The Cost of Club Work, the Price of Black Feminism," in Nancy A. Hewitt and Suzanne Lebsock, eds., *Visible Women: New Essays on American History* (Urbana: University of Illinois Press, 1993), 247–69.

35. RCT, "My Life."

36. David Levering Lewis, *When Harlem Was in Vogue* (1979; reprint, New York: Oxford University Press, 1981), 106; Souvenir Scrapbook, Second Annual Ball, [1926], LC/APR Box 54; *Messenger* 10 (1927): 29.

37. "Souvenir Program" [1926]; *Black Worker* (July 1935): 2; APR, "The Brotherhood's Anniversary," *Messenger* 8 (1926): 265.

38. RCT, "My Life"; APR to MPW, May 29, 1927, CHS/BSCP Box 2.

39. "Cooperation Plan of the Women's Economic Council," SCH/BSCP 87-53 Box 1.

40. APR to "Brother," Oct. 25, 1929, and "Group Plan of Organization" (ca. Oct. 25, 1929), UCB/CLD Box 9; APR to MPW, Aug. 10, 1928, CHS/BSCP Box 3; for more on the plan see chapter 4.

41. RCT, "My Life"; ALT to APR Aug. 29, 1935, LC/APR Box 1; Festival of American Folklife, 1983 and 1984, recordings of retired sleeping car porters, SI/OFP; see also CLD to C. Beridon, Feb. 18, 1938, UCB/CLD Box 6: "No, the sisters cannot vote in the Brotherhood election and . . . the porters cannot participate in the Auxiliary election."

42. J. A. Koupal to A. V. Burr, memo, Sept. 19, 1927, "Propaganda," PCOP; "St. Louis," *Messenger* 10 (1927): 335. Gilmore is not mentioned in T. D. McNeal's or E. J. Bradley's version of the division history, LC/APR Box 10, although she is mentioned in contemporary reports.

43. J. A. Koupal to A. V. Burr, Sept. 19, 1927, PCOP.

44. Ibid.

45. LeRoy, "Founding Heart," 37; *Black Worker* (Feb. 1930): 2; (Aug. 1930): 2; (Mar. 1938): 2; RCT, "My Life"; "Souvenir Program."

46. RCT, "My Life."

47. Ibid.; EJB, "Some of My Early Experiences"; "Souvenir Program."

48. Ada Dillon and Sara Harper, "New York Local Organized Oct. 1925," LC/BSCP Box 74.

49. *Messenger* 11 (1928): 16, and 10 (Dec. 1927): 358; also MPW to APR, Mar. 28, 1927, CHS/BSCP Box 2.

50. "Women's Economic Council of Los Angeles," *Messenger* 11 (Jan. 1928): 15; Santino, *Miles of Smiles*, 2; *Messenger* 10 (Dec. 1927): 359.

51. Chicago *Defender,* Dec. 12, 1928, cited in Sterling D. Spero and Abram L. Harris, *The Black Worker: The Negro and the Labor Movement* (1931; reprint, New York: Antheneum, 1969), 457; APR to MPW, Oct. 4, 1928, CHS/BSCP Box 3; APR to CLD, Feb. 14, 1940, UCB/CLD, Box 4; MPW to APR, Mar. 15, 1928, CHS/BSCP Box 3; see also MPW to APR, Sept. 4, 1928, CHS/BSCP Box 3; APR to Robert Linton, May 12,

1932, CHS/BSCP Box 4. The rented Chicago headquarters were used for offices, overnight sleeping quarters, and a recreation hall. APR to MPW, June 26, 1928, and MPW to APR, Oct. 1, 1928, CHS/BSCP Box 3; MPW to Moore, Mar. 4, 1929, and MPW to Moore, Feb. 18, 1929, UCB/BSCP Box 393; "Souvenir Program"; CLD to W. B. Holland, Apr. 5, 1935, UCB/CLD Box 5.

52. Albrier, *Determined Advocate,* 80–81; RCT, "My Life"; Naomi DesVerney, "Speech Made at Second Anniversary in New York City" *Messenger* 11 (1928): 40.

Chapter 3: Striking for the New Manhood Movement

1. Henry Louis Gates Jr., "The Trope of the New Negro and the Reconstruction of the Image of the Black," *Representations* 24 (Fall 1988): 129–54; Sterling D. Spero and Abram L. Harris, *The Black Worker: The Negro and the Labor Movement* (1931; reprint, New York: Antheneum, 1969); Carroll Smith-Rosenberg, "The New Woman as Androgyne: Social Disorder and Gender Crisis, 1870–1936," chapter in *Disorderly Conduct: Visions of Gender in Victorian America* (New York: Oxford University Press, 1985), 245–96.

2. Frank Crosswaith, "Toward the Home Stretch," *Messenger* 9 (1926): 196; APR, "An Open Letter to Mr. E. F. Carry," *Messenger* 8 (1926): 10; Brailsford Brazeal, *The Brotherhood of Sleeping Car Porters: Its Origin and Development* (New York: Harper and Brothers, 1946), 215.

3. *The Pullman Porter,* 12; see also *Social Service Bulletin* 17 (Apr. 1927): 7; and "The Pullman Porters' Attempts to Organize," Information Service Department of Research and Education, Federal Council of Churches of Christ in America; reprint, *Messenger* 9 (1927): 164–65; 7 (1925): 289, original emphasis; "A Reply to Pullman Propaganda," *Messenger* 8 (1926): 293.

4. Dorothy Sue Cobble, *Dishing It Out: Waitresses and Their Unions in the Twentieth Century* (Urbana: University of Illinois Press, 1991), 41–42. Chinese women working as Pullman maids faced this same complex of opinions, since whites held similar sexually exploitative attitudes toward Asian women. See Evelyn Nakano Glenn, "From Servitude to Service Work: Historical Continuities in the Racial Division of Paid Reproductive Labor," in Ellen DuBois and Vicki Ruiz, eds., *Unequal Sisters: A Multicultural Reader in U.S. Women's History,* 2d. ed. (New York: Routledge, 1994), 405–35.

5. Cobble, *Dishing It Out,* 41–42; "Petitioner's Brief on Motion to Dismiss," *Brotherhood of Sleeping Car Porters v. Pullman Company,* Docket No. 20,007, Oct. 20, 1927, Interstate Commerce Commission, MSRR; Hearing Transcript, *BSCP v. the Pullman Company,* Jan. 21, 1928, Washington, D.C., CHS/BSCP Box 3; Brazeal, *The Brotherhood,* 70–71.

6. William H. Harris, *Keeping the Faith: A. Philip Randolph, Milton P. Webster, and the Brotherhood of Sleeping Car Porters, 1925–37* (Urbana: University of Illinois Press, 1977, 1991), 96.

7. APR, "The Abolition of the U.S. Railroad Labor Board," *Messenger* 9 (1926): 164; Harris, *Keeping the Faith,* 58; Spero and Harris, *Black Worker,* 124–25, 311–12, 459–60.

8. Harris, *Keeping the Faith,* 101–4; Brazeal, *The Brotherhood,* 70–75; Spero and

Harris, *Black Worker,* 455, claim Pullman spent over one million dollars to defeat the strike.

9. "Instructions to Organizers of Brotherhood of Sleeping Car Porters on Handling Strike Situation," n.d., CHS/BSCP Box 2; Jervis B. Anderson, *A. Philip Randolph: A Biographical Portrait* (1973; reprint, Berkeley: University of California Press, 1986), 200–201. The BSCP also drafted terms for settling the strike (see "Order of Negotiation," n.d. [ca. 1928] UCB/CLD Box 20).

10. *Messenger* 11 (1928): 112.

11. Brazeal, *The Brotherhood,* 212; Harris, *Keeping the Faith,* 63–64; "Souvenir Program, BSCP Silver Jubilee Anniversary and Seventh Biennial Convention," Sept. 10, 1950, RCTP.

12. Maids Service Records Box; telegram, APR to Dad Moore, Oct. 29, 1927; telegram APR to George C. Grant, Oct. 30, 1927; both in "Propaganda," PCOP; Harris, *Keeping the Faith,* 40–41; "Souvenir Program"; APR, "Ladies Auxiliary Convention," *Black Worker* (Sept. 1938): suppl. 3; Annie Foster and APR correspondence, July 14, 1939, July 20, 1939, Sept. 1940, LC/BSCP Box 75.

13. RCT, "My Life." See Santino, *Miles of Smiles,* 44–45, for a slightly different version of this story.

14. Harris, *Keeping the Faith,* 106–7; Brazeal, *The Brotherhood,* 83–84.

15. Harris, *Keeping the Faith,* 112–13; APR to MPW, June 13, 1928, quoted in Brazeal, *The Brotherhood,* 81.

16. Brazeal, *The Brotherhood,* 221–23.

17. Harris, *Keeping the Faith,* 127–29, 143–44, 150–51; Brazeal, *The Brotherhood,* 171.

18. MPW to CLD, Dec. 1, 1930, and Constitution and General Rules of the Brotherhood of Sleeping Car Porters, eff. Oct. 15, 1930, UCB/CLD Box 23.

19. Constitution and General Rules of the Brotherhood of Sleeping Car Porters, eff. Oct. 15, 1930, UCB/CLD Box 23; "Program for the Colored Women's Economic Council," n.d. (ca. 1928), UCB/CLD Box 9.

20. Naomi DesVerney, "Speech Made at Second Anniversary in New York City," *Messenger* 9 (1926): 40, 45.

21. CLD to APR, Dec. 7, 1935, UCB/CLD Box 4.

22. "National Convention," press release, n.d. (ca. 1929), UCB/CLD Box 10.

23. "By-Laws of the Colored Women's Economic Council, Ladies Auxiliary to the Brotherhood of Sleeping Car Porters," n.d. (ca. 1929), LC/APR Box 11.

24. Ibid.

25. "Program for the Colored Women's Economic Council."

26. Ibid.

27. "Division Notes, New York" *Black Worker* (Feb. 15, 1930); Pittsburgh Auxiliary Notes, *Black Worker* (April 1943): 2; Dallas Auxiliary Notes, *Black Worker* (Dec. 1947): 7; Darlene Clark Hine, "The Housewives' League of Detroit: Black Women and Economic Nationalism," in Nancy A. Hewitt and Suzanne Lebsock, eds., *Visible Women: New Essays on American History* (Urbana: University of Illinois Press, 1993), 223–41; William Muraskin, "The Harlem Boycott of 1934: Black Nationalism and the Rise of Labor Consciousness," *Labor History* 13 (Summer 1972): 361–73; Gary J. Hunter, "Don't Buy Where You Can't Work: Black Depression, 1929–1941" (Ph.D. diss., University of Michigan, 1977); Lerner, *Black Women in White America,* 443–47, 458–59, 477–88.

28. "Program for the Colored Women's Economic Council," n.d. (ca. 1928), UCB/CLD Box 23; see chapters 6 and 8.

29. "Group Plan of Organization," n.d. (ca. Oct. 25, 1929), UCB/CLD Box 9; "Analysis of Job to Control the Organization Operation Conservation of the Los Angeles District Brotherhood of Sleeping Car Porters," n.d., LC/APR Box 10.

30. "Group Plan of Organization," n.d. (ca. Oct. 25, 1929), UCB/CLD Box 9; MPW to APR, July 20, 1928, CHS/BSCP Box 3; Harris, *Keeping the Faith*, 128–29; Mattie Mae Stafford, "Comments on the Brotherhood," *Black Worker* (Oct. 1935): 3; see also Mattie Mae Stafford to President, Women's Economic Council, Sept. 30, 1936, UCB/CLD Box 2.

31. CLD to C. Beridon, Feb. 18, 1938, UCB/CLD Box 6; RCT, "My Life"; Mazie Sandle and C. V. Austin to APR, July 9, 1939; Mazie Sandle and Mrs. C. V. Austin to APR, Aug. 12, 1939; and APR to Mrs. Sandle and Mrs. Austin, Aug. 18, 1939; Lottie Moore to APR, May 10, 1940; APR to Lottie Moore, May 23, 1940, all in LC/BSCP Box 75.

32. "By-Laws of the Colored Women's Economic Council."

33. APR to "Brother," Oct. 25, 1929; Harris, *Keeping the Faith*, 163–64; Paula F. Pfeffer, *A. Philip Randolph, Pioneer of the Civil Rights Movement* (Baton Rouge: Louisiana State University Press, 1990), 37.

34. Anderson, *A. Philip Randolph*, 127–29; Darlene Clark Hine, "The Housewives' League of Detroit: Black Women and Economic Nationalism," in Hewitt and Lebsock, eds., *Visible Women*, 223–45.

35. See generally, Nancy J. Weiss, *Farewell to the Party of Lincoln: Blacks in the Age of FDR* (Princeton: Princeton University Press, 1982); Robin D. G. Kelley, *Hammer and Hoe: Alabama Communists in the Great Depression* (Chapel Hill: University of North Carolina Press, 1990); David Levering Lewis, *When Harlem Was in Vogue* (1979; reprint, New York: Oxford University Press, 1981); Harvard Sitkoff, *A New Deal for Blacks: The Emergence of Civil Rights as a National Issue: The Depression Decade* (New York: Oxford University Press, 1978).

36. Anderson, *A. Philip Randolph*, 78, 82, 150; Theodore Kornweibel, *No Crystal Stair: Black Life and the Messenger, 1917–1928* (Westport, Conn.: Greenwood Press, 1975), 30, 53; Peter Wallenstein, "Lucille Campbell Green Randolph," s.v. *Black Women in America*, ed. Darlene Clark Hine (Brooklyn, N.Y.: Carlson Publishing Co., 1993).

37. Geraldine Smallwood Jackson to APR, Feb. 8, 1955, LC/BSCP Box 106; see also William Smallwood to CLD, June 18, 1935, and Geraldine Dorthulla Smallwood, Recording Secretary, to CLD, Aug. 13, 1935, UCB/CLD Box 6.

38. Geraldine Dorthulla Smallwood to APR, Feb. 8, 1955, LC/BSCP Box 106; "In Memoriam," *Black Worker* (Sept. 1939): 2.

39. ALT, *Report of Proceedings of the Seventh Biennial Convention and Silver Jubilee, Ladies Auxiliary . . . Held at New York, N.Y., Sept. 11 to 13, 1950*, 156–57, RCTP.

40. Ibid., 20; *Report of the Proceedings of the First National Convention of the Ladies Auxiliary . . . Held at Chicago, Ill., Sept. 24 to 27, 1938*, CHS/BSCP Box 27; LeRoy, "Founding Heart," 32–36.

41. EJB, "Some of My Early Experiences"; APR to Ashley L. Totten, Mar. 26, 1942, LC/APR Box 9.

42. Harris, *Keeping the Faith*, 179–89; Brazeal, *The Brotherhood*, 101–2, 141–42.

43. Brazeal, *The Brotherhood*, 10–11.

44. Harris, *Keeping the Faith*, 199–201; Brazeal, *The Brotherhood*, 144–45; Spero and Harris, *Black Worker*, 284–86, 300.

45. Harris, *Keeping the Faith*, 203. If Crawford or Pullman Company officials had been aware of the AFL's decision, they might have continued to ignore the BSCP or begun negotiations with the Order of Sleeping Car Conductors (with which they had signed a contract in 1922) on behalf of the porters and maids. Whatever the case, Crawford was obviously unaware of the AFL's deliberations.

46. Harris, *Keeping the Faith*, 204.

47. CLD to W. B. Holland, July 9, 1935, UCB/CLD Box 5; Harris, *Keeping the Faith*, 206–7; Brazeal, *The Brotherhood*, 106–11; *Black Worker* (July 1935): 2.

48. Fannie Caviness, *Report of the Proceedings of the First National Convention of the Ladies Auxiliary . . . Held at Chicago, Ill., Sept. 24 to 27, 1938*, 25–26, CHS/BSCP Box 27; "Meet the Family of Porter J. L. Caviness," *Pullman News* (Oct. 1948): 34–35; "Souvenir Program, Brotherhood of Sleeping Car Porters Silver Jubilee Anniversary and Seventh Biennial Convention," Sept. 10, 1950, RCTP.

49. Anderson, *A. Philip Randolph*, 9–10; Joseph F. Wilson, ed., *Tearing Down the Color Bar: An Analysis and Documentary History of the Brotherhood of Sleeping Car Porters* (New York: Columbia University Press, 1989), 45–47.

50. MPW, "The Brotherhood Case and the Mediation Board," *Black Worker* (Feb./Mar. 1936): 4. A. Sagittarius, a columnist for *The Messenger* and *The Black Worker*, continued to write articles about manhood, however. See, for example, "The Brotherhood as an Aid to True Manhood," (Dec. 1936): 2.

Chapter 4: "The First International Ladies' Auxiliary to the First Negro Trade Union in the World"

1. The railroad brotherhood auxiliaries, as well as other trade unions, usually called themselves "women's" auxiliaries. "Ladies Auxiliaries" were more common among men's service and veterans' organizations.

2. Marjorie Murphy, *Blackboard Unions: The AFT and the NEA, 1900–1980* (Ithaca: Cornell University Press, 1990), 83, 163–65, 172–73; Ethel Payne interview, Washington, D.C., Apr. 10, 1991; TTP to CLD, Apr. 8, 1938, and TTP to CLD, Aug. 22, 1938, UCB/CLD Box 2; "Conference on Domestic Service," May 19–22, 1938, CHS/BSCP Box 5; Brailsford Brazeal, *The Brotherhood of Sleeping Car Porters: Its Origin and Development* (New York: Harper and Brothers, 1946), 183.

3. RCT, "My Life As I Have Lived It," (ca. 1980), RCTP; HW, "Welcome Address," *Report of the Proceedings of the First National Convention of the Ladies Auxiliary to the Brotherhood of Sleeping Car Porters . . . Held at Chicago, Ill., September 24 to 27, 1938* (Chicago: International Ladies' Auxiliary, 1938), 13–15 (hereinafter, *First National Convention*).

4. Mary Ann Clawson, "Nineteenth Century Women's Auxiliaries and Fraternal Orders," *Signs* 12 (Winter 1986): 40–61.

5. CLD to Mattie Mae Stafford, May 7, 1936, UCB/CLD Box 5; CLD to Mrs. F. E. Thompson, Jan. 14, 1938, UCB/CLD Box 9; CLD to K. W. Phillips, June 25, 1938, UCB/CLD Box 6.

6. *Black Worker* (Nov. 1935): 2; (Mar. 1936): 2; (Feb./Mar. 1937): 2; (Apr. 1937): 2; Minutes, Chicago BSCP Division, Oct. 29, 1936, CHS/BSCP Box 4.

7. *Black Worker* (July 1935): 2; (May 1935): 2; (Jan. 1943): 3.

8. "Negro Women Turn Attention to Problems of Labor," *Black Worker* (Mar. 1932): 1, in LC/APR Box 54; T. L. Williamson, "Opening Processional," 1940, CHS/BSCP Box 27.

9. "Fifth Annual Membership Inspirational Tea and Candle-lighting Service," *Black Worker* (Apr. 1938): 2.

10. *Black Worker* (Nov. 1936): 2; (Oct. 1935): 2.

11. *Black Worker* (May 1936): 1.

12. M. C. Oglesby, "Your Opportunity, My Opportunity" *Black Worker* (June 1937): 2.

13. Mrs. Bennie [Hazel] Smith, "The Negro Woman Faces the Future," *Black Worker* (Feb. 1938): 2; (Mar. 1938): 2.

14. Smith, "Negro Woman," 2.

15. A. Sagittarius, "With the Ladies' Auxiliary," *Black Worker* (Jan. 1936): 3.

16. A. Sagittarius, "The Stuff is Here," *Black Worker* (Oct. 1937): 7.

17. Ibid.

18. *Black Worker* (June 1935): 2; (Sept. 1935): 2; (June 1936): 2; Robin D. G. Kelley, *Hammer and Hoe: Alabama Communists in the Great Depression* (Chapel Hill: University of North Carolina Press, 1990), 18, 85, 124, 178.

19. *Black Worker* (July 1935): 2; (Feb./Mar. 1936): 2; "Miss Cuthbert Counsels Union of All Workers," *Black Worker* (Aug. 1936): 8; (May 1936): 2; (Nov. 1936): 2; (Jan. 1937): 1; RCT, "Report," *Black Worker* (May 1938): 2; (July 1938): 3; see also *New Negro Alliance v. Sanitary Grocery Company,* 303 U.S. 552, 58 S.Ct. 703 (1938) and *Green v. Samuelson,* 168 Md. 421, 178 A. 109 (1935); Rosalyn Terborg-Penn, "Survival Strategies among Afro-American Women," in Ruth Milkman, ed., *Women, Work, and Protest: A Century of Women's Labor History* (Boston: Routledge & Kegan Paul, 1985), 139–55.

20. *Black Worker* (May 1938): 2; (Aug. 1936): 7.

21. *Black Worker* (Nov. 1935): 2.

22. APR, *Black Worker* (Sept. 1938): suppl. 6; *Black Worker* (Aug. 1936): 6.

23. *Black Worker* (Aug. 1936): 6; Harvard Sitkoff, *A New Deal for Blacks: The Emergence of Civil Rights as a National Issue: The Depression Decade* (New York: Oxford University Press, 1978), 167; Kelley, *Hammer and Hoe,* 198–204; Pfeffer, *A. Philip Randolph,* 34–43; *Black Worker* (June 1938): 2.

24. *Black Worker* (Jan. 1937): 2; Paula S. Fass, *The Damned and Beautiful: American Youth in the 1920s* (New York: Oxford University Press, 1979), 213–15.

25. Lester B. Granger, "The Negro—Friend or Foe of Organized Labor?" in Joanne Grant, ed., *Black Protest: A Documentary History* (New York: Fawcett, 1972), 236. Rye seems to be the same person as "Fry" in *Black Worker* (Feb./Mar. 1936): 2; (Dec. 1936): 2; (Sept. 1935): 2; (May 1937): 2; (June 1937): 2; (Mar. 1940): 2.

26. *Black Worker* (Feb./Mar. 1937): 3; Ada V. Dillon, "My Work on a WPA Project," *Black Worker* (Feb./Mar. 1936): 1, in RCTP.

27. *Black Worker* (July 1935): 2; Ruth Bogin, "Crystal Bird Fauset," s.v., *Notable American Women: The Modern Period,* ed. Edward T. James et al. (Cambridge, Mass.: Belknap Press of Harvard University, 1971).

28. Program, BSCP Labor Mass Meeting, Dec. 6–11, 1936; Tucker to Mary Anderson, Nov. 19, 1936, both in NARA/W Box 52; Mary Mason Jones, "The Negro Woman As a Factor in the Economic Life of America," *Black Worker* (Aug. 1938): 2, and (Oct. 1938): 2.

29. BSCP and Worker's Education Bureau, "Labor and the National Recovery Program," handbill, ca. July 20, 1934, LC/APR Box 54; "Gertrude MacDougald," *Black Worker* (Aug. 1938): 2, and (Dec. 1938): 2.

30. Pauli Murray, *Song in a Weary Throat: An American Pilgrimage* (New York: Harper & Row, 1987), 105–7; see generally APR-Murray correspondence (some unidentified) in LC/APR Boxes 2 and 24.

31. "Principle File Including Minutes, History of Porters' Agreement of Oct. 1, 1937," PCOP File 2095–9 (hereinafter "Principle File"); see also CLD to Charles Upton, June 10, 1937, UCB/CLD Box 30, and CLD to "Members of the Pacific Coast Division, BSCP," July 23, 1935, UCB/CLD Box 20.

32. "Principle File."

33. "Calling Passengers," *Instructions for Porters, Attendants and Busboys* (Chicago: Pullman Company, 1952), 46–47; Minutes, Apr. 7, 1937, in "Principle File"; see also Patricia and Fredrick McKissack, *A Long Hard Journey: The Story of the Pullman Porter* (New York: Walker, 1989), 21.

34. L. M. Greenlaw, file memo, July 19, 1937, "Principle File"; "Agreement between the Pullman Company and the Porters, Maids, Attendants and Bus-Boys represented by the Brotherhood of Sleeping Car Porters, eff. Oct. 1, 1937," LC/BSCP Box 52; this point was central in the aborted 1928 strike, see [BSCP] "Order of Negotiation," n.d. (ca. 1928), UCB/CLD Box 20.

35. BSCP's Proposed Agreement, Oct. 1, 1935, "Principle File"; see also [BSCP], "Order of Negotiation"; see also CLD to W. B. Holland, Sept. 8, 1938, UCB/CLD Box 5.

36. William H. Harris, *Keeping the Faith: A. Philip Randolph, Milton P. Webster, and the Brotherhood of Sleeping Car Porters, 1925–37* (Urbana: University of Illinois Press, 1977, 1991), 214–15; Minutes, Apr. 14, 1935 [*sic:* 1937], "Principle File"; Edward Berman, Ph.D., "Brief for the Brotherhood of Sleeping Car Porters," n.d. [1936], CHS/BSCP Box 4.

37. Minutes, Apr 7, 1937; Minutes, Apr. 14, 1935 [*sic:* 1937]; both in "Principle File."

38. Minutes of meeting with Mediator Cole, Apr. 6, 1937; Minutes, Apr. 14, 1935 [*sic:* 1937]; Minutes of joint meeting, May 19, 1937, all in "Principle File."

39. "Record of Grievance of Maid Y. J. Drye," Feb. 1937, UCB/CLD Box 12; "Current Grievances," *Black Worker* (July 1937): 3; see also MPW to CLD, Aug. 1, 1933, UCB/CLD Box 34; CLD to MPW, Mar. 31, 1937, CLD to MPW, Apr. 8, 1937, CLD to MPW, Sept. 10, 1937, all in UCB/CLD Box 4.

40. CLD to MPW, Sept. 10, 1937; CLD to MPW, Mar. 24, 1937, CLD to MPW, Mar. 31, 1937, CLD to APR, Nov. 8, 1937, CLD to MPW, Nov. 10, 1937, all in UCB/CLD Box 4.

41. Vroman, Lary, and Ruddy to Carry, memo, "Disputed rules of porters agreement," July 23, 1937; L. M. Greenlaw to Champ Carry and H. R. Lary, memo, Aug. 19, 1937; both in "Principle File."

42. Minutes, Aug. 25, 1937, 10:40 A.M., Present: APR, MPW, ALT, CLD, EJB,

Bennie Smith, Robert Cole, Champ Carry, George A. Kelly, Frank Vroman, Mr. Ruddy, H. R. Lary, in "Principle File"; Harris, *Keeping the Faith,* 215; Harry E. Jones, *Railroad Wages and Labor Relations, 1900–1952: An Historical Survey and Summary of Results* (New York: Bureau of Information of the Eastern Railways, 1953), 106–7, notes that on Aug. 25, 1937, the National Mediation Board negotiated a national agreement providing a five cent per hour wage increase for all non-operating workers in the Big Five Brotherhoods. On that same date, engine and train service workers began voting to strike should the NMB fail to produce a similar contract for them.

43. "Agreement between the Pullman Company and porters, attendants, and maids in the service of the Pullman Company in the United States of America and Canada, represented by the Brotherhood of Sleeping Car Porters, effective Oct. 1, 1937"; Dellums reported the Southern Pacific refused to allow its three working maids to be included in the bargaining unit during 1942 contract negotiations, CLD to APR, Apr. 9, 1942, UCB/CLD Box 4.

44. CLD to APR, Apr. 9, 1942, UCB/CLD Box 4.

45. Preston Valien, "The Brotherhood of Sleeping Car Porters," *Phylon* 3 (1940): 235; Industrial Relations Division, Pullman Company, memo, Aug. 25, 1937, PCOP; "The Friends We Make," *Pullman News* (Oct. 1943): 67; Charles Upton to CLD, Oct. 4, 1937, UCB/CLD Box 30; Ernest Smith to MPW, Feb. 21, 1940, CHS/BSCP Box 6. Although seniority rosters give the names of maids, few apparently had regular work; compare "Maids' Seniority Roster, San Francisco District, Jan. 1, 1941," UCB/CLD Box 22, listing twenty-five women, with CLD to MPW, Feb. 27, 1941, UCB/CLD Box 4, noting the Pacific Zone had "575 Porters and Attendants *on the payroll* and no maids" (my emphasis). See also State of California, Department of Industrial Relations, Division of Labor Statistics and Law Enforcement, "Organized Labor Questionnaire," June 1, 1941, UCB/CLD Box 1.

46. *Black Worker* (Nov. 1935): 4.

47. Frances Mary Albrier, *Frances Mary Albrier: Determined Advocate for Racial Equality,* interview conducted by Malca Chall. Women in Politics Oral History Project (Berkeley: Regional Oral History Office, Bancroft Library, University of California, 1979), 88, 98–102.

48. "Diagram of Structure and Affiliations," [ca. 1938] LC/BSCP Box 67; Brazeal, *The Brotherhood,* 171–95.

49. In a panel discussion, "Women in the Early Years of the Civil Rights Movement: The 1930s–1950s," at the University of Virginia, June 1, 1989, Modjeska Simpkins commented succinctly, "White women were ladies, black females were 'women.'"

50. "Midwestern Regional Conference of the Ladies' Auxiliary," *Black Worker* (Oct. 1937): 4; Lillian Herstein, *First National Convention, 1938,* 41–43.

51. Lillian Herstein, *First National Convention, 1938,* 41–43; Vice President E. J. Bradley represented the St. Louis Council by proxy; as Brazeal noted, "Study of the names of Auxiliary delegates, as compared to those of delegates to the Brotherhood's convention reveals that very few indicated that they belonged to wives of Brotherhood delegates." Brazeal, *The Brotherhood,* 191–92.

52. APR, "The Ladies Auxiliary," *Black Worker* (Sept. 1938): suppl. 3.

53. APR, "Opening Address," *First National Convention, 1938,* 4.

54. Edwards, *First National Convention, 1938,* 44; TTP to CLD, Apr. 8, 1938, and TTP to CLD, Aug. 22, 1938, UCB/CLD Box 2.

55. Herstein, *First National Convention, 1938,* 39.

56. APR, *First National Convention,* 9, 7.

57. Ibid., 9.

58. Ibid., 10, 12.

59. Ibid., 12.

60. Greetings, *First National Convention, 1938,* 27, 26, 22.

61. Ibid., 25.

62. Herstein, *First National Convention, 1938,* 39, 41–43; Susan Ware, *Beyond Suffrage: Women in the New Deal* (Cambridge: Harvard University Press, 1981), 79, 117–19; and Ware, *Holding Their Own: American Women in the 1930s* (Boston: Twayne Publishers, 1982), 27–29.

63. Herstein, *First National Convention, 1938,* 43.

64. See also Paul H. Douglas, *Wages and the Family* (Chicago: University of Chicago Press, 1925). Douglas served as an advisor to the BSCP during its 1935–37 contract negotiations; Harris, *Keeping the Faith,* 210–11; and Martha May, "The Historical Problem of the Family Wage: The Ford Motor Company and the Five Dollar Day," in Ellen Carol DuBois and Vicki L. Ruiz, eds., *Unequal Sisters: A Multi-Cultural Reader in U.S. Women's History* (New York: Routledge, Chapman & Hall, Inc., 1990), 275–91; Murphy, *Blackboard Unions,* 172–73.

65. RCT, "My Life"; RCT, *First National Convention, 1938,* 28.

66. "Constitution and By-Laws of the International Ladies' Auxiliary to the Brotherhood of Sleeping Car Porters," Art. 5, *First National Convention, 1938,* 52.

67. Ibid.

68. Ibid., Art. 12, p. 57.

69. "Report of the Committee on Workers' Education," in *First National Convention, 1938,* 46. The reading list included the magazines *Consumers' Union* and *Consumers' Guide;* M. C. Phillips, *Skin Deep;* Ruth DeForest Lamb, *The American Chamber of Horrors;* Stuart Chase, *Your Money's Worth,* "and books similar to above." Also recommended were pamphlets from the Central States Cooperative League, "A Short Introduction to Consumers' Cooperation" and the Consumers' Cooperative Services, "The Story of Toad Lane."

70. Resolutions, *First National Convention, 1938,* 68–71.

71. APR, Resolution No. 8, *First National Convention, 1938,* 70; the Auxiliary joined the NCNW in 1943 for one year, but withdrew when dues were raised; HW and APR thought NCNW failed to address economic issues sufficiently.

72. Deborah Gray White, "The Price of Club Work, the Price of Feminism," in Hewitt and Lebsock, eds., *Visible Women,* 247–69.

73. *First National Convention, 1938,* 82–84; Edith Bell Bailey to CLD, Nov. 5, 1941, UCB/CLD Box 9.

Chapter 5: "A Bigger and Better Ladies' Auxiliary"

1. MPW to CLD, July 21, 1939, CLD to MPW, Aug. 22, 1939, and MPW to CLD, Aug. 25, 1939, all in UCB/CLD Box 4; Anon. to CLD, Jan. 30, 1939, Florence

Thompson to CLD, Jan. 30, 1939, Florence Thompson to CLD, Feb. 19, 1939, UCB/CLD Box 7; "Do Not Separate the Groups," *Black Worker* (Jan. 1942): 4.

2. HW to Members, n.d. (ca. Mar. 1941), UCB/CLD Box 39; APR, "Concerning Dual Ladies' Auxiliary Organizations," n.d. (ca. Mar. 1941), LC/BSCP Box 74; APR to CLD, Mar. 4, 1941, UCB/CLD Box 4; H. Dumas to CLD, Mar. 2 [1941?], UCB/CLD Box 6; APR to Osmond Cole, Nov. 24, 1953, LC/BSCP Box 80; HW to Lucille Jones, Jan. 26, 1942; HW to local Secretary-Treasurers, Oct. 22, 1940; HW to Mrs. S. W. Austin, Nov. 26, 1942, all in CHS/BSCP Box 27.

3. International Ladies' Auxiliary Bulletin, June 5, 1939, and International Ladies' Auxiliary Bulletin, ca. 1938, both in LC/BSCP Box 74.

4. Dellums commented on this point: "History has always depicted the action of men, as being based on a background where women played an important part, and no doubt with the women injected internationally in this movement, they are going to play an important part in this movement, either good or otherwise." CLD to TTP, April 13, 1939, UCB/CLD Box 2. See Elizabeth Faue, *Community of Suffering and Struggle: Women, Men, and the Labor Movement in Minneapolis, 1915–1945* (Chapel Hill: University of North Carolina Press, 1991), 67–99; and generally, Barbara Melosh, "Manly Work: Public art and masculinity in Depression America," and Melissa Dabakis, "Gendered Labor: Norman Rockwell's *Rosie the Riveter* and the discourses of wartime womanhood," in Melosh, ed., *Gender and American History since 1890* (New York: Routledge, 1993), 155–204; La'Tonya Rease, " 'The sink had belonged to someone else': Representations of Black Women's Work in *The Street* and *Brown Girl, Brownstones," Truth: Newsletter of the Association of Black Women Historians* 11:3 (Spring 1994): 20–28.

5. K. Sue Jewell, *From Mammy to Miss America and Beyond: Cultural Images and the Shaping of U.S. Social Policy* (London: Routledge, 1993), 22, 37–44; Patricia Morton, *Disfigured Images: The Historical Assault on Afro-American Women* (Westport, Conn.: Greenwood Press, 1991), 7–10; Gloria Joseph and Jill Lewis, *Common Differences: Conflicts in Black and White Feminist Perspectives* (Garden City, N.Y.: Anchor Press, 1981). Note also that in 1939, Hattie Gossett won an Academy Award for her portrayal of "Mammy" in *Gone With the Wind,* the first African American to be recognized for acting.

6. HW to Local Secretary-Treasurers, Oct. 22, 1940, LC/BSCP Box 27; Rhonda Y. Williams, "Does this Work Ever End?: Toward a Historiographical Synthesis of Black Women's Work Experiences," Spring 1994, University of Pennsylvania, unpublished paper, copy in author's possession.

7. HW to APR, Oct. 21, 1942; HW to APR, Nov. 18, 1942; HW to APR, Aug. 5, 1943, and HW to APR, Dec. 20, 1943, all in CHS/BSCP Box 7; Louise Myers, *Report of the Proceedings of the Southwestern Zone Conference, BSCP, Houston, Texas, April 24–29, 1949,* 23.

8. APR, *Black Worker* (Sept. 1938): suppl. 5.

9. Ibid., 6.

10. Ibid., 5; RCT, speech "Delivered 11/6/52," RCTP.

11. CLD to TTP, Nov. 29, 1938, CLD to TTP, Mar. 28, 1939, CLD to TTP, April 13, 1939, UCB/CLD Box 2; CLD to MPW, May 20, 1940, UCB/CLD Box 4; Charles Upton to CLD, May 24, 1939, UCB/CLD Box 30; Bennie Smith to APR, Oct. 2, 1944, LC/APR Box 8.

12. Letitia Murray to APR, Mar. 15, 1938, LC/BSCP Box 73; *Report of the Proceedings of the First Biennial Convention of the Ladies Auxiliary . . . Held at New York, N.Y., Sept. 15 to 20, 1940,* 1–2, RCTP. When the El Paso Auxiliary notified Dellums of its intention to disband, he wrote letters to all BSCP and Auxiliary officials, asking them to reconsider; see CLD to Mrs. G. L. Lopez, Mar. 5, 1940, CLD to HW, Mar. 5, 1940, CLD to King Philips, Mar. 5, 1940, all in UCB/CLD Box 9; see the appendix for membership figures.

13. "Smokers" were typically male-only events, see CLD to W. B. Holland, Nov. 6, 1939, UCB/CLD Box 30; and ALT to CLD, Oct. 21, 1939, UCB/CLD Box 3; *Black Worker* (October 1939): 1.

14. HW to Member, Feb. 13, 1941, CHS/BSCP Box 27; other Auxiliary activities in Oklahoma City are discussed in Lessie Bennet and Emma C. Jones to APR May 23, 1941, LC/BSCP Box 74; APR to Mrs. Carrie Edwards, Jan. 27, 1948, LC/APR Box 20; APR to Mrs A. Stewart, Jan. 27, 1948, LC/APR Box 21; Mrs. Carrie L. Edwards to APR, Feb. 9, 1948, LC/APR Box 21.

15. *Black Worker* (Apr. 1941): 3; Emma Starks to HW, Feb. 1, 1942, CHS/BSCP Box 27; Brailsford Brazeal, *The Brotherhood of Sleeping Car Porters: Its Origin and Development* (New York: Harper and Brothers, 1946), 221. See also the appendix.

16. Letitia Murray to APR, Dec. 17, 1938; Letitia Murray to APR, Dec. 26, 1938, both in LC/BSCP Box 73; Letitia Murray to CLD, May 24, 1939; Letitia Murray to CLD, July 28, 1939, UCB/CLD Box 9; MPW to CLD, Mar. 4, 1939, UCB/CLD Box 4; "Financial Report, July 1, 1940 to Dec. 31, 1940," RCTP; Brazeal, *The Brotherhood,* 222.

17. CLD to APR, July 5, 1946, UCB/CLD Box 4.

18. Bennie Smith to HW, Feb. 26, 1943, CHS/BSCP Box 29.

19. V. I. Petgrave, "A Saga of the Sleeping Car Porters of the Canadian Pacific Railway Company," *Black Worker* (May 1945): 3, and (June 1945): 2.

20. *Report of the Proceedings of the First Biennial Convention of the International Ladies Auxiliary to the Brotherhood of Sleeping Car Porters . . . Held at New York, N.Y., September 15 to 20, 1940* [Chicago: International Ladies' Auxiliary, 1940], 104.

21. "Oath," n.d., UCB/CLD Box 24; RCT to Secretary-Treasurer, n.d. (ca. 1939), UCB/CLD Box 39; *First Biennial Convention, 1940,* 104–5.

22. Rosina Corrothers-Tucker, *Marching Together* (n.p., 1939); Letitia Murray, *First Biennial Convention, 1940,* 38–39, RCTP; *Black Worker* (Aug. 1942): 3. Other popular Brotherhood songs included "John Brown's Body" and "We Shall Not Be Moved." The Cleveland Auxiliary also sang "Workers' Lullaby" and "Union Maid," "Cleveland BSCP and Ladies Auxiliary Program," Aug. 17, 1946, CHS/BSCP Box 10.

23. HW to Velmer Coward, Dec. 11, 1942, CHS/BSCP Box 28.

24. RCT, speech "Delivered 11/6/52," RCTP.

25. International Ladies' Auxiliary Bulletin, ca. 1938, LC/BSCP Box 74.

26. "Bulletin of Instruction, Decisions and Orders of the First Convention of the Ladies' Auxiliary and International Executive Board," ca. Oct. 1938, CHS/BSCP Box 27; Letitia Murray to CLD, Dec. 6, 1939, UCB/CLD Box 6; CLD to Letitia Murray, Dec. 13, 1939, UCB/CLD Box 9; *Black Worker* (Aug. 1939): 4.

27. TTP, *First National Convention, 1938,* 21.

28. APR, *Black Worker* (Sept. 1938): suppl. 6; CLD to Letitia Murray, July 3, 1940, UCB/CLD Box 9; John R. Commons et al., *History of Labor in the United States* (New

York: Macmillan, 1935); John R. Commons, *Trade Unions and Labor Problems* (1905); E. E. Cummins, *The Labor Problem in the United States* (New York: D. Van Nostrand Co., 1935); Selig Perlman, *A Theory of the Labor Movement* (New York: Macmillan Co., 1928); Norman L. Ware, *Labor in Modern Industrial Society* (Boston: D. C. Heath and Co., 1935); Ira De A. Reid, *Negro Membership in American Labor Unions* (National Urban League, Dept. of Research and Community Projects, 1930); Charles H. Wesley, *Negro Labor in the United States* (New York: Vanguard Press, 1927); Charles Lionel Franklin, *The Negro Labor Unionist of New York* (New York: Columbia University Press, 1936); Charles S. Johnson, *The Negro in American Civilization* (New York: Henry Holt & Co., 1930); Herbert R. Northrup, *Organized Labor and the Negro* (New York: Harper & Brothers, 1944); Brazeal, *The Brotherhood;* APR to McLaurin, May 25, 1944, LC/APR Box 7.

29. Letitia Murray to APR, July 1, 1939, LC/BSCP Box 73; the *Black Worker* ran the syndicated column, "Labor Library," from September 1944 through July 1945, and occasionally thereafter; *Black Worker* (Sept. 1946): 7.

30. HW, "Organized Labor and the Ladies' Auxiliary," *Black Worker* (October 1947): 7; Alice Kessler-Harris, *Out to Work: A History of Wage-Earning Women* (New York: Oxford University Press, 1982), 40–41, 82.

31. HW, "Organized Labor and the Ladies' Auxiliary"; HW, "Women and the Labor Movement," *Black Worker,* (Jan. 1940): 2; [HW], untitled ms., n.d., CHS/BSCP Box 27; see also HW to Velmer Coward, Dec. 11, 1942, CHS/BSCP Box 28; HW to local Secretary-Treasurers, Oct. 22, 1940, LC/BSCP Box 27.

32. HW to Lucille Jones, Feb. 12, 1940, CHS/BSCP Box 27.

33. Ibid.; APR to Mrs. Napier, Aug. 5, 1939, LC/BSCP Box 73.

34. HW to Lucille Jones, Feb. 12, 1940, CHS/BSCP Box 27.

35. HW to Mrs. S. W. Austin, Nov. 26, 1941, CHS/BSCP Box 27; *Black Worker* (Aug. 1939): 4.

36. APR to Mrs. Napier, Aug. 5, 1939, and Napier to APR, May 5, 1939, both in LC/BSCP Box 73.

37. *Black Worker* (Sept. 1938): suppl. 6, original emphasis. The guest list for the Silver Tea surpassed the planners' expectations. Lady Margaret McWilliams, wife of lieutenant governor of Manitoba Province, officially opened the party with Madame Wen Tao Weng, wife of the consul of the Republic of China, also in attendance. Representatives attended from the Fur and Leather Workers' Union, the Glove Makers' Union; the Eastern Star; the Local Council of Women; the Polish Federation of Canada; British War Wives Association; Bethel A.M.E. Mission; Cooperative Commonwealth Federation Labor Party; Pilgrim Baptist Church; Wee Hour Club; Maple Leaf Lodge No. 22 of the Ladies' Auxiliary to the Canadian Brotherhood of Railroad Employees; and Victoria Temple Daughters of Elks Lodge. The premier of Manitoba, the mayor of Winnipeg, and members of the city council were patrons of the event. *Black Worker* (July 1945): 2.

38. *Black Worker* (Apr. 1938): 2; (Nov. 1945): 5; (June 1946): 7; (Feb. 48): 7; (Dec. 1948): 7; (May 1949): 7; (Dec. 1949): 7; HW to Dear Member, July 12, 1948, LC/BSCP Box 75. BSCP officers were also concerned that union "entertainments" reflect the organization's standing; see for example, Minutes, Chicago Division BSCP, May 16, 1939, CHS/BSCP Box 6; and Minutes, Nov. 27, 1942, CHS/BSCP Box 7; Eva Swait, *Southwestern Zone Conference, 1949,* 23; but see Kathryn J. Oberdeck, " 'Not Pink

Teas': The Seattle Working-Class Women's Movement, 1905–1918," *Labor History* 32 (Spring 1991): 193–230.

39. HW to Member, July 12, 1948, LC/BSCP Box 75; Lillian Herstein, *First National Convention, 1938, 42.*

40. Nate Brown, "We Assist a Ladies' Auxiliary," *Compiled Narrative Reports of Workers' Service Program,* Nov. 1–30, 1941, 14, copy in LC/BSCP Box 31.

41. HW to Velmer Coward, Dec. 11, 1942, CHS/BSCP Box 28; HW, "To All Past and Present Auxiliary Members Everywhere," *Black Worker* (Mar. 1945): 3.

42. Auxiliary members also questioned BSCP officials about the salaries Wilson and Tucker received for their work; see CLD to MPW, Mar. 28, 1939, and CLD to APR, Mar. 28, 1939, both in UCB/CLD Box 4. Rosina Tucker did see herself as a worker, especially during her separations from her husband, see RCT, "My Life."

43. Elizabeth Craig to HW, Jan. 1, 1944, CHS/BSCP Box 34.

44. HW, "Women and the Labor Movement," *Black Worker* (Jan. 1940): 2.

45. Ibid.

46. Mae Dailey, Southwestern Zone Report, *Report of the Proceedings of the Second Biennial Convention of the Ladies Auxiliary . . . Held at St. Louis, Sept. 15 to 19, 1942,* 56; Mrs. C. M. [Susanna D.] Lester, "Women in Organized Labor," *Black Worker* (Nov. 1944): 3.

47. CLD to P. J. Gallagher, Sept. 19, 1939, UCB/CLD Box 20; CLD to Charles Real, Teamsters Brotherhood Local No. 70, Nov. 4, 1942, and CLD to Director of Admissions, University of California, Berkeley, Mar. 6, 1939, UCB/CLD Box 1; CLD to Harry Kingman, Nov. 22, 1944, UCB/CLD Box 23; CLD to Harry T. Kraus, Feb. 19, 1952, and CLD to John F. Fisher, July 3, 1952, UCB/CLD Box 2; Frances Mary Albrier, *Frances Mary Albrier: Determined Advocate for Racial Equality,* interview conducted by Malca Chall. Women in Politics Oral History Project (Berkeley: Regional Oral History Office, Bancroft Library, University of California, 1979), 128–35.

48. Throughout 1944 and 1945, attendance at Auxiliary meetings declined according to reports in the *Black Worker;* Letitia Murray, Pacific Zone Report, *Report of the Proceedings of the Fourth Biennial Convention of the Ladies' Auxiliary . . . Held at Cleveland, Ohio, Sept. 18 to 20, 1944,* [Chicago: The International Ladies Auxiliary to the BSCP, 1944], 65–68; *Black Worker,* (Feb. 1945): 2; (July 1946): 7.

49. Katherine Lassiter, *Fourth Biennial Convention, 1944,* 56; *Black Worker* (Nov. 1944): 2; HW to Myrtle Haskins, Oct. 28, 1943, CHS/BSCP Box 29.

50. "Jamaica, L.I. members" to APR, June 24, 1945, LC/BSCP Box 74; TTP to HW, Apr. 20, 1942, CHS/BSCP Box 27. Union membership on Long Island was substantial enough to station a field agent there.

51. HW to McLaurin, Apr. 27, 1943, CHS/BSCP Box 27; HW to APR, Dec. 5, 1945, CHS/BSCP Box 7; HW to Sara Harper, Jan. 28, 1946, LC/BSCP Box 76.

52. Katherine Lassiter, "Report of Eastern Zone Tour," *Report of the Proceedings of the Fifth Biennial Convention of the Ladies Auxiliary . . . Held at Chicago, Ill., Sept 16 to 18, 1946,* CHS/BSCP Box 30; Lumattie DeBerry, President to HW, "1946," CHS/BSCP Box 30.

53. RCT, "Visits," n.d., RCTP.

54. Letitia Murray to APR, CLD, and HW, Oct. 8, 1940, UCB/CLD Box 9; APR to Letitia Murray, Oct. 18, 1940, and Letitia Murray to APR, Oct. 25, 1940, LC/BSCP

Box 73; see also CLD to APR, Dec. 3, 1940, UCB/CLD Box 4; Charles Upton to CLD, Aug. 9, 1939, and CLD to Charles Upton, Aug. 17, 1939, both in UCB/CLD Box 5.

55. Mabel Brown to Bennie Smith, Mar. 18, 1943, CHS/BSCP Box 29. HW to APR, Oct. 13, 1944, LC/BSCP Box 76. HW asked if she should expunge the convention minutes of remarks made by the Winnipeg delegate "to the effect that the Brotherhood local was requesting money from the Auxiliary so its members could have monthly beer parties." APR permitted the deletion, APR to HW, Oct. 15, 1944, LC/BSCP Box 76. Art. 27, "Location of Offices," covered all Auxiliary offices, but not meeting places, *Constitution and By-Laws of the International Ladies' Auxiliary to the Brotherhood of Sleeping Car Porters,* rev. 1940 [Chicago: the International Ladies' Auxiliary]. Cleanliness and use of the BSCP union hall was frequently an issue elsewhere; see for example, CLD to Charles Upton, July 19, 1938, UCB/CLD Box 5; CLD to J. C. Martin, July 2, 1938, UCB/CLD Box 6; Charles Upton to CLD, Mar. 17, 1939, UCB/CLD Box 30; Charles Upton to CLD June 20, 1939, UCB/CLD Box 5; Ardella Nutall to CLD, Feb. 25, 1949, UCB/CLD Box 8; CLD to Ardella Nutall, Mar. 10, 1949, UCB/CLD Box 2; HW to CLD, Nov. 30, 1954, UCB/CLD Box 9.

56. Mabel Brown to Bennie Smith, Mar. 18, 1943, CHS/BSCP Box 29.

57. Ibid.

58. "Constitution and By-Laws," organized Feb. 28, 1926, revised and adopted Oct. 2, 1930, Laura Dillard, Chairman, LC/BSCP Box 74.

59. Mabel Brown to Bennie Smith, Mar. 18, 1943, CHS/BSCP Box 29.

60. Article 27, "Ladies' Auxiliary," *Constitution and General Rules of the Brotherhood of Sleeping Car Porters,* rev. 1940, [New York: BSCP, 1940], RCTP.

61. Mabel Brown to Bennie Smith, Mar. 18, 1943, CHS/BSCP Box 29.

62. Joseph Richard Hudson Jr. to Bennie Smith, Mar. 19, 1943, LC/APR Box 8.

63. Ibid.

64. APR to CLD, June 13, 1939, UCB/CLD Box 4; CLD to Charles Upton, Aug. 17, 1939, UCB/CLD Box 5; APR to Letitia Murray, Oct. 18, 1940, LC/BSCP Box 73.

65. HW to Members, Nov. 10, 1941, CHS/BSCP Box 27; see also "Do Not Separate the Groups," *Black Worker* (Jan. 1942): 4.

66. Helen Iola Hudson to HW, Feb. 22, 1944, CHS/BSCP Box 29.

67. BSCP membership also grew, see "Financial Report of Dues Paying Members as of Mar. 31, 1945," UCB/CLD Box 17. Of 9,393 sleeping car porter members, 65.5 percent were financial, having paid all dues, taxes, and special assessment through the end of 1944; the BSCP also had 1,142 car cleaners; 1,088 chair and train porters; and 470 firemen-brakemen-switchmen.

Chapter 6: "The Duty of Fair Representation"

1. Walter Licht, "The Dialectics of Bureaucratization: The Case of Nineteenth-Century American Railway Workers," in Charles Stephenson and Robert Ashers, eds., *Life and Labor: Dimensions of American Working Class History* (Albany: State University of New York Press, 1986), 92–114; Plaintiffs' First Amended Brief, *King v. Boggs* (Brotherhood of Railroad Trainmen, Order of Railway Conductors, Brotherhood of Locomotive Firemen, Brotherhood of Locomotive Engineers, Brotherhood of Locomotive Firemen and Enginemen), Circuit Court, City of St. Louis,

copy in LC/BSCP Box 73; *Constitution and General Rules of the Brotherhood of Sleeping Car Porters,* rev. Sept. 21, 1936, [New York: BSCP, 1936], Art. 26, copy in RCTP; Philip S. Foner and Ronald L. Lewis, eds., *Black Workers: A Documentary History from Colonial Times to the Present,* abr. ed. (Philadelphia: Temple University Press, 1988), 509; Joseph F. Wilson, ed., *Tearing Down the Color Bar: An Analysis and Documentary History of the Brotherhood of Sleeping Car Porters* (New York: Columbia University Press, 1989), 188.

2. David R. Roediger, *The Wages of Whiteness: Race and the Making of the American Working Class* (New York: Verso, 1991).

3. Wilson, *Tearing Down the Color Bar,* 48; Jervis B. Anderson, *A. Philip Randolph: A Biographical Portrait* (1973; reprint, Berkeley: University of California Press, 1986), 138–50; Brailsford Brazeal, *The Brotherhood of Sleeping Car Porters: Its Origin and Development* (New York: Harper and Brothers, 1946), 227–31; Randolph quoted in Paula F. Pfeffer, *A. Philip Randolph, Pioneer of the Civil Rights Movement* (Baton Rouge: Louisiana State University Press, 1990), 217.

4. "Pullman Comfort Pleases Tennessean's Passengers," *Pullman News,* 20 (Jan. 1942): 99–100; CLD to E. D. Moody, Feb. 10, 1945, UCB/CLD Box 9; "Nurse Stewardesses: Nursing Takes to the Railroad," *American Journal of Nursing* 37:1 (Jan. 1937): 38. I am indebted to Suzanne Kolm for this reference.

5. "Nurse Stewardesses," 19; Frances Mary Albrier, *Frances Mary Albrier: Determined Advocate for Racial Equality,* interview conducted by Malca Chall. Women in Politics Oral History Project (Berkeley: Regional Oral History Office, Bancroft Library, University of California, 1979), 83.

6. "Nurse Stewardesses," 18–19; Darlene Clark Hine, *Black Women in White: Racial Conflict and Cooperation in the Nursing Profession, 1890–1950* (Bloomington: Indiana University Press, 1989), 109–20.

7. "Nurse Stewardesses," 18–19; "Welcoming the Nation," *Independent Woman* 17:2 (Feb. 1938): 40; "Women on Wheels," *Time,* Aug. 16, 1937, 38.

8. Jack Santino, *Miles of Smiles, Years of Struggle: Stories of Black Pullman Porters* (Urbana: University of Illinois Press, 1989), 130–31; Dorothy Sue Cobble misses this point in her discussion on the replacement of black waiters with white waitresses, *Dishing It Out: Waitresses and Their Unions in the Twentieth Century* (Urbana: University of Illinois Press, 1991); Suzanne Kolm, paper presented at Smithsonian National Museum of American History and Technology Fellows Workshop, January 1990; Phyllis Palmer, *Domesticity and Dirt: Housewives and Domestic Servants in the United States, 1920–1945* (Philadelphia: Temple University Press, 1989).

9. "Nurse Stewardesses," 18; "Women on Wheels," 48; photograph, *Pullman News* (Apr. 1950): 6; Brazeal, *The Brotherhood,* 152–53; "Pullman Comfort Pleases," 99–100. The Baltimore and Ohio Railroad, the Rock Island Line, the Southern Pacific, the Santa Fe, and the Pullman Company also employed stewardess-nurses; the Southern Pacific also employed maids; see "Memorandum of Agreement between the Southern Pacific Company and . . . the Brotherhood of Sleeping Car Porters . . . eff. July 1, 1942," UCB/CLD Box 9.

10. Pullman prosecuted porters who fraternized with its white female railway employees for "misconduct"; see for example,TTP to APR, June, 6, 1944, LC/APR Box 7; MPW to CLD, June 18, 1949, UCB/CLD Box 3.

11. Marjorie Murphy, *Blackboard Unions: The AFT and the NEA, 1900–1980* (Ith-

aca: Cornell University Press, 1990), 101, and Nancy Cott, *The Grounding of Modern Feminism* (New Haven: Yale University Press, 1988), 235–37, discuss the class and gender tensions between professional, feminist women and union leaders. See also Roediger, *Wages of Whiteness*, 11–13; Daniel J. Walkowitz, "The Making of a Feminine Professional Identity: Social Workers in the 1920s," *AHR* 95 (Oct. 1990): 1051–75; Foner and Lewis, eds., *Black Worker: A Documentary History*, vol. 7, 239–49.

12. American Federation of Labor, *Convention Proceedings, 1938*, 358–60, quoted in Brazeal, *The Brotherhood*, 152–53; *Black Worker* (Oct. 1938): 3; see also CLD to Anna Beachman, Nov. 22, 1941, UCB/CLD Box 1.

13. "Pullman Comfort Pleases Tennessean's Passengers."

14. Harry E. Jones, *Railroad Wages and Labor Relations, 1900–1952: An Historical Survey and Summary of Results* (New York: Bureau of Information of the Eastern Railways, 1953), 98–99; Herbert Northrup, *Organized Labor and the Negro* (New York: Harper & Brothers, 1944), 1–8; Edgar Edgerton Tucker, "Brotherhood of Sleeping Car Porters, 1945–1961" (M.A. diss., Howard University, 1963), 99–100; Paul M. Taillon, " 'By Every Tradition and Every Right': Fraternalism and Racism in the Railway Brotherhoods, 1880–1910," paper presented at the American Studies Association Annual Meeting, Baltimore, Maryland, Nov. 1, 1991; William H. Harris, *The Harder We Run: Black Workers since the Civil War* (New York: Oxford University Press, 1982), 118.

15. *Graham v. Brotherhood of Locomotive Firemen and Enginemen*, 338 U.S. 232 at 238 (1949); *Report of Proceedings of the Conference for Colored Locomotive Firemen Held at . . . Washington, D.C., on March 28 and 29, 1941*, 55, RCTP; Anderson, *A. Philip Randolph*, 283–316; Pfeffer, *A. Philip Randolph*, 89–133.

16. Originally scheduled for December 1942, the hearings were finally held after President Franklin Roosevelt issued Executive Order 9346, specifically prohibiting labor unions from discriminating, the resignation of several members (including Charles H. Houston), and an "indefinite" postponement; Louis C. Kesselman, *The Social Politics of the FEPC: A Study in Reform Pressure Movements* (Chapel Hill: University of North Carolina Press, 1948), 19, 21, 31; Genna Rae McNeil, *Groundwork: Charles Hamilton Houston and the Struggle for Civil Rights* (Philadelphia: University of Pennsylvania Press, 1983), 164–65; William H. Harris, *Keeping the Faith: A. Philip Randolph, Milton P. Webster, and the Brotherhood of Sleeping Car Porters, 1925–37* (Urbana: University of Illinois Press, 1977, 1991), 118–19; Pfeffer, *A. Philip Randolph*, 94.

17. McNeil, *Groundwork*, 157–75; *Steele v. Louisville and Nashville R.R.*, 323 U.S. 192, 204 (1944); *Graham v. BLFE*; Derrick A. Bell, *Race, Racism and American Law*, 2d. ed. (Boston: Little, Brown and Co., 1980), 601–2. In 1957, a Michigan state case ruled that sex discrimination was within the "wide range of reasonableness" allowed by the U.S. Supreme Court. *Cortez v. Ford Motor Co.*, 349 Mich. 108, 84 N.W. 523 (Sup. Ct. Mich., 1957), cited in Barbara Allen Babcock, Ann E. Freedman, Eleanor Holmes Norton, and Susan C. Ross, *Sex Discrimination and the Law: Causes and Remedies* (Boston: Little, Brown and Co., 1975), 365; as late as 1974, the court had not extended the duty of fair representation to women (ibid.).

18. McNeil, *Groundwork*, 163; Anderson, *A. Philip Randolph*, 9, 258–59; *Graham v. BLFE*, 338 U.S. 232 (1949); Tucker, "Brotherhood," 102.

19. Eric Arneson, " 'Like Banquo's Ghost, It Will Not Down': The Race Ques-

tion and the American Railroad Brotherhoods, 1880–1920," *AHR* 99 (Dec. 1994): 1,619; Roediger, *Wages of Whiteness,* 11–13.

20. *Proceedings of the Fifth National Convention of the Brotherhood of Sleeping Car Porters, 1938,* 83–84. *Black Worker* (Sept. 1943): 3; Tucker, "Brotherhood," 98–99; "Central Zone, New York Central Yards," *Pullman News* (Oct. 1944): 67; Howard W. Risher Jr., *The Negro in the Railroad Industry,* Report No. 16 (Philadelphia: Wharton School of Finance and Commerce, University of Pennsylvania, 1971), quotes one federal researcher, "Helpers only became craftsmen after everyone else had died" (77).

21. "This is the Way We Clean Our Cars," *Pullman News* (Oct. 1946): 16–17; see also Maurine Weiner Greenwald, *Women, War and Work: The Impact of World War I on Women Workers in the United States* (1980; reprint, Ithaca: Cornell Paperbacks, 1990), 106–16.

22. *Black Worker* (July 1943): 2; *Pullman News* (July 1946): 5; (Oct. 1953): 2–7; and (Oct. 1951): 181–83; ALT to APR, Jan. 19, 1942, LC/APR Box 9.

23. Tucker, "Brotherhood," 98; Brazeal, *The Brotherhood,* 226–27, 232.

24. Tucker, "Brotherhood," 98; "In the Matter of Representation of Employees of the Pullman Company," Case no. R-1625, cert. Dec. 24, 1946, NMB.

25. Minnie Lou Sellers to APR, Feb. 8, 1946, LC/BSCP Box 84; C. D. Miller to APR, Mar. 17, 1946, LC/BSCP Box 87; see also Edward Melton to CLD, Mar. 26, 1945, UCB/CLD Box 6.

26. C. D. Miller to APR, Mar. 17, 1946.

27. Mattie Hooks to APR, Apr. 16, 1945, LC/BSCP Box 14.

28. Elizabeth Davis to APR, Jan. 19, 1945, LC/BSCP Box 11; see also Susie Farrow Calumet to BSCP, Nov. 27, 1946, CHS/BSCP Box 7.

29. Minnie Lou Sellers–APR correspondence, 1945–47, LC/BSCP Box 84.

30. Minnie Lou Sellers to APR, July 16, 1945, LC/BSCP Box 84.

31. "Transcript of Hearing Accorded Mrs. Minnie Rincon, Cleaner, Oakland Yards, on May 18, 1946," UCB/CLD Box 10.

32. Ibid., "Statement of E. E. Gilday." Note that "language becoming a Pullman employee" meant using an honorific title to refer to white supervisors, but not when referring to Mrs. Rincon.

33. CLD to MPW, Oct. 5, 1945, UCB/CLD Box 4; "Statement of Mrs. Viola Perry," Nov. 24, 1943, and MPW to APR, Nov. 30, 1943, LC/APR Box 9.

34. Alma Illery, Housewives Cooperative Guild, Pittsburgh, to MPW, Committee on Fair Employment, Oct. 26, 1942, CHS/BSCP Box 22; Lois I. Stalland[?] to MPW, Dec. 26, 1941, Blanche Lee to MPW, Feb. 17, 1942, CHS/BSCP Box 20; LC/APR Boxes 18–21 contain many letters from women complaining of racial discrimination. As a member of the Fair Employment Practices Committee, Milton P. Webster received letters from several women applying for positions with the committee (see for example, E. Pauline Myers to MPW, June 13, 1942, CHS/BSCP Box 21; Elizabeth McDougald to MPW, July 5, 1942, CHS/BSCP Box 22; Ethel Payne to MPW, July 25, 1943, CHS/BSCP Box 24; Anna Belle Douglas to MPW, Feb. 2, 1945; Anna Belle Douglas to Malcolm Ross, Feb. 22, 1945, CHS/BSCP Box 25. Although Webster wrote to Ethel Payne that "the hiring of personnel is exclusively out of the jurisdiction of Committee members" on August 2, 1943, two days later he appealed to FEPC Chair Msgr. Francis Haas to hire three men, David Grant, Theodore Brown, and Robert E. Brown (Aug. 4, 1943, CHS/BSCP Box 24).

35. Elmer W. Henderson to Louis Taylor, Oct. 20, 1943, PCOP Box 335-1; Carry to Crawford, Memo, Oct. 27, 1942, PCOP Box 335-1.

36. Carry to Crawford, Memo, Oct. 27, 1942.

37. Risher, *Negro in the Railroad Industry,* 63-66.

38. Ibid., table 12, 75. Susan Hirsch, "Rethinking the Sexual Division of Labor: Pullman Repair Shops, 1900-1969," *Radical History Review* 35 (1986): 24-48, does not sufficiently differentiate between the employment opportunities Pullman provided white women and its restrictions on African American women's employment.

39. *Black Worker* (Oct. 1944): 4; "Mrs. Leslie Oliver Retires," *Black Worker* (Mar. 1947): 6; "Provisional Committee of the BSCP for the Organization of Pullman Car Cleaners and Yard Forces," and "Inside Committee," June 7, 1945, CHS/BSCP Box 7; Brazeal, *The Brotherhood,* 223; APR to Anne Mae Dantzler, July 5, 1947, LC/BSCP Box 11; "Car Cleaners Secretary-Treasurer Dies," *Black Worker* (Mar. 1947): 6.

40. *Black Worker* (July 1945): 2; (Sept. 1944): 4; E. D. Nixon to APR, Aug. 12, 1943, LC/BSCP Box 84.

41. Minnie Lou Sellers to APR, July 16, 1945; Oscar Soares reported that Pullman took similar retaliatory measures against Mrs. Jones in Los Angeles (Oscar Soares to CLD, Nov. 26, 1946, UCB/CLD Box 5).

42. MPW to CLD, Oct. 17, 1946, UCB/CLD Box 4.

43. "Representation of Employees of the Pullman Company," Case No. R-1625, cert. Dec. 24, 1946, National Mediation Board, Washington, D.C.; APR to Minnie Lou Sellers, January 6, 1947; Minnie Lou Sellers to APR, Jan. 14, 1947, both in LC/BSCP Box 84.

44. International BSCP, "Bulletin Concerning the Brotherhood's Fight for the Carmen," Dec. 8, 1948, UCB/CLD Box 8.

45. Karen Tucker Anderson, "Last Hired, First Fired: Black Women Workers during World War II," *JAH* 69 (June 1982): 82-97; Philip S. Foner, *Women and the American Labor Movement: From the First Trade Unions to the Present* (New York: The Free Press, 1982), 344-57, 364; Foner and Lewis, eds., *Black Workers,* 521-22; see also Greenwald, *Women, War and Work,* 106-16.

46. TTP to APR, Mar. 16, 1944, LC/APR Box 7. The Union Pacific also employed porterettes during the war; see CLD to MPW, Dec. 11, 1945, UCB/CLD Box 4.

47. A. N. Peters to H. W. Snowden [*sic:* A. Philip Randolph], Oct. 23, 1946, and B. F. McLaurin to Henry Epstein, Dec. 26, 1946, LC/BSCP Box 112.

48. T. D. McNeal to Benjamin McLaurin, Jan. 14, 1947, and Benjamin McLaurin to T. D. McNeal, Jan. 17, 1947, LC/BSCP Box 112; "Certification of Election," *BSCP v. United Transportation Service Employees of America,* Case no. R-1949, Nov. 28, 1947, National Mediation Board, Washington, D.C.

49. Henry Epstein to Benjamin McLaurin, Dec. 28, 1946, LC/BSCP Box 112. "Agreement between the Baltimore and Ohio Railroad and . . . the Brotherhood of Sleeping Car Porters, eff. Jan. 1, 1947," LC/BSCP Box 35.

50. *Southern Pacific R.R. Co. v. Arizona,* 325 U.S. 761 (1945); Joseph L. Rauh, "Applicability of Ohio General Code Sec. 1008-1 . . . to Porterettes Employed on Interstate Carriers," Memo, Feb. 1, 1957, LC/BSCP Box 78.

51. APR to E. H. Burgess, draft of letter, Feb. 1, 1957, LC/BSCP Box 78; Frank J. Goebel to APR, May 10, 1957; APR to Frank J. Goebel, May 15, 1957; Frank J. Goebel

to APR, May 27, 1957; APR to Frank J. Goebel, June 28, 1957; Frank J. Goebel to APR, July 8, 1957; APR to Frank J. Goebel, Aug. 6, 1957; Frank J. Goebel to APR, June 16, 1958; Frank J. Goebel to Joseph L. Rauh Jr., June 16, 1958, all in LC/BSCP Box 35; Joseph L. Rauh, "Notes of the Conference with Mr. Randolph and Mr. McLaurin," Nov. 5, 1956, LC/BSCP Box 23; LC/BSCP Box 35.

52. *Rosenfel v. Southern Pacific R.R. Co.*, 444 F.2d 1219 (9th Cir. 1971), quoted in Babcock et al., *Sex Discrimination and the Law: Causes and Remedies* (Boston: Little, Brown and Co., 1975), 268–69.

53. The BSCP also pursued litigation on behalf of African American porter-brakemen in *King v. Boggs* (Brotherhood of Railroad Trainmen, Order of Railroad Conductors, Brotherhood of Locomotive Firemen, Brotherhood of Locomotive Engineers, Brotherhood of Locomotive Firemen and Enginemen), Plaintiffs' First Amended Brief, Circuit Court, City of St. Louis, copy in LC/BSCP Box 73, essentially a class-action race-based wage discrimination case that sought to expand the duty of fair representation. See M. Melinda Chateauvert, "'Marching Together': Women of the Brotherhood of Sleeping Car Porters, 1925–1957" (Ph.D. diss., University of Pennsylvania, 1992), 256–59.

Chapter 7: Union Wives, Union Homes

1. Mae Dailey, "The Ladies' Auxiliary: The Part it Can and Should Play in Building and Maintaining Strong and Effective Local Divisions," *Report of the Proceedings of the Southwestern Zone Conference of the BSCP, Houston, Texas, April 24–29, 1949*, 20–22; Jean Gardiner, "Women's Domestic Labor," and Batya Weinbaum and Amy Bridges, "The Other Side of the Paycheck: Monopoly Capital and the Structure of Consumption," in Zillah R. Eisenstein, ed., *Capitalist Patriarchy and the Case for Socialist Feminism* (New York: Monthly Review Press, 1979), 173–205; Heidi Hartmann, "Capitalism, Patriarchy, and Job Segregation by Sex," *Signs* 1 (1976): 3, pt. 2: 137–69; and "The Family as the Locus of Gender, Class, and Political Struggle: The Example of Housework," *Signs* 6 (Spring 1981): 366–94; Lydia Sargent, ed., *Women and Revolution: A Discussion of the Unhappy Marriage of Marxism and Feminism* (Boston: South End Press, 1981); Alice Kessler-Harris, *Out to Work: A History of Wage-Earning Women* (New York: Oxford University Press, 1982), 321–23.

2. The BSCP gave female unionists complementary membership in the Auxiliary; International Ladies' Auxiliary Bulletin, Oct. 10, 1940, LC/BSCP Box 74; APR, "The Women's Economic Council," *Black Worker* (Sept. 1938): suppl. 3.

3. HW, "A Story of Labor," *Black Worker* (Dec. 1948): 7; Bureau of the Census, *Population: Families; Types of Families, Size of Family and Age of Head, Employment Status, and Family Wage or Salary Income in 1939* (Washington, D.C.: Government Printing Office, 1943), table 14; E. Franklin Frazier, *Black Bourgeoisie: The Rise of a New Middle Class* (New York: The Free Press, 1957), 51, and passim.

4. E. Franklin Frazier, *Black Bourgeiousie: The Rise of a New Middle Class* (New York: The Free Press, 1957), 43–59; Saunders Redding, *The Lonesome Road: A Narrative History of the Black American Experience* (1958; reprint, Anchor Books, 1973), 236; Allan G. Spear, *Black Chicago: The Making of a Negro Ghetto, 1890–1920* (Chicago: University of Chicago Press, 1967), 13ff.; St. Clair Drake and Horace R. Cay-

ton, *Black Metropolis: A Study of Negro Life in a Northern City,* rev. and enl. ed., vol. 1 (New York: Harcourt, Brace, and World, 1962); Lynn Weber Cannon, "Trends in Class Identification among Black Americans, 1951-1978," *Social Science Quarterly* 65 (Mar. 1984): 112-26.

5. *Black Worker* (Jan. 1941): 3.

6. HW, "New Year's Greetings from the International Ladies' Auxiliary," *Black Worker* (Jan. 1950): 7.

7. *Black Worker* (Feb. 1940): 2; (Dec. 1940): 2; Layle Lane, "I'm On My Way," *Black Worker* (Nov. 1938): 4; *Black Worker* (Feb. 1940): 2; (Aug. 1947): 7.

8. *Black Worker* (Apr. 1939): 2; (Nov. 1939): 2; (Jan. 1940): 2; (Dec. 1941): 2; (May 1942): 3; (Feb. 1943): 3; (May 1939): 2; (June 1939): 2; Winifred Wandersee, "The Economics of Middle-Income Family Life: Working Women during the Great Depression," in Lois Scharf and Joan M. Jensen, eds., *Decades of Discontent: The Woman's Movement, 1920-1940* (Boston: Northeastern University Press, 1987), 45-58.

9. HW, "Ladies' Auxiliary," n.d., but marked "1945" CHS/BSCP Box 30; "The Cooperative Movement among Negroes," *Messenger* 2 (1918): 23-24; MPW to APR, Feb. 18, 1928, CHS/BSCP Box 3; "Cooperatives Are One of 'Four Democracies,'" *Prosveta,* English section, (Jan, 6, 1944), in LC/APR Box 57; Bulletin, reprint of Helen Norton and Mark Starr, "The Worker as Consumer" (International Ladies' Garment Workers' Union, Education Dept.), n.d., UCB/CLD Box 24.

10. HW to "Dear Sister," Feb. 20, 1942, CHS/BSCP Box 27.

11. HW, "Consumers Cooperative Movement," *Black Worker* (Feb. 1942): 2; see also HW to Mrs. Corinne Watts, June 17, 1942, CHS/BSCP Box 27.

12. Layle Lane, "I'm On My Way," *Black Worker* (Oct. 1938): 5, and (Nov. 1938): 4.

13. Lane, "I'm On My Way," *Black Worker* (Nov. 1938): 4.

14. "Citizens' Committee for Jobs for Negroes," Rev. H. T. S. Johnson and Esterline Williams to "Ladies' Auxiliary, Dorothy Williams," June 3, 1940, UCB/CLD Box 39; William Muraskin, "The Harlem Boycott of 1934: Black Nationalism and the Rise of Labor Consciousness," *Labor History* 13 (Summer 1972): 361-73; see generally, Gary J. Hunter, "Don't Buy Where You Can't Work: Black Depression, 1929-1941" (Ph.D. diss., University of Michigan, 1977).

15. *Report of the Proceedings of the First National Convention of the Ladies Auxiliary . . . Held at Chicago, Ill., Sept. 24 to 27, 1938,* 46-48; Elizabeth Craig to HW, Jan. 31, 1944, CHS/BSCP Box 34; Mary Gregory to HW, June 8, 1944, CHS/BSCP Box 34; S. I. Hayakawa, "Second Thoughts," *Black Worker* (Feb. 1944): 4; Mary Allen, "How Can the Cooperative Movement Help Workers?" *Black Worker* (Mar. 1948): 5, see also *Black Worker* (Mar. 1947): 1; HW, "Cooperation: The Middle Way of Sweden," *Black Worker* (Dec. 1947): 6, and "The ABC's of Consumer Cooperatives," (Apr. 1948): 7; Obituary, S. I. Hayakawa, *New York Times,* Feb. 27, 1992; *Black Worker* (May 1939): 2; *Black Worker* (June 1939): 2; (Feb. 1947): 7; (Sept. 1940): 2; (Aug. 1943): 2.

16. HW, "The Consumers' Cooperative Movement," *Black Worker* (Jan. 1942): 1, 3; E. P. Thompson, *The Making of the English Working Class* (New York: Vintage Books, 1966), 779-807, and passim; HW, "More about the Rochdale Cooperative Principles," *Black Worker* (May 1942): 3.

17. Hayakawa, "Second Thoughts," 4. Other African American cooperatives in Chicago included Peoples', the Ida B. Wells', Thrift, and Morgan Park Coopera-

tives, *Black Worker* (Mar. 1944): 2; "Negro Cooperatives," July 15, 1942, CHS/BSCP Box 34; Agnes Thornton to Central States Cooperative, July 15, 1943, CHS/BSCP Box 34; *Black Worker* (June 1948): 7; (Aug. 1944): 7; HW, "Report on Cooperatives and Credit Unions," *Report of the Proceedings of the Fifth Biennial Convention of the Ladies Auxiliary . . . Held at Chicago, Ill., Sept 16 to 18, 1946,* CHS/BSCP Box 30.

18. *Black Worker* (Aug. 1942): 3; (Feb. 1942): 3; HW to Mrs. Warner Foster, Mar. 12, 1945, CHS/BSCP Box 34; Agnes Thornton, "Brief History of the Brotherhood Consumer Cooperative Store," n.d. [1948], CHS/BSCP Box 34.

19. *Black Worker* (July 1943): 3; membership list, "Consumers Cooperative Buying Club," 1943, CHS/BSCP Box 34.

20. *Black Worker* (Oct. 1944): 2; (July 1944): 2; (Feb. 1944): 4; Cooperative Buying Club to Dear Member, Apr. 24, 1944, CHS/BSCP Box 34.

21. Membership list, Consumers Cooperative Buying Club, 1943, CHS/BSCP Box 34; Financial Statement, LC/BSCP Box 75.

22. Letitia Murray, *Report of the Proceedings of the Second Biennial Convention of the International Ladies Auxiliary to the Brotherhood of Sleeping Car Porters . . . Held at St. Louis, September 17 to 19, 1942* [Chicago: International Ladies' Auxiliary, 1942], 72; see also Letitia Murray to HW, Jan. 20, 1942, CHS/BSCP Box 34.

23. Agnes Thornton, *Second Biennial Convention, 1942,* 74.

24. Nannie Wells, *Second Biennial Convention, 1942,* 76.

25. Ibid., 77.

26. In *Women's Paid and Unpaid Labor* (Philadelphia: Temple University Press, 1993), 3–28, Nona Glazer uses the term "work transfer" to discuss how capitalists have increased profit margins through the growth of "self-service," based largely on increasing women's work as consumers. I suggest here that during World War II the federal government engaged in a similar transfer of work by rationing domestic goods and expecting women, particularly housewives, to scavenge for other necessary products; "Soldiering," *AFWAL Newsletter* (Mar. 1944): 1; Letitia Murray, *Second Biennial Convention, 1942,* 81.

27. *Black Worker* (Feb. 1946): 4, 3, 2; (Apr. 1946): 1; (May 1945): 2; "Government Expert Demonstrates Canning to Ladies' Auxiliary," Washington *Tribune,* May 23, 1942, 21, copy in RCTP; Elizabeth Craig to HW, Jan. 30, 1943, CHS/BSCP Box 29; Elizabeth Craig to HW, Jan. 1, 1944; Solon C. Bell to HW, n.d.; Elizabeth Craig to HW, Apr. 28, 1944; see also HW to Marion Leslie, June 2, 1943; HW to Senator Scott Lucas, and HW to Senator C. Wayland Brooks, Dec. 14, 1943, all in CHS/BSCP Box 34.

28. Frances Williams, "Analysis of Reports on Negro Participation in the Work of War Price and Rationing Boards, April 30, 1945," Office of Price Administration, copy in RCTP; see also Frances Williams to HW, n.d. (ca. Mar. 1, 1944), CHS/BSCP Box 34.

29. *Black Worker* (Jan. 1943): 3; (Jan. 1945): 7; (Feb. 1945): 2; "History of the St. Louis Ladies' Auxiliary," *Black Worker* (Feb. 1946): 7; (May 1946): 5; (July 1943): 2.

30. Nannie M. Wells to HW, Mar. 25, 1946, CHS/BSCP Box 30; *Black Worker* (July 1945): 3; (May 1946): 5.

31. "Denver Ladies' Auxiliary: A Job Well Done," *Black Worker* (Apr. 1946): 7.

32. *Black Worker* (Dec. 1945): 2.

33. HW to Mayor Edward J. Kelly, Sept. 3, 1941, CHS/BSCP Box 27.

34. Chicago Ladies' Auxiliary, "Rental List," Sept. 12, 1941; HW to Alderman Arthur G. Lindell, Mar. 4, 1942, both in CHS/BSCP Box 27; Mrs B. L. [Halena] Wilson, "Opinion of the People," and Benjamin Wilson to Office of Housing Expediters, Sept. 21, 1951, both in CHS/BSCP Box 33.

35. For BSCP wages, see chapter 3; Harry E. Jones, *Railroad Wages and Labor Relations, 1900-1952: An Historical Survey and Summary of Results* (New York: Bureau of Information of the Eastern Railways, 1953), 194.

36. HW to Member, Oct. 20, 1941, CHS/BSCP Box 27; Philip M. Klutznick to HW, Mar. 15, 1943, CHS/BSCP Box 29; *Fifth Biennial Convention, 1946,* 139; *Report of Proceedings of the Sixth Biennial Convention of the Ladies' Auxiliary . . . Held at Detroit, Mich., Sept. 13 to 15, 1948,* 157; Clarence R. Walton to Franklin Delano Roosevelt, Jan. 12, 1940; John A. Garber to C. R. Walton, June 12, 1940; C. R. Walton to [MPW], Oct. 11, 1940, CHS/BSCP Box 6; Maggie Friday and Virgie Lee, "Portland [History]" *Black Worker* (Sept. 51): 7; Mary Crump to APR, Feb. 12, 1940, LC/BSCP Box 74; "Emergency Price Control; Statement of Mrs. Thomasina Walker Johnson, Legislative Representative of the National Non-Partisan Council on Public Affairs of Alpha Kappa Alpha Sorority . . . before the House Banking and Currency Committee," June 13, 1945, copy in RCTP; RCT, "Legislative Report," *Fifth Biennial Convention, 1946,* 167–69; RCT, "Legislative Report," "1950," RCTP.

37. Robert Stanford, *Fifth Biennial Convention, 1946,* 120.

38. *Black Worker* (July 1948): 7; (May 1948): 7; (Dec. 1948): 7; see also HW to Elizabeth Craig, May 3, 1945, CHS/BSCP Box 34.

39. *Black Worker* (July 1948): 7; (Sept. 1949): 7; (June 1950): 7; (Feb. 1951): 7.

40. Chester Bowles, "Can We Have Higher Wages without Higher Prices?" *Black Worker* (Mar. 1946): 8; *Black Worker* (Dec. 1945): 6; (Jan. 1946): 7; Edith Christiansen, *Fifth Biennial Convention, 1946,* 135; "Save the OPA," *Black Worker* (July 1946): 1; Anne Mason to HW, Mar. 21, 1946, LC/BSCP Box 76; *Fifth Biennial Convention, 1946,* 155; *Sixth Biennial Convention, 1948,* 165; *Seventh Biennial Convention, 1950,* 173.

41. Lucille Coward to HW, Apr. 28, 1948, CHS/BSCP Box 31.

42. Ibid.; *Black Worker* (June 1948): 7; (July 1948): 7; (Jan. 1948): 7.

43. RCT to National Bank of Washington, Jan. 10, 1971, RCTP; "Average Family Never Lays up a Cent," *Black Worker* (Apr. 1938): 7; (Sept. 1947): 3.

44. Velmer Coward, *Fifth Biennial Convention, 1946,* 114–15; Coward to APR, Mar. 5, 1943, LC/BSCP Box 73.

45. Joyce L. Kornbluh, *A New Deal for Workers' Education: The Workers' Service Program, 1933–1942* (Urbana: University of Illinois Press, 1988), 120–23; Marjorie Murphy, *Blackboard Unions: The AFT and the NEA, 1900–1980* (Ithaca: Cornell University Press, 1990), 150–74.

46. *Black Worker* (Oct. 1939): 3; (Nov. 1937): 2; (Jan. 1938): 2; (Apr. 1942): 3; "Junior Auxiliary," 1945, CHS/BSCP Box 30; HW, "NAM Changes Its Tactics," *Black Worker* (Mar. 1946): 7 (quotations mark text Wilson took from the publication "In Fact").

47. HW, "NAM Changes Its Tactics."

48. "Proposed Constitution and Rules and Regulations for Junior Auxiliary," and "Program," n.d, LC/BSCP Box 76; APR to Walter Frank, May 27, 1942, LC/BSCP Box 73; "Constitution of the Youth Council and Junior Auxiliary to the BSCP,"

1945, CHS/BSCP Box 30; HW to "Dear Parent," June 27, 1945, CHS/BSCP Box 29; Gilbert Jones to APR, Dec. 13, 1955, APR to Jones, Dec. 21, 1955, Jones to APR, Feb. 29, 1956, all in LC/BSCP Box 106; James Gilbert, *A Cycle of Outrage: America's Reaction to the Juvenile Delinquent in the 1950s* (New York: Oxford University Press, 1986), 1–17, 197–211.

49. Special Notice from HW, October 15, 1948, LC/BSCP Box 75; HW to APR, July 25, 1949, LC/BSCP Box 75; *Black Worker* (Dec. 1943): 2; (July 1944): 2; Thornton, "Brief History"; HW to APR, July 25, 1949; HW to Brotherhood Coop Buying Club Members, Special Bulletin, July 11, 1949; APR to HW, July 22, 1949, all in LC/BSCP Box 75.

50. HW to APR, July 6, 1945, LC/BSCP Box 76; APR to HW, Aug. 29, 1945; Elaine Faulkner (HW's secretary) to APR, January 19, 1948; HW to APR, Jan. 22, 1948; C. J. McLanahan to HW, July 26, 1948; HW to APR, July 25, 1949, all in LC/BSCP Box 75.

51. APR to HW, Sept. 9, 1949, LC/BSCP Box 75; HW to Member [APR], Feb. 3, 1950, LC/BSCP, Box 7.

52. *Black Worker* (Oct. 1951): 7.

53. Special letter, Wilson to Friend, Mar. 13, 1952, CHS/BSCP Box 33.

54. I. M. Ornburn, "Victory Veterans and American Standards," *Black Worker* (Dec. 1944): 3; "Labels in Uniforms," (Jan. 1945): 4; *AFWAL Newsletter* (Jan. 1950): 1; CLD to Union Label Committee, May 15, 1956, UCB/CLD Box 2.

55. CLD to L. B. Thompson, Mar. 15, 1951; Anne Sweet to APR, May 8, 1951; Anne Sweet to CLD, Nov. 2, 1951; CLD to Anne Sweet, Nov. 17, 1951; Anne Sweet to CLD, Nov. 20, 1951, all in UCB/CLD Box 5; "Trade Union Agreement, Alameda County," Mar. 1953, UCB/CLD Box 2; HW, *Fifth Biennial Convention, 1946,* 138; HW to APR, Oct. 18, 1944; APR to HW, Oct. 30, 1944, both in LC/BSCP Box 76; Bulletin, Nov. 15, 1939, UCB/CLD Box 39.

56. Jesse J. Myers to APR, Apr. 28, 1949, LC/BSCP Box 82.

57. *Black Worker* (Apr. 1948): 7; (Jan. 1948): 8; (June 1948): 8.

58. Unidentified photograph, A. Philip Randolph Collection, Prints and Photographs Division, Library of Congress, Washington, D.C.; R. Norman to MPW, June 7, 1941, CHS/BSCP Box 6; *Black Worker* (June 1930): 2; (Apr. 1938): 2; (May 1942): 3; (June 1942): 4; (Oct. 1944): 6; (July 1947): 7; (July 1948): 7; (May 1949): 7; (Oct. 1951): 7; (December 1955): 7; Vance Packard, *The Status Seekers* (New York: Pocket Books, 1959), 115–19, citing Bernard Barber and Lyle S. Lobel, "Fashion in Women's Clothes and the American Social System," *Social Forces* (Dec. 1952); Paul K. Edwards, *The Southern Urban Negro as a Consumer* (1932; reprint, College Park, Md.: McGrath Publishing Co., 1969), 79–99; Frances Williams, *Report of the Proceedings of the Second Biennial Convention of the Ladies Auxiliary . . . Held at St. Louis, Sept. 17 to 19, 1942,* 68; see also Evelyn Brooks-Higginbotham, "Beyond the Sound of Silence: Afro-American Women's History," *Gender & History* 1 (Spring 1989): 50–67; Susan Willis, "I Shop Therefore I Am: Is There a Place for Afro-American Culture in Commodity Culture?" in Cheryl A. Wall, ed., *Changing Our Own Words: Essays on Criticism, Theory, and Writing by Black Women* (New Brunswick, N.J.: Rutgers University Press, 1989), 173–85; Patricia K. Hunt, "Clothing as an Expression of History: The Dress of African American Women in Georgia, 1880–1915," in Darlene Clark Hine et al., eds. *'We Specialize in the Wholly Impossible': A Reader in*

Black Women's History (Brooklyn, N.Y.: Carlson Publishing, 1995), 393–404; Rayna Rapp and Ellen Ross, "The 1920s: Feminism, Consumerism, and Political Backlash," in Judith Friedlander et al., eds., *Women in Culture and Politics: A Century of Change* (Bloomington: University of Indiana Press, 1986), 55.

59. RCT, diary, 1957–1960, RCTP; "Look before You Sign," *Black Worker* (May 1939): 2; Editorial, "What of the Future?" *Black Worker* (Sept. 1947): 3; *Report of Proceedings of the Seventh Biennial Convention and Silver Jubilee, International Ladies Auxiliary to the Brotherhood of Sleeping Car Porters . . . Held at New York, N.Y., September 11 to 13, 1950,* 145; Dana Frank, *Purchasing Power: Consumer Organizing, Gender, and the Seattle Labor Movement, 1919–1929* (New York: Cambridge University Press, 1994), 10.

60. Jones, *Railroad Wages*, 64–66.

61. Brailsford Brazeal, *The Brotherhood of Sleeping Car Porters: Its Origin and Development* (New York: Harper and Brothers, 1946), 209–11; Nixson Denton, *History of the Brotherhood of Railway and Steamship Clerks, Freight Handlers, Express and Station Employees* (Cincinnati: George M. Harrison Biographical Committee, 1965), 70–71; Sterling D. Spero and Abram L. Harris, *The Black Worker: The Negro and the Labor Movement* (1931; reprint, New York: Antheneum, 1969), 124.

62. Bureau of the Census, *The Social and Economic Status of the Black Population in the United States: An Historical View: 1790–1978* (Washington, D.C.: Government Printing Office, n.d.), 30; St. Clair Drake and Horace R. Cayton, *Black Metropolis: A Study of Negro Life in a Northern City*, rev. and enl. ed., vol. 2 (New York: Harcourt, Brace, and World, 1962), 526–63; Brazeal, *The Brotherhood*, 215; Jones, *Railroad Wages*, 194.

"Comparable" is used here in the same way as used by women's pay equity experts. Assistant passenger conductors and sleeping car porters required comparable education, experience, skills, and responsibilities, but because the Order of Railway Conductors' constitution barred African American members, porters' classes were not considered apprenticeships; further, porters often ran "in-charge," doing conductors' work, but solely because of race, could not hold the job. See Eric Schnapper, "Perpetuation of Past Discrimination," *Harvard Law Review* 96 (1983): 828–64; Winn Newman and Lisa Vonhof, " 'Separate but Equal'—Job Segregation and Pay Equity in the Wake of *Gunther*," *University of Illinois Law Review* (1981): 269–332; Martha Blaxall and Barbara Reagan, eds., *Women and the Workplace: The Implications of Occupational Segregation* (Chicago: University of Chicago Press, 1976).

63. Jones, *Railroad Wages*, 134, 164–65; Howard W. Risher Jr., *The Negro in the Railroad Industry,* (Philadelphia: Wharton School of Finance and Commerce, University of Pennsylvania, 1971), 31.

64. See table 2, chapter 4; Jones, *Railroad Wages*, 164–65.

65. Elizabeth E. Hoyt, Margaret G. Reid, Joseph L. McConnell, and Janet M. Hooks, *American Income and Its Use* (New York: Harper and Brothers, 1953), 167–210; Alice Kessler-Harris, *A Woman's Wage: Historical Meanings & Social Consequences* (Lexington: University Press of Kentucky, 1990), 8–13, provides a succinct discussion of these definitions, but gives insufficient consideration to the impact of this ideology on African American women; see discussion in introductory chapter. BSCP leaders believed women needed less money than men, see CLD to W. B. Holland, Sept. 8, 1938, UCB/CLD Box 5.

66. According to Edgar Edgerton Tucker, "The Brotherhood of Sleeping Car Porters, 1945–1961" (M.A. diss., Howard University, 1963), 131, in 1946, porters received $2,254.80 for 2,460 working hours. "Findings of Fact," *J. T. and Emma Lowe v. Commissioner of Internal Revenue,* U.S. Tax Court, copy in LC/BSCP Box 76; "Porters' Seniority Roster, New Orleans Dist., Jan. 1, 1939," LC/BSCP 85.

67. Obituary, Etta [*sic*] Catlett Lowe, New Orleans *Times-Picayune,* Apr. 2, 1960, 11; "Findings of Fact."

68. "The City Worker's Family Budget," *MLR* 66:2 (1948): 152; A. Ford Hinrichs, "The Budget in Perspective" *MLR* 66 (1948) 2: 131. The sexism in the assumptions of such budgets has been commented upon by Martha May, "The Good Managers: Married Working Class Women and Family Budget Studies, 1895–1915," *Labor History* 25 (1984): 351–72; see also Dorothy S. Brady, "Scales of Living and Wage Earners' Budgets," *Annals* (1951): 32–38.

69. "City Worker's Family Budget," 148; "Findings of Fact."

70. "City Worker's Family Budget," 136.

71. "Findings of Fact"; "City Worker's Family Budget," 135, 160.

72. Hoyt et al., *American Income and Its Use,* 194.

73. Obituary, Etta [*sic*] Catlett Lowe; "Findings of Fact"; "City Worker's Family Budget," 153; see also CLD to H. Lawder, Oct. 26, 1946, requesting a ticket refund for his wife when the Pullman agent in San Antonio refused to acknowledge her reserved ticket on account of race.

74. From Frazier's *Black Bourgeoisie,* 51, the Lowes' were in the top 5 percent of southern African American families; Jones, *Railroad Wages,* 194; Bureau of the Census, *Historical Statistics of the United States: Colonial Times to 1970,* pt. 1 (Washington, D.C.: Government Printing Office, 1975), 170; Denton, *History of the Brotherhood,* 70–71. See table 1, chapter 4, and Brazeal, *The Brotherhood,* 219.

75. "Income . . . Received by each Fifth and Top 5 Percent of Black and Other Race and White Families for Selected Years: 1947 to 1974," in *Social and Economic Status of the Black Population,* 35; Frazier, *Black Bourgeoisie,* 51–59. BSCP porters averaged $4,145 in 1956, well above income earned unskilled and semiskilled African American men. A settlement house worker's survey of "complete families" conducted in Rosina Tucker's Washington, D.C., neighborhood provided these examples: "(a) a family of five living on a yearly income of $2300, father a laborer; (b) a family of seven living on $3500, father a night watchman; (c) a family of 8 living on $3000, father a laborer; (d) a family of 9 living on $3000, father a store-porter; (e) a family of 9 living on $2600, father a laborer; (f) a family of 5 living on $2900, father a painter's helper." "East Capitol Area Citizens Youth Project, (Area P of the Commissioner's Youth Council) Report of the Research Committee," Oct. 21, 1954, RCTP; Venzie P. Witt, "A Tribute to A. Philip Randolph" *Black Worker* (Nov. 1938): 4; for similar views, see W. S. Anderson (Sept. 1940): 2.

76. *Black Worker* (Dec. 1955): 7; (Jan. 1955): 7; (Oct. 1951): 7; Ethel L. Payne, "Knight of the Road, Porter Golden William Smith," *Pullman News* (Apr. 1952): 10–14; on automobile ownership, see for example CLD to Charles Upton, June 23, 1938, UCB/CLD Box 5, and RCT, "My Life As I Have Lived It," RCTP. The BSCP fought Pullman's attempts to abolish the Tucson district in part because over half of the porters owned homes, see E. A. Woods to CLD, Jan. 11, 1947, and Jan. 12,

1947; E. A. Woods to "Member," Feb. 4, 1950; Gladys Haynes to CLD, July 7, 1950; Edward Melton to CLD, Jan. 22, 1951, UCB/CLD Box 7.

77. Maureen Honey, *Creating Rosie the Riveter: Class, Gender, and Propaganda during World War II* (Amherst: University of Massachusetts Press, 1984), 51–52, 61–65, 79; Sonya Michel, "American Women and the Discourse of the Democratic Family in World War II," and Ruth Milkman, "American Women and Industrial Unionism during World War II," in Margaret Randolph Higonnet et al., eds., *Behind the Lines: Gender and the Two World Wars* (New Haven: Yale University Press, 1987), 154–67, 168–81; Karen Tucker Anderson, *Wartime Women: Sex Roles, Family Relations, and the Status of Women during World War II* (Westport, Conn.: Greenwood Press, 1983); Glazer, *"Women's Paid and Unpaid Labor,"* note 26.

78. HW, "The Brotherhood Auxiliary, Its Aim and Purpose," *Black Worker* (Feb. 1950): 7.

79. Sharon Harley, "When Your Work Is Not Who You Are: The Development of a Working-Class Consciousness among Afro-American Women," in Noralee Frankel and Nancy S. Dye, eds., *Gender, Race, and Class in the Progressive Era* (Lexington: University Press of Kentucky, 1991), 42–55; Glenna Matthews, *"Just a Housewife": The Rise and Fall of Domesticity in America* (New York: Oxford University Press, 1987), 193–222.

80. Chicago Auxiliary, "A Skit," 1951, CHS/BSCP Box 33.

Chapter 8: "We Talked of Democracy and Learned It Can Be Made to Work"

1. The prohibition against politics was adopted apparently to prevent the Auxiliary from joining organizations tied to the Communist Party. Although Randolph, C. L. Dellums, Ashley Totten, and Benjamin McLaurin, as well as several Auxiliary members, were quite active in the National Negro Congress, Randolph and Tucker, chair of the constitution committee, perhaps feared that the political naivete of many porters' wives would lead to inappropriate alliances. The dangers of communist infiltration remained a concern. Randolph routinely rejected Auxiliary leaders' requests to participate in various organizations and political action committees, on the grounds they might be "communist-dominated and controlled." Red-baiting appears to have served as a convenient explanation to deny Brotherhood women political autonomy; women who individually participated in purportedly Communist organizations could also be removed from office in the Auxiliary; see for example, Theresa C. Ehrlich to HW, Mar. 9, 1944; HW to APR, Mar. 16, 1944; APR to HW, April 14, 1944, all in LC/BSCP Box 76. The policy was not well-understood, even by Auxiliary officials. International President Wilson, for example, ordered Dorothy Gray Williams of Oakland to withdraw from Labor's Non-Partisan League, despite Randolph's suggestion that the Auxiliary support the organization. HW to Dorothy Williams, May 13, 1940; Letitia Murray to Dorothy Williams, May 18, 1940, both in UCB/CLD Box 39, and CLD to HW, May 20, 1940, UCB/CLD Box 9; see also Charles Upton to CLD, July 11, 1939, UCB/CLD Box 5; Charles Upton to CLD, Apr. 25 [1940?], UCB/CLD Box 30; CLD to E. A. Woods, Oct. 22, 1946 and E. A. Woods to CLD, Oct. 29, 1946, UCB/BSCP Box 7; APR to HW, Feb 24, 1949; RCT to HW, Mar. 4, 1949; RCT to APR, Mar. 14, 1949, all in LC/BSCP Box

75. Randolph wrote all of the Auxiliary's convention resolutions on political issues until 1942, when President Wilson took over the task. Even then, however, drafts of proposed resolutions received Randolph's approval long before the International officers read them.

2. The National Negro Congress, founded in 1936, did not originate in the BSCP but drew together existing organizations to represent African American economic interests during the Depression. However, many BSCP and Auxiliary members belonged to the NNC, as a cross-listing of Oakland membership lists revealed. Among the women were Dorothy Gray Williams, secretary-treasurer of the Ladies' Auxiliary and former BSCP maid Frances Mary Albrier; Sponsor Members, East Bay Section, NNC, n.d.; Mailing List, NNC, n.d.; [East Bay Council, NNC], "To the Worker," n.d.; Local Executives, East Bay Council, NNC [letterhead], n.d.; all in UCB/CLD Box 23; Ladies Auxiliary Mailing List, n.d. [ca. 1940], UCB/CLD Box 9; APR, "Call to Negro America," *Black Worker* (May 1941): 1; Richard M. Dalfiume, "The 'Forgotten Years' of the Negro Revolution," *JAH* 55 (1968): 90–106; Paula Pfeffer, *A. Philip Randolph, Pioneer of the Civil Rights Movement* (Baton Rouge: Louisiana State University Press, 1990), 32–43; Jervis B. Anderson, *A. Philip Randolph: A Biographical Portrait* (1972; reprint, Berkeley: University of California Press, 1986), 229–40.

3. APR, "Keynote Address to the Policy Conference of the March on Washington Movement," Sept. 26, 1942, in August Meier, Elliott Rudwick, and Francis L. Broderick, eds., *Black Protest Thought in the Twentieth Century,* 2d ed. (Indianapolis: Bobbs-Merrill, 1971), 226; Joseph F. Wilson, ed. *Tearing Down the Color Bar: An Analysis and Documentary History of the Brotherhood of Sleeping Car Porters* (New York: Columbia University Press, 1989), 198–99; Dalfiume, "'Forgotten Years,'" 93, quoting the Pittsburgh *Courier,* Feb. 14, 1942; March on Washington Movement [letterhead]; "MOWM Book Store Price List," UCB/BSCP Box 23.

4. Robert Fredrick Burk, *The Eisenhower Administration and Black Civil Rights* (Knoxville: University Press of Kentucky, 1984), 24–29; Pfeffer, *A. Philip Randolph,* 94, 97–98; E. Pauline Myers, "The March on Washington Movement Mobilizes a Gigantic Crusade for Freedom" (New York: March on Washington Movement, n.d. [1943]), lent by the author.

5. RCT, "My Life As I Have Lived It," RCTP.

6. David Brinkley, *Washington Goes to War* (New York: Knopf, 1988), i, 78–83; RCT, "My Life"; Harvard Sitkoff, *A New Deal for Blacks: The Emergence of Civil Rights as a National Issue: The Depression Decade* (New York: Oxford University Press, 1978), 317, 320–21; E. Pauline Myers, interview by author, Washington, D.C., May 15, 1991; Anderson, *A. Philip Randolph,* 258–59; Pfeffer, *A. Philip Randolph,* 50.

7. Louis Ruchames, *Race, Jobs and Politics: The Story of the FEPC* (New York: Columbia University Press, 1953), 164.

8. Louis Coleridge Kesselman, *The Social Politics of the FEPC: A Study in Reform Pressure Movements* (Chapel Hill: University of North Carolina Press, 1948), 15–24; Richard Bardolph, *The Civil Rights Record: Black Americans and the Law, 1849–1970* (New York: Thomas Y. Crowell Co., 1970), 302; Lee Finkle, *Forum for Protest: The Black Press during World War II* (Rutherford, N.J.: Farleigh Dickinson University Press, 1975), 97.

9. Anderson, *A. Philip Randolph,* 259; Ellen Tarry, *The Third Door: The Autobi-*

ography of an American Negro Woman (1955; reprint, Westport, Conn.: Negro Universities Press, 1972), 192–93; APR to Ada Dillon, June 22, 1942; APR to Rachel Corrothers, June 22, 1942; both in LC/APR Box 24; "Program for Mass Meeting of the March on Washington Movement, Madison Square Garden, June 10, 1942," CHS/BSCP Box 7; Memorandum, Crystal Bird Fauset to Congressman [John W.] McCormack, July 23, 1942, copy in CHS/BSCP Box 22.

10. "9,000 attend Rally to March on Plan," *St. Louis Argus,* Aug. 21, 1942, 1; "10,000 Attend FEPC March on Washington Meet," *Pittsburgh Courier,* Aug. 22, 1942, 1; Dona Blakely, "Woman's Role in the March on Washington Movement," *Chicago Defender,* Aug. 22, 1942, n.p., all in FEPC Scrapbook, St. Louis, CHS/BSCP; MPW to CLD, June 30, 1942, UCB/CLD Box 4. For a discussion of the problems of women organizers in the Chicago and Washington rallies, see M. Melinda Chateauvert, "'Marching Together': Women of the Brotherhood of Sleeping Car Porters, 1925–1957" (Ph.D. diss., University of Pennsylvania, 1992), 412–17; Pfeffer, *A Philip Randolph,* 52–53. In Chicago, the principals included Milton P. Webster and Charles Wesley Burton, Neva Ryan, Ethel Payne, Gloria Eason, and Irene McCoy Gaines.

11. Pauli Murray, *Song in a Weary Throat: An American Pilgrimage* (New York: Harper and Row, 1987), 168, 164–65, 171; *Black Worker* (June 1941): 3; (April 1942): 3; Ashley L. Totten to All Secretary-Treasurers, BSCP, Dec. 2, 1940, UCB/CLD Box 3; APR to CLD, June 30, 1942, UCB/BSCP Box 10; Layle Lane to APR, July 6, 1942, LC/APR Box 24; HW to APR, July 3, 1942, CHS/BSCP Box 7; Ethel Payne to APR, April 3, 1942, LC/APR Box 25. The Auxiliary also protested the impending execution of the Martinsville Seven in 1951, asking President Truman "save the lives of these men"; HW to President Harry Truman, Jan. 1, 1951, CHS/BSCP Box 33.

12. Half of the ninety delegates at the "We Are Americans, Too" convention were women, including International Auxiliary President Halena Wilson, Mrs. Milton P. (Elizabeth) Webster, Miami Car Cleaners' President Minnie Lou Sellers, Mrs. Bennie (Hazel) Smith of Detroit, Nashville Auxiliary President Davie Della Phillips, Thelma Freeman of the Denver Auxiliary, and Maizie Sandle, president of the Washington, D.C., Auxiliary, "Report of Credentials Committee to National Secretary," "We Are Americans, Too Confab," in St. Louis Scrapbook, 1942–44, CHS/BSCP; Burk, *Eisenhower Administration,* 24–29; Pfeffer, *A. Philip Randolph,* 94, 97–98; see generally, Kesselman, *Social Politics of FEPC.*

13. MPW to CLD, July 14, 1943, UCB/CLD Box 4; Neva Ryan to APR, n.d., LC/APR Box 25; Interview with E. Pauline Myers, conducted by author, June 12, 1991; March on Washington Movement, National Executive Committee, Oct. 26, 1943, UCB/CLD Box 23; Negro March-on-Washington Committees, n.d., and Local Units of the March on Washington Movement, May 24, 1943, LC/APR Box 25; RCT, "My Life," RCTP.

14. "Call Meeting: Indianapolis," July 29, 1944, LC/APR Box 1; "March on Washington Movement Indianapolis," [1946?], LC/APR Box 25, with penciled note "49 Pullman Porters included at that time, all young porters. I hope you will keep this be a record." Kesselman, *Social Politics of FEPC,* 67–83.

15. APR, "Keynote Address to the Policy Conference," Sept. 26, 1942, in August Meier, Elliott Rudwick, and Francis L. Broderick, eds., *Black Protest Thought in the Twentieth Century* (Indianapolis: Bobbs-Merrill, 1971), 227–28; *Black Worker* (May 1942): 1; see also note 1.

16. E. Pauline Myers, "March on Washington Movement and Non-Violent Civil Disobedience," *Black Worker* (Feb. 1943): 3. The microfilm copy is missing this portion of the text; Miss Myers provided me with her copy, published as, "The March on Washington Movement Mobilizes a Gigantic Crusade for Freedom" (New York: March on Washington Movement, n.d. [1943]). Pfeffer misspells Myers's name as "Meyers" in *A. Philip Randolph*.

17. E. Pauline Myers, interview by author, Washington, D.C., May 15, 1991; *Black Worker* (Sept. 1944): 2; E. D. Nixon to APR, Aug. 12, 1943, LC/BSCP Box 84; E. D. Nixon to HW, Feb. 10, 1948; E. D. Nixon to HW, Aug. 20, 1948, both in CHS/BSCP Box 31; "Report of Credentials Committee to National Secretary," "We Are Americans, Too Confab"; "Souvenir Program, Feb. 15, 1954, Honoring Mr. Edgar Daniel Nixon," LC/BSCP Box 85; see also "Negroes Defy Race-Baiting in Southern Primaries," *Black Worker* (July 1946): 1.

18. APR to Blanche Lee, Oct. 1, 1944, LC/APR Box 25.

19. Constance McLaughlin Green, *The Secret City: A History of Race Relations in the Nation's Capital* (Princeton: Princeton University Press, 1967), 258–60; Genna Rae McNeil, *Groundwork: Charles Hamilton Houston and the Struggle for Civil Rights* (Philadelphia: University of Pennsylvania Press, 1983), 171–72, 175; Merl E. Reed, *Seedtime for the Modern Civil Rights Movement: The President's Committee on Fair Employment Practice, 1941–1946* (Baton Rouge: Louisiana State University Press, 1991), 332–37.

20. APR to T. D. McNeal, Mar. 26, 1943, LC/APR Box 7; "Not to Let Up in Fight for Defense Jobs," *St. Louis Argus,* June 22, 1942, in FEPC Scrapbook, CHS/BSCP; [T. D. McNeal] March on Washington Movement, "Statement of Facts," n.d., LC/APR Box 25; see also Paul Dennis Brunn, "Black Workers and Social Movements of the 1930s in St. Louis" (Ph.D. diss., Washington University, 1975), 763–65.

21. "Three Young Women: They Walked Past Jim Crow at Grand-Leader Lunch Counter" *The American,* May 25, 1944, in St. Louis FEPC Scrapbook.

22. Ibid.; T. D. McNeal, interview with Richard Resh, Oral History Program, University of Missouri at St. Louis, quoted in Brunn, "Black Workers and Social Movements," 763; August Meier and Elliott Rudwick, *CORE: A Study in the Civil Rights Movement, 1942–1968* (New York: Oxford University Press, 1973), 63, discuss CORE's efforts to desegregate the downtown eating places in 1947 and 1948.

23. "Colored Women Crusaders Attack Downtown Dept. Store Cafeteria Discrimination," unidentified clippings; "Civil Rights Groups Demonstrate at 2 Downtown Stores," *Globe Democrat,* July 9, 1944; Henry Winfield Wheeler, "Citizens' Civil Rights Committee Demonstration Dramatic," *The American,* July 13, 1944; "Silent Protests Staged by Loyal American Citizens in Downtown Department Stores; Mother with Five Sons in Army is among Those in Group Denouncing Discrimination," unidentified clipping; Loretta Owens, "FEPC to Rule on Injustices," *St. Louis Argus,* Aug. 3, 1944; "For Action in Behalf of Democracy on the Home Front," *The American,* Sept. 21, 1944; all in St. Louis Scrapbook, CHS/BSCP. In 1953, Alberta Williams, president of the Dallas Auxiliary, began to work with "a committee to abolish discrimination against Negro women in department stores," *Report of Proceedings of the First Triennial Convention of the International Ladies Auxiliary to the Brotherhood of Sleeping Car Porters . . . Held at Los Angeles, Cal., October 5 to 9, 1953,* 71.

24. APR and Allan Knight Chalmers, Call for Conference, Jan. 4, 1944; *Proceedings of the "Save The FEPC Conference" Held in Washington, D.C.*, LC/APR Box 17; Kesselman, *Social Politics of FEPC*, 29–35, 47–53.

25. Reports from New Orleans, Shreveport, St. Louis, Dallas, Fort Worth, San Antonio, Seattle, Los Angeles, Columbus, Louisville, and Chicago auxiliaries, *Report of the Proceedings of the Fifth Biennial Convention of the International Ladies Auxiliary, 1946*, 75–99. Jacksonville, Indianapolis, Fort Worth, Oakland, Los Angeles, Seattle, and Portland reported contributions in 1948, *Report of Proceedings of the Sixth Biennial Convention of the International Ladies' Auxiliary 15, 1948*, 77–80, 84–87, 123–27; HW to Members, Jan. 9, 1942, CHS/BSCP Box 27; Mattie Owens to HW, Jan. 22, 1942, CHS/BSCP Box 34; G. C. Garran, C. M. Lester, and V. O. Duncan to APR, Oct. 6, 1944, LC/APR Box 25; V. O. Duncan to APR, Oct. 24, 1953, LC/BSCP Box 85; Charles Wesley Burton to CLD, July 18, 1945, UCB/CLD Box 1; *Black Worker* (Feb. 1945): 7; (Feb. 1946): 7; (May 1946): 7; (Aug. 1946): 7; and (Oct. 1948): 7; Anna R. Hughes to HW, Aug. 30, 1946, CHS/BSCP Box 30; A. F. Booth to APR, Aug. 22, 1947; A. F. Booth to APR, May 1, 1949; A. F. Booth to APR, Sept. 11, 1949; A. F. Booth to "Chief," Mar. 11, 1957, all in LC/APR Box 20; A. F. Booth to CLD, Oct. 18, 1948 [note letterhead] UCB/CLD Box 7; A. F. Booth to APR, Sept. 17, 1954, LC/BSCP Box 85; Herbert Garfinkel, *When Negroes March: The March on Washington Movement and the Organizational Politics for FEPC* (Glencoe, Ill.: 1959; reprint, New York: Antheneum, 1969), 170–74, 171ff.

26. Velmer Coward to APR, July 6, 1943, LC/APR Box 25.

27. Velmer Coward to APR, Nov. 23, 1942, LC/BSCP Box 73.

28. Ibid.; APR to Velmer Coward, Nov. 27, 1942, LC/BSCP Box 73; HW to Velmer Coward, Dec. 11, 1942, CHS/BSCP Box 28.

29. APR to Velmer Coward, Nov. 27, 1942; Bennie Smith to APR, July 10, 1943, LC/APR Box 25; Velmer Coward to APR, Mar. 5, 1943, LC/BSCP Box 73.

30. Robin Winks, *The Blacks in Canada* (New Haven: Yale University Press, 1971), 335–36, 418; APR to Velmer Coward, Nov. 27, 1942, LC/BSCP Box 73; Bennie Smith to APR, July 10, 1943, LC/APR Box 25; Velmer Coward to APR, Sept. 27, 1944, LC/BSCP Box 73.

31. Velmer Coward to APR, Sept. 27, 1944, LC/BSCP Box 73; "Randolph Speaks at Symposium," *Black Worker* (Nov. 1944): 3.

32. "Calgary Herald Apologizes," *Black Worker* (Oct. 1945): 1, 5; (Nov. 1944): 3; (May 1947): 7; (Sept. 1949): 7.

33. Winks, *Blacks in Canada*, 424–27, credits the BSCP for this legislation, but considering the overlap of officers in the league, BSCP, and Auxiliary, his confusion is understandable; Frank Doyle to APR, June 2, 1949, LC/APR Box 20.

34. "Minutes of Proceedings of Conference Called by A. Philip Randolph . . . William Townsend; Morris Milgram; Wilfred H. Kerr . . . in Order to Formulate a Program of Action to End Race Segregation and Discrimination by the Armed Services," Apr. 28, 1945, LC/APR Box 15; Resolutions, *Report of the Proceedings of the Second Biennial Convention of the Ladies Auxiliary . . . Held at St. Louis, Sept. 17 to 19, 1942*, 90–91; Thomasina R. Johnson to APR, Sept. 19, 1942; Frank Knox to Algernon Black, Mar. 5, 1943, both in LC/APR Box 25.

35. In Montgomery, African American passengers paid their fares in front, and then reboarded through the rear, according to JoAnn Gibson Robinson, *The Mont-*

gomery *Bus Boycott and the Women Who Started It: The Memoir of JoAnn Gibson Robinson* (Knoxville: University of Tennessee Press, 1987), 20–22, 32–33; Mabel Staupers to APR, Oct. 7, 1942; APR to [Alabama] Governor Dixon, Oct. 16, 1942, both in LC/APR Box 24; "Legislative Bulletin," Feb. 28, 1945, LC/APR Box 76; see also Florence Culkin, "WAC Humiliated on Southern Railroad," *Black Worker* (Sept. 1945): 5.

36. APR to HW, July 14, 1948; APR to Lela M. Lee, Aug. 13, 1948; APR to Ada Dillon, July 14, 1948, all in LC/APR Box 16; HW to President Franklin D. Roosevelt, Sept. 22, 1942, CHS/BSCP Box 28; "To the President of the United States of America," *Black Worker* (Oct. 1942): 3; HW to APR, July 19, 1948; Grant Reynolds to HW, July 24, 1948; APR to HW, July 29, 1948; APR to HW, Aug. 20, 1948; all in CHS/BSCP Box 10.

37. Mattie Mae Stafford to Franklin Delano Roosevelt, copy in LC/APR Box 25.

38. Mary Frances Berry and John W. Blassingame, *Long Memory: The Black Experience in America* (New York: Oxford University Press, 1982), 329–30; Green, *Secret City,* 321.

39. *Black Worker* (July 1946): 7; (Aug. 1946): 7; Committee to End Jim Crow, "American Mother of 1946 Calls U.M.T. Bill 'Public Enemy No. 1'," press release, Dec. 21, 1947, LC/APR Box 16; Louisville Auxiliary to APR, telegram, May, 9, 1946, LC/BSCP Box 73; Pfeffer, *A. Philip Randolph,* 145–46; Dr. Clement joined the Committee to End Jim Crow in 1947.

40. Blakely, "Woman's Role"; E. N. Davis, "10,000 Attend March on Washington Meet," *Pittsburgh Courier,* Aug. 22, 1942; "9,000 attend Rally to March on Plan"; "Negro Women will Fight too," [photo] *St. Louis Argus,* Aug. 21, 1942; all in FEPC Scrapbook, CHS/BSCP.

41. HW, "Fair Employment Practice and Jim Crow in the Armed Services," *Black Worker* (Dec. 1950): 7; see also Roy Wilkins to HW, July 27, 1948, CHS/BSCP Box 10.

42. APR to James B. Cook, Dec. 11, 1944, LC/APR Box 18; *Manuscript,* no. 59; Ruth Calvin to Staff, Apr. 22, 1946, LC/APR Box 21; Ethel Payne, interview by author, Washington, D.C., Mar. 7, 1991; McLaurin to APR, Feb. 27, 1943, LC/APR Box 7; Pauline Myers, interview by author, Washington, D.C., June 10, 1991; Senora Lawson to APR, July 18, 1945, LC/APR Box 18; Anderson, *A. Philip Randolph,* 266–67; Chateauvert, "'Marching Together,'" 419–23, 432–42; MPW to APR, June 2, 1944, LC/APR Box 9; Earline Wright to APR, May 29, 1945, LC/APR Box 18; FEPC memoranda, LC/APR Box 19; Pfeffer *A. Philip Randolph,* 109, incorrectly identifies Elmer Henderson as executive secretary, he was in fact executive director, 116–17; Kesselman, *Social Politics of FEPC,* 82–83; Hedgeman to Allan Knight Chalmers, May 19, 1947, LC/APR Box 19; Sidney Wilkinson, "Press Release," Aug. 27, 1946, LC/APR Box 22; C. Herbert Marshall to APR, Feb. 27, 1947, and APR to C. Herbert Marshall, both in LC/APR Box 19; Anna Arnold Hedgeman to Allan Knight Chalmers, Mar. 19, 1947, LC/APR Box 19.

43. Webster commented to Dellums, "Incidentally, Mrs. Roosevelt has ordered [Randolph] down to Washington to discuss FEPC. Am wondering why the big boss [FDR] lets the madam do all his heavy discussing. His committee [FEPC] of which I am a member has been trying to get a conference with him for a year . . . but I guess he does not think much of his committee." MPW to CLD, Nov. 14, 1944,

UCB/CLD Box 4. Dellums vied with Frances Mary Albrier for political power among African Americans in California; see for example, Augustus Hawkins to CLD, Oct. 22, 1940; George P. Miller to Augustus Hawkins, Oct. 15, 1940; Augustus Hawkins to George P. Miller, Oct. 21, 1940; copies in UCB/CLD Box 1; H. W. Wheeler, "Three Young Women." Instructions for nonviolent protesters often included admonitions to present a decent appearance; see for example, "Integrated Bus Suggestions," in Joanne Grant, ed., *Black Protest: History, Documents, and Analyses* (New York: Fawcett Books, 1968), 283–84.

44. K. Sue Jewell, *From Mammy to Miss America and Beyond: Cultural Images and the Shaping of U.S. Social Policy* (London: Routledge, 1993), 45.

45. See particularly, Dixon's *The Leopard's Spots* (1908?) and D. W. Griffith's film version of the book, "Birth of a Nation" (1913). Closer to the period, Margaret Mitchell's "Gone With the Wind" (1937) and the film version (1939) also depicted African American elected officials of the Reconstruction period as illiterate and intemperate, intent on enriching themselves by selling off the South's assets to northern carpetbaggers.

46. E. Franklin Frazier, *The Negro Family in the United States* (Chicago: University of Chicago Press, 1939). Frazier introduces his chapter on "The Matriarchate" by castigating African American women for their political courage in 1868: "If a freedman, having obtained [a campaign badge of Grant], lacked the courage to wear it at home on the plantation in the presence of 'ole marsa and missus' or of the 'overseer,' his wife would often take it from him and bravely wear it upon her own breast. If in such cases, the husband refused to surrender it, as was sometimes the case, and hid it from her or locked it up, she would walk all the way to town, as many as twenty or thirty miles sometimes, and buy, beg, or borrow one, and thus equipped return and wear it openly, in defiance of husband, master, mistress, or overseer." This woman asserted a "male" standard for female equality: political participation; as a consequence, her fitness as a mother is questioned. One of the solutions suggested by Daniel Patrick Moynihan for the matriarchal household was to draft African American men for the armed services, where they could experience a real masculine world, Lee Rainwater and William L. Yancey, eds., *The Moynihan Report and the Politics of Controversy; Including the Full Text of "The Negro Family: The Case for National Action" by Daniel Patrick Moynihan* (Cambridge: MIT Press, 1967), 42; see also Ruth Feldstein, " 'I Wanted the Whole World to See': Race, Gender, and Constructions of Motherhood in the Death of Emmett Till," in Joanne Meyerowitz, ed., *Not June Cleaver: Women and Gender in Postwar America, 1945–1960* (Philadelphia: Temple University Press, 1994), 263–303.

47. *Black Worker* (July 1948): 7; (May 1948): 7; (Dec. 1948): 7; *Black Worker* (Nov. 1938): 4; *Black Worker* (Feb. 1940): 2; Paul Ornburn to RCT and Washington, D.C., Ladies' Auxiliary, Nov. 11, 1954, RCTP; HW to APR, Oct. 14, 1942; HW to APR, Oct. 20, 1942; APR to HW, Oct. 24, 1942, all in CHS/BSCP Box 7; HW to RCT, Nov. 4, 1942; RCT to HW, Nov. 9, 1942, CHS/BSCP Box 28; HW to Mary McLeod Bethune, Oct. 29, 1943, CHS/BSCP Box 29; Natalie Moorman to HW, Oct. 16, 1944, LC/BSCP Box 76; see also HW to Elizabeth Craig, May 3, 1945, CHS/BSCP Box 34; RCT, "Visits," Sept. 4, 1956, RCTP; RCT to Anon., Apr. 26, 1946, RCTP; see also HW to Bethune, Sept. 3, 1942; Jeanetta Welch Brown to HW, Sept. 24, 1943; Bethune to HW, Oct. 4, 1943; Brown to HW, Oct. 16, 1943; RCT to Brown, Oct. 29, 1944; Bethune

to HW, Jan. 25, 1945; HW to Brown, Sept. 29, 1943; HW to Bethune, Jan. 4, 1945, all in NCNW Box 1; Mary McLeod Bethune to HW, Sept., 7, 1950, CHS/BSCP Box 33; RCT to C. Vivian Mason, May 16, 1956, NCNW Box 3; and Mason to APR, Feb. 16, 1956, NCNW Box 106. *Fifth Biennial Convention 1946,* 141–42; *Sixth Biennial Convention 1948,* 8–9, 150, 161–66; *Report of Proceedings of the Seventh Biennial Convention and Silver Jubilee, International Ladies Auxiliary to the Brotherhood of Sleeping Car Porters . . . Held at New York, N.Y., September 11 to 13, 1950,* 9–12, 151; Florence Bryant, "Report of the Seventh Biennial Convention," n.d., UCB/CLD Box 24; *First Triennial Convention 1953,* 5–8, 41–42, 106–9.

48. Mamie Willis, Scholarship Report, 1946, CHS/BSCP Box 30.

49. Betty Boynton to CLD, July 17, 1941, UCB/BSCP Box 1; Mildred Scruggins, Scholarship Report, 1946, CHS/BSCP Box 30; HW to APR, July 9, 1948, CHS/BSCP Box 10.

50. Lela Jackson, Scholarship Report, [1947], CHS/BSCP Box 31.

51. Julia Burwell and Evelyn Ford, Scholarship Reports, [1946], CHS/BSCP Box 30.

52. HW, "In the Legislative Field," *Black Worker* (Feb. 1946): 4.

53. Ibid.

54. HW to APR, Oct. 10, 1942, CHS/BSCP Box 7.

55. *Fourth Biennial Convention, 1944,* 12–27, 86–107; *Fifth Biennial Convention, 1946,* 20–36, 120–46; *Sixth Biennial Convention, 1948,* 15–32, 73–96; *Seventh Biennial Convention, 1950,* 7–31, 86–113; *First Triennial Convention, 1953,* 104–6, 114–15, 126.

56. *Sixth Biennial Convention, 1948,* 13, 190.

57. Ibid., 15; Robert H. Zieger, *American Workers, American Unions, 1920–1985* (Baltimore: Johns Hopkins University Press, 1986), 118–19, 121.

58. "Soldiering," *AFWAL Newsletter* (Mar. 1944): 1; HW to Sara Allen, Aug. 20, 1942, CHS/BSCP Box 28; *Black Worker* (Aug. 1945): 2; RCT, "My Life," RCTP; "1949 Annual Report of the Chicago Ladies' Auxiliary," CHS/BSCP Box 32; Maida Springer, *Seventh Biennial Convention, 1950,* 118.

59. HW to APR, Apr. 11, 1956; APR to HW, Apr. 19, 1956; HW to APR, May 7, 1956; all in LC/BSCP Box 74; APR, *Report of Proceedings of the Second Triennial Convention of the International Ladies Auxiliary to the Brotherhood of Sleeping Car Porters . . . Held at St. Louis, September 10 to 12, 1956,* 2–7, 46, 54–55.

60. HW to APR, July 3, 1942, CHS/BSCP Box 22; HW to APR, Sept. 2, 1942, CHS/BSCP Box 4; *Black Worker* (Dec. 1943): 2; (Jan. 1945): 2; (Nov. 1945): 2; HW, "Report of the Chicago Ladies' Auxiliary to the WTUL Conference," Dec. 2, 1951, CHS/BSCP Box 33.

61. HW, *Fifth Biennial Convention, 1946,* 137.

62. Ibid.; Mary Frances Berry, *Why E.R.A. Failed: Politics, Women's Rights, and the Amending Process of the Constitution* (Bloomington: Indiana University Press, 1986), 60f.

63. Wilson, *Fourth Biennial Convention, 1944,* 17.

64. "Sister Maggie Hudson," *Black Worker* (Oct. 1944): 5; Leo Kanowitz, *Women and the Law: The Unfinished Revolution* (Albuquerque: University of New Mexico Press, 1969), 114–17; Barbara Allen Babcock, Ann E. Freedman, Eleanor Holmes Norton, and Susan C. Ross, *Sex Discrimination and the Law: Causes and Remedies* (Boston: Little, Brown and Co., 1975), 239–54; see also chapter 7.

65. *Sixth Biennial Convention, 1948,* 12, 154–55; *First Biennial Convention, 1940,* 98; *Second Biennial Convention, 1942,* 96; *Fourth Biennial Convention, 1944,* 14, 95, 97; *Seventh Biennial Convention, 1950,* 149, 171; Wilson, *Sixth Biennial Convention, 1948,* 12–13; Edmund F. Wehrle, "'For a Healthy America': Labor's Struggle for National Health Insurance," *Labor's Heritage* 5:2 (Summer 1993): 28–45; RCT, "Legislative Report," *Sixth Biennial Convention, 1948,* 189; RCT, "Some Serious Thinking about Serious Problems," n.d., RCPT.

66. RCT, "My Life," RCTP; RCT, "Radio broadcast, The Public Interest Civic Association," April 10, 1955; RCT, "To the Board of Commissioners of the District of Columbia," Oct. 17, 1946; RCT to Alice C. Hunter, D[istrict of] C[olubmia], Recreation Board, June 21, 1949; RCT, "To The Members of the Board of Education," June 29, 1929 [*sic:* 1949], Social Service and Welfare Committee Report, Apr. 26, 1946, all in RCTP; "Brother Anderson Protests against New Jim Crow Ruling," *Black Worker* (Sept. 1945): 2; Green, *Secret City,* 263–64, 269–73, 286–90, 291–95, 310–11.

67. Eileen Brooks to RCT, Mar. 11, 1946; [F.C.A., Social Services Committee], "Summary of Findings" (ca. 1951); Minutes, United Community Services, Subcommittee on Institutions, Committee on Public Welfare Services, Feb. 9, 1951; Recommendations, Industrial Home for Colored Children and Industrial Home School for Colored Girls, formerly National Training School for Girls, Subcommittee on Institutions, Apr. 25, 1952; Program, "Junior Village, D.C., Department of Public Welfare . . . Dedicated by Commissioners of the District of Columbia, Sept. 9, 1956," RCTP; "District Challenge to Lift 450,000 Out of Their Heritage of Poverty," "This is Life in Junior Village: Lonely, Crowded, Hopeless," "Junior Village Report Proposals," "3 Agencies Fill Junior Village," *Washington Post,* Nov. 29, 1959, clippings in RCTP; Report of the Research Committee, Area P, Oct. 21, 1954, RCTP.

68. Lassiter, *Second Triennial Convention 1956,* 24; CLD to Zilica Williams, Feb. 19, 1957, UCB/CLD Box 2. The International Auxiliary adopted two black West Virginia schools, Itmann School in Mullen, and Glen Morrison School in Glen Forks, for which it raised money and donated clothing through the Rural School Program, directed by Rae Brandstein (misidentified in Joseph F. Wilson, *Tearing Down the Color Bar* as "Ray"). In 1948, the Auxiliary raised $426, allowing the teacher at Glen Morrison to "serve more than 1000 hot meals, purchase 65 primary text books and other essentials." See HW, *Sixth Biennial Convention, 1948,* 237–65; Financial Statement for Mar. 1955 to Aug. 1955, RCTP; McLaurin to HW, Feb. 11, 1947, and Feb. 26, 1948, both in CHS/BSCP Box 31; "Special Letter," HW to Members, Mar. 22, 1951; HW to Chicago Transit Authority, July 12, 1951, both in CHS/BSCP Box 33.

Chapter 9: *"Disharmony within the Official Family"*

1. Kenneth T. Jackson, *Crabgrass Frontier: The Suburbanization of the United States* (New York: Oxford University Press, 1985), 190–218, 232–45; Bennie Smith, "Detroit Notes," Dec. 13, 1950, LC/BSCP Box 25; RCT, "Report to International Executive Board," Aug. 1954, RCTP; "Southwestern Regional Zone Conference," *Black Worker* (May 1949): 4; Nixson Denton, *History of the Brotherhood of Railway and Steamship Clerks, Freight Handlers, Express and Station Employees* (Cincinnati: George

M. Harrison Biographical Committee, 1965), 256–57; Harold Barger, *The Transportation Industries, 1889–1946: A Study of Output, Employment, and Productivity* (New York: National Bureau of Economic Research, 1951), 153.

2. Mrs. E. D. Nixon to APR, Dec. 19, 1951; APR to Mrs. E. D. Nixon, Jan. 2, 1952, LC/BSCP Box 85; William Adelman, *Touring Pullman: A Study in Company Paternalism: A Walking Guide to the Pullman Community in Chicago, Illinois* (Chicago: Illinois Labor History Society, 1972), 44.

3. ACL, "Notice to Train Maids"; "In Re: Claim of the ACL Maids B. L. Jay, L. V. Thorpe, et al."; Seniority roster, 1951 ACL Maids, LC/APR Box 13; W. S. Baker to APR, Nov. 23, 1951, LC/APR Box 13. The BSCP did not originally seek to represent the ACL maids, but in a representation grievance with the company union, the National Mediation Board granted the BSCP jurisdiction in February 1941. In negotiations with the ACL, the BSCP made no specific wage demands for the maids, although it requested a 30 percent increase for "train porters, chair car porters, and attendants." Again, the NMB decided in the BSCP's favor, and signed a contract that included maids in April 1943. The union later won retroactive wage increases for attendants and maids and a vacation agreement, LC/BSCP Box 34; Harry E. Jones, *Railroad Wages and Labor Relations, 1900–1952: An Historical Survey and Summary of Results* (New York: Bureau of Information of the Eastern Railways, 1953), 152. One of the layed-off ACL maids was Capitola Minyard (see chapter 2).

4. APR to "Women's Organizations," Mar. 24, 1952; APR to W. S. Baker, Dec. 6, 1951; "Case of the Train Maids"; *Gertrude Payne v. ACL*, Award No. 738, National Railroad Adjustment Board, Fourth Division, Oct. 12, 1951; APR to Frank Pace, Mar. 7, 1952; Case no. 75–314, awarded, Dec. 3, 1952, and APR to ACL, Dec. 3, 1952, all in LC/APR Box 13.

5. William H. Harris, *Keeping the Faith: A. Philip Randolph, Milton P. Webster, and the Brotherhood of Sleeping Car Porters, 1925–37* (Urbana: University of Illinois Press, 1977, 1991), 225; Mrs. E. D. Nixon to APR, Dec. 13, 1951, LC/BSCP Box 85.

6. APR to Mrs. E. D. Nixon, Jan. 2, 1952. Dellums reported no female union members for 1948, 1952, and 1953; see State of California, annual Organized Labor Questionnaires, UCB/CLD Boxes 2, 8.

7. Georgia Painter Nielson, *From Sky Girl to Flight Attendant: Women and the Making of a Union* (Ithaca, N.Y.: ILR Press, 1982). Suzanne Kolm's forthcoming dissertation (Brown University) examines the airlines' decision to hire white women, rather than African American men; Martha W. Griffiths to APR, Oct. 4, 1960, LC/BSCP Box 13; Iris Peterson to APR, Feb. 2, 1961, LC/BSCP Box 23.

8. Financial reports, 1945, RCTP; Brailsford Brazeal, *The Brotherhood of Sleeping Car Porters: Its Origin and Development* (New York: Harper and Brothers, 1946), 222, (estimated for 1945) provides membership figures for the union through 1943 only. No other record of BSCP membership appears to be available.

9. HW to Bennie Smith, Apr. 14, 1952, CHS/BSCP Box 33; Lassiter, *Report of the Proceedings of the Fourth Biennial Convention of the Ladies Auxiliary, 1944*, 57; *Report of the Proceedings of the Seventh Biennial Convention of the Ladies Auxiliary, 1950*, 102–6, 193–97; *First Triennial Convention, 1953*, 49–55, 148–53; *Second Triennial Convention, 1956*, 80–83; see also CLD to MPW, Aug. 22, 1939, UCB/CLD Box 4, for comments on HW's speaking style.

10. RCT, "Visits," n.d., RCTP; *Constitution and By-Laws of the International La-*

dies' Auxiliary to the Brotherhood of Sleeping Car Porters, rev. 1940, as amended, *Report of the Proceedings of the First Triennial Convention of the International Ladies Auxiliary, 1953,* 110–14, 116–17; *Report of the Proceedings of the Second Triennial Convention of the International Ladies Auxiliary, 1956,* 56–58, 60–66.

11. RCT, "Visits." See, for example, Wilson's correspondence with Dallas Secretary-Treasurer Olevia Rawlston to retrieve the Auxiliary's financial records, HW to Olevia Rawlston, Aug. 12, 1947; HW to APR, May 4, 1948; APR to HW, May 7, 1948, all in LC/BSCP Box 76; HW to Rawlston, May 11, 1948; Rawlston to HW, May 20, 1948, LC/BSCP Box 73; HW to Rawlston, June 10, 1948, LC/BSCP Box 75.

12. CLD to HW, Nov. 1951, UCB/BSCP Box 24.

13. HW to CLD, Jan. 9, 1953, UCB/BSCP Box 9; Howard W. Risher Jr., *The Negro in the Railroad Industry,* Report No. 16 (Philadelphia: Wharton School of Finance and Commerce, University of Pennsylvania, 1971), 72–73.

14. HW to Velmer Coward, Dec. 11, 1942, CHS/BSCP Box 28; HW to Member, Oct. 14, 1955, CHS/BSCP Box 34; *Second Triennial Convention, 1956,* 22–23; RCT to BSCP International Executive Board, May 9, 1951, and BSCP International Executive Board, Minutes, May 16, 1951; in LC/APR Box 11; see also HW to CLD, and members of the BSCP International Executive Board, Apr. 1, 1954, UCB/CLD Box 9; and CLD to W. B. Holland, Sept. 8, 1939, UCB/CLD Box 5.

15. RCT, "Visits"; see also HW to CLD, Nov. 30, 1954, UCB/CLD Box 9.

16. HW to BSCP International Executive Board, May 16, 1956, LC/BSCP Box 74.

17. Wilson, *Report of the Proceedings of the Second Triennial Convention of the BSCP, Held at St. Louis, 1956,* 6–7.

18. BSCP International Executive Board, Minutes, Sept. 7, 1956, LC/APR Box 11; Resolution, "Reorganization of the Ladies' Auxiliary," BSCP International Executive Board Resolution, n.d. (Sept. 17, 1956), RCTP.

19. APR, *Second Triennial Convention, Ladies' Auxiliary, 1956,* 42.

20. Ibid.

21. Ibid., 43, 44; *Second Triennial Convention, BSCP, 1956,* 51, 253.

22. *Second Triennial Convention, 1956,* 44–45; RCT to APR and BSCP International Executive Board, Sept. 12, 1956, LC/BSCP Box 75.

23. Ella Johnson to RCT, Oct. 4, 1956, RCTP.

24. RCT to APR, Nov. 27, 1956, LC/BSCP Box 75.

25. HW to M. L. Stillerman, Mar. 11, 1952, CHS/BSCP Box 33; HW to CLD, Jan. 25, 1955, UCB/CLD Box 9; APR to HW, Jan. 1, 1955, LC/BSCP Box 74; APR to Mrs. Taylor, LC/BSCP Box 73; RCT to Velma King, Aug. 26, 1957, RCTP; David L. Lewis, *King: A Critical Biography* (Baltimore: Penguin Books, 1970), 89–90.

26. APR to RCT, July 2, 1957, LC/BSCP Box 75.

27. RCT to "Dear Sisters," July 5, 1957, RCTP.

28. APR to RCT, Oct. 22, 1957, RCTP; RCT to APR, Aug. 15, 1957; APR to RCT, Oct. 22, 1956; RCT to APR, July 18, 1957, all in LC/BSCP Box 75; RCT to Ted Brown, Aug. 15, 1957, RCTP.

29. APR to HW, Jan. 17, 1956, LC/BSCP Box 74; "Testimonial Banquet Honoring Presidents' Ladies Auxiliary, Washington Division," Nov. 18, 1966, RCTP.

30. From the mailing labels of RCT's copies of the *Black Worker,* it appears that not even she received her own copy. RCT recounted the opinions of old Pullman porters who "used to get together and brag about how *little* they let their wives

know. 'Well, I don't let my wife leave the house without me,' one might say, and 'I don't even let mine *talk* without asking my permission,' another might say. In fact, many men seemed to think that they owned their wives. 'I paid five dollars for you!' was a common remark (referring to the marriage license) made at any display of independence on the wife. It was amusing, however, how some of the porters bragged about how they bossed their wives, how meek and henpecked they were in the actual presence of their spouse." RCT, "My Life As I Have Lived It," RCTP; see also Charles Upton to CLD, Oct. 15, 1939, UCB/CLD Box 5; CLD to Theodore E. Brown, July 12, 1951, UCB/CLD Box 8; E. A. Woods to CLD, Feb. 13, 1950, UCB/CLD Box 7; but on *Black Worker* readership, compare CLD to APR, Dec. 7, 1938, UCB/BSCP Box 4.

31. Ashley L. Totten to APR, Oct. 9, 1942, LC/APR Box 9; see also RCT, "My Life."

32. RCT, "My Life."

33. RCT, "Report [Eastern Zone Tour]," Aug. 1954, RCTP.

34. "Halena Wilson," biographical statement, and "Testimonial Banquet Honoring Halena Wilson," Nov. 18, 1954, both in CHS/BSCP Box 34; RCT, "Report [Eastern Zone Tour]."

35. "Youth and Education," *BSCP Fiftieth Anniversary Year Luncheon Honoring A. Philip Randolph,* June 25, 1975, LC/APR Box 9; Harold B. Anderson to APR, Mar. 17, 1958, LC/BSCP Box 84.

36. Paula Pfeffer, *A. Philip Randolph, Pioneer of the Civil Rights Movement* (Baton Rouge: Louisiana State University Press, 1990), 176–85.

Index

MELINDA CHATEAUVERT teaches in the Afro-American Studies Program at the University of Maryland, College Park. She holds a B.A. and an M.A. in women's studies from the University of Massachusetts at Amherst and George Washington University, respectively. As research director for the Pay Discrimination Institute, a nonprofit legal defense fund, she developed expert historical testimony for race- and sex-based wage discrimination cases. She completed a Ph.D. in U.S. history at the University of Pennsylvania in 1992.

The Female Economy: The Millinery and Dressmaking Trades, 1860–1930
Wendy Gamber

"Negro and White, Unite and Fight!": A Social History of Industrial Unionism in Meatpacking, 1930–90   *Roger Horowitz*

Power at Odds: The 1922 National Railroad Shopmen's Strike   *Colin J. Davis*

The Common Ground of Womanhood: Class, Gender, and Working Girls' Clubs, 1884–1928   *Priscilla Murolo*

Marching Together: Women of the Brotherhood of Sleeping Car Porters
Melinda Chateauvert

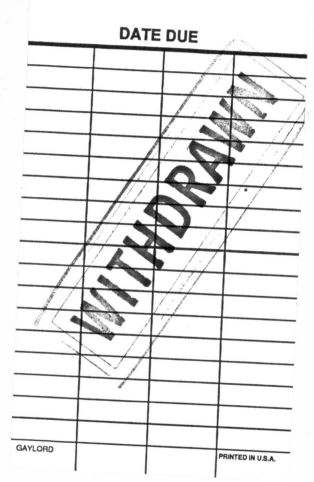

DATE DUE